Chasing Traces

CHASING TRACES

History and Ethnography in the Uplands of Socialist Asia

EDITED BY

Pierre Petit

AND

Jean Michaud

University of Hawai'i Press

Honolulu

Library of Congress Cataloging-in-Publication Data

Names: Petit, Pierre, editor. | Michaud, Jean, editor.
Title: Chasing traces : history and ethnography in the uplands of socialist
  Asia / Pierre Petit, Jean Michaud.
Description: Honolulu : University of Hawai'i Press, [2024] | Includes
  bibliographical references and index.
Identifiers: LCCN 2023036413 (print) | LCCN 2023036414 (ebook) | ISBN
  9780824895556 (hardback) | ISBN 9780824897901 (trade paperback) | ISBN
  9780824897758 (epub) | ISBN 9780824897765 (kindle edition) | ISBN
  9780824897741 (pdf)
Subjects: LCSH: Socialism—China, Southwest—History. |
  Socialism—Vietnam—History. | Socialism—Laos—History. |
  Ethnohistory—China, Southwest. | Ethnohistory—Vietnam. |
  Ethnohistory—Laos.
Classification: LCC HX376.A6 C495 2024 (print) | LCC HX376.A6 (ebook) |
  DDC 320.53/1095—dc23/eng/20230824
LC record available at https://lccn.loc.gov/2023036413
LC ebook record available at https://lccn.loc.gov/2023036414

Cover photograph: A research assistant interviewing a centenarian Hmong
woman with the help of the latter's daughter (left), about the story of the
prophet Pa Chay Vue. © Sarah Turner

CONTENTS

Acknowledgments

The editors wish to thank the Fund for Scientific Research (FRS–FNRS) of Belgium, the journal *Civilisations* (Université libre de Bruxelles), as well as the Social Sciences and Humanities Research Council of Canada for their financial support in the production of this volume.

The two anonymous readers of University of Hawai'i Press have provided generous and extremely helpful comments. Similarly, participants to the 2019 and 2020 workshops who could not join the publication project should be mentioned for their intellectual contribution: Yves Goudineau, Oliver Tappe, and Lukas Christian Husa. This book project has also been discussed critically with several colleagues, including Stevan Harrell, Rosalie Stolz, Vanessa Frangville, and Rian Thum. It has also been debated over public presentations at two EuroSEAS conferences (Berlin and Paris), the Canadian Council for Southeast Asian Studies conference in Québec City, the EHESS in Paris, Bielefeld University, and the Institut für Ethnologie, Universität Heidelberg. So many ideas resulted from these scholarly and friendly exchanges and played a major role in fine-tuning this volume.

Isabelle Renneson and Cassandre Voituron (in Belgium) and graduate students Peter Garber, Simon Bilodeau, Dominic Roberge, Stéphane Pelletier, and Mysaëlle Lavoie-Lemieux (in Canada) deserve to be wholeheartedly acknowledged for their assistance in various editorial tasks.

Thanks to all!

INTRODUCTION

Pierre Petit and Jean Michaud

A COMPULSION TO PRESERVE and pass on the memory of the past has gripped Western European societies since at least the Industrial Revolution (Nora 1997). By contrast, among the upland societies living in the area covered by this book—that is, the connected highlands of China, Vietnam, and Laos—the urge to investigate and own the past is not even remotely as pressing. These three countries of the communist "red brotherhood" (Evans and Rowley 1984) have gone through economic openings that have increasingly connected them with global flows and the market economy, tourism, heritage industry, and digital technologies. But recalling the past in this region remains highly sensitive. Among the local societies of the uplands, many may actively avoid recalling the past for fear of endangering themselves and others. Such contrast begs for careful investigation.

A similar level of complication arises regarding the material traces of the past.[1] After the communist revolutions, artifacts and monuments associated with the so-called feudal period had to be destroyed for the sake of building the modern socialist society. Years later, the language of "heritagization" of upland "cultures" has saturated the national discourse in China, Vietnam, and Laos. This discourse has crystallized in a selective way requiring total compliance with the national historical narrative: some institutions formerly banned have now resurfaced, but mainly under the benign guise of "living fossils of the nation," to use the expression popularized by Chinese bureaucrats in relation to the "ethnic minority cultures" (*shaoshu minzu*).

James C. Scott's (2009) *The Art of Not Being Governed: An Anarchist History of Upland Southeast Asia* fostered, more strongly than any prior publication, an interest in the so far neglected history of this highland region (which he calls Zomia), and especially in the relations between the lowland centers of power and their mountainous peripheries. Scott's daring thesis triggered vigorous debates, as in the special issues of the *Journal of Global History* (Michaud 2010b) and the *Asia Pacific Journal of Anthropology* (Tappe 2015), and inspired more indirectly a recent special issue of *Social Anthropology* (Stolz and Tappe 2021).[2] Now, fifteen years after the release of his book, it is time to uncouple the debate from Scott's germane hypotheses and consider the making of history itself as a central challenge.

Working from disciplinary margins raises epistemic awareness, and the very project of historical anthropology is by nature a perpetual inducement to "rethink our practices of knowledge production" (Axel 2002, 33). Producing history, ethnohistory, historical anthropology, and historical geography in the Southeast Asian highlands raises significant questions relating to methodology, epistemology, and ethics, for which most researchers in the fields of social sciences and the humanities are often ill prepared. There is still no single reference book on how to navigate the margins between the fields of history and social anthropology, where oral traditions and rare archives remain the main avenues to visit the past.

Our initial questions were manifold. How can scholars manage to competently access information about the past? How do local societies produce and store their stories in their own terms, terms that are often ill at ease with national and Western categories? How is the memory of the past transmitted—or not—and with what logic? Regarding oral testimony, who exactly are the "wise ones" researchers are routinely directed to for their interviews? How can one handle the oft-reported male authority on historical information, and how can historical narratives better reflect the different voices behind the authoritative versions of those in charge? How should one cope with key informants but also with gatekeepers when working with minorities under authoritarian regimes? How can historical statements be addressed as situated speech acts and not mere "data"? And how is one to capture history-in-the-making through events, rituals, and performances rather than interviews and surveys, including the telling of life stories and micro-stories?

Similar questions arise when perusing archives. If written archives are the staple of historians, how should social scientists use them? Should they proceed in the same way as historians, or should they develop a specific method and agenda? How does archival research intersect with fieldwork, and what kind of added value might it bring to it? Is access to national or regional archives restricted for political motives? If so, what are the costs and possible compromises needed to access them?

And in terms of positionality, by what right can Western and/or "white" scholars dig into the past of societies other than their own? This is an unsettling question that came to the fore amid debates on reflexivity and decoloniality, one that has become unavoidable and for which there is no simple answer.

The necessity of working with a variety of dissenting sources across disciplinary boundaries represents a common experience for those working on history in the highland regions of Asia. One must then find out how to use oral and textual information together—or, rather, the conditions for their synergy. The same question can arise about archives from different holding funds, from different epochs, written in different languages, for different readerships, or managed and ordained by different political regimes with intentions often outside scholarly consideration. Historical criticism, reflexivity, and methodological triangulation are simply essential in this context. And once all has been gathered and put together in a meaningful way, the final production of history as texts, films, or exhibitions creates, in turn, a new flow of historical information that will one way or another feed back into the local scenes. Are those retroactions common or exceptional? In them, who speaks for whom and in what languages and scripts? How does the work of scholars—national or international—when fed back to their original owners, impact the local sense of history and self? What can be said on the ethics of anonymity, authorship, censorship, and self-censorship? Historical analysis in the shape of a scientific discourse that refracts ideological injunctions can easily annoy the powers that be, gatekeepers, and pundits, who develop and support canonical narratives about the past they claim to be common (and beneficial) to the whole nation. When producing knowledge that challenges such orthodoxies, scholars are not the only ones who could find themselves in the line of fire, even if unwittingly or by unfamiliarity with national canons—their informants and collaborators could be too.

Facing such complications, this volume is intended as a guiding companion for those confronted with such multifarious and at times daunting challenges. It is based on experiences and reflections rooted in decades of work in the three Marxist-Leninist states who share portions of the Southeast Asian Massif: China, Vietnam, and Laos (see map 1). We are convinced of the relevance of reaching out beyond

Map 1. Location of authors' fieldwork in upland socialist Asia, with respective chapter number. © P. Petit and I. Renneson.

national borders not only because populations and fluxes straddle these porous boundaries, but also because heuristic exogamy is the best way to refresh perspectives on research. Seventy-five percent of the indigenous highland populations of the Massif are concentrated in these three countries (Michaud 2016, 3). The challenges of social science fieldwork in that area have been addressed in a volume edited by Sarah Turner (2013a). With the present volume, we want to focus particularly on history and the social sciences as fields of inquiry shared by a dozen researchers with different backgrounds, mindsets, and perspectives, with the aim of launching a constructive discussion about common stakes—and mistakes.

Moreover, and most unexpectedly, our collection has recently acquired a timely quality. A few months after we launched this editorial project, the COVID pandemic took off, changing everything. Traveling for research became severely restricted, to the point that fieldwork and ethnography became inaccessible to most researchers. Then, the war in Ukraine and its unpredictable side effects and long-term ripples further increased the threat to international mobility. Last but not least, scholars working in China, be they nationals or outsiders, currently face increasing research and access limitations imposed ever more strictly by the present regime. Over what could turn into a lengthy period, many among our colleagues have no idea about when they may be allowed to resume their fieldwork, and they feel confused. Facing these major obstacles, many researchers practicing ethnographic fieldwork had to change their methods and turn to alternative sources of information. This has become a time for many to delve into online ethnography and archival work. In this context of multifaceted change, researchers have need of guidelines for alternative ways to document and reflect upon Asian highland societies when access has become, at best, limited. Our book can help to cope with this challenging situation.

Ten Issues Addressed in This Book

To bring order to these liminal remarks, we propose a list of ten key issues recurring throughout this book. Before enumerating this list, however, it is necessary to clarify how the term "history"—beyond its practical use referring to the past by contrast to the present—has been used throughout the volume. "History" can refer to a very specific way to record and analyze the past, with a focus on chronology;

history would thus be the specific domain of chroniclers, specialists, and trained historians. Alternatively, it refers to any narrative about the past: a song, a ritual, an oral tale about origins, a story prompted by a mnemonic device, chronicles written in archives, a book by a local or professional historian, a personal memory of a past event. It can narrate the past using not only chronological but also mythical and genealogical means (Daniel 1996; Harrell 2001). This empirical, extensive meaning from the ground up is the one that has been favored by all our contributors, and it acts as a methodological foundation for this book.

This distinction recalls the one drawn by Maurice Halbwachs between memory and history ([1950] 1997, 130–142). In Halbwachs's view, memory is more popular, multiple, tied to emotions, embodied, and collective, and only concerned by elements of the past that are relevant for the present. History is by contrast more constructed, erudite, objective, conceptual, and all-embracing, and hovers above human groups. In this sense, our book would be, for the most part, a contribution to the study of the former: collective memory in the highlands.

But this still leaves another important dimension unaddressed: the engagement people have with knowledge about the past. Rian Thum (2014, 1–2) insightfully remarked that memory denotes a passive, "mostly involuntary participation" in the recollection of the past. By contrast, the Uyghurs, who were at the center of Thum's research, were driven by curiosity, intentionality, effort, and active engagement in their relationship to the past. Thum argues that this active attitude is a defining feature of the practice of history and hence considers that the relation of Uyghurs with their past has more to do with history than with memory. We endorse this view, as it certainly applies to many situations described in the next chapters. Defining history by engagement rather than by methods is a creative way to address the conceptual issue we now discuss in this first point.

1. A "Duty of Remembrance"

We begin with a critical reflection on the way scholars themselves relate to this past, with a reference to what is widely called in French *devoir de mémoire*. This reflexive stance sees social scientists as constituents of the research process, which helps avoid the trappings of "othering" the host societies through their projection into a time of their own, different from the present of the researcher (Fabian 2014).

Pierre Nora's (1997) *Realms of Memory* captures the "duty of remembrance" that pervades late industrial societies in Europe and most Western countries. This fascination with the past goes well beyond the sphere of scholars; it is noticeable in everyday practices, including the way Western tourists plan to visit a city by delving into historical tourist literature without which their experience would be deemed incomplete.

The contributors to this volume share elements of this implicit concern and see the task of empowering highland communities with their own history as a laudable endeavor. However, the intrinsic value of the past, of historical evidence, and of witnesses' testimonies is not to be assumed. If modern Western scholars take for granted that historical knowledge is to be shared and the "truth" to be unveiled, this commitment is not shared by all societies, and even less by all their members. It may come as a surprise to many, but some highland groups have little interest (not to be confused with capability) in preserving and transmitting their history. And far from being an exception, this might even be the norm for some of them. According to James Scott (2009, chap. 6½; Michaud 2020a), this oblivion could be a defining trait of Zomian societies. Neglecting the production of a history of self protects one from the burden of carrying the past on one's back, from self-proclaimed legitimacies, and, ultimately, from the grip of the state, from whom crucial information is withheld. The Bru of the Central Highlands in Vietnam discussed by Gábor Vargyas are an excellent example of this notion, as we will see in issue 4 below. For some, the past is only cautiously evoked, as in the chapter by Vanina Bouté, where the old institutions of the Phunoy are explicitly stigmatized by the subjects themselves as archaic, counterrevolutionary, and superstitious. Such stigmatization even made it difficult for her to elicit comments on that period beyond prudent lip service conforming to the official state version.

But who are we to demand "the truth"? Do Western and/or white scholars have the moral right to explore the depth of history among Asian societies who have not conducted (or have not been seen to conduct, or have refused to conduct) this search by themselves? We strongly adhere to the view that local history should be explored primarily by, or at least jointly with, the holders of memory and not merely rely on extracting data (Tuhiwai Smith 1999). But with different cultures having drastically different visions of what history means and what purpose it serves, many of which are unrelated to the principles of the European Enlightenment, collaboration raises real challenges. As argued above, revealing the past publicly and precisely is not as widespread an objective as one might think, and local upland groups under authoritarian regimes are definitely not to be held solely to the standards of scientific positivism. That said, such an argument does not suffice to stop any scientific consideration of the history of the Other in its tracks, especially when that Other's history is being seized and edited by an internal elite to perpetuate forms of social inequality, or when it is enmeshed with that of dominant societies that enforce contradictory and sometimes conflictual narratives about a so-called common past onto local groups.

The issue becomes further complicated when research is conducted among/about/with ethnic minorities in former colonies by scholars coming from former colonial powers and their associates. Recent examples include India with the subaltern studies debate (Chaturvedi 2012), and the Americas with the push for "decolonizing" research among indigenous subjects by agents seen as connected to the former oppressor (Quijano 2007). Without digging too deeply into a debate that exceeds the parameters of this book (see Axel 2002), we find that refraining from conducting social science research in authoritarian Asian countries purely on moral grounds (not being the right persons, from the right countries, collaborating with an "unjust" polity, and so on) and in the absence of indigenous voices who have the right to be heard, would only encourage guilty complicity. Such research may foster a tacit collaboration with the systematic operation of silencing "national minority" groups conducted by state agents, whose role is to produce a normative story coherent with the national political narrative (as will be unpacked in issue 7 below). Currently, scholars devoting their energy to the Uyghurs or the Tibetans will understand immediately what we mean here—"carrying a voice." As an adapted response to this moral dilemma, the strategy known as engaged or public anthropology (Low and Merry 2010; Besteman 2013) has been sympathetically viewed by various scholars working in the region, including several contributors to this book. Beside the production of science, further carrying the voice of minorities under duress becomes an aim and a powerful incentive to mindful researchers. Their work will not be perfect, but an imperfect history conducted prudently is better than a falsified one meant to suit ideological purposes.

Such moral commitment may even stimulate applied projects aiming to reactivate historical memory within specific groups, guided by the concern that writing and diffusing local history should reinforce the agency of subaltern groups and those who have routinely been muted. This was the explicit objective of the project undertaken by Sarah Turner and Sarah Delisle; young Vietnamese Hmong were asked to collect life stories of elders from their group. The stories formed the basis of a website intended to transmit history in a context where intergenerational knowledge-sharing seemed at risk.

2. *"Incidental" Historians*

Compared to historians who are generally focused on the past, social scientists are primarily interested in the present. Their analyses substantially aim to understand social relations, institutions, material culture, and subjectivities in human societies based on ethnographic fieldwork—that is, on participant observation and various forms of interlocution. The chapters in this volume make it clear: social scientists, and in particular social and cultural anthropologists, do not investigate the past as an aim in itself; rather, they explore it as a way to better root their understanding of today's society. In this sense, they become "incidental" historians, much in the same way Western missionaries became "incidental" ethnographers in this same region (Michaud 2007).

In this book, interest in the past mainly takes two forms. First, social scientists can simply not ignore the events that led to the current situation. The concept of "regressive history," a term coined by historian Marc Bloch (1964), captures this movement: to make sense of the present, one needs to shed light on the previous state of things and see the continuities and ruptures. Understanding current kinship hierarchies, agricultural landscapes, or the morphology of highland villages is pointless without a sound historical background. To analyze a ritual performed today without considering the impacts of wars, communist revolutions, the ensuing state policies framing religious practices, and the recent call for tourist heritagization would be plainly misleading. This is the argument of Sylvie Beaud in this volume. Beaud's anthropological research on the Guan Suo Opera, now performed in a village in Yunnan, supposes not only unpacking the troubled past that followed the Communist takeover of 1949, but also unearthing of deeper layers of history relating to the presence of imperial troops in the region during the nineteenth century. Neglecting such layers of history could produce only folkloristic vignettes resting on a fallacy of cultural simplicity and presumed continuities. Such is precisely the way state ethnography has proceeded in many instances in the three countries under investigation, with the view to dehistoricize and depoliticize upland cultures (McElwee 2004; Petit 2008; Michaud 2009, 2022; Mullaney 2011).

Besides the need to historicize today's societies, social scientists have found another interest in the past. This time, researchers focus on the memories people keep of the past and on the past's various uses as a resource. If the first, "regressive" movement aimed to understand the present by looking into the past (the past being embedded in the present), the second movement aims to decipher the intricacies of the present in the recounting of the past (the present being in the past-as-a-narrative). Indeed, history provides a frame to make sense of and justify present institutions. Any reference to tradition or culture supposes assertions on origins. This can lead to unabashed instrumentalization of the past, as when communist states reconstruct local history to have it toe the party line. But often, the process is not as blatant: the past is progressively, incrementally, subtly, and even partly unknowingly remodeled to fit with the current views of those in charge of narrating it. For instance, the oral traditions collected by Wang Ming-ke in the Aixigou Valley of Sichuan describe the migration of the Qiang using the trope of brothers founding different villages. It is doubtful that this is an actual fact; rather it is a way to shape the Qiangs' experience of the local world and to frame the relations of alliance, distinction, and confrontation between communities.

In sum, any discourse on the past is related to the current time, to the views and stakes of the society voicing it. This simple assertion explains in part why historical memory is selective in forgetting or obliterating elements; the past will be remembered only when it is deemed relevant to and consistent with the present. This selective memory further causes the discrepancy between the scientific work on history, which maximizes the critical recollection of historical sources to produce thick knowledge, and the vernacular memory of the past in highland Asia as elsewhere, which has adapted to meet the needs of intelligibility and legitimacy for the group today in an economical way. As argued by Pierre Petit in his chapter, the minimalist ways in which local societies record history presents a challenge for social researchers, creating "hollows" that are more extensive than positive information. This situation is very different from more usual forms of ethnography where information can be produced abundantly over time.

3. An Iterative Process Based on Multiple Sources

Whether their interest in the past stems from their wishes for a regressive history to contextualize the present or from a willingness to understand how current discourses instrumentalize the past as a resource, social scientists have no choice but to come to terms with history. This is often unexpected, and scholars usually confess that they improvise with this requirement.

To answer the challenge, most contributors to this volume combine written and oral sources, and they praise the benefits gained from doing so. The benefits of this crossover are many. Combining sources can confirm information, add details, and pose questions. Disparities between written and oral sources often act as teasers for researchers, pointing to unexpected directions to investigate and new questions to address. In his chapter, Petit explains that the information he found in the French colonial archives of Aix-en-Provence were instrumental in designing new questions about colonial times to ask during fieldwork, notably regarding past economic activities and trade routes. These refined questions prompted significantly more comments from informants than his previous, less precise ones. Conversely, when Petit cross-checked the oral narratives he collected during fieldwork with data he gathered in the archives, further speculation ensued, moving back in time to events up to the early nineteenth century, which incidentally demonstrate the historical depth of oral traditions in the region.

In most instances covered in this book, the iterative process began with ethnographic field research, subsequently complemented and energized by an exploration of archives and written documents. For example, Vanina Bouté and Wang Ming-ke explain how merging oral and written sources was key to shedding new light on ethnogenesis among the Phunoy and the Qiang/Rma. Vatthana Pholsena proceeded similarly to analyze the rise in power of the Phu Tai in Central Laos from the seventeenth century onward. For Christian Lentz, on the other hand, while his work started in archives, he also underscores the benefits of his regular travels to the Điện Biên Phủ region, where he gained a sense of scale, agricultural cycles, evolving toponyms, interethnic backgrounds, and open-ended state interventions—in short, of the various "historical rhythms" of that area. In his view, these intimate field experiences enabled him to mentally reconstruct what happened in the 1940s and 1950s, when the region was progressively reframed as part of the nascent Vietnamese state.

Archives are unique windows into the past, but historical criticism is mandatory to contextualize the documents (Stocking 1991; Pels and Salemink 1999; Salemink 2003; Michaud 2007; Stoler 2009). Jean Michaud notes that the field reports he collected were authored by

French military officers and showed the predictable stereotypes typical of the French colonial project. That said, he also notes that the ethnographies were usually written with care and provide consistent descriptions of the highland societies at that time like no other contemporaneous source. In terms of methods, Michaud insists on patience and organization when conducting in-depth archival search, as collections can be scattered in diverse institutions governed by different bodies, each with their own sets of access and use rules. Both Michaud and Lentz point out that luck plays a significant role when dealing with archives, and they recommend that researchers keep snooping beyond and beside the intended targets.

Historical information can be drawn from a wide array of starting points. Magnus Fiskesjö demonstrates that anthropological history can benefit from an inspection of names and anthroponyms; Bouté and Wang do the same with ethnonyms, as do Lentz, Bouté, and Beaud with toponyms. These are all rich sources on the past, locales having often been (re)named through time following major as much as minor events. The landscape can also serve as a starting point for historical interpretation (Pholsena and Tappe 2013), and the technique of photo analysis can play a similar role, as exemplified by Michaud in weaving the story of a Hmong messiah from pictures (2020b). Ghost stories, legends, or "solidified" rumors linking historical events to hidden powers can also be used as starting points for grasping the local sense of history (Kwon 2008; High and Petit 2013).

Such diversity of sources and foci presents a real challenge for untrained researchers. Faced with this trial, contributors to this book seem to relish—and sometimes possibly indulge—in this largely unexpected change of registers, protocols, and disciplinary mind frames for their work. Eclecticism can become a treat to researchers, and their curiosity, rekindled by new and unexpected material, added to the body of their research and energizing it further. Enjoyment and pleasure are also needed for carrying out research in the long term. Curiously, social scientists are rather discreet, in their writings at least, about the pleasure they can derive from doing research, as if it were an improper or shameful topic.

4. History—or Lack of History—from Below

Fifty years ago, in the *Annual Review of Anthropology*, Robert M. Carmack took stock of the field of "ethnohistory," aiming to capture the various definitions, methods, and objectives allotted to this subdiscipline. The final set of definitions he discussed equated ethnohistory with "folk history"—that is, the way local populations conceive history in their own terms, in the same sense that ethnobotany is the endogenous botany developed by a specific society (Carmack 1972, 239–242). We propose that such considerations have not aged one bit and still usefully inform the way human groups construct their own history, and that they should be dealt with more attentively. For instance, E. Valentine Daniel (1996) talked about "historical" vs. "mythical" representations of the past, and Stevan Harrell (2001) contrasted a Chinese "historical" representation with a Nuosu "genealogical" one. What are the representational, lexical, and material frames people activate when addressing their past? What is an emic standpoint on history?

Several authors in this volume examine this issue, which is surprisingly not frequently addressed in reference works on historical anthropology (for instance, Axel 2002). In some societies, history does not seem to be a topic at all. Doing fieldwork in the 1980s among the Bru of Central Vietnam, Gábor Vargyas was utterly surprised by their lack of interest in things of the past. This Bru community had no local specialists of collective memory, no genealogies or yesteryears' heroes, and no oral tradition or public storytelling related to the past. Besides casual comments addressed to the passing anthropologist, funerals seemed to be the only public circumstance when the past could be rekindled, though in a generic way: the ancestors had to be called to safely conduct the process of turning the "recent" dead into ancestors. Otherwise, all seemed to indicate that the Bru formed a history-repellent society, so to speak. Michaud (2020b) has also argued a very similar point about the Hmong, expressed through the potentially strategic absence of a common script into which their past could be recorded.

On the other hand, Pascale-Marie Milan shows that the Na of the Yunnan-Sichuan frontier favorably appraise the capacity to retell the past, which is evenly distributed across the population and straddles the borders of gender. "Telling stories about the past is useful today" was a saying often repeated to her. The Na use lexical categories in relation to this aptitude. And the Tai Vat discussed by Petit refer to the narratives of the main events of their past as *pavat*, a word they share with their Lao neighbors. *Pavat* has a meaning close to a chronicle in European historiography. For the male elites of the Tai Vat, being able to publicly tell stories about the past is a valued asset to gain respect.

Sometimes, when there is no specific term to refer to historical narratives, the latter may still appear as a practical category. According to Wang Ming-ke, among the Qiang/Rma of Yunnan, there is no specific word to convey the western meaning of history. Yet, people use the expression "long ago" (*zegvea*) when they engage in narrating the past, sometimes repeated twice to refer to the very distant past. Milan noticed expressions used by the Na in conversation to underline the historical character of what they were saying: "this is how we say" or "my mother (or grandmother) told me the story like that." The role of such locutions when recalling the past emphasizes that discussions on history are always situated speech acts (Austin 1962). They rely on codes, are performative, and are determined by considerations well beyond the urge to pass on factual information about the past.

Back to our discussion on ethnohistory as folk history, favoring an emic perspective also creates a distance from logocentric approaches often favored in Western historical analysis. History from below and without written text can be conveyed by means other than language alone, like material supports and corporal performances. Beaud shows that the Guan Suo opera performances send viewers back to the imperial era in Yunnan. Fiskesjö recommends that physical supports of various kinds must also be considered when probing historical memory, as the skull alleys built by the Wa at the entrance of their villages, where the bones of vanquished enemies are set on display to remind everyone of the fighting deeds of the community—until the Chinese Communist regime put an end to them.

Research in the field of folk history has also long underscored issues of a more encompassing nature, like the global perspectives on history developed by different groups. Or the "cultural attitude a people have with regard to the passage of time itself" (Carmack 1972, 239), a concern illustrated by Benjamin Whorf's (1956) famous discussion on the conceptualization of time among the Hopi, and by Marshall Sahlins (1985) in *Islands of History*. Some contributors to this volume address related concerns. Beaud highlights the cyclical dimension of local history in the Yunnan villages where she worked, a feature she had to face to disentangle what seemed like inconsistencies from a chronological point of view. Fiskesjö points to the sense of decline pervading the Wa's conception of their own history. The Wa see themselves as the original humans on Earth and believe that this makes them the keepers of ritual stability for all of humankind, a burden that they carry on despite the ungratefulness of others. The loss of their former autonomy due to their forced inclusion into the Chinese nation has caused a deep feeling of alienation, triggering anxieties about the present and, by the same token, about what the future has in store for them.

5. A Gendered Access to the Past—and Writing about It

Pascale-Marie Milan, a single woman researching the matrilineal society of the Na in China, convincingly illustrates what many have demonstrated before and elsewhere—that is, how the gender of the researcher impacts access to channels of knowledge, which also entails different experiences and, ultimately, gendered outputs. It is no coincidence that in this book, women's voices have been collected and transmitted mostly by female researchers. While no chapter in this volume is specifically dedicated to the gendered dimension of memory, nearly all chapters show that authors as well as a number of informants, aware of their positionality, do factor in the implications of being (and being categorized as) gendered.

In Asian upland societies that view knowledge on the past as an asset, this domain can be the preserve of a few endogenous authorities, in particular male elders in power and/or ritual positions. Such experts can have no desire or pressing interest in sharing this privilege, as shown in chapters by Magnus Fiskesjö and Pierre Petit. Often, knowledge about times gone by is not treated as a common good in the highlands. The romantic representation of local societies as a milieu where the elders generously hand over traditions to the youth is generally mistaken. Typically, elders use this license sparingly and only amid their peers or to form the next generation of similar elites.

Gender asymmetries relate to access to knowledge in general, including things of the past. In Jean Michaud's study of French colonial archives, it became clear that not only were all the French ethnographers who were recording data at the turn of the twentieth century male officers, but all their informants were notables, meaning indigenous male leaders. And internally, among the Tai Vat, the spatial context where history is usually evoked favors transmission between elder men: younger men and women of all ages are not to be within hearing distance of these discussions. In Petit's chapter, as in Bouté's about the Phunoy of northern Laos, women interviewed on the past nearly always defer to men—except for some women married to local leaders, who partook in the daily practice of power through this relationship.

This obvious gender disparity regarding historical knowledge leads to a further question: what could a history of the highlands recorded and retold in a properly women-centered perspective be like? In all our chapters, there is little evidence of literary genres produced or retold by women, such as songs or oral traditions related to historical contents. However, Turner and Delisle report having had rich oral history conversations with elder Hmong women who could answer a broad range of questions with similar assurance as elder Hmong men. They also identified fields of knowledge through time that appear to be typically women-focused and on which men had little to say; this has more to do with cultural transmission than with historical memory, properly speaking, but the two processes are partly entwined. Another notable exception is life stories: Milan, Pholsena, and Turner and Delisle gathered women's biographies during their research, revealing a women-centered historical competency—see also Gail Hershatter (2011) on female historical memory among northern China rural peasants. We suggest that it is imperative to investigate this neglected field further.

Besides gender, other social divides, such as age, lineage, ethnicity, religion, and socioeconomic levels, may play a role in the unequal distribution of historical knowledge in highland societies. Moreover, these factors would all be promising entry points for new research. How do young highlanders appraise the local history of their group and their region? How do they make sense of the past, caught as they are between the national schoolbooks and the conversations they catch from elders, as noted by Delisle and Turner? This question consequently demands taking notice and addressing the coexistence of different narratives on the past that will be further unpacked in issue 7 below.

6. War and Violence

The legacies of warfare and violence are variables lurking behind this whole book. It is an uncommon situation that three countries with common borders could repeatedly share simultaneous occurrences of wars that were not fought primarily against each other. In China, Vietnam, and Laos, this refers to wars against imperial powers: in Vietnam and Laos, against France, and in China, against Japan and to a lesser degree several European powers entrenched on its coastline. These gradually morphed into civil wars fought internally between pro- and antirevolutionary factions. They devastated all three for decades, involving the active participation of foreign powers of the first order—the United States and the USSR with their respective allies, of course, and China as one of the covert protagonists in the Indochina Wars. This situation was particularly tricky as many of the upland groups were fighting other nationals, not foreigners or even parts of their own groups, blurring the limits of trust for a long time.

Besides the wars, self-created internal violence based on ideological principles caused massive waves of diasporic flows combined with forced internment and communist reeducation of dissidents. In China, the Great Leap Forward and the Cultural Revolution triggered the death of tens of millions. Concurrently, the American embargo promoted hunger and suppressed economic development in Vietnam for two more decades after 1975, with the implosion of the USSR starving that country as well as Laos for a decade. As if that was not enough, cross-border wars directly involved upland populations, such as the Sino-Vietnamese conflict of 1979 and Vietnam's invasion of Cambodia in 1979.

Thus, it is necessary to consider life anywhere in these countries as connected to warfare and violence: this has marked the landscape and socio-scape of the region, in all senses of the terms (Pholsena and Tappe 2013). Jean Michaud's chapter addresses this aspect the most directly by focusing on the intelligence the colonial military needed to gather about upland cultures and social organizations. War and ideological repression also appear prominently in the chapters by Vatthana Pholsena, directing the spotlight on war veterans; by Christian Lentz with the national and international fame of his subject, the Điện Biên Phủ battles and the discourse about it today; and by Gábor Vargyas with the war and postwar anxiety regarding recalling the past. In the other chapters, war and forced socialist normalization are always lingering in the background.

Tellingly, the China-based chapters less explicitly raise issues of violence, in part because a certain idea of "peace" has been imposed on the Chinese population after 1949 and has strongly impacted local discourses on the past. This absence might also, it could be argued, derive from the dominant state narrative in China that now deliberately discards the "diseases" of the past (chiefly feudalism) and promotes a unified "happy" image of its populations on the margins. It is then in subtle daily dealings, as shown in Magnus Fiskesjö's and Pascale-Marie Milan's chapters, that the issue of structural violence keeps arising, rarely obvious but always forcefully effective.

7. Local Stories versus National Metanarratives

"Distance-demolishing technologies" (Scott 2009, 11) have contributed to the integration, willingly or not, of highland communities into modern nation-states based on lowland cultural standards. Inclusion into the national network of physical and virtual communication has greatly facilitated the generalization of mandatory schooling for all children and, by the same token, the dissemination of an official vision of history throughout the highlands. Also contributing greatly to the spread of national narratives are television news and programs, advertisements, monuments, tourist infrastructure, and official speeches. The coexistence of a national narrative with local versions of history is explicitly addressed in over half the chapters.

The general script of official national history is largely shared by the three Marxist-Leninist states, in particular when it relates to dealing with upland minority groups, the "minority nationalities" (Michaud 2009). History is appraised through moral and evolutionary lenses, and the socialist revolution is presented as having rescued a powerless population from feudal domination, colonial indolence—and violence—and social backwardness. The "Liberation Wars" in China, Vietnam, and Laos have been made the central trope of this narrative, amounting to no less than the triumph of good over evil—"a tale of national salvation" (Tappe 2013, 437). Communist parties are now leading the three nations toward science, progress, prosperity, and the brightest possible future. As this official narrative hinges on the successful (re)unification of previously disunited countries, references to any rift along ethnic lines are strictly prohibited and, if need be, actively censored (Vargyas, this volume; Petit 2013; Michaud 2022). This (r)evolutionary metanarrative becomes the only possible version of history; it lays the foundations of the single-party state and legitimates the regime, which is the heir to the heroes of the liberation struggle. Therefore, anyone questioning this official history is liable to be deemed unpatriotic and a threat to the nation.

Local versions of history are impacted by the increasing pressure of the national narrative. Depending on context and power balance, these local versions coexist and often hybridize with the national one, or they are progressively demolished by the state's informational steam roller. Pascale-Marie Milan describes the coexistence of two sets of historical narratives among the Na of China. These are depicted in the official account of the Na as a surviving primitive matriarchal society, which is consistent with the evolutionist perspective of Marxist social history. Seeing an opportunity to partake in the tourist bonanza, the Na adapt to this situation by making onstage performances that fit the mainstream Chinese tourist expectations, notably that of going back to the latter's own ancient roots in a kind of internal orientalism (Schein 1997). But a backstage also exists for the insiders, as the Na are keenly aware of the fallacy of what they pretend to be for tourist consumption.

Local learned notables, with knowledge and/or texts about the past of their communities, play a pivotal role in articulating together the different historical narratives. Often doubling as local historians, these (mostly men) can promote a particular version of the local history and tune it more or less precisely to the national metanarrative. This is illustrated by Vatthana Pholsena, who details how a Bru officer of the Lao Front for National Construction interviewed his informants according to the script of the national historiography. Such figures fully participate in the ongoing local discussion about the past, influencing not only the vernacular traditions but also, to various degrees, the official story. Such elites become more and more common with the ongoing stratification of upland societies and increased access to (higher) education. Certainly, the category of "local historians" is an abstraction that covers a diversity of situations, ranging from the schoolmaster who jots down the genealogy of the village founding families as documented by Petit, to state officers who, following an administrative request or by their own volition, embark on writing the "true" history of the area where they work and sometimes originate from, as shown by Bouté and Pholsena. These histories often glorify the local heroes of the Liberation Wars, sometimes even faulting the "mainstream" histories for underestimating the role of their group in the national history (Harrell and Li 2004). The situation is different when such historians write from abroad, as discussed by Fiskesjö in this volume, or when war refugees of the diaspora feel free to express themselves unreservedly on behalf of their group, or when they entrust a Western scholar with these refugees' historical drama (Jonsson 2014).

8. From Revolutionary Destruction to the Glorification of National Heritage

Relating to the past in these uplands has never been a simple or stable affair. All three countries experienced a revolutionary watershed during which everything connected with the "feudal" past was deemed undesirable and condemned as anachronisms founded on superstitions that could impede the harmonious development of the new socialist nation. In Vietnam, friends of ours who were children in the 1980s confess that when playing in local temples, they sometimes willingly broke artifacts; such iconoclasm was considered cute and revolutionary by many adults (see also Kwon 2006, 106–107).

But after this frenzy of obliteration of the visible signs of a shameful ancient regime, prerevolutionary monuments and symbols started being restored in what can be considered an ambiguous process, taking place in ways that shrewdly evade the full rehabilitation of their former status and symbolism. While this revisionism applies to the national level, it also pervades in the highland margins. In the latter, the restored cultural assets must obey a new, ascribed status of "heritage," or of "living fossil" (*huo huashi* in China). Sylvie Beaud describes how the Guan Suo Opera was reshaped as valued local heritage after decades of proscription as an archaic superstition earmarked for eradication. On the Yunnan-Sichuan border, as explained by Milan, the Na also had to adapt elements of their culture to become acceptable to Han cultural canons, turning them into a pretty "living fossil" suitable for consumption by national tourists. Wang shows that the Qiang are undergoing a similar process in relation to ethnic tourism, which induces the branding of their aboriginality and magnifies their presumed backwardness, putting them "at the edge of history."

Summoning or restoring prerevolutionary times is hence thinkable, but only along lines that make it harmless to the current regime. What is thus kept alive boils down to "lovely" customs, "ravishing" architecture, "colorful" dress, and "exotic" ritual survivals that honor the deep historical roots of the socialist nation, along entirely apolitical means (Nyiri 2006; Petit 2008; Michaud 2009). In the longer term, will such symbols of the past and the diversity of the nation, duly tuned to the glory of the harmonious multiethnic but single-minded socialist nation, remain forever under the control of the state? Could some upland groups divert and even subvert them to fit their own agenda, perhaps only surreptitiously? In any case, it is plausible that the emerging strategy of heritage-making can be increasingly harnessed by local groups to unexpected ends. This is also true for the inscription of local histories into national narratives by local historians, as we have mentioned in the last section.

9. Reflexivity and Positionality in Authoritarian Situations

In *The Ethnography of Vietnam's Central Highlanders,* Oscar Salemink (2003) vividly described the embeddedness of ethnography in the political, economic, and sometimes militaristic context of its time. On a more global scale, Andrew Willford and Eric Tagliacozzo (2009) explored the evolving relations between history and anthropology, and argue for the necessity of situating these relations in the broader political context of the colonial and postcolonial world. No one speaks from nowhere. A critically reflexive posture combined with transparent and explicit positionality consideration has been agreed upon by all authors in this book, stressing the practical, political, and cultural processes of their research and analyses. Gender, age, ethnicity and racial ascription, nationality, language(s), religion(s), and other assigned categories all impact interactions in the course of any research, and this book is no exception (Bamo, Harrell, and Lunzy 2011; Meadow 2013; Turner 2013a; Schnegg 2014). We consider it essential to make the readers aware of the conditions of our work, while carefully dodging the type of near narcissism that could sometimes surface during the heyday of postmodernist social science.

As we hope to have made abundantly clear above, handling history under socialist regimes requires great care. History is heavily politicized as a body of instrumental knowledge, and hence, it is a treacherous terrain to tread for individual social scientists. When addressing delicate topics regarding ethnic minorities in sensitive borderlands for whom top-down administration is the norm, potential pitfalls multiply. Scholars' frequent proclamations on the innocuous character of their research, buttressed by their individual good will, do not take reality fully into account and could even be called naïve. This then leads to the additional conundrum of deciding what to publish and in what shape, languages, scripts, and types of media.

The stakes in accessing the field are discussed by about half our contributors, their arguments connecting to issues raised in books on fieldwork in the region (Heimer and Thøgersen 2006; Turner 2013a). A wide range of postures have been taken by researchers in relation to state gatekeepers policing access to field sites and local populations. Choice can be very narrow at times, and many situations stand beyond researchers' grasps; at other times, these postures can be adjusted through changing circumstances. Among our authors, some prefer to keep a healthy distance from the representatives of state power. Vanina Bouté did her best to escape the tutelage of the state officers who accompanied her in villages and hindered her research. Sarah Delisle and Sarah Turner, along with Jean Michaud, tried to associate with local state officials as little as feasible, knowing from experience that the former's presence would trigger reservations, self-censorship, and truncated information among their Hmong and Mien participants. Pascale-Marie Milan took great care not to become even narrowly connected with state representatives during her field research. Such prudence does not prohibit linkages with national scholars, but these are elected first for their higher degree of ideological as much as intellectual independence. Formal and routine associations with state-controlled organizations are treated with care.

Nonetheless, other researchers consider that it makes little sense to pretend not to be working "in the footsteps of the communist party," in countries where state control is ubiquitous and where official surveys are common (Hansen 2006). Vatthana Pholsena, Christian Lentz, Wang Ming-ke, Gábor Vargyas, and Pierre Petit have all worked in effective collaboration with state institutions—large organizations, national universities, national academies, and district officers—as it seemed to be the only way to access their field sites. The visibility of this tutelage becomes instrumental in preserving researchers from suspicions of espionage by the administration at all levels. This clearly does not mean these researchers endorse the standards and ideologies of the authoritarian state; it is a pragmatic strategy that can be tweaked daily at the level of personal rapport, which, with time and the gradual building of trust, can often develop into something less intimidating and restrictive than initially suggested. Here, Gábor Vargyas details the conditions he faced in the late 1980s as a researcher from an Eastern European socialist country (Hungary) conducting collaborative work in a "brother country" (Vietnam). His intimacy with the socialist state of mind allowed him and his local colleagues from the Vietnamese Academy of Social Sciences, once trust had been established, to share common views on the bureaucracy and the police-like surveillance system they had to obey. In turn, this community of experience triggered a strong sense of solidarity at the personal level. Among this book's contributors, it is this unique experience that led us to position Vargyas's chapter as a sort of thought-provoking epilogue to this volume.

Inside this atmosphere of state control and permanent surveillance, all researchers experience various degrees of anxiety and fear. These emotions could relate to not being able to reach one's field site, being expelled from the field, concern for collaborators' safety during fieldwork and after publication, and self-censorship (by local and foreign scholars alike) as a means to dull potential threats. One step further, chapters by Bouté and Fiskesjö also stress the disarray each experienced operating in societies victim to various forms of violence—physical, cultural, structural, and symbolic—worsened by the society's marginal status.

Consequently, it should not come as a surprise that a large majority of the scholars from the People's Republic of China or the Socialist Republic of Vietnam invited to join this book as authors, whom we cannot name for obvious reasons, did not feel comfortable enough to take up the opportunity. Since its authoritative turn, the government of Xi Jinping is highly suspicious of any critical take on the relation between the central state and the internal peripheries, and the prospect of bearing the brunt of the state's wrath have made many very cautious. This pressure is so strong that even some non-Chinese scholars working on China were also wary of joining a project requesting them to show critical reflexivity and making positionality explicit. And understandably so, in terms of safeguarding the right to return to their study sites in the socialist uplands.

All this said, this book proves that field research can still take place under restricted circumstances and, as Michaud (2010a) discussed in relation to Vietnam, that building relations of trust based on reciprocity is a key to success. In his chapter, Lentz vividly describes how he managed to break the ice with the employees of the archive center where he worked in Hanoi. Being an American working on the Indochina Wars is not a stress-free position in Vietnam. But after a rocky start, he managed to join everyday interactions and become involved in the staff's discussions about their professional concerns. This relationship required sharing breaks and snacks with the staff, joining in with a few dance steps, providing help to repair the air-conditioning system, and contributing to a trilingual edition of the user manual for the archive's holdings. Other related forms of everyday exchange and working cooperation are mentioned throughout the volume, notably in the contribution by Vargyas, who engaged in helping scholars of the Vietnamese Academy of Social Sciences to access funding to travel abroad.

10. Ethics

It flows from the previous points that the elephant in the room here—ethics—matters greatly when conducting research with groups at risk within ideologically rigid states. We are not merely talking about procedural ethics following the development of ethics boards across North America and beyond; we are above all concerned with the deeper matter of moral ethics, individual as much as collective (Harrell and Li 2003; Guillemin and Gillam 2004; Dowling 2010).

Under regimes where the rule of law is not fully functioning, individual rights are always at risk, and protecting research assistants and research participants becomes a high priority. There is often a dilemma between the option—or sometimes the Western institutional requirement—to anonymize information, cover tracks, and protect people from retaliation, and the commitment to duly acknowledge all people involved in the research process. Answering these two imperatives is a balancing act: anonymity is imprecise, unfair, frustrating, and possibly unscientific, while nominal acknowledgment wields the potential to inflict grievous harm. In our view, interaction with trusted persons and research assistants in the field, discussion with colleagues facing similar issues, and finding inspiration in codes of ethics like the one popularized by the American Anthropological Association can all be of value in making informed decisions. We are concerned that the growing bureaucratic requirements in Europe, the Americas, and Australasia regarding the use of official procedures and forms (for instance, written informed consent) might induce a guilt-relieving treatment where boxes are ticked and official permissions granted, putting personal morals to rest. Our collective experience in China, Vietnam, and Laos rather pleads for a sensible, reflexive, context-driven, locally informed, peer-discussed, and iterative way of dealing with ethical issues, far from the mere rubber-stamping based on bureaucratic principles.

The pitfalls of field research for collaborators and researchers alike appears clearly in Gábor Vargyas's chapter. In 1989, he secretly interviewed a Bru man who ended up on the wrong (i.e., South Vietnam/American) side during the Second Indochina War. This interview happened only due to trust between the two men. The interviewee at first proclaimed that if his story was to be disclosed, "the Kinh (the Vietnamese ethnic majority) will slaughter me." The series of nightly discussions resulted in a lengthy recording whose transcription and translation, due to strategic and ethical considerations, was only completed in 2007 after the death of the interviewee. Due to a tense political situation in Vietnam's Central Highlands at the time, Vargyas always feared that local policemen might enquire more insistently and learn of the content of the interview. This could have resulted in harmful consequences for Vargyas himself and for relatives and acquaintances of the late interviewee.

Vargyas also faced the dilemma of how to make this material reach the public eye. More than thirty years after its collection, he has decided to publish the life story in full. With the interviewee now gone, along with presumably the whole generation of those who have been involved in the events, the potential harmful consequences stand at a lower level. The process is still challenging for various reasons, and far from completion.

Finally, ethical concerns also have much to do with our institutional collaborators, especially with our local research assistants, whatever their ethnicity might be. How can we make sure no harm is done to them in the process? How can we help them in their career as they do for us (Turner 2013b)? How can we make sure that despite anonymity, reciprocity remains key in avoiding the stigma of extractive research? These questions remain open.

Concluding Thoughts

Considering the authors assembled in this book and the rich experiences they have shared with us, we believe it matters greatly to keep in mind that long-term, in some cases lifelong, research devoted to a society of limited demography and territory—one peripheral to the larger dominant cultures of a region—can be hard to sell to short-term and result-oriented funding bodies, universities, and sometimes even colleagues. We believe this book will provide arguments for a reasoned answer reaching beyond statistical weight, normativity, and supposedly immanent macroscopic truths. It is a plea for the individual, the hidden, and the infrequent, in other words for what life is really like on the ground, as opposed to imagined homogeneity, recurrence, legibility, and unambiguousness. It is a plea to embrace the challenge of complex thinking. Social scientists interested in micro-societies on the margins of strong centralized states can be derided by other, often state-focused scientists, as unpractical idealists and dreamers—"basket weavers."[3] Historians engaged in micro-history, in comparison with those involved in the more classical approaches of their discipline, can also be routinely reproved. Yet, the most central benefit of a historical reading in the social sciences applied to highland societies in Asia has been most fittingly underscored by historian Victor Lieberman, in his comments on Scott's *The Art of Not Being Governed:* "Scott's central achievement, then, is to bring hill peoples into the mainstream of regional history by uncovering their relation to lowland states and societies. [. . .] Scott has rescued hill peoples from assumptions of stasis, primitivism, essentialism, and isolation" (Lieberman 2010, 36). In short, he has carried their voices and highlighted their agency.

Scott was not the first one to do that of course, but he is the most widely read scholar to have done so. Indeed, conducting historical anthropology is instrumental in multiplying standpoints on historical processes that have otherwise been approached solely from the perspective of the dominant polities controlling the fertile and heavily populated lowlands, thus depriving local upland subjects from their capacity for original agency. This is all the more visible in relation to matters like ethnogenesis or wars in the near as much as distant past. This also fosters substantial knowledge on the relationship between dominated societies and the nation-states with which they now find their destiny enmeshed. In this sense, the contributions to this volume substantiate what is arguably the central project of historical anthropology: "show(ing) up the ways that the supposed margins and metropoles, or peripheries and centers, fold into, constitute or disrupt one another" (Axel 2002, 2).

Beyond the reductionist binary of submission versus resistance, there is ample and inviting room for other relations made of vernacularization, hybridization, accommodation, tweaking, and coexistence on many different scales. To be bluntly realistic, in situations of political and demographic weakness and cultural vulnerability, forms of accommodation are mandatory for the smaller players. There is no possibility to escape the heavy presence of the state—strongly encouraged by international bodies and global strategies—as well as the symbolic and institutional straitjacket it imposes on subaltern societies dwelling in borderlands and internal peripheries. This is as true for upland Southeast Asia as it is for aboriginal Australia or indigenous Americas.

Biographies are highly relevant in producing a change in the scale of analysis (Waterson 2006). They help bring information to the fore that would remain totally invisible when adopting solely a macroscopic appraisal of history. Vatthana Pholsena provides a fine example of that potential with her chapter based on life stories of Lao women engaged in the Revolutionary War. She argues that such an approach sheds light on local lives that would have otherwise remained below the radar if examining history through an event-oriented bias or a focus on politics and institutions. With her view from below, we see in all clarity that oral history is a way to investigate the gray zone between the factuality of events and what lies inside the witnesses' minds. This approach promotes a rich way to explore the subjectivity of experience in history, its phenomenology, but also the agency of the various actors taking part in the events.

This, in truth, is what this whole book is about.

Notes

1. Including through archaeology. The field of archaeology is yet to expand into much of the highlands of Southeast Asia (Michaud 2016, 13–14) and it was therefore left out of this discussion.

2. Although, it would not be fair to ascribe the whole scholarly production on history in the highlands to the influence of Scott's book. For instance, monographs authored since the 2000s include Vargyas (2000), Michaud (2007), Bouté (2011, 2018), Le Failler (2014), Davis (2017), Lentz (2019), Nguyễn (2019), and Petit (2020), underscoring the vitality of historical anthropology in this highland region.

3. This was actually how some political scientists cheekily labeled social anthropologists in the Centre for South-East Asian Studies at the University of Hull, UK, when Jean Michaud worked there in the late 1990s.

References

Austin, John L. 1962. *How to Do Things with Words.* London: Oxford University Press.

Axel, Brian Keith. 2002. "Introduction: Historical Anthropology and Its Vicissitudes." In *From the Margins. Historical Anthropology and Its Futures,* edited by B. K. Axel, 1–44. Durham, NC: Duke University Press.

Bamo Ayi, Stevan Harrell, and Ma Lunzy. 2011. *Fieldwork Connections: The Fabric of Ethnographic Collaboration in China and America.* Seattle: University of Washington Press.

Besteman, Catherine. 2013. "Three Reflections on Public Anthropology." *Anthropology Today* 29 (6): 3–6.

Bloch, Marc. 1964. *Apologie pour l'histoire ou Métier d'historien.* Paris: Armand Colin.

Bouté, Vanina. 2011. *En miroir du pouvoir: Les Phounoy du Nord-Laos; Ethnogenèse et dynamiques d'intégration.* Paris: École française d'Extrême-Orient.

———. 2018. *Mirroring Power: Ethnogenesis on the Margins of the Lao State.* Chiang Mai: Silkworm Books.

Carmack, Robert M. 1972. "Ethnohistory: A Review of Its Development, Definitions, Methods, and Aims." *Annual Review of Anthropology* 1: 227–246.

Chaturvedi, Vinayak, ed. 2012. *Mapping Subaltern Studies and the Postcolonial.* London: Verso and New Left Review.

Daniel, E. Valentine. 1996. *Charred Lullabies: Chapters in an Anthropography of Violence.* Princeton, NJ: Princeton University Press.

Davis, Bradley C. 2017. *Imperial Bandits: Outlaws and Rebels in the China-Vietnam Borderlands.* Seattle: University of Washington Press.

Dowling, Robyn. 2010. "Power, Subjectivity, and Ethics in Qualitative Research." In *Qualitative Methods in Human Geography*, edited by I. Hain, 26–39. Oxford: Oxford University Press.

Evans, Grant, and Kelvin Rowley. 1984. *Red Brotherhood at War: Indochina since the Fall of Saigon.* London: Verso.

Fabian, Johannes. 2014. *Time and the Other: How Anthropology Makes Its Object.* New York: Columbia University Press.

Guillemin, Marilys, and Lynn Gillam. 2004. "Ethics, Reflexivity, and 'Ethically Important Moments' Research." *Qualitative Inquiry* 10 (2): 261–280.

Halbwachs, Maurice. (1950) 1997. *La mémoire collective.* Paris: Albin Michel.

Hansen, Mette Halskov. 2006. "In the Footsteps of the Communist Party: Dilemmas and Strategies." In *Doing Fieldwork in China*, edited by S. Thøgersen and M. Heimer, 81–95. Copenhagen: NIAS Press.

Harrell, Stevan, ed. 2001. *Perspectives on the Yi of Southwest China.* Berkeley: University of California Press.

Harrell, Stevan, and Li Yongxiang. 2003. "The History of the History of the Yi, Part II." *Modern China* 29 (3): 362–396.

Heimer, Maria, and Stig Thøgersen, eds. 2006. *Doing Fieldwork in China.* Copenhagen: NIAS Press.

Hershatter, Gail. 2011. *The Gender of Memory: Rural Women and China's Collective Past.* Berkeley: University of California Press.

High, Holly, and Pierre Petit. 2013. "Introduction: The Study of the State in Laos." *Asian Studies Review* 37 (4): 417–432.

Jonsson, Hjorleifur. 2014. *Slow Anthropology. Negotiating Difference with the Iu Mien.* Ithaca, NY: Cornell University.

Kwon, Heonik. 2006. *After the Massacre: Commemoration and Consolation in Ha My and My Lai.* Berkeley: University of California Press.

———. 2008. *Ghosts of War in Vietnam.* Cambridge: Cambridge University Press.

Le Failler, Philippe. 2014. *La rivière Noire: L'intégration d'une marche frontière au Vietnam.* Paris: CNRS.

Lentz, Christian C. 2019. *Contested Territory. Điện Biên Phủ and the Making of Northwest Vietnam.* New Haven, CT: Yale University Press.

Lieberman, Victor. 2010. "A Zone of Refuge in Southeast Asia? Reconceptualizing Interior Spaces." Review of *The Art of Not Being Governed: An Anarchist History of Upland Southeast Asia,* by James C. Scott. *Journal of Global History* 5 (2): 333–346.

Low, Setha M., and Sally Engle Merry. 2010. "Engaged Anthropology: Diversity and Dilemmas." *Current Anthropology* 51 (S2): S203–S226.

McElwee, Pamela. 2004. "Becoming Socialist or Becoming Kinh? Government Policies for Ethnic Minorities in the Socialist Republic of Vietnam." In *Civilizing the Margins: Southeast Asian Government Policies for the Development of Minorities,* edited by C. R. Duncan, 182–213. Ithaca, NY: Cornell University Press.

Meadow, Tey. 2013. "Studying Each Other: On Agency, Constraint, and Positionality in the Field." *Journal of Contemporary Ethnography* 42 (4): 466–481.

Michaud, Jean. 2007. *"Incidental" Ethnographers: French Catholic Missions on the Frontier of Tonkin and Yunnan, 1880–1930.* Leiden: Brill Academic.

———. 2009. "Handling Mountain Minorities in China, Vietnam, and Laos: From History to Current Concerns." *Asian Ethnicity* 10 (1): 25–49.

———. 2010a. "Research Note: Fieldwork, Supervision, and Trust." *Asia Pacific Viewpoint* 51 (2): 220–225.

———. 2010b. "Zomia and Beyond." *Journal of Global History* 5 (2): 187–214.

———. 2016. "Seeing the Forest for the Trees: Scale, Magnitude, and Range in the Southeast Asian Massif." In *Historical Dictionary of the Peoples of the South-East Asian Massif,* 2nd ed., edited by J. Michaud, M. Byrne Swain, and M. Barkataki-Ruscheweyh, 1–40. Lanham, MD: Rowman & Littlefield.

———. 2020a. "The Art of Not Being Scripted So Much: The Politics of Writing Hmong Language(s)." *Current Anthropology* 61 (2): 240–263.

———. 2020b. "Is This Pa Chay Vue? A Study in Three Frames." *Journal of the Royal Asiatic Society* 31 (2): 1–29.

———. 2022. "Ethnography in the Northern Vietnamese Highlands." In *Routledge Handbook of Contemporary Highland Asia,* edited by J. Wouters and N. Heneise, 430–450. London: Routledge.

Mullaney, Thomas S. 2011. *Coming to Terms with the Nation: Ethnic Classification in Modern China.* Berkeley: University of California Press.

Nguyễn Đặng Anh Minh. 2019. "Land Property, Land Politics: A History of the Bahnar in Kon Tum (1820–1945)." PhD diss., Ecole Pratique des Hautes Etudes.

Nora, Pierre. 1997. *Les lieux de mémoire.* Paris: Gallimard.

Nyíri, Pal. 2006. *Scenic Spots: Chinese Tourism, the State, and Cultural Authority.* Seattle: University of Washington Press.

Pels, Peter, and Oscar Salemink, eds. 1999. *Colonial Subjects: Essays on the Practical History of Anthropology*. Ann Arbor: University of Michigan Press.

Petit, Pierre. 2008. "Les politiques culturelles et la question des minorités en RDP Laos." *Bulletin des séances de l'Académie royale des sciences d'outre-mer* 54 (4): 477–499.

———. 2013. "The Backstage of Ethnography as Ethnography of the State: Coping with Officials in the Lao People's Democratic Republic." In *Red Stamps and Gold Stars: Fieldwork in Upland Socialist Asia*, edited by S. Turner, 143–164. Vancouver: UBC Press.

———. 2020. *History, Memory, and Territorial Cults in the Highlands of Laos: The Past Inside the Present*. London: Routledge.

Pholsena, Vatthana, and Oliver Tappe. 2013. *Interactions with a Violent Past: Reading Post-Conflict Landscapes in Cambodia, Laos, and Vietnam*. Singapore: National University of Singapore Press.

Quijano, Aníbal. 2007. "Coloniality and Modernity/Rationality." *Cultural Studies* 21 (2–3): 168–178.

Sahlins, Marshall. 1985. *Islands of History*. London: Tavistock Publications.

Salemink, Oscar. 2003. *The Ethnography of Vietnam's Central Highlanders: A Historical Contextualisation, 1850–1990*. London: Routledge Curzon.

Schein, Louisa. 1997. "Gender and Internal Orientalism in China." *Modern China* 23 (1): 69–98.

Schnegg, Michael. 2014. "Epistemology: The Nature and Validation of Knowledge." In *Handbook of Methods in Cultural Anthropology*, 2nd ed., edited by H. Russell Bernard and C. C. Gravlee, 21–53. Lanham, MD: Rowman & Littlefield.

Scott, James. 2009. *The Art of Not Being Governed: An Anarchist History of Upland Southeast Asia*. New Haven, CT: Yale University Press.

Stocking, George W., Jr., ed. 1991. *Colonial Situations: Essays on the Conceptualisation of Ethnographic Knowledge*. Madison: University of Wisconsin Press.

Stoler, Ann Laura. 2009. *Along the Archival Grain: Epistemic Anxieties and Colonial Common Sense*. Princeton, NJ: Princeton University Press.

Stolz, Rosalie, and Oliver Tappe, eds. 2021. "Upland Pioneers: Aspiration, Future-Making, and Emerging Elites in Upland Southeast Asia." Special issue, *Social Anthropology/Anthropologie Sociale* 29 (3).

Tappe, Oliver. 2013. "Faces and Facets of the *Kantosou Kou Xat*: The Lao 'National Liberation Struggle' in State Commemoration and Historiography." *Asian Studies Review* 37 (4): 433–450.

———, ed. 2015. "Frictions and Fictions—Intercultural Encounters and Frontier Imaginaries in Upland Southeast Asia." Special issue, *Asia Pacific Journal of Anthropology* 16 (4).

Thum, Rian. 2014. *The Sacred Routes of Uyghur History*. Cambridge, MA: Harvard University Press.

Tuhiwai Smith, Linda. 1999. *Decolonizing Methodologies: Research and Indigenous Peoples*. London: Zed Books.

Turner, Sarah, ed. 2013a. *Red Stamps and Gold Stars: Fieldwork Dilemmas in Upland Socialist Asia*. Vancouver: UBC Press.

———. 2013b. "The Silenced Research Assistant Speaks Her Mind." In *Red Stamps and Gold Stars: Fieldwork Dilemmas in Upland Socialist Asia*, edited by S. Turner, 220–238. Vancouver: UBC Press.

Vargyas, Gábor. 2000. *À la recherche des Brou perdus, population montagnarde du Centre Indochinois*. Paris: Les cahiers de Péninsule.

Waterson, Roxana. 2006. *Southeast Asian Lives: Personal Narratives and Historical Experience*. Singapore: NUS Press.

Whorf, Benjamin Lee. 1956. "An American Indian Model of the Universe." In *Language, Thought, and Reality: Selected Writings of Benjamin Lee Whorf*, edited by J. B. Carroll, S. C. Levinson, and P. Lee, 57–64. Cambridge, MA: MIT Press.

Willford, Andrew, and Eric Tagliacozzo. 2009. *Clio/Anthropos: Exploring the Boundaries between History and Anthropology*. Stanford, CA: Stanford University Press.

CHAPTER 1

The Archive, the Road, and the Field Between

Toward a Geography of Vietnam's Black River Region

Christian C. Lentz

ON THE FRONT PAGE OF A RESEARCH NOTEBOOK I kept at Vietnam's National Archives—and right above my name and phone number in Hanoi—are the serial numbers, manufacturer name, and parent company of a commercial air-conditioning unit. Fourteen years later I still remember the spring 2006 day when I recorded this information so seemingly superfluous to my studies. I was sitting in the reading room of Archives Center 3 when a good-natured man summoned me to follow him and his coworker. Although I did not know either's job, exactly, we had regularly shared tea, tobacco, and small talk over breaks among security guards and other workers near the front gate. As the three of us rode the elevator up, he asked for my help translating some technical English into Vietnamese. Stepping out onto the roof, we were momentarily blinded by the tropical sun and blasted by the heat. Once our eyesight adjusted to the glare, he directed me to a massive American-made machine that, he explained, was malfunctioning. Could I help fix it? I cautioned him that air-conditioning repair was not my specialty. But, noting that the manufacturer happened to be near my home university, I recorded the technical details and offered to help as best I could.

It was another quirky day in the archives, but it was more than that. Standing on the roof, I gained a panoramic view from the archives onto Vietnam's capital: in the foreground sat the zoo graced with green, the grandiose Daewoo Hotel, sidewalk cafes, embassies and guard posts, and blocks and blocks of concrete, including my apartment building; in the background barges floated the Red River's bend, West Lake glimmered gray, and construction cranes loomed and swung; all around us were roadways coursed by cars, buses, and motorbikes, the beeps of which punctuated the roar of airplanes overhead.

The everyday experience changed my research perspective in fundamental and lasting ways. I realized where the archive was situated in a thriving city, how it connected with the country, and the ways it was run by people with everyday concerns distinct from the documents, files, and permission slips that preoccupied me. Though the workers figured out how to repair the air-conditioning unit on their own, our experience thinking about how to fix it together was the first of what became many collaborative projects and reciprocal exchanges. The minutes I spent standing there, blinking in the sun, and grasping for technical terms fostered relations that increased my access to and understandings of the archives' collections. Even more, my time on the roof transformed how I located my work: the field was not out there in Điện Biên Phủ, waiting for me when I finished my archival work. Rather, Hanoi was the field too, as were the archives, roads, and rivers that connected one to the other and both to distant places, radical ideas, and transformative processes.

This chapter offers a methodological reflection on the mixed-method research underlying my recently published book, *Contested Territory: Điện Biên Phủ and the Making of Northwest Vietnam* (Lentz 2019). Whereas the book's empirical foundation rests on archival documents dating to the 1940s–1950s from Vietnam and France, "The Archive, the Road, and the Field Between" discusses the ethnographic fieldwork conducted to collect those documents and resituates them in their generative context of the Black River region, now known as the Northwest (Tây Bắc). Unfolding in spurts since 2004 and lasting over two years in total, this fieldwork was multisited, involving sojourns in the national archives and residential life in Hanoi, interviews in government offices in Điện Biên Phủ, travel around the rural region, and immersion in the social life of ethnically diverse montane villages.

Tacking between sites led me to think about the making of Vietnam in a historic borderlands and the contested construction of its nation, state, and territory there. Moving across field and archive, what Bernard Cohn (1980, 220) called "the diagnostic work place[s] of the historians and anthropologists," placed me in the same geographic relationship I aimed to study. Furthermore, expanding a sense of "the field" to encompass the archive as well as the infrastructure and landscapes connecting these far-flung sites enabled me, as advocates of such interdisciplinarity suggest, to "elucidat[e] structures of power," including the archive itself (Tagliacozzo and Willford 2009, 19). Finally, participant observation in communities distant from one another did not simply highlight the differences in mainland Southeast Asia between lowland and highland places, as though a relic of what scholars have theorized as "Zomia" (Michaud 2010; Scott 2009; Van Schendel 2002). Rather, working at the interstices between places that my oral and textual sources alike called "upstream and downstream" immersed me in the spatial relations, powerful exchanges, and cultural forms that have long tied them together.

The chapter's first substantive section explains how a contrapuntal research design produced knowledge iteratively and contingently, a methodology realized after the fact. The sections that follow focus on several moments in the longer research process, beginning with the archives, then rural field sites, and, finally, the road between them. Moments include informal labor exchanges with archival leadership, visiting a farmer's household accompanied by officials, impromptu conversations with veterans, and travel on a road built in 1954. Each moment led me to consider my own positionality as a young, male American researcher working in a former conflict zone. Taken together, these experiences generated a sense of place, empathic understanding, reciprocal commitments, and appreciation for ethnolinguistic diversity that both informed the book project and, I argue, renewed a geographic dialogue between history and anthropology in the highlands of Southeast Asia.

Contrapuntal Research Design and Iterative Knowledge Production

Much like the processes of state and territory formation analyzed in *Contested Territory*, the trajectory of my research in and on Vietnam makes sense only in retrospect. By contrast, between February 2006 and April 2007, when I was working in the archives and the field on my dissertation, very little of what I had planned actually turned out as expected. In fact, the path of my research and its role in my book hinged on unforeseen circumstances and outcomes largely beyond my control, underlining the "contingencies of knowledge production" that lurk behind truth claims levied by states and scholars alike (Tagliacozzo and Willford 2009, 1). Arriving at this critical insight stemmed from adopting a flexible methodology and adaptive approach consistent with qualitative inquiry and ethnographic methods (Hancké 2009). Now, looking back at this formative fifteen-month period, I recognize a contrapuntal research design operating along distinct but interrelated geographic and methodological axes. Since 2007—while I started a family, filed my dissertation in 2011, and advanced on the tenure track—my visits to overseas research sites have become less frequent but more focused, occurring mostly in the summer season. All along, I have developed an iterative approach to knowledge production that adapts research questions to diverse forms of textual, oral, and visual data.

My research design emerged contingently through negotiations with local sponsors at multiple sites in Hanoi and Điện Biên Phủ. I did not plan—much less "design"—this approach from the outset. In fact, both my first attempt at identifying a sponsor and my initial methodology failed in face of the formidable challenges associated with research in Vietnam (Scott, Miller, and Lloyd 2006; Lentz 2014). A graduate student in development sociology at the time, I first visited Vietnam in summer 2004 as a participant in an intensive language program for American university students.[1] In addition to daily Vietnamese lessons, another PhD student and I endeavored to secure a sponsor for our upcoming dissertation research before leaving Hanoi. Armed with a letter of introduction from the program director, we met the head of a research academy and explained our intent. He agreed to take us on, asking for our assistance in the meantime by editing a paper. Though both of us delivered written comments to his office, he responded to neither of our many emails after we had left for the United States, leaving us temporarily without institutional support. Fortunately, another student put me in touch with a university in Hanoi. A center director there generously responded to my email inquiry, agreed to sponsorship, welcomed me to his campus, and introduced me to students, faculty, and researchers. However, because of the suspicion that I—a young, white American man—would likely arouse due to legacies of the Second Indochina War (1955–1975), he and his colleagues cautioned against my plans to conduct long-term ethnographic participation and household surveys in rural areas. Their advice, which I adopted, was to "act like a cadre" and take month-long, periodic trips to my field site while maintaining residence in Hanoi and using the archives between trips.

Looking back, and before explaining what became of them methodologically, these introductory experiences were significant in three ways. First, local sponsorship for foreign scholars is required in Vietnam but not always easy to secure. Modeled on the Soviet Union, the university system there is intended for education and the academies for research. I was very lucky to get connected with a university that was not only as interested in research as education but also welcomed international scholars like me. Second, Vietnamese-language training was and remains crucial to doing research in Vietnam. Whenever I used Vietnamese in introductory meetings with sponsors, my efforts were greeted with a mix of relief (that we did not have to speak my native language) and respect (for the effort spent learning theirs). Moreover, Vietnamese-language facility opened new insight into the everyday ways and words through which diverse peoples understand their social worlds, especially the political dimensions of community and space associated with Vietnam. Had I become proficient in languages common in the Black River region, such as Tai, Khmu, or Hmong, I would have learned more still. Finally, the academy's head had proposed a reciprocal arrangement: in exchange for assistance editing an English-language article, he would help sponsor our research. That he did not reciprocate nonetheless foreshadowed more productive exchanges to come, including my vetting as an air-conditioner repairman.

As introduction gave way to immersion, I found myself working across co-configured forms of geographic and epistemic difference. Tacking between Hanoi and Điện Biên Phủ and traveling the Black River region immersed me in geographic relationships reminiscent of those I studied in the archives. Read in Hanoi, archival documents dating to Vietnam's 1945 revolution discussed how activists, soldiers, officials, and cadres allied with the nascent Democratic Republic of Vietnam attempted to recruit, mobilize, and govern residents of the Black River region during and after the First Indochina War (1946–1954). Fifty years later, encountering farmers, officials, veterans, traders, and specialists in Điện Biên Phủ evoked these historic subjects and helped me understand the cultural differences and physical distances that their contemporaries, too, must navigate in everyday ways. Traveling the region while studying maps schooled me in a complex landscape marked by high mountains, racing rivers, cultivated slopes, and terraced hollows, all populated by peoples patterned by ethnolinguistic diversity. Epistemically, comparing the actual landscape with its cartographic representations educated me in the multiple place names used for a given location, how local meanings vary, and why toponyms still coexist alongside one another. For example, whereas Điện Biên Phủ means "border post prefecture" in

Vietnamese, its local name Muang Thanh means "heavenly place" in Tai, underlining how the site figures marginally in Kinh/Việt space but centrally in Tai space. Reflecting on the convergence or divergence of meaning offered insight into political contests, infrastructure developments, and population movements that continue to this day. As such, peregrinations and bipolar residencies placed me in geographic relationships not only similar to but, moreover, a direct legacy of those I studied in the archives.

Methodologically, moving back and forth between archives and field sites enabled me to ask questions and seek answers unavailable in either data source alone. My first visit to Điện Biên Phủ occurred in 2004 when I was studying Vietnamese and was curious about a momentous battle that took place there a half-century earlier. The many monuments, memorials, museums, and cemeteries on display told a story of long, fierce combat ending with Vietnam's final victory over French forces on May 7, 1954. Yet what read on the former battlefield as a story of military triumph and radical rupture with colonialism echoed only faintly with what archival documents told of a longer period of tense political organizing and the broader context in which these relationships unfolded. Trained in textual and contextual analysis (Cohn 1980), I knew that bringing these narratives into correspondence required thinking carefully about the provenance of data sources, authorial motivations, and intended audiences. But working in a region often written about but poorly understood meant I kept asking myself seemingly simple but actually baffling questions about what had happened where, in what sequence, and why there and in that order. Fortunately, I found informed answers among archivists and local interlocutors whose expertise was based either in the documents they managed or in the very ground under their feet. Posing the same questions to people in different social positions yielded a geographic method of triangulation, confirming some findings, casting doubt on others, and raising more questions for further inquiry (Warshawsky 2014).

Moving between sites and thinking across methods formed the basis of iterative knowledge production. Thinking in this recursive mode meant revisiting the same places at different times, reviewing sources based on new information, and nurturing relationships that evolved with my changing interests and research questions. Acting like a cadre in line with my sponsor's advice, I visited Điện Biên Phủ four times over fifteen months and stayed, on average, for a month each time. In doing so, I encountered interlocutors at different moments in a seasonal calendar guiding their agricultural production, cultural activities, and official duties. Meeting village heads in August at a time of meager meals and annual food scarcity (*giáp hạt*)—when maize had yet to mature and rice was still ripening—contrasted with October when everyone, myself included, participated in harvesting rice and celebrating the renewal of household stores. In the meantime, officials regulated where I stayed overnight, whom I met, and what data I saw, forcing me to refine my inquiry but alerting me to ongoing practices of state formation (Lentz 2015). Given these limits, I abandoned a village-based study and refocused on the archives, where my access was greater. Nonetheless, what I learned in varied villages about agroecological cycles, food production, agricultural policy, development projects, and interethnic relations helped me understand how the same seasonal rhythms had structured early state interventions dating to the 1940s and 1950s. Though I wound up focusing on this transformative period in my book—when the Black River region became known and governed as Vietnam's "Northwest"—I could not have understood the historical rhythms and seasonal shifts without encountering them ethnographically in the field.

Reciprocity in the Archives

Around the time when I played the short-lived role of air-conditioning repairman, the woman who delivered my files at Archives Center 3 invited me to join an afternoon dance lesson. Feeling shy and not being a graceful dancer, I demurred. But after a day or two, the pulsing music, the emptiness of the reading room, and the friendly archivist's repeated entreaties led me to reconsider. I packed up a bit early, joined the lessons, and wound up dancing the rumba awkwardly but happily (Lentz 2020). Participation in the social event put my two left feet on display to the dismay of my partner but the delight of everyone else, including the center's leadership in attendance. More than providing still another, even quirkier, day in the archives, the dance lesson embedded me deeper into the archives' community. What felt like a step outside my comfort zone was, in fact, an extension of my ethnographic approach and the third occasion I had mixed with the archives staff socially—and far from the last. Little did I know that being a participant-observer in the archives' social world would initiate a sustained process of reciprocal exchange resulting in successful scholarly collaborations and wider access to newly available holdings.

Before I could even dream of dancing there, my early forays to the National Archives in Hanoi required learning more about the institutions and rules of access than the content I sought. I took heart in the advice of a dissertation adviser who had warned that all archives are different from one another, requiring close work with archivists and close attention to institutional norms. Indeed, I quickly realized that even Hanoi's two centers differed widely not just in their collections but also in their regulations governing access and reproduction. Whereas Archives Center 1 holds French-language documents from the colonial era, Archives Center 3 holds Vietnamese-language documents dating to the Democratic Republic's birth in 1945. Both centers require a research proposal and a sponsor's letter to gain entrance, completion of one form to read individual files, and completion of another to photocopy documents, all of which must be approved by higher levels in the bureaucracy. Neither center allowed the use of computers or cameras nor the copying of maps. But these surface similarities disguised sharply differential norms regarding file access and reproduction. Center 1, for example, rejected requests to view files on colonial-era opium production in Laos and on a journey by the resident-superior of Tonkin to the Mekong River because they "do not relate to the topic of research." It only permitted photocopies of part of a file, not its whole contents. By contrast, Center 3 rejected multiple file requests but without giving a reason. It did allow photocopying of whole files. Moreover, and perhaps because of my emergent exchange relations and a growing openness to international scholars there, Center 3's interpretation of my topic and its relevant geographic area were broader, allowing the former to change and the latter to expand over time.

Negotiating access filled my archival notebooks not just with information on record groups, file numbers, and document titles but also with notes on rules, regulations, archivist names, and spoken remarks, including the quote above from an archivist at Center 1. Because a given request might take days, weeks, or even months to register approval or denial, simply keeping track of my own requests challenged my record-keeping capabilities. Further, awaiting word and fearing rejection from anonymous higher-ups worried me, an emotional response that balanced the satisfaction I felt about making good finds. Over time, I learned to take more detailed notes on content, quoting directly in the source language as much as possible in order to hedge against rejected photocopy requests and to remind myself why the document had seemed important. To this day, working in Vietnam's archives still produces mixed feelings, toggling between relief about fulfillment and worry about denial.

Although my notebooks register a consistently mixed affect on my part, they also record a distinct shift in June 2006, when routine ethnographic work contributed to a larger intellectual exchange. On the month's first day, I arrived at Center 3 and took a break to buy cigarettes. Out on the street, it happened to be market day, and the lychees looked delicious. So I bought a couple of kilograms to share with the archivists. Back inside, I presented the fruit to the reading room's head, who then called in his staff for a small, impromptu party. Our conversation meandered over familiar topics, ranging from the price I had paid for the lychees (fair), to my family status (married), parental background (acrimonious divorce), place of residence (North Carolina), and the like. A woman whom I had considered standoffish turned out to be hilarious: she said that if I were not married already, then it would be a "waste" (*phê*) of me. Recalling my wife's visit earlier that spring, the head commented on her beauty, intelligence, and outsized presence. "They really appreciated the fruit," I wrote, implying also the social life that my sharing of it had encouraged.

A few hours later, back at my desk reading files, an archivist approached to say that the center's directors wanted to see me in their office upstairs. A bit nervous at first, I wondered if I had done something wrong by straying beyond my approved topic, bringing fruit into the building, or something else entirely. Perhaps noticing my discomfort, the two directors tried to set me at ease by joking about whether I had found a girlfriend yet (no). Steeped in masculine norms—the question was common among men in my neighborhood as well—their inquiry marked their comfort with me even as they treated me as a (male) scholar (Farmer et al. 2019). Pivoting in response to questions about my experience thus far, I praised the supportive reading room head, noting that I had agreed to his request to "share information" (*tuyên truyền*; lit. propagandize) about the center with other foreign scholars. Gradually, they raised the issue that, evidently, had been their reason for summoning me: they had a trilingual archives guide in the works and needed help with the English-language portion. Would I be willing to help? Was ten days enough time? Not knowing at all what I was getting into, I agreed.

Shortly thereafter, the two directors sent me a very large computer file, and I got to work. Quickly overwhelmed by the size and complexity of the task, I stayed home from the archives to devote myself to poring over dozens of documents and translating them one by one. When I reported to a director that prioritizing the translation project would take time away from my own research, she offered to expedite my requests with a staffer. "I guess that's how it works," I wrote, noting an incipient form of labor exchange. In the meantime, owing to the vocabulary's specialized and archaic nature, many words were not only new to me but unavailable in contemporary dictionaries. So, I reached out via email to senior scholars who had written about relevant historical topics, explained the project, and asked for help rendering key words into English. Reading emails one day in a smoky internet café near my apartment, I came across one response that gave me pause: a colleague at the Hanoi branch of the French School of Asian Studies (ÉFEO) said, basically, please stop what you are doing and call me immediately.

What unfolded over the following weeks and months was an intensely collaborative project involving ÉFEO scholars, international donors, directors and archivists at Center 3, and the center's parent agency, the State Records and Archives Department. Before my arrival in Hanoi, all these parties had been working together to produce definitive, trilingual guides to the National Archives' center-based collections, including descriptions of holdings by record group, procedures for access, and other information relevant to patrons. They had already published a guide to Archives Center 1 (Ngô 2001) and had now turned to Center 3. After calling by phone, I learned that my colleagues at the ÉFEO had long waited for the delivery of the very same computer files that, for some reason, I now had in my hands. My colleagues and I then worked long hours every day for two weeks, producing draft translations into English and French of Center 3's Vietnamese-language collections that I delivered to the director at Center 3 with thanks from the ÉFEO. Published later that same year, the volume (Phạm et al. 2006) listed me as a member of its English-language advisory board.

A process fascinating in its own right, translation became my principal contribution to the center's intellectual and public life. I routinely assisted reading room staff with their own projects, including those of their family members. Later in 2006, I collaborated again with Center 3's directors to stage an exhibit at the Hồ Chí Minh Museum presenting the memorabilia of northern soldiers, medics, and cadres who had

traveled south to participate in the Second Indochina War. As with specialized or outdated terms, I frequently encountered words revealingly
hard to translate. Not simply a one-to-one transfer of meaning, I realized the multiple valences of Vietnamese words, their etymology and
morphology, and how their meanings changed over time. Furthermore,
words carry concepts that may resist translation. I committed to practicing what qualitative researchers call "grounded theory," an inductive
method through which concepts emerge from assembling and analyzing data (Guba and Lincoln 1994). For example, my book *Contested
Territory* analyzes Vietnamese-language concepts such as "people's
laborer" (*dân công*), "anxiety" (*thắc mắc*), and "watching over" (*theo dõi*)
to plumb culturally significant meanings too often absent from English-
and French-language scholarship.

In addition to these intellectual benefits, participating in translation
work with Center 3 changed my relationships with staff and the conditions of my access there in lasting ways. As promised, the director asked
her staff to expedite my requests, and my files did come faster than
before. Nonetheless, I continued to worry about receiving a large and
growing pile of photocopies in time for my trip back home. But all was
well by late March 2007, when I hosted a farewell party with archivists
and readers at a local restaurant. Not until years later did other benefits come to fruition. On a brief visit in January 2011, the director said
to me, "You must return here and use the collections before I retire."
Understanding the generosity of her offer to reciprocate our exchange,
I returned in summer 2012 for a deep dive back into the collections.

In and Out of Villages

My introduction to Noong Nhai village in August 2006 began like any
other village tour arranged by my local sponsors in Điện Biên district.
Departing from quarters in the Province Guest House, I rode my motorcycle to the district's Economic Service, met my minder and a junior
cadre at 7:00 a.m., formed a caravan of three bikes, and drove south
out of town for a few kilometers. We rallied at the offices of Thanh
Xương commune, located at the heart of the Muang Thanh plain and
just behind a memorial to the 444 villagers killed there in an explosion
during the battle of Điện Biên Phủ in April 1954. Inside the office, my
minder introduced me to commune officials, explained my interest in
agriculture and rural society, indicated that I spoke Vietnamese, and,

referring to an official letter that had preceded our visit, requested assistance visiting a village in their jurisdiction. The chairman of the commune People's Committee confirmed the letter's receipt and said he had no problem with my program. He told how irrigation had brought prosperity to an ethnically diverse commune composed of majority Tai and minority Kinh, Khmu, and Hmong peoples. We discussed how Vietnam's rural territorial administration—ranging from province down through district, commune, and village to team and household—compared with that in the United States. Taking our leave, two commune cadres joined our caravan. The five of us rode into Noong Nhai, where we met the village head, talked about agriculture and infrastructure, and gathered population data.

Acting like a cadre, I came to realize, meant learning as much about the construction and performance of state power as what I had intended to study about agrarian change. As I have written elsewhere (Lentz 2014), negotiating permission to do research, navigating a complex administrative hierarchy, interviewing farmers accompanied by officials, and collecting household data all implicated me and my interlocutors in a micropolitics of state formation. Ethnography offered a method to understand my Janus-faced role as both a participant in powerful state-making practices and an observer of their effects on rural society. Crucially, I realized that cadres have long been doing similar work. My minder, for example, worked as an agricultural extension agent until his boss in the Economic Service assigned him to watch over me. He was also an outsider of sorts among the Tai and Khmu peoples we met: hailing from Thái Bình Province, he was one of a coterie of upstream Kinh officials with downstream roots. More generally, Kinh officials by and large held the reins of Điện Biên's province- and district-level bureaucracies, dominating leadership and predominating in line agencies, like those under the Ministry of Agriculture and Rural Development. At the commune level, official positions were more mixed, including higher numbers of so-called local cadres (*cán bộ địa phương*), most often Tai. In the villages, village heads and party leaders tended to reflect the unit's relevant ethnic composition, whether Tai, Kinh, Hmong, or Khmu (Lentz 2014). Incorporating these ethnographic insights into my analysis of archival documents helped me understand a complex geography of state-making, including the ways in which culturally distinct spaces, especially the Tai *muang* (governed spatial unit) and diverse village spaces, became integral to Vietnamese territory.

What set that day in August apart from other chaperoned village tours in Điện Biên stemmed from a tip by the village head, who, noting my interest in history, referred us to a knowledgeable neighbor. Our slow-moving motorcycle gang wound over muddy tracks, past waving groves of bamboo, between timber houses on stilts, through gates, and into a yard that opened onto emerald wet-rice fields stretching to hills on the horizon. At a large house, one of the commune officials shouted greetings in Tai, and a tall man stepped onto the porch, raising his hand in welcome. As we parked our bikes, he beckoned me to move mine under the shade. Fumbling awkwardly, I ran over a red plastic basin, crushing it. He waved away my mortified apology. We mounted the stairs, removed our shoes, drank tea, and began the customary greetings. This time, because it was his bailiwick, a commune official introduced me and my fellow district travelers. The tall man said it was his honor to host us. Now retired but still farming, he told how in his prime he had served as head of the Farmers Association (*Hội Nông dân*), leading collectivization during the Second Indochina War. Then, perhaps owing to his service as a cadre, something strange happened: all the escorting officials politely took leave and left us alone. As we talked about the village's history and his biography, I could see the four cadres wandering the yard, admiring a fish pond and the lovely view. We conversed in Vietnamese nonetheless because my Tai was inadequate. He invited me back.

Impressed as much by his prodigious memory as his evident kindness, I took him up on his offer just a few days later on a visit with my wife, becoming a student of oral history in the process (Lee 2015). I brought a new plastic basin to replace the one I had crushed. Thanking me, he again beckoned me to park under his porch, where, I noted, someone had cleverly patched up and continued to use the broken basin. Inside, I introduced my wife, an American historian, who happened to be visiting me for several weeks. He, in turn, introduced his wife, granddaughter, and parents. Serving rice wine, not tea, he explained, signaled welcome and good cheer. We settled into a conversation, and I asked questions about the region's intricate ethnolinguistic situation, including relations between Tai groups. He responded, "White Tai and Black Tai are really the same, truly only one, but because of fighting became two." Their languages were mutually comprehensible, he added, varying slightly by regional dialect. By contrast, he continued, Tai people needed several years to master the "Kinh language" (*tiếng Kinh*). Prior to "liberation" in 1954, he explained, there were very few Kinh people in the area, only those who worked with the French. "No one else spoke Kinh," he declared, referring to a language I had always been taught to call Vietnamese. Though the soldiers and settlers who arrived in 1954 learned Tai quickly, he gradually learned the Kinh language in school, "like you learned English."

This conversation about language, ethnicity, and settlement helped transform my understanding of Vietnam's construction in historically Tai spaces. I realized that Vietnam was a political project still under construction along the rugged frontier with China and Laos, where, furthermore, Vietnamese is this project's most pronounced cultural dimension. Rather than calling it the "national" or "common" (*phổ thống*) language, as was normal downstream, the retiree's telling reference to "the Kinh language" associated it with a specific ethnolinguistic group, if one now dominant in a territorial nation-state. Likewise, Tai women in Điện Biên's many markets often noted my facility speaking "Kinh." But Kinh women there still referred to my Vietnamese, revealing a nationalist norm steeped in ethnocentricity. More broadly, other Tai and non-Tai peoples there routinely employed Tai as the lingua franca. If local peoples had acculturated to Vietnamese in school, then the retiree and I had experienced its official practice in company of the cadre convoy. In other words, Vietnamese or "Kinh" was not the first language for either me or the Tai retiree but, rather, a lingua franca endowed with national significance. After I left, my interlocutors and his neighbors would surely revert to linguistic customs registered in Tai. In short, all these local Tai speakers had flipped the script: even as Kinh peoples are a cultural force and numerical majority in the Vietnamese nation, Tai peoples remain a cultural force and numerical majority in the Black River region (Cầm 1978; Mukdawijitra 2007).

Understood as a cultural artifact with political overtones, Vietnamese-language facility indicated patterns of Kinh migration initiated in the 1950s and still operating on an ancient, multilingual society grounded in Tai socio-spatial forms. In this light, the 1954 battle of Điện Biên Phủ inaugurated an era of state-sponsored Kinh migration from lowland centers to Vietnam's montane borderlands with Laos, China, and Cambodia (Hardy 2002). Even the battlefield itself—that is, the arable Muang Thanh plain—had figured in a long-standing rivalry between Tai elites in Lai Châu (often glossed as "White Tai") allied with the French, and Tai elites in Thuận Châu and Sơn La (often glossed as

"Black Tai") allied with the Democratic Republic of Vietnam (McAlister 1967; Le Failler 2011). Ultimately, the territorial prize went to the Tai-Kinh alliance, becoming an irrigated rice bowl as a result of subsequent irrigation projects, agrarian mobilizations, and development projects, including wartime collectivization led by my interlocutor (Lentz 2011; Dao 2015). Through it all, the Tai *muang* endured as a kind of cultural bedrock both stabilizing more recent cultural formations and influencing other groups, especially Khmu and Hmong neighbors but also Kinh migrants, through long-standing processes of Tai-ization (Turton 2000). Ethnographically, I had glimpsed a small example of Tai power when the cadres left me alone with a prominent former official and respected community member. In subsequent visits to Noong Nhai village, neighbors recognized his social position by way of deference to his authority and comments about his wealth. His accumulated status overflowed the Tai *muang*'s traditional boundaries, saturating Vietnamese territory as well (Condominas 1976; Lentz 2019).

These and other ground-level experiences in and around Điện Biên Phủ taught me to pay closer attention to the subtle but routine gestures, language, and customs that also registered, albeit dimly, in the archives. In order to protect local informants, *Contested Territory* does not cite oral and ethnographic data, foregrounding instead close readings of newly available documents. Nonetheless, what I learned from my informants shed new light on rich source material in files dating to the late 1940s. Written by Tai cadres from elite families, the documents described relations between peoples in the Black River region and the Red River delta in terms of "upstream" (*miền ngược*) and "downstream" (*miền dưới*), respectively. Echoing across the river basins of Southeast Asia, the riverine idiom predates European colonialism and nationalist anticolonialism, suggesting continuous processes rather than ruptures with the past (Bronson 1978). More prosaically, the Vietnamese-language documents contained spelling and grammatical errors that indicated the author's struggles to learn a third or fourth language, which, at the time, was itself a revolutionary activity led by Việt Minh cadres on literacy campaigns. As such, *Contested Territory* begins in World War II, when powerful Tai cadres worked with these and other "downstream cadres" to build postcolonial Vietnamese territory by incorporating old *muang* relations into new administrative structures. Much like the retired head of the Farmers Association, these "local cadres" had brokered regional relations in a time of war, building bridges between Tai and Kinh social formations, negotiating with other ethnic groups, and, ultimately, securing Vietnamese territory (Ha 2016). Not simply climbing the hills, as the literature on Zomia would have it, I came to argue that Tai elites had pulled Kinh civilization into the Black River region as well.

On the Road Again

In November 2006, shortly after returning from a month upstream, I shared a draft beer with friends in my old downstream neighborhood back in Hanoi. Located just off a busy road in Hai Bà Trưng, the alleyway was home to many veterans who had fought in any one of the three Indochina Wars. We got along well once we had established that I was as interested in their lives and stories as they were in mine (Lentz 2015). That day, as we sat in plastic chairs, sipped draft beer, and snacked on peanuts, I told them about riding my motorcycle to and from Điện Biên Phủ. They were surprised, concerned perhaps, that I had traveled alone on the five-hundred-kilometer journey on dangerous roads in unfamiliar places. I assured them of my safety but admitted that the two-day return trip had exhausted me. Standing in attendance, an older man spoke up: "Two days, huh?" He continued: "Back when we went that way, it took us thirty days marching by night." We all paused, and I felt the gulf between his experience and my own.

Even though we had traveled the same road, the veteran of the First Indochina War threw into sharp relief the distance and dangers he had negotiated during the epic Điện Biên Phủ Campaign. His journey was typical of those traveled by People's Army soldiers in 1953–1954. Mobilized in downstream areas, they packed their own rations, firearms, and ammunition on foot. Walking by night over mountains and sheltering by day in the forest, they avoided the warplanes that strafed supply routes and river crossings. At the end of the line, they faced an elite French force dug into fortifications. Far fewer soldiers survived the bitter siege to make the month-long journey home.

Traveling by land from Hanoi to Điện Biên Phủ and listening to stories such as these resonated in concrete ways with the documents I read in the archives. Before World War II, upstream and downstream communities, as the terms imply, were connected by the Black River (Sông Đà), which joins the Red River at Việt Trì just west of Hanoi. But the treacherous journey upriver took weeks in favorable conditions, and summer monsoons rendered it impassable (Le Failler 2014, 30). In fact, much of what is today National Road 6 was built during the campaign by Vietnamese soldiers, engineers, and "people's laborers" (*dân công*), including a ninety-kilometer section from Tuần Giáo to Điện Biên Phủ that the French had called a "mule track" (Shrader 2015, 348). Militarily, the two armies' logistics strategy pitted porters plying long overland routes under constant construction against airplanes flying short hops between air bases. To the consternation of the French generals who trusted victory to superior technology, the pedestrian strategy won. To this day, travel by plane on this route is deceptively simple, requiring only fifty minutes in the air. By contrast, travel by car, bus, or motorcycle exposes the traveler to long-standing geographic barriers of climate, culture, and topography. Nonetheless, road construction continues to close the distance, connect far-flung communities, and overcome these barriers.

Only by traveling the tarmac they built did I gain an appreciation for the herculean infrastructural labors performed sixty-some years ago. In 2006–2007, National Road 6 was again under construction to widen the road, straighten switchbacks, and strengthen crossings. Overland traffic might halt for hours near Thuận Châu at the foot of a mountain pass called Pha Đin, a Tai name meaning "sky land." Stretching over thirty kilometers at altitudes above 1,000 meters, the pass had been a chokepoint during the campaign when airplanes subjected youth pioneers, soldiers, and civilian laborers to withering fire. They prevailed in no small measure because of the upstream local people, many of whom were women, who helped build these roads and feed their downstream compatriots. Half a century later, engineers and workers again used dynamite to blast a new route over the pass, cutting travel time significantly. I rode up and up, passing dump trucks, excavators, fallen trees, and drainage pipes before reaching into the clouds and entering a thick fog. At the summit, the fog lifted and the clouds melted away. The sun peeked through, opening onto checkered swidden fields, scattered Hmong houses, and grassy pastures, one dented by a bomb crater. Switching back and forth steadily downward, the road wound past Tai homes nestled amid terraced wet-rice fields before flattening into the town of Tuần Giáo, the site of a storage depot during the campaign. My overland journey was a walk in the park compared to the same journey in 1954, but my understanding of the landscape grew nonetheless from traveling it ethnographically and investigating its construction historically.

Conclusions

Good scholarship requires movement, immersion, and flexibility. I could not have written *Contested Territory* by simply collecting documents in Hanoi, Paris, or Aix-en-Provence. Only by listening carefully at multiple sites to varied sources did I start to hear and slowly understand stories that located archival documents in their generative context, in this case the Black River region of Vietnam. Doing research across all these sites brought old state documents into the same analytical frame as the contemporary villages, offices, memorials, and rice fields of Điện Biên Phủ. Through careful listening at each site, I heard voices and observed gestures that spoke of a context still enmeshed in the same historic processes under study, namely acculturation, nationalization, and territorialization.

Conditioned by circumstance and recognized in retrospect, this contrapuntal methodology came into focus through an iterative process of knowledge production. My research questions evolved in relation to data emerging through the scholarly collaborations, unforeseen obstacles, and other contingencies that structure research access in Vietnam, as elsewhere. Adjusting to regulations and adapting to insights required flexibility as well as years of patient inquiry. I asked the same questions of different sources, returned to the same sources with different questions, and recorded all manner of textual, verbal, and nonverbal responses. As a participant-observer in everyday social life, I built relationships with a range of interlocutors, including the cadres and archivists who regulated my access. Doing so enabled forms of reciprocal exchange that sometimes worked in my favor but more often exceeded any instrumental purpose.

Altogether, taking these archival and ethnographic steps helped me trace the geographic linkages that multiethnic actors forged in the First Indochina War between the Black River region and Red River delta. In an ethnographic way, I found myself in Tai *muang* spaces that undergird contemporary Vietnamese territorial administration. In an archival way, I excavated the everyday labors of the numerous and anonymous civilian laborers who did the logistical and infrastructural work that helped clinch Vietnam's victory over France at Điện Biên Phủ in 1954. In a very concrete sense, traveling the roads between downstream archives and upstream field sites grounded me in the economic, cultural, and political connections that, like Vietnamese territory more broadly, remain under construction to this day.

Notes

1. Known as VASI (Vietnamese Advanced Summer Institute), now defunct.

References

Bronson, Bennett. 1978. "Exchange at the Upstream and Downstream Ends: Notes towards a Functional Model of the Coastal State in Southeast Asia." In *Economic Exchange and Social Interaction in Southeast Asia: Perspectives from Prehistory, History, and Ethnography*, edited by Karl Hutterer, 39–52. Ann Arbor: Michigan Papers on South and Southeast Asia.

Cầm Trọng. 1978. *Người Thái Ở Tây Bắc Việt Nam* (The Tai people of Northwest Vietnam). Hà Nội: Nhà Xuất bản Khoa học Xã hội.

Cohn, Bernard. 1980. "History and Anthropology: The State of Play." *Comparative Studies in Society and History* 22 (2): 198–221.

Condominas, George. 1976. "Essai sur l'évolution des systèmes politiques thaïs" (Essay on the evolution of Tai political systems). *Ethnos* 41 (1–4): 7–67.

Dao, Nga. 2015. "Political Responses to Dam-Induced Resettlement in Northern Uplands Vietnam." *Journal of Agrarian Change* 16 (2): 291–317.

Farmer, Ashley, Gretchen Heefner, Rebecca Herman, Lien-Hang Nguyen, and Kirsten Weld. 2019. "How Gender Affects the Experience of Archival Research and Field Work." *Modern American History* 2 (2): 193–200.

Guba, Egon, and Yvonna Lincoln. 1994. "Competing Paradigms in Qualitative Research." In *Handbook of Qualitative Research*, edited by N. Denzin and Y. Lincoln, 105–117. Thousand Oaks, CA: Sage.

Ha Viet Quan. 2016. "Brokering Power in Vietnam's Northwest: The Case of Ethnic Tai Cadres." PhD diss., Australian National University.

Hancké, Bob. 2009. *Intelligent Research Design: A Guide for Beginning Researchers in the Social Sciences*. New York: Oxford University Press.

Hardy, Andrew. 2002. *Red Hills: Migrants and the State in the Highlands of Vietnam*. Singapore: Nordic Institute of Asian Studies.

Lee, Mai Na. 2015. *Dreams of the Hmong Kingdom: The Quest for Legitimation in French Indochina, 1850–1960*. Madison: University of Wisconsin Press.

Le Failler, Philippe. 2011. "The Đèo Family of Lai Châu: Traditional Power and Unconventional Practices." *Journal of Vietnamese Studies* 6 (2): 42–67.

———. 2014. *La rivière Noire: L'intégration d'une marche frontière au Vietnam* (The Black River: The integration of a Vietnamese borderland). Paris: CNRS.

Lentz, Christian C. 2011. "Mobilization and State Formation on a Frontier of Vietnam." *Journal of Peasant Studies* 38 (3): 559–586.

———. 2014. "The King Yields to the Village? A Micropolitics of Statemaking in Northwest Vietnam." *Political Geography* 39: 1–10.

———. 2015. "Encountering Everyday Perspectives on the American War." *Geopolitics* 20 (4): 753–756.

———. 2019. *Contested Territory: Điện Biên Phủ and the Making of Northwest Vietnam.* New Haven, CT: Yale University Press.

———. 2020. "Dancing in the Archives." In *Overseas Research: A Practical Guide,* 3rd ed., edited by C. Barrett, J. Casson, and E. Lentz, 84–85. New York: Routledge.

McAlister, John T. 1967. "Mountain Minorities and the Viet Minh: A Key to the Indochina War." In *Southeast Asian Tribes, Minorities, Nations,* edited by P. Kunstadter, 771–844. Princeton, NJ: Princeton University Press.

Michaud, Jean. 2010. "Editorial—Zomia and Beyond." *Journal of Global History* 5: 187–214.

Mukdawijitra, Yukti. 2007. "Ethnicity and Multilingualism: The Case of the Ethnic Tai in the Vietnamese State." PhD diss., University of Wisconsin, Madison.

Ngô Thiếu Hiệu, ed. 2001. *Sách Chỉ Dẫn Các Phông Lưu Trữ Thời Kỳ Thuộc Địa /Guide des Fonds d'Archives d'Époque Coloniale* (Guide to colonial-era archival collections). Hanoi: NXB Thông tin.

Phạm Thị Bích Hải, Vũ Thị Minh Hương, Trần Thị Hương, Philippe Le Failler, and Nguyễn Minh Sơn. 2006. *Sách chỉ dẫn các phông lưu trữ bảo quản tại Trung tâm Lưu trữ Quốc gia III* (Guide to the Collections of National Archives Centre III). Hanoi: NXB Văn hoá Thông tin.

Scott, James C. 2009. *The Art of Not Being Governed: An Anarchist History of Southeast Asia.* New Haven, CT: Yale University Press.

Scott, Steffanie, Fiona Miller, and Kate Lloyd. 2006. "Doing Fieldwork in Development Geography: Research Culture and Research Spaces in Vietnam." *Geographical Research* 44 (1): 28–40.

Shrader, Charles. 2015. *A War of Logistics: Parachutes and Porters in Indochina, 1945–1954.* Lexington: University Press of Kentucky.

Tagliacozzo, Eric, and Andrew Willford. 2009. "History and Anthropology: Strange Bedfellows." In *Clio and Anthropos: Exploring the Boundaries between History and Anthropology,* edited by E. Tagliacozzo and A. Willford, 1–26. Stanford, CA: Stanford University Press.

Turton, Andrew. 2000. *Civility and Savagery: Social Identity in Tai States.* Richmond, UK: Curzon Press.

Van Schendel, Willem. 2002. "Geographies of Knowing, Geographies of Ignorance: Jumping Scale in Southeast Asia." *Environment and Planning D: Society and Space* 20: 647–668.

Warshawsky, Dan. 2014. "The Potential for Mixed Methods: Results from the Field in Urban South Africa." *Professional Geographer* 66 (1): 160–168.

CHAPTER 2

With Military Precision

A Reflexive Examination of Colonial Ethnography in Upland Tonkin

Jean Michaud

BETWEEN 1897 AND 1904, French colonial infantry officers compiled extensive "ethnographic" reports on the highland peoples of what is now the northern frontier of the Socialist Republic of Vietnam. Colonial military ethnography was never a popular topic in social anthropology. It has been considered biased and unscientific, a crude tool for furthering the colonial agenda and deepening the domination of the colonized. Furthermore, as Remco Raben (2009, 556) put it, "There was a time when perusing [...] archives was an extremely suspect, if inevitable, activity that often gave rise to bitter comments on the limitations and bias of such documents." I present in this chapter a case that disrupts that narrative.

I focus on the ethnic minority societies in the high borderlands of northern Vietnam, a linguistic and cultural composite of over 3.3 million individuals today, whose principal commonality is their distinction from the national ethnic majority, the Kinh. In a region where oral societies typically have left very little in terms of text and archeology, the tangible result of this military ethnographic push—eight thousand pages of handwritten reports, pictures, and maps—forms a significant body of ethnographies regarding early information on this high region and its inhabitants; nothing is even close to being comparable.

I do not seek to dive into the details of these ethnographic records in this chapter; I have done that elsewhere (Michaud 2013, 2015; Michaud and Turner 2016). For what remains to be analyzed regarding these records, I address this in a book manuscript that is currently under construction. For this chapter, in step with the overarching issues Pierre Petit and I have underlined in the introduction, I focus on the progression of unearthing this military ethnography; putting this endeavor against a background of its critical, methodological, and ethical implications; and paying particular attention to logic and embedded practices. I take up the duty of remembrance for lost ethnography by these unambiguously incidental and gendered authors for whom such labels contributed to keeping their production in the shadows.

Critical reflexivity, with some storytelling, is a common thread throughout this chapter. But being critically reflexive can turn into a precarious affair. Social anthropology has insisted on its practitioners developing a sixth sense to foresee the methodological, ethnocentric, ethical, and empiricist snags that can damage or even scuttle their intellectual ship (Stocking 1991; Pels and Salemink 1999). Dealing reflexively with early ethnography thus presents robust challenges.

From reading and reflecting over the years on the forces of modernization in isolated upland societies in several Asian countries, I contend that when pushing this ethnological and historical data through the sifter of critical scholarship on egalitarian societies, layers of implications can be peeled. Discussing these colonial archives provides evidence of an early crystallization of power differentiation and, in the process, creates questions concerning context and methods that bring the moral dimension of any historical anthropology enterprise to the fore.

The Military as Incidental Ethnographers

My long-term research on upland groups of northern Vietnam during the colonial period involves the performance of an ethnography of ethnographers. In itself, this entails interesting gymnastics. While the true subjects of my research are the societies historically dwelling in the uplands, by ricochet, archives have led me to widen my gaze and include the colonial agents who came to the uplands, visited the locals and their homes, recorded their livelihoods, and, when they moved on, left behind evidence of people and places rarely discussed before.

Military colonial ethnography performed competently has not been very common around the world, but here is one interesting case. Let me address it through a short detour. When I investigated French missionary ethnographic texts from the colonial era twenty years ago (Michaud 2004,

2007), I was aware that reliability was going to be an issue. Catholic missionaries sent to Tonkin, as colonial northern Vietnam was then called, did not want nor need to care excessively for facts. Having internalized the wants of the Church, self-censorship operated effectually, and such writers ended up composing narratives that would primarily help their mission obtain more resources from their vicariate as much as from devout parishioners back in the motherland. With their exoticized stories, many missionaries assisted the Church hierarchy by making stronger cases to attract recruits. Enrollment from the French countryside came through the publication of colorful and somewhat fantasist accounts appealing to the believers' emotions and, if nothing else, made them reach for their pocket. It is only exceptionally uncommon that recruits like Paul Vial (1898), Alfred Liétard (1913), and François-Marie Savina (1924) went on to produce ethnographic writing venturing beyond the instrumentality of conversion and institutional reproduction to reach the level of genuine ethnography—by the day's standard, that is, as promoted for instance by the journal *Anthropos* from 1906 onward.

By comparison, for the military ethnographers of the years 1897–1904, it was security, precision, and political supremacy that were paramount. And unlike the Catholic Church, the colonial infantry had no need to generate its financial support or muster recruits.

As should be the case in such a tightly run and unequivocally hierarchical ship, military orders were to be followed scrupulously. This discipline resulted in diligently answering the detailed commands from the governor-general of Indochina, and as a foretold consequence, "each [military] sector without exception provided a notice accompanied by a map." Then, "the notices of the sectors centralized in the chief town of each Territory, were submitted to the examination of an experienced officer, who made an overall report on the [Military] Territory" (Maître 1905, 200).

Unlike their missionary counterparts, the French military sought facts, not opinions, stories, wants, or hopes. Yes, individual officers still had their own agendas, which sometimes tainted their prose, but it was undeniably secondary to military reason and to the orthodoxy of organizational efficiency rather than answering to individual distinction—beyond subordinates wishing to make an impression on their commanding officers. Moreover, the top brass in Tonkin kept strict watch on data crunching, and the production of a final blend of reports for the general staff was meant to be accurate and tactical and ensure an efficient use of military resources (see fig. 2.1).

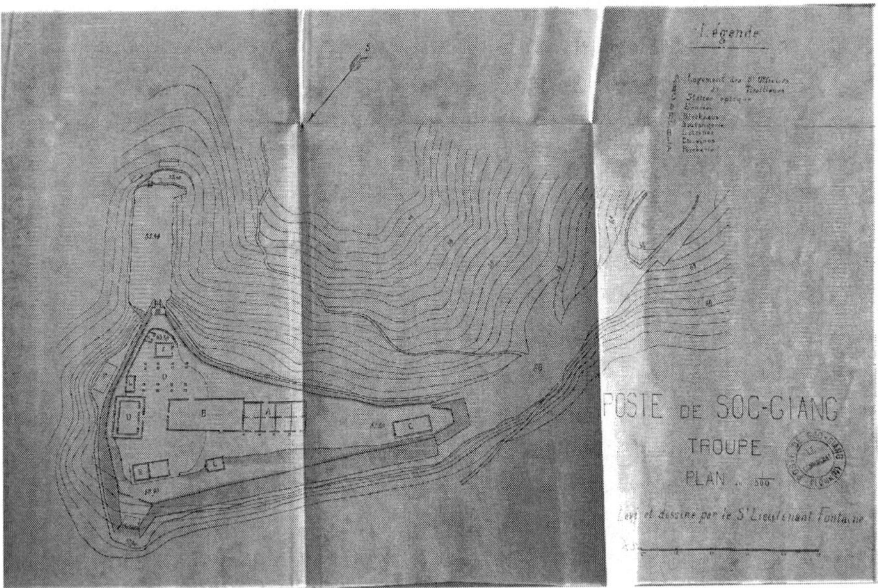

Figure 2.1. Methodical: A plan of the French military post of Soc-Giang (ANOM, 1898, GGI 66103). © J. Michaud.

A Methodological Challenge

Scores of such handwritten pages very precisely located in time and space have been sitting in vaults ever since; while a few of the original reports have been brought to light on occasion, most have been entirely forgotten, never translated or analyzed. Yet, this record contains a distinctive body of firsthand observations that says something unuttered about these remote societies; it is precious information in view of the paucity of reliable ethnographic data available in any language before European contact.

To get a sense of their content and atmosphere, I let these primary documents briefly speak for themselves. First, we find dozens of original and for the most part never before seen photographs that adorn many reports (see fig. 2.2). In truth, most do not differ much in style and intention from contemporaneous pictures of "tribes" and "savages" found in European colonies, but they come from distant locations where pictures had never been taken before. A serious analysis of such images clearly needs to take place.

Figure 2.2. Exotic: A photograph from
a sector report of 1903 (ÉFEO, ME 318.
Quan-Ba). © J. Michaud.

Along with photographs, a striking outcome of the 1903–1904 survey
in particular was ethnolinguistic cartography. Handmade color maps
locating each ethnicity were formally requested from all sector officers
and duly created. Sadly, many originals have been lost or can no longer
be located in archives. Figure 2.3 shows a remaining example from the
Ba-xat Sector, 4th Military Territory. From this material, Commander
Lunet de Lajonquière had a summary map drawn for the entire northern borderlands for his 1904 volume (Lunet de Lajonquière 1904),
which became the first-ever ethnolinguistic map of northern Tonkin.

Then, in terms of the texts themselves, here are five telling samples
illustrating the diverse methods and degrees of professionalism found
in the field reports.

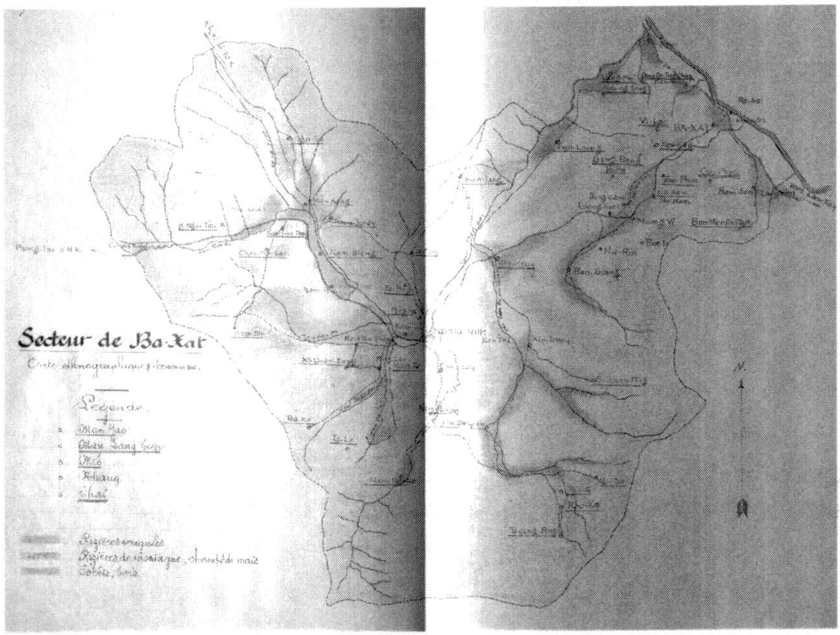

Figure 2.3. Agreeable: Hand-drawn ethnolinguistic and economic map of 1903 (ÉFEO, ME 331. Ba-Xat). © J. Michaud.

Vignette 1: Samples of Ethnography

The Man, who are great hunters and who can fish too, have the equipment necessary to engage in these kinds of exercises. We see these hanging in a corner of their homes: first a primitive crossbow, then a fork to spear the fish, and finally this strange gun that the Man Méo Tam make themselves from scratch, a matchlock with elongated barrel and without a stock, which cannot be shouldered and which one simply places against the cheek to aim. [...] They use these guns to hunt predators and other animals that come prowling around their homes or cause damage to their crops. (Sector of Dong Khe, ÉFEO, ME 301, 1903)

The Méo is a great hunter. With his matchlock he is not afraid to take on large predators and he can stalk a deer for days. For small birds he uses a blowgun with a stock. (Sector of Dong-Van, ÉFEO, ME 315, 1903)

The fauna of the region includes: tiger, tiger cat, bear, wild boar, deer, otter, porcupine, armadillo, monkey, and weasel. The main birds are: the eagle, the raven, the dove, woodcock, snipe, partridge, wild rooster and hen, the ordinary pheasant, and the silver pheasant. The natives hunt with rifles or using snares. During the year 1897 they brought to the Coc Rau post four tigers, a half-dozen tiger cats, weasels, deer, a porcupine, and an armadillo. (Sector of Coc-Rau, ANOM, GGI 66104, 1898)

To the inhabitant of the upper regions of Tonkin, to the montagnard, the forest is actually the *alma parens*, the great benefactor. He knows her every nook and cranny. In the troubled moments of his history, when war was plaguing villages in the plains with its horrors and devastation, it is to the forest that, poor, defeated, powerless to defend himself, he came to seek asylum and protection. She has sheltered him in her safe hidings, him with his family, his cattle, his provisions. When the rice ran out, she fed him, she gave him unreservedly her bamboo shoots, her succulent roots, all of the resources known only to the mountain folks. Thus, he loves her, he respects her, and only just does he preserve his fields against her attacks. (Sector of Bang Hanh, ANOM, GGI 66104, 1898)

**Vignette 2: *Mercuriales* (market price lists)
for the Sector of Ba-Xat (ANOM, GGI 66105, 1897).**

| | | Price list per marketplace in piastres [$] and sapèques [sap.] | | | Average price in sector |
| | | Ban-Qua | Muong-Hum | Trinh-Thuong | |
Merchandise	Unit				
Rice	picul (60 kg)	$2.65	$3.00	$2.50 to $3.00	$2.80
Paddy	picul (60 kg)	$1.50	$1.50	$1.50	$1.50
Maize	picul (60 kg)	$1.25	$1.25	$1.25	$1.25

(continued)

Merchandise	Unit	Price list per marketplace in piastres [$] and sapèques [sap.]			Average price in sector
		Ban-Qua	Muong-Hum	Trinh-Thuong	
Quartered pork	annamite kilo (0.6 kg)	120 sap.	100 sap.	100 sap.	107 sap.
Quartered buffalo	annamite kilo (0.6 kg)	64 sap.	60 sap.	60 sap.	61 sap.
Pork fat	annamite kilo (0.6 kg)	130 sap.	120 sap.	120 sap.	123 sap.
Chicken	annamite kilo (0.6 kg)	120 sap.	100 sap.	100 sap.	107 sap.
Fish	annamite kilo (0.6 kg)	50 sap.	50 sap.	45 sap.	48 sap.
Duck	per item	400 sap.	350 sap.	350 to 450 sap.	400 sap.
Rice alcohol	bottle	70 sap.	60 sap.	80 sap.	70 sap.
Salt	picul (60 kg)	$4.00	$4.00	$6.00	$4.66
Opium, raw	annamite 100 g	$2.65	$3.00	$2.50 to $3.00	$2.80
Chinese tobacco	annamite 100 g	$0.08	$0.10	$0.10	$0.09
Matches	pack	$0.07	$0.10	$0.10	$0.09

Vignette 3: Sample of Ethnocentric Thinking

For two years, great efforts have been made both in Cao Bang and in the sectors, to bring Natives to cultivate special products, which later, under the leadership of European settlers, may also enjoy a great development and can definitely ensure the region's wealth: coffee, tobacco, opium. But, despite our own example and advice, we only encountered negative results with the Natives, whose laziness and carelessness are ill-suited for the care and time that these cultures require. (Circle of Cao-Bang, ANOM, GGI 66103, 1898)

Vignette 4: Methods Made Explicit

The information given in the second part [the catalogue of "races"] has been collected: 1) For the Chinese, directly by the Sector's Commander from a Chinaman in Ba-xat who can speak French; 2) For the Thaïs, directly by the Sector's Commander from the Tia-Tian of Van-xéou, the Ly-truong of Muong Hum serving as the interpreter; 3) For the Nhangs, directly by the Sector's Commander from the Ly-truong of Ba-xat, who can speak some French. (Sector of Ba-Xat, ÉFEO, ME 331, 1903)

And for the fifth vignette, Commander Auguste Bonifacy, the officer closest to qualifying as a proper ethnologist at the time, expresses his intelligence of the situation in resolutely reflexive terms. Here, he brings to light the positionality of actors in the field and highlights the distinction between descriptions of material culture, farming, and other aspects of everyday life, which we can assume to be accurate, and those about ethnological institutions and concepts, which in truth standard officers would have no reason to know about.

Vignette 5: Limitations of the Ethnography

Data relating to psychological life is often wrong. [Ethnic Vietnamese] interpreters habitually cannot admit that the natives may think differently, and consider certain of their customs as immoral and simply do not translate the information relating to these. [. . .] In addition, the officers conversant in ethnography and ethnology and owning books on these matters are very rare.

As a consequence, the details given are sometimes worthless, while the facts pertaining to customs that have great importance for an ethnographic perspective are ignored. [. . .] In addition, some remains of primitive customs—group marriage, levirate, endogamy, exogamy, etc.—have not been researched, the officers not knowledgeable in ethnology generally ignoring these customs. Same with what belongs to the social life; the types of property, the formation of clans, rules relating to justice: ordeals, judicial evidence, have generally not been treated, sociology still being a little-known science. (Ha-Giang Military Territory, ÉFEO, ME 313, 1903)

My Positionality in the Shape of Storytelling

Back to the story of this body of archives, I have come upon it by accident. During my first visit to the national CAOM (Centre des Archives d'Outre-Mer) in Aix-en-Provence in 1996, since renamed ANOM (Archives Nationales d'Outre-Mer), I stumbled on a report showcasing military ethnography. I did not make much of it, as my eyes were set on other targets. For readers not familiar with the ANOM, it is worth sharing a few particulars on research methods.

Once the researcher has been assigned a seat in the modern and spacious reading room, the standard procedure is then to be handed one protective archive box, a bulky object containing the document one has asked to see from the catalogue, selected by its title and the series it belongs to. That box hosts the document requested but also dozens of others belonging to the same numerical sequence, despite them usually having nothing to do with each other; these documents just happened to be filed on the same day in the same office in colonial Hanoi. Looking for a particular document, I often found that it did not live up to the enticing outline jotted down in the catalogue. But by regulation, only one box can be in hand at any given time, with a maximum of only a few consecutive boxes per day, with wide gaps between official times of release from the storage desk. Thus, when the initial target proves disappointing, and unlike older times when one was not allowed to photograph anything and thus made good use of these gaps to record by hand, researchers today take pictures for later examination. There is thus time to cruise through other papers that simply happen to live in the box they have in hand, biding time until they could swap this box for a new one with its fresh promises. As everyone eventually comes to realize, it can pay to be nosy.

Over following visits, I bumped in this way into two more ethnographic reports from the Military Territories, this time dutifully writing down the references for future consideration, but still clueless as to the bigger picture (see fig. 2.4). Concurrently over the same ten years or so, I was also visiting other archives, including those of École française d'Extrême-Orient (ÉFEO) in Paris. There, I likewise ran into an intriguing stream of military reports from the northern frontier showing resemblances with the ones in Aix-en-Provence, though all were dated a few years later. At the ÉFEO, these military documents were easier to spot as all had been catalogued together. Still busy chasing other rabbits, I initially assumed that these were simply copies of the ANOM reports that I had already spotted in Aix. That is, until that fine day in 2010, when the penny finally dropped: the reports I had encountered so far in the ANOM were dated 1897–1899, and the ones at ÉFEO were all from 1903–1904. They were not copies of each other, and they had ended up in different repositories because they had been handled by different colonial bodies. Indeed, they turned out to be two entirely separate lots from two distinct initiatives, even if at times involving some of the same officers in the field. At last I had connected the dots and realized the full scale of the matter: two major investigations had closely followed each other in exactly the same locations, involving between them a total of seventy military officers posted all over the northern highlands, who penned over eighty-five separate reports of entirely original material. I eventually published the story of their making in the *Journal of Vietnamese Studies* (Michaud 2013).

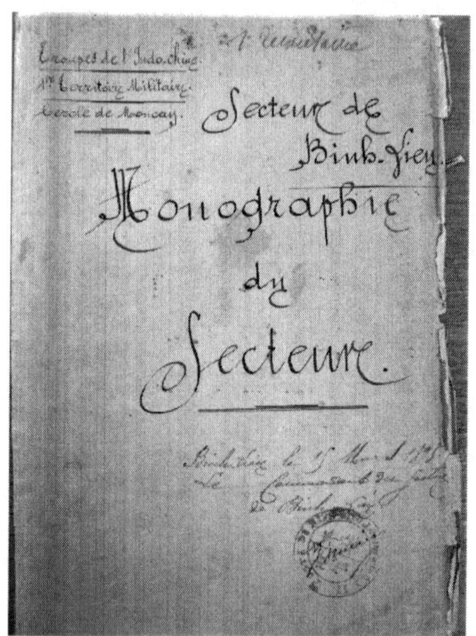

Figure 2.4. Informative: A typical sector report cover from 1898 (ANOM, GGI 66102). © J. Michaud.

This unintended turn in my journey through the archives later struck me as an illustration of one of the most mysterious features of research, combining curiosity and a pinch of opportunism with sheer luck (see fig. 2.5). Initially, I did not have the project to dive into this ethnographic material or write about it. But gradually, when faced with this wealth of ethnography that contrasts so sharply with the paucity of other sources dealing with these remote populations at that time, I had to accept that I just could not ignore the significance of this material. But why me, a social anthropologist? Could these documents not have waited for proper historians to come to the repositories and perform their magic? The fact, however, is that historians' interest in stateless and often aliterate peoples is modest at best.[1] Outside the subfields of École des Annales and micro-history (Ginzburg, Tedeschi, and Tedeschi 1993; Brooks, DeCorse, and Walton 2008), a majority of historians still put their focus on documents: their nature, their authority, their details, the context of their

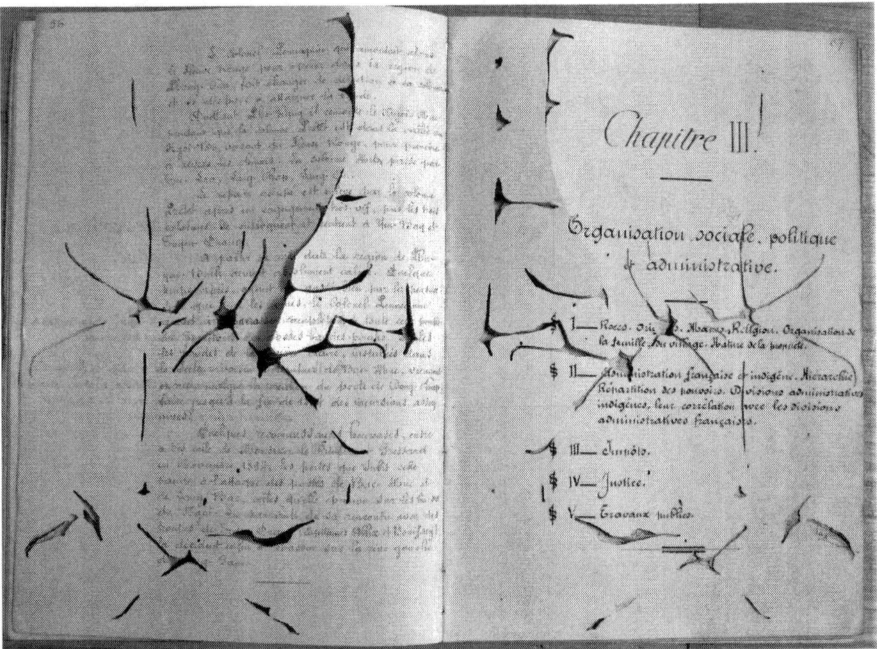

Figure 2.5. Adding a twist: Bookworms . . . (ANOM, GGI 66104. Phuyen-Binh). © J. Michaud.

production, their authorship, even their textual quality. Through such text, the aim is to investigate a particular event thoroughly without exceeding the boundaries assigned to the said event by the limits of the material available. By contrast, the broader picture of cultures and identity of those whom the documents depict, their belief systems, their social organization, their vision of the world, their emotions and aspirations—all that could be read between the lines, as it were—would not be of primary importance and often labeled as unscientific vagaries.

For social anthropologists, however, that is where the good stuff lies. Their attention is aimed at the subjects and practices depicted in archives, and a scarcity of documents is not a motive to stop pondering, thus providing space for elaboration and challenging hypotheses. Like many, and as the partially overlapping subfields of ethnohistory and micro-history exemplify, I am convinced that historians and anthropologists have compatible and largely complementary methodologies. In a situation like this one, as I have argued before (Michaud 2010, 188–193), the common subjects of historians' and anthropologists' research can benefit from their joint efforts. Making archives "speak" is the bread and butter of trained historians, and when what little there is takes an ethnographic turn, anthropological methods and tools can help refine, and also broaden, the picture significantly (Willford and Tagliacozzo 2009).

Beyond the substantial amount of time I spend exploring colonial archives, a large portion of my enterprise has been resting on my experiences with and my writings about highland societies in several countries of highland Asia. In terms of language abilities, French is my mother tongue. Unlike most social anthropologists working in highland Asia, I have not specialized on one particular society (even if I am more familiar with one, the Hmong). I have focused on what connects groups rather than on each one's distinctive culture, rituals, and ontologies. My methods reflect a macroscopic, cross-cultural, and supranational stance, the possible shortcomings of which I accept fully.

This research effort thus is an enterprise in physical, political, and intellectual border crossing. Methods are geared toward applied cross-disciplinarity, cross-border field sites, a fluid personal itinerary, and the will to bring it all together. Patently, this plasticity raises multiple questions about expertise, accountability, and ethics.

The Perils of Early Ethnography

Early ethnography of upland Vietnam at the time of European contact falls prey to tropes rooted in a period about which not as much can be known as one might like. Nothing, or just about, was known about societies dwelling in the high region (Michaud 2022). Not only is ethnography inescapably bound to time, space, and cultural logics, it also unavoidably involves, then as today, a degree of bias depending on methods, preparations, circumstances, morals, mind frames, and strategies played by all parties in the ensuing interpersonal transactions. In this way, bias is not solely borne by ethnographers, the whole context also matters.

Produced by untrained colonial agents such as explorers, administrators, and missionaries, the scholarly appreciation of early productions has understandably been either negative or tentative (Stocking 1991; Pels and Salemink 1999; Chafer and Sackur 2001; Goodman and Silverstein 2009; Johnson 2017). These hesitations have much to do with the fact that the observers were active in the years before professional ethnographic methods were devised and tested. There are also doubts about the gender, intellectual, religious, and class preconceptions on the part of the colonial observers that are reputed to taint or warp their prose, sometimes to the point of rendering it scientifically worthless—examples abound (Salamone 1977; Said 1989; Pels 1997; Michaud 2004). European explorers and fortune seekers in Tonkin, like Francis Garnier (1873) and Jean Dupuis (1879), for example, were mostly trying to make a name for themselves. Their motivation was sensationalist and self-serving, and the ethnographic parts of their texts ought to be treated with utmost caution. Administrators, except for truly unique ones such as Auguste Pavie (1908) and Pierre Lefèvre-Pontalis (1892), were rarely in the physical presence of the northern highland populations, and if they were, the contact periods were far too brief and the language and culture gaps too extensive to support dependable testimonies. As for missionaries in the Tonkinese highlands, most were from the Société des Missions étrangères de Paris, which, by the end of the nineteenth century, was recruiting chiefly from the peasantry in rural France. Their seminary education was certainly solid, but it was exclusively directed at steering candidates towards the service of God, with little room for doubt or notions of scientific thinking (Michaud 2007).

Thus, to concretely grapple with the problem of colonial ethnography among upland societies of Tonkin, one must be aware of the ethnographers' profiles: their origin, social class, ethnicity, cultural fabric, religious thinking, education, intentions, desires, biases, and position in the colonial hierarchy. One must also bear in mind the context of the surveys and carefully factor in the historical and political forces that affected their course.

Compared with their predecessors, the military officers sent to the northern outposts of Tonkin, who were eventually ordered to reinvent themselves briefly as ethnographers, were a rather different kettle of fish, particularly among the Military Territories' commanders and sub-commanders (see fig. 2.6). Bearing the ranks of infantry lieutenant and captain, all had comfortable or even affluent family backgrounds that allowed them to use their social capital and wealth to secure a solid education and an officer's commission. This combination of class and formal education promoted a capability for organized reasoning and critical thinking, although whether it was likely to venture beyond mere conformity to the colonial military cause remained unsure. In that era of anticlericalism typical of the French Third Republic (1870–1940), such a middle- to upper-class upbringing combined well with a scientifically designed survey and a rigid work ethos, helping to produce unusually consistent and steady outputs. Yet, many other shades of subjectivity and biases remained, arguably in a lower concentration than in the "ethnography" performed by explorers and missionaries.

Figure 2.6. Pensive: A lone French officer near his upland post of Pho-Bang (Abadie 1924, plate 2). © J. Michaud.

With its peculiar nature, military ethnography is seen by many scholars to be particularly suspect due to the rigidity inherent in military thought and action, its ideological as much as power-driven agenda, and its culture of secrecy.[2] So, in an attempt to balance the blessings and the trials, and while I unequivocally share the calls for caution, the decisive factor to bring to the fore in colonial military ethnographies here relates to the scarcity of voices speaking about the former identities of these mostly aliterate societies—some of which being also devoid of a formal mode of remembering their own collective past (see Vargyas, this volume). It leads me to believe that mining these archives, trying hard to decipher them, and meticulously cross-checking their content with the rare other sources available constitutes an authentic endeavor while being also a substantial challenge. In many cases, and despite obvious partialities dictated by the epochs and the mind frames tinting military ethnography, it can only be accepted that these imperfect texts represent firsthand observations that ought to be studied.

What Scholars Were Saying at the Time

Beyond my own judgments regarding the soundness of such a legacy, it might be helpful to consider what contemporary scholars have said of this work and its authors. In the preface to infantry officer Maurice Abadie's 1924 ethnography of the northern highlands, entitled *Les races du Haut-Tonkin de Phong-Tho à Lang-Son,* French scholar Paul Pelliot (1924, 5) wrote: "You belong to the lineage of Diguet, Lunet de Lajonquière, Bonifacy, and so many officers in the Military Territories whose names were never cited, but whose conscientious investigations, humbly transmitted through the hierarchy, have helped to build our ethnographic knowledge of Upper Tonkin on a solid foundation." Pelliot was referring by name to the higher-ranking officers who contributed to the rare publications stemming from the two military surveys discussed here. First and foremost are Étienne-Edmond Lunet de Lajonquière's twin volumes issued in 1904 and 1906, which fed directly on the 1903–1904 field reports handed to him by the colonial hierarchy with a request to produce two summary volumes. The 1904 one was intended for internal use and bore the title *Ethnographie des Territoires militaires (Rédigée sur l'ordre du Général Coronnat [. . .] d'après les travaux de M. M. le Lieutenant-Colonel Diguet, le Commandant Bonifacy, le Commandant Révérony, le Capitaine Fesh etc.).* The 1906 volume, called *Ethnographie*

68   Chapter 2

du Tonkin septentrional, was an expanded version also including northern lowland provinces and was aimed at a civilian audience.[3] Auguste
Bonifacy, whom we met briefly above, was a ranking officer, commander
of the 3rd Military Territory, who spent many years accumulating a
deep knowledge of the mountain groups and languages along the Clear
River watershed. This experience allowed him to produce several summaries of many of the 1903–1904 survey reports then used by Lunet
de Lajonquière to write his two volumes. Over the next two decades,
Bonifacy also went on to publish his independent ethnography and
analyses of the northern highlands in dozens of scholarly articles. In
1908, Lieutenant-Colonel Edouard Diguet, after his active involvement in the 1903–1904 survey, independently published his own *Les
Montagnards du Tonkin,* based on his experiences and the personal notes
he took as commander of the 2nd Military Territory. Eminent diplomat
Auguste Pavie signed the preface to Diguet's 1908 volume, Pavie and
Diguet having met fourteen years earlier in the Tai domain of *Sip Song
Chau Tai,* where the latter was a commanding officer and the former was
conducting a political study of the local population for the benefit of
the colonial administration (Pavie 1908, v; Le Failler 2014). In his preface, Pavie (1908, xv) predicted that Diguet's *Les Montagnards du Tonkin*
"will always remain a precious help to all those wanting to know the
upper regions of Tonkin."

As for Paul Pelliot, this scholar was among the first prominent intellectuals to see the importance of this body of early field data. A sinolo-
gist, anthropologist, archeologist, INALCO linguist, member of ÉFEO,
and professor at Collège de France since 1911, Pelliot had the highest
academic credentials available in France, and as such, his 1924 endorse-
ment of the works by the original officers involved in the surveys carried
weight. Among other qualities, Pelliot underscored that these ethnographies followed methodological and intellectual standards fitting the
contemporary expectations for ethnological research. And sixty years
after their publication, Frank M. Lebar, Gerald C. Hickey, and John K.
Musgrave in their *Ethnic Groups of Mainland Southeast Asia* (1964) refer
abundantly to Lunet de Lajonquière's work, along with Abadie and
Diguet's, declaring these to be the most reliable sources available on
the early ethnography of upland Tonkin.

Still, others were less convinced. Antoine Cabaton (1907, 339), in his
generally positive review of *Ethnographie du Tonkin septentrional* (Lunet
de Lajonquière 1906), also lamented that it contained "official reports

of very unequal and sometimes insufficient value." Young sociologist
Marcel Mauss, who had helped design the questionnaire used for the
1903–1904 survey long before he would reach academic fame (Salemink
2003, 74–75; Michaud 2007, 205–206), rightly remarked in his review of
Lunet de Lajonquière's 1906 opus that "this book has all the virtues,
all the faults also of such work imposed by a hierarchy concerned with
something other than science" (Mauss 1906, 241).

It is significant to note that these assessments were all based solely
on Lunet de Lajonqière's two summary volumes, plus the few follow-up
pieces made public by other officers, some of whom had been active
in the surveys. Crucially, none of the commentators from that time
appeared to have seen or have a chance to appraise the bulk of original
field reports informing these published compendiums. By the time they
had printed their opinions, the reports themselves had already been
tucked away and would not resurface for decades.

Buried Data

It is telling that the colonial government of French Indochina did not
see value in publishing more from this sizeable initiative than just the
two overlapping 1904 and 1906 summaries by Lunet de Lajonquière.
As Mauss had rightly perceived in 1906, the ethnographic initiative had
served its purpose of state control through knowledge production, and
the state's gaze moved on. The budding French military anthropology
of colonial subjects was redirected at other targets for "pacification,"
such as in Africa and Polynesia. Accordingly, demand quickly died out
for what Tonkin's military reports had brought up. Within a few years,
even the Military Territories themselves had run their course and were
handed over to civilian administration, while the frontline actors and
witnesses of the 1897–1904 efforts had been redeployed to other battle-
fields and occupation zones within Indochina and beyond.[4]

Since then, a very busy century has unfolded and the science of
anthropology has expanded accordingly. Against today's expectations
of methods and ethics, the colonial administrators and ideologues must
still be treated as having produced this knowledge as weapon of control (notwithstanding its truly scientific potential), to bury it as soon
as it was judged obsolete. Having now retrieved it, we are able to see
that this material, once sensibly sifted, adds a new layer of knowledge
about a poorly known, underdocumented, ancient, and multifaceted

social constellation in the early stages of a transition to the globalized
world order. With regard to some of the other themes of this book, such
knowledge might even also feed retroactively into to local people's own
narratives of their own pasts.

Lowland imperial powers surrounding the northern highlands initiated the transition of kinship-based upland societies toward modernity,
which was then catalyzed by French colonial occupation. Remarkably,
the early advent of globalization was promoted by both capitalism and
communism alike, and in the post-collective era, rapid market integration became the driver. Even with reality imperfectly perceived and
expressed through Eurocentric biases, this archival data opens a win-
dow into this longitudinal landscape of practices, beliefs, representations, compliance, opportunism, and defiance among and between
endogenous and exogenous societies, dominant and dominated groups,
regions, valleys, and hamlets, and even among kin.

Again, one-off surveys conducted relatively speedily by inexpe-
rienced external agents embedded in a rigid ideological framework
will inevitably display a contingent mindset conditioned by subjectivities and positionalities of a rather extreme sort: the military psyche.
Officers can only report what they see, hear, or are told in connection
with the pre-set questions they asked; they can only write what they
grasp and what is acceptable to their hierarchy. Moreover, they might
leave out the rest uncritically, as Bonifacy had wisely noted above. The
ultimate historical, anthropological, and linguistic portrait painted in
these two flawed, yet unique surveys lies in the raw frontline transcripts
of the sector reports, penned in the field in a consistent manner by
dozens of eyewitnesses. It provides verifiable factual data contained in
abundant demographic tables, glossaries, maps, and photographs. It
is this material's integration, horizontally across the whole region and
vertically following common mindsets, structure, and method, that
confirms its significance.

The Challenges Ahead

One can argue whether the seventy or so officers who contributed to
the surveys can be branded ethnographers. I have no decisive answer
to that. Yet in my mind, the texts they produced are without a doubt
ethnographic in nature. It is the rigorous enforcement of military
discipline and norms that places these texts in a different category

from contemporary missionary accounts and the embellished diaries of travelers and explorers (Salemink 2003, 58–72; Glover et al. 2012). The uniformity of the officers' descriptions, cemented by their common educational as well as cultural backgrounds, constitute a rare and verifiable DNA.

For scholars and for the heirs of the uplanders themselves, the sum of these fine-grained accounts represents an unanticipated achievement in viewing the kaleidoscope of agency, desires, intentions, and down-to-earth logic among dominated groups faced with multiple forms of adversity. With the complexity they reflect, these testimonies provide both a foundation and a milestone for a more reliable reading of social and cultural behavior through time. These accounts could also help reiterate the social intricacy and cultural uniqueness of a past that continues to play a role in today's construction of identity with its connected negotiations and struggles. With such germane discovery comes a moral duty for the social scientist aware of its scale and potential. This duty is to make this material bear fruit by heralding its existence, cataloguing its content, cross-checking its substance, verifying its soundness against known data, and making the results of this endeavor available to the broader and local communities alike (Johnston 2010; Low and Merry 2010).

Or, put in a reflexive way—literally—I do not think I would be able to look at myself in a mirror having learned about the existence and potential of these documents and then choosing to sit on my hands. This, thus, becomes a case where a quiet archival search can unexpectedly morph into a long-term commitment, turning without warning a detached and predictable scientific search into a subjective, engaged, and morally binding practice. As I pointed out at the start of this chapter, I may not be, for an array of reasons, the best person on this planet to conduct this endeavor; but it seems that I am among the few willing to step forward—for the time being.

Looking ahead, the methodological challenge now lies in cross-checking this relatively ancient and well-situated material with contemporaneous texts yet to be brought up from Asian archives and possibly from other European ones too—most likely from Spain and Britain as far as Tonkin is concerned. Endogenous archives in Vietnamese, Chinese, and vernacular scripts from these highlands, such as Thái, Tày, and Nùng, if such texts exist, could also yield unique data and should not be overlooked. Here again, the active contribution of (indigenous?) historians would be needed.

Beyond textual evidence and corroboration, as several authors in this collective book underline, oral history should be explored, although my efforts regarding this method have mostly drawn blanks so far (Michaud 2012, 2021). Despite its usual pitfalls already known to historical anthropologists, listening to the memories of living elders is not just a way of learning more, but also of participating actively in the expression, appropriation, or reappropriation of local history by the very people who were themselves at its heart, but who have been silenced or disconnected by grand narratives attuned to concerns not entirely their own (as the chapter by Turner and Delisle illustrates handsomely).

Another challenge will be to bring this material to engage with today's world. Doing so involves rereading the upland situation one century ago from this previously little-known perspective. I have made a start through the particular lens of livelihoods studies, but much more remains to be done from several additional angles. What kind of endogenous knowledge model could these texts reveal? In what ways are these endogenous knowledge models similar to, or different from, colonial models produced and promoted by others, such as explorers, administrators, or Vietnamese intellectuals of the imperial and colonial eras (Michaud 2022)?

A century may have passed, but many threads are still being woven as we speak, at times in similar directions and sometimes in radically different ones, depending on what is at stake for the agents involved. The heartening news is that there is now evidence available for a fresh and possibly more adequate, more respectful consideration and discussion of the history of Vietnam's northern highlands' societies.

Notes

1. A few recent and distinguished exceptions exist in northwest Vietnam, with the pioneering works of Philippe Le Failler (2014), Bradley Camp Davis (2017), and Christian Lentz (2019), whose work I salute.

2. To be convinced of this, one needs only to try accessing the military archives at the Fort de Vincennes' Service Historique de la Défense, starting with being summoned in front of an officer in uniform and *képi*, who will decide on the suitability of your credentials and quest.

3. Claude-Eugène Maître (1905, 200), an Orientalist and the future director of ÉFEO, wrote the following after reviewing the 1904 volume by Lunet de Lajonquière: "We must especially praise the positive results

obtained by the good organization of work, regulated by the General Staff, and the zeal displayed by the commanders of the territories, some of whom had already been noted before for their remarkable studies." The 1906 opus was reviewed favourably by INALCO professor Antoine Cabaton (1907), and by S. W. B. (1907) in the British *Journal of the Royal Asiatic Society.*

4. With a few notable exceptions, such as Auguste Bonifacy, who retired in Hanoi and carried on with his intellectual pursuit until his death in 1931.

References

Archives

1897–1898 Documents. Archives Nationales d'Outre-Mer (ANOM), Aix-en Provence, France. Series Gouvernement Général de l'Indochine (GGI)
Reports from the 1st Military Territory: GGI 66102
Reports from the 2nd Military Territory: GGI 66103
Reports from the 3rd Military Territory: GGI 66104
Reports from the 4th Military Territory: GGI 66105

1903–1904 Documents. Archives of the École française d'Extrême-Orient (ÉFEO), Maison de l'Asie, Paris, France. Series Manuscrits en langues européennes (ME), most numbered in the 300s.

Published Works

Abadie, Maurice. 1924. *Les races du Haut Tonkin de Phong-Tho à Lang-Son (Races of Upper Tonkin from Phong Thố to Lạng Sơn).* Paris: Société d'Éditions Géographiques, Maritimes et Coloniales.

Brooks, James F., Chris DeCorse, and John Walton, eds. 2008. *Small Worlds: Method, Meaning, and Narrative in Microhistory.* Santa Fe: School of American Research Press.

Cabaton, Antoine. 1907. Review of *Ethnographie du Tonkin septentrional,* by E. Lunet de Lajonquière. *Anthropos* 2 (2): 336–339.

Chafer, Tony, and Amanda Sackur, eds. 2001. *Promoting the Colonial Idea: Propaganda and Visions of Empire in France.* New York: Palgrave.

Davis, Bradley Camp. 2017. *Imperial Bandits: Outlaws and Rebels in the China-Vietnam Borderlands.* Seattle: University of Washington Press.

Diguet, Édouard J. J. 1908. *Les Montagnards du Tonkin.* Paris: Librairie Maritime et Coloniale, Augustin Challamel.

Dupuis, Jean. 1879. *L'ouverture du Fleuve Rouge au commerce et les événements du Tong-Kin, 1872–1873.* Vol. 2, *Journal de voyage et l'expédition.* Paris: Challamel ainé.

Garnier, Francis. 1873. *Album pittoresque.* Part I of *Atlas du voyage d'exploration en Indo-Chine.* Paris: Librairie Hachette.

Ginzburg, Carlo, John Tedeschi, and Anne C. Tedeschi. 1993. "Microhistory: Two or Three Things That I Know about It." *Critical Inquiry* 20 (1): 10–35.

Glover, D. M., S. Harrell, C. F. McKhann, and M. B. Swain, eds. 2012. *Explorers and Scientists in China's Borderlands, 1880–1950.* Seattle: University of Washington Press.

Goodman, J. E., and P. A. Silverstein, eds. 2009. *Bourdieu in Algeria: Colonial Politics, Ethnographic Practices, Theoretical Developments.* Lincoln: University of Nebraska Press.

Johnson, D. H. 2017. "Political Intelligence, Colonial Ethnography, and Analytical Anthropology in the Sudan." In *Ordering Africa: Anthropology, European Imperialism and the Politics of Knowledge,* edited by A. S. Thompson and J. M. MacKenzie, 309–335. Manchester: Manchester University Press.

Johnston, Barbara Rose. 2010. "Social Responsibility and the Anthropological Citizen." *Current Anthropology* 52 (S2): S235–S247.

Lebar, F. M., G. C. Hickey, and J. K. Musgrave, eds. 1964. *Ethnic Groups of Mainland Southeast Asia.* New Haven, CT: Human Relations Area Files Press.

Le Failler, Philippe. 2014. *La rivière Noire: L'intégration d'une marche frontière au Vietnam.* Paris: CNRS.

Lefèvre-Pontalis, Pierre. 1892. "Notes sur quelques populations du nord de l'Indo-Chine (1ère série)." Extrait du *Journal asiatique.* Paris: Ernest Leroux.

Lentz, Christian C. 2019. *Contested Territory: Dien Bien Phu and the Making of Northwest Vietnam.* New Haven, CT: Yale University Press.

Liétard, Alfred. 1913. *Au Yun-nan: Les Lo-lo p'o. Une tribu des aborigènes de la Chine méridionale.* Münster: Aschendorffsche Verlagsbuchhandlung, Anthropos Bibliothek.

Low, S. M., and S. E. Merry. 2010. "Engaged Anthropology: Diversity and Dilemmas." *Current Anthropology* 51 (S2): S203–S226.

Lunet de Lajonquière, Étienne-Edmond. 1904. *Ethnographie des territoires militaires (Rédigée sur l'ordre du Général Coronnat Commandant supérieur des Troupes du Groupe de l'Indo-Chine, d'après les travaux de M. M. le Lieutenant-Colonel Diguet, le Commandant Bonifacy, le Commandant Révérony, le Capitaine Fesh etc.).* Hà Nội: F. H. Schneider.

———. 1906. *Ethnographie du Tonkin septentrional, Rédigée sur l'ordre de M. P. Beau, Gouverneur Général de l'Indo-Chine Française, d'après les études des administrateurs civils et militaires des provinces septentrionales.* Paris: Ernest Leroux.

Maître, Claude Eugène. 1905. "Recension de: Commandant Lunet de Lajonquière: Ethnographie des territoires militaires." *Bulletin de l'Ecole française d'Extrême-Orient* 5: 199–207.

Mauss, Marcel. 1906. "Recension de Ethnographie du Tonkin septentrional par E. Lunet de Lajonquière." *L'Année Sociologique* 10: 241–243.

Michaud, Jean. 2004. "French Missionary Expansion in Colonial Upper-Tonkin." *Journal of Southeast Asian Studies* 35 (2): 287–310.

———. 2007. *"Incidental" Ethnographers. French Catholic Missions on the Frontier of Tonkin and Yunnan, 1880–1930.* Leiden: Brill Academic Publishers.

———. 2010. "Editorial: Zomia and Beyond." *Journal of Global History* 5 (2): 187–214.

———. 2013. "French Military Ethnography in Colonial Upper Tonkin (Northern Vietnam), 1897–1904." *Journal of Vietnamese Studies* 8 (4): 1–46.

———. 2015. "Livelihoods in the Vietnamese Northern Borderlands Recorded in French Colonial Military Ethnographies 1897–1904." *Asia Pacific Journal of Anthropology* 16 (4): 343–367.

———. 2021. "Is This Pa Chay Vue? A Study in Three Frames." *Journal of the Royal Asiatic Society* 31 (2): 363–391.

———. 2022. "Ethnography in the Northern Vietnamese Highlands." In *Routledge Handbook of Contemporary Highland Asia,* edited by J. Wouters and N. Heneise, 430–450. London: Routledge.

Michaud, Jean, and Sarah Turner. 2016. "Tonkin's Uplands at the Turn of the 20th Century: Colonial Military Enclosure and Local Livelihood Effects." *Asia Pacific Viewpoint* 57 (2): 154–167.

Pavie, Auguste. 1908. "Préface." In *Les Montagnards du Tonkin,* edited by Édouard J. J. Diguet, v–xv. Paris: Librairie Maritime et Coloniale, Augustin Challamel.

Pelliot, Paul. 1924. "Lettre-préface." In *Les races du Haut Tonkin de Phong-Tho à Lang-Son,* edited by Maurice Abadie, v–vi. Paris: Société d'Éditions Géographiques, Maritimes et Coloniales.

Pels, Peter. 1997. "The Anthropology of Colonialism: Culture, History, and the Emergence of Western Governmentality." *Annual Review of Anthropology* 26: 163–183.

Pels, Peter, and Oscar Salemink, eds. 1999. *Colonial Subjects: Essays on the Practical History of Anthropology.* Ann Arbor: University of Michigan Press.

Raben, Remco. 2009. "Debate: Ambiguities of Reading and Writing." *Bijdragen tot de Taal-, Land- en Volkenkunde* 165 (4): 551–567.

Said, Edward. 1989. "Representing the Colonized. Anthropology's Interlocutors." *Critical Inquiry* 1 (5): 205–225.

Salamone, E. A. 1977. "Anthropologists and Missionaries: Competition or Reciprocity?" *Human Organisation* 36 (4): 407–412.

Salemink, Oscar. 2003. *The Ethnography of Vietnam's Central Highlanders: A Historical Contextualization, 1850–1990.* Honolulu: University of Hawai'i Press.

Savina, François Marie. 1924. *Histoire des Miao.* Hong Kong: Imprimerie de la Société des Missions-Etrangères.

Stocking, George W., Jr., ed. 1991. *Colonial Situations: Essays on the Conceptualisation of Ethnographic Knowledge.* Madison: University of Wisconsin Press.

S. W. B. 1907. "Notice of Book: Ethnographie du Tonkin Septentrional by E. Lunet de Lajonquière." *Journal of the Royal Asiatic Society of Great Britain and Ireland,* n.s., 39 (1): 198–200.

Vial, Paul. 1898. *Les Lolos: Histoire, religion, mœurs, langue, écriture.* Shanghai: Imprimerie de la mission catholique.

Willford, Andrew, and Eric Tagliacozzo, eds. 2009. *Clio/Anthropos: Exploring the Boundaries between History and Anthropology.* Stanford, CA: Stanford University Press.

CHAPTER 3

Wa History

Agency and Victimization

Magnus Fiskesjö

THE WA PEOPLE OF THE BURMA-CHINA BORDERLANDS, who are about a million strong today, have striking indigenous traditions not only regarding their own origins and history but also with respect to those of humankind as a whole. These traditions contrast with narratives about history now imposed on them from outside, especially from the powerful modern states of China and Burma, which in the 1950s each annexed about a half of the independent Wa lands. Even before this loss of de facto independence and their reduction to the status of a "minority" in China and in Burma, the Wa were, of course (like all other people of the region), entangled in complex relations with these states and other neighbors. Yet at the same time, they managed to preserve their self-determination and historical identity to a very high degree, and some of their traditions continue even now.

Recent and Dramatic Changes in the Wa Lands

I will introduce the indigenous Wa traditions of history-making and history-telling in more detail below, building on my own understanding gained through conversations with Wa people during my fieldwork in this area as well as through the comparative study of Chinese, British, Shan, and other documents. First, however, I will seek to paint a better picture of the setting of the Wa. With dramatic transformations influencing almost every aspect of life in the China-Burma borderlands, illustrating this social landscape in turmoil is necessary to understand how indigenous Wa historical imaginaries have recently come under assault, and how these imaginaries have changed. Above all, the Wa have lost their armed autonomy and self-rule—the hallmarks of independence that they previously enjoyed in the central Wa lands until the 1950s.

Broadly, the Wa live in the lands to the east of the Burmese cities of Lashio and Mandalay, west of the Chinese tea outpost known as Pu'er, and north of the former Shan realm of Kengtung.[1] Chronicles and accounts of this kind compiled by Shan lords, by Shan Buddhist temple clergy, and by Chinese, Burmese, and British writers are all relevant for the study of Wa history, insofar as they mention the Wa as neighbors, adversaries, trading partners, or otherwise.[2]

The Wa were able to uphold their autonomy in core areas, despite attempts from earlier Burmese and Chinese regimes to extend their rule here (by way of taxation, conscription of labor and soldiers, etc.). In fact, during the last Chinese empire, a court report noted that the Wa were one of the only peoples never included in it. Even with Burma under its colonial rule until 1947, Britain had also failed, in the late nineteenth and early twentieth centuries, to incorporate and colonize the Wa (Fiskesjö 2000).

After the end of British rule in Burma, the postcolonial (or arguably neocolonial) states of newly independent Burma and the People's Republic of China (hereafter referred to as China) then sought to divide up the Wa autonomous lands that still remained between themselves. Burma and China, for the first time in history, imposed a delineated border between each other, without asking the Wa, cutting the ancient Wa lands in two.

At first, the new Chinese Communist government actually sought to claim all the Wa lands west to the Salween River and, from the early 1950s on, optimistically sent in forward military teams to prepare for annexing and administer large parts of these claims. However, Burma rejected this and instead negotiated to give China more land to the north. By the early 1960s, the two new nation-states finally established the current international border, which has formally split the Wa lands between Chinese and Burmese territories and designated Wa people as either Chinese or Burmese citizens.

Even on the Burmese side of the border, however, Chinese influence has been predominant. Such influence has stemmed from the Chinese Communist Party's (CCP) proxy in Burma, the Burmese Communist Party (BCP), which had been fighting a Maoist-like struggle in Burma with Chinese support. After losing its bases in central Burma, the BCP entered Wa lands and subdued the Wa to build a new base. Notably, the BCP cadres were just as eager as their CCP mentors to rid the Wa of their social and political institutions that had sustained their autonomy.

Thus, on both sides of the new border, important elements of Wa society and culture were upended. The large log drums that had been kept in every Wa village as ritual focal points of society, and which also functioned as a means of communication in wartime, were thrown out and burned. The old fortifications surrounding almost every settlement in the Wa's central territory were razed. The native political offices of the Wa were canceled, and Chinese-style rule by Party officers was imposed. Characteristically, these actions aimed to transform the formerly proud warrior Wa into peasants of the Chinese or Burmese socialist states. Such subjugation was a major break with the past, not least as there had not been any central authority or kingdom administrating Wa territory; there had been only self-ruling, armed communities that would unite against common enemies—much like the "ordered anarchy" famously described by E. E. Evans-Pritchard.[3]

The trajectory of the Wa's post-autonomous history took another turn after 1989. While the world's attention was focused elsewhere, the aging and now largely irrelevant BCP was replaced in a coup of sorts, staged by some of the Wa soldiers the BCP had recruited (Lintner 1990). These soldiers now seized the BCP's Chinese-supplied arms and regrouped as an ethno-nationalist army called the United Wa State Army (UWSA), which was named for the new "Wa State" within Burma's borders.[4] Today, the UWSA (along with its political arm, the United Wa State Party) asserts that this Wa state is still formally part of Burma, but, like other ethno-nationalist insurgent armies in Burma, they also demand semi-independence in a future federalized Burma. The UWSA maintains deep links with China: Chinese commerce, as well as Chinese language, currency, and so on, is so widespread here that many Burmese citizens think of the area as already being Chinese owned.

Despite this profound Chinese influence, the Wa State in Burma, like the Wa areas in China, remains distinctly "Wa." Among the many ethno-nationalist insurgencies that have arisen since Burma's independence, the Wa state actually maintains the largest and most well-armed army among all of these insurgencies, and the Burmese government has only managed to establish a ceasefire. The failure of Burma's military to control its national territory (despite its brutal, decades-long effort) can seem hard to understand and has led some to theorize that China has been undermining such efforts, similar to Russia's strategy of maintaining numerous "frozen conflicts" along its borders (regarding geopolitics, see Lintner 2021).

While I have traveled extensively throughout Wa country, my research has focused on the once central portion that today is just inside the Chinese side of the international border. For my dissertation fieldwork, I based myself in an old ancestral village called Yong Ou (Village Founded by Ou), which was the center of a grouping of roughly thirty villages related by kinship until its autonomy was broken in 1958 (the Chinese Communist military launched a drive to confiscate weapons, which led to a minor war, after which the Chinese destroyed the local Wa political leaders).

Such kinship-based entities possessed strong political significance and were known in Wa as *jaig' qee* (realm), a term that the British translated using a similar Shan word meaning "circle." In Communist Chinese parlance, it was a *buluo* (tribe). The limits of its territory were also the limits of the forest agriculture and opium farming practiced by the entire kin-bound cluster or circle of villages. Beyond these limits, infringement by outsiders, whether fellow Wa or others, could be a cause for war.

The *jaig' qee* today have been dissembled and overwritten by new borderlines on new Chinese maps, which typically do not recognize the traditional boundaries that today live on only in the memory of local Wa. Moreover, Chinese authorities intentionally rearranged the political geography to splinter old Wa centers, such as by demoting the key founder-villages to outposts, and elevating less significant places to house Chinese administrative offices. All these acts served to disrupt Wa social structures that had existed before and had once sustained Wa historical imagination, identity, and self-worth.

Previously, the centers of a circle held particular ritual significance. The *o lang* ("chief," and head ritualist) of a founder-village would be especially revered throughout the realm, and even beyond. Although without executive powers, through officiating at the grandest ceremonies, he formed a living link to a hallowed past when the pioneer-founders first came to the area and began to hunt, gather, and cultivate as well as maintain services to the local gods. Even after many years since the Chinese takeover, in the one such founder-village I know well, no one would build on the site where the house of the *o lang* had once stood. Half a century after the neocolonial Chinese authorities destroyed the institution of the *o lang*, everyone still knew who the living legitimate successor was who could inherit the post of the *o lang* in case the tradition could be revived.

Realistically, the position and responsibilities cannot be easily revived. At most, the title of the *o lang* has been cynically recycled by Chinese tourist entrepreneurs, as exemplified in the name of a Chinese-owned restaurant at a theme park in the nearby town of Ximeng, the Chinese trading and administrative seat of the new, nominally "autonomous" Chinese county. Areas where non–Han Chinese ethnicities dominate demographically are designated as the "autonomous" areas of these ethnicities and must have an ethnic governor or mayor. However, real power is held by the Communist Party secretary, who shadows and dominates every level in this new hierarchy.

Whereas the Wa used to rule themselves, they are now ruled by others. They were once the owners of the land, but most have now—on both sides of the border—become peasants working the same land for someone else, or they have become long-distance migrant workers leaving for the factories of eastern China.

History from the Wa Perspective

For the Wa, every inquiry about history inevitably becomes entangled in the post-1950s reality, split between their proud past autonomy and present-day Chinese domination. Asking about Wa history today may engender vastly different narratives of the past: some may emphasize the proud, powerful self-rule that some still remember; others may echo the newly imposed Chinese state-sponsored narrative of the supposed primitive backwardness (and incoherence) of the Wa, necessarily dependent on the more modern Chinese people. There might also be a mix of such perspectives.

Let me first introduce the past according to some indigenous Wa terms, which I learned about through my field research, listening to local Wa people. For the most part, this field research was conducted in the Wa language, and although I could not understand everything, over the two years (on and off) of my first stay, I did manage to learn the local Wa dialect (called A Vex) well enough to be able to speak freely with Wa people. Learning the language was especially helpful when speaking with elderly folks who never used any Chinese, many of whom engaged in conversation with me about things past and present, and often took pains to explain Wa concepts to me. I also was privileged to take part in many aspects of everyday life (farming, house construction, and so on) and in various ceremonies that punctuate rural life (such as weddings, funerals, and the various sacrifices aimed at helping the sick), all of which helped me to gain a fair understanding regarding Wa ideas of history in their own context. All this is still, of course, my own interpretation for which I am responsible as a researcher.

Elsewhere (Fiskesjö 2013a, 2021), I have discussed the conditions of my fieldwork in more detail, including how people understood my presence (sometimes with healthy suspicion), and my self-declared ethnographic mission to understand and learn to appreciate Wa history, language, and culture. Unexpectedly for me, Wa people understood that I and other outsiders were already indebted to them—in their understanding, a debt incurred due to the Wa's standing as the first people on Earth, and therefore humanity's custodians of the deities stationed at the ground zero of humankind.

I came to understand the related Wa origin myths and stories as fundamental to the local conception of history. In Wa society, even now, Wa kinship genealogy serves as the scaffold of both personal and communal history—always connected back to the origins of the Wa, and thus always situating every Wa person in relation to these origins and their retellings.

According to widely known and still circulating versions of Wa origin myths, the history of humanity began right in the heart of Wa country. Most versions say that humans first emerged on Earth from a hole in the ground, although some stories speak of an original gourd, a feature in many similar stories among Mon-Khmer speaking peoples elsewhere in the region (Proschan 2001).

In my area of research, this origination event is called the Sigang Lih (Emergence [Lih] from the Primordial Opening [Sigang]). Many local Wa people believe this hole in the Earth is still open, at a site called Blag Dieh, which is close by (within a day's walk) and now in Burma. In current retellings of this myth, the Wa people came up first through this hole onto the surface of the Earth, and other members of the human family came later. The others include the Wa's neighbors, such as the Siam (Shan or Tai), Gui (Lahu), Houx (Chinese), Man (Burmese), and all others mentioned last, if at all. Indians and Europeans are traditionally known as Grax, along with all other people not included in the usual shortlist, and are all amenable to be appended at the tail end of this story of originary emergence.

Importantly, the Wa, having emerged first, settled ground zero. This, as it was sometimes explained to me, is why foreigners (both Asians like the Chinese, and non-Asians) live far away: when the others emerged from the hold, they had to move farther afield, since the land at ground zero was already settled by the Wa. There may well be a factual basis for this: all of the Wa's neighbors agree that the Wa were there before the others.[5]

I also speculate that the way this story is construed in Wa mythology may very likely follow the logic of their *ecological* history. Itinerant forest agriculture comprised the original livelihood of the Wa when they first came to these areas, and they have practiced it for centuries (Fiskesjö 2009; Yin 2001). In the more distant (and now heavily idealized) past, anyone arriving in an area already settled by others would have to move on into virgin forests, where they would establish new settlements. Today, as virgin land has run out (or come under the control of hostile powers), this more ancient logic has been redeployed by the Wa to assert prior ownership of this region and to account for the more recent history of encroachments by outsiders like the Chinese, whose recent possessions can be framed as an unjust reverse expansionism and as an undeserved homecoming.

Having been the first on Earth is a mixed blessing for other reasons as well, according to many local Wa people I spoke to. In their view, the Wa are still paying heavily for the twist of fate that made their people the elders of humankind. They must care for the deities and other spirit-beings that inhabit their mysterious land, by "feeding" or "nurturing" them on behalf of all others. They speak of the *muid' eei eix gon A Vex* (the supreme deities [*muid'*] that we Wa feed), which Wa people feed through sacrifice (*yuh si niee,* making sacrifices) on behalf of the rest of humanity. The latecomers who escaped this fate got off lightly. These outsiders live easily, in their *nqieh* (downhill, "in the valleys") homes where they have enriched themselves, while the Wa remain saddled with this formidable, thankless burden. In the words of some Wa I spoke with, the lowlanders "don't even know how to sacrifice any more" (*ang li raong tei yuh si niee*)—sacrifice here conceptualized as the giving up of something that otherwise could have belonged to oneself (Valeri 2001).

Additionally, in Wa country, most deities, spirits, or entities that receive sacrifices are not understood to reward or help people; they are never benign and always present a threat (Fiskesjö 2017). With the exception of ancestor spirits, which linger around the settlement as a collective entity, and to some extent the *muid'*, which lord over specific places, most spirits are considered to be disconnected from and unconcerned with human affairs—unless humans inadvertently get in their way or annoy them somehow. The only exception is the *muid'*, which sometimes mysteriously endow individual humans, almost only women, with seeing powers, which they can use to help their fellow villagers as oracle mediums. With the exception of the ancestor spirits, all the spirits are not humanlike or more-than-human anthropomorphized beings (as they might be for people in other regions of the world); these spirits are rather other than human, of their own mind, and largely unknowable. Nevertheless, one must deal with them as best one can, including the ancestral spirits and *muid'* of the land.

This conception of Wa history casts the Wa in a position of responsibility that creates a relationship of indebtedness with outsiders, something I also encountered on a personal level during my fieldwork. Let me explain that while this way of framing (macro-)history is new, it is modeled on old notions of propriety. Customarily, the eldest brother is supposed to remain in his birth home, nurturing both its elders *and* its spirits (which include people who transformed into ancestral spirits after death). In contrast, younger siblings typically leave their homes to either settle new villages or, especially in recent centuries, become tradesmen or migrant workers (Fiskesjö 2011).

As for brothers fanning out over the landscape, this is not unique to the Wa but rather common among peoples whose history is conceived as a series of migration waves. For example, compare the brother-settler historical narrative pattern described by Wang Ming-ke (2006, see also this volume) from Tibetan-speaking areas of Sichuan, Southwest China (Wang contrasts them with the unique, lone cultural hero legends constructed by states and civilizations, such as China).

In the Wa context, the ancient formula of brothers and their fateful tasks has now been redeployed to explain and present arguments about present-day relations with ethnic "others" as well. The Wa insist on their senior role as the *ai* (elder brother), and other people as *nyi, soi* (younger siblings, according to the birth order sequence in the complex Wa naming system) (Fiskesjö 2009). This is thus one more reason why other people, including myself as an outsider, owe the Wa respect as a senior people, in addition to their responsibility as the caretakers of humanity's birthplace.

Personal genealogy represents another fundamental, generative framework of Wa history. Personal genealogy is designed and practiced so that it regenerates each person's connection to ground zero as well as the moral obligation that goes with it. As a result, each Wa person is historically connected to the Wa community and to its fate.

Every Wa person is a member of an exogamous patrilineal clan, within which one cannot marry. Each clan also has its specific name, but the existence and consequences of the arrangement of these clans are so obvious and self-evident to local residents that the clans themselves are rarely referred to in everyday life. The clan names even go unmentioned during many ceremonial occasions (for a fuller explanation, see Fiskesjö 2009).

Instead, and in keeping with the Wa people's continued penchant for egalitarianism and personal autonomy, each man and woman is commonly known by their personal name. Notably, Wa personal names are constructed from a birth-order system, coupled with a second component that is usually the name of the weekday on which an individual was born.[6]

Each person memorizes their genealogy by tracing it back to the Sigang Lih (Emergence from the Primordial Opening). This genealogy is called a *ndax ntoung* (tracks of the clan). This is the *full* answer to the question "Who are you?" and serves as a sort of highly formal and most complete form of personal identification. It begins with one's name, followed by the name of one's father, his father, and onward (or, backward, if you wish), until one "arrives at the Sigang Lih." This is how every Wa individual's genealogy must conclude—with the emergence of humanity, followed by the ancestors of the particular individual.

One's genealogy thus serves as a mnemonic device that reinforces the personal genealogy of the individual who is reciting this information. Genealogies also place individuals in direct relation to all other fellow Wa, by way of signaling membership in the general social arrangement of the Wa (membership in a clan), and also as an "elder brother Wa" who remain tasked with taking care of the gods of ground zero.

The above summary is an outline of the grand framework of Wa history as it was perceived before Chinese domination. Events in recent, actual history will be (or used to be, until recently) framed within it. For example, as mentioned in a common story, when a neighboring immigrant Lahu settler let a gourd grow a vine that accidentally extended into the territory of the Wa and bore fruit there, the fruit would have customarily belonged to the native Wa "elders," yet a Lahu person plucked it. This story now serves as an explanation for why Wa and Lahu communities have been enemies at times.

Tales like this are often be known as *groung kod* (tales of elders), which convey knowledge about history beyond the province of mythology proper (which deals with pre-human affairs, namely how the world was initially set up as a stage for human endeavors). This example, whereby historical neighborly relations are framed, is not associated with a year and a date. Such records do not exist, and even the identity of the original planter and other details like the exact place are obscure in the surviving story. Rather, the narrative has become a historical account that explains and reaffirms the historical Wa understanding of their universe of ethnic relations, coexistence, and enmity as well as the parameters of conflict within their claimed realm.

Obviously, this conceptualization of history—known by the general term *nqu ga* (generations past)—differs from the chronological understanding of history privileged in modern Western thinking, or even in the longstanding Chinese and Burmese conceptualizations of history as a sequence of named dynasties succeeding one another. In this sense, the Chinese settler woman who once stopped me getting off a bus at the trading town bus station and asked me point-blank "Are you the foreigner who says he is studying Wa history?" (which is indeed what I had been telling people) was right. When I answered yes, she countered with another question: "How can you study their history, when they don't have any?" This built on what she had been taught: the Chinese notion that primitives without writing would thus be without history, forever dancing in a circle, outside of time. I could only reply: "But they do have their own history."

One example of Wa "unwritten" history, which is largely unknown to the Chinese and missed by most researchers, relates to certain aspects of their famous war practices. Historically, the central Wa cultivated their military prowess as a deterrent, successfully branding themselves as headhunters and instilling fear in others. They did this not just by waging war but also by arranging the skulls of unlucky intruders in rows displayed on posts along village approach roads; in this way, enemies would see them, as would villagers on their way to working the fields.

Although the main function of these "skull avenues" was to frighten the next would-be intruder, I discovered that a chronological history of the associated events was also "written" into the arrangement of the skulls (Fiskesjö 2021, chap. 6) for the benefit of the local audience. Since there was no writing system in use, the warriors could not have their names inscribed on the posts of the enemies they each had killed. However, this did not prevent the cultivation of a historical memory. The sequential order of installation revealed not only which was the most recent, and thus most alive in the memories of locals passing by, but they were also grouped by the clan from which the victorious warriors hailed. The local Wa audience (not outsiders) would thus have been able to use these arrangements as mnemonic devices, enabling them to constantly recall and remember the warriors, their respective clan affiliations, the historical events of the conflict that once led to war, and to the victorious killing of certain enemies. As I understand it, this kind of information would survive for generations through oral retelling, being constantly rekindled in conversations prompted by the material remains that people would often pass by.

Importantly, this also functioned on a community-wide level: each skull avenue, with its particular distinctions and groupings, belonged to a particular village and would be managed and modified only by locals from that village. New villages would seek to establish their own avenues as well, in order to establish their visible historical memorial or record.

I once saw the remains of one such newly established skull avenue. This was in the 1990s, forty some years after the skull avenues would last have been set up and in use. The remains of the posts, and some traces of human remains, could still be seen, but were no longer maintained and left to the forest. Thus vanished one of the communities' main historiographical devices.

Through the example of these skull avenues of the past, we can see how built memorials may serve as a fertile foundation for historical memory, even in (or perhaps especially in) a society without writing, taking forms akin to the history of dates, thought to exist only in the "civilized" world. However, in the current situation, when a half century of disuse has separated the events from the structures, such nonwritten insights become more and more difficult to access. Eyewitnesses pass away, material remains degrade, and practices like building settlement walls, drum shrines, or skull avenues will become irrelevant to younger generations. This was especially true in my area of study, where no one wished to revive any of these traditions and instead preferred to let the remains simply *hram* (rot away in the forest).

Eventually, the only method for outsiders to find out about such remains would be the combination of other outsiders' observations (including old reports that noted such skull avenues) and archaeological methods (such as excavating and painstakingly interpreting the remains of skull avenue sites, some of which were made with stone posts, tasks that have never been done). But even archaeology in itself, the "anthropology without informants," is necessarily limited in what it can address. When possible, the best methods will still be those of listening to and interviewing living people on site, while also combining such methods with visual investigation and soliciting interpretations from living people about how they understand their own past—if they even want to remember it.

There are other places where people include the process of decay directly into the structure of the memorial itself. For example, some Northwest Coast "totem poles" serve as memorials for the recent dead, but these were not meant to outlast the grief of the living. Instead, they were meant to fall and rot away, as any fallen tree would, in the forest where they were first raised. This process was mentioned in the set of films Gil Cardinal (2008) made about the return of a Haisla totem pole illicitly taken to Sweden in the 1920s. The totem pole was repatriated in the 2000s, and while it was never raised again, it was given a new role as a "heritage" and token of history that has been preserved by the community.

The fading of Wa memorials, in comparison, was a consequence of how outsiders in the 1950s and 1960s successfully destroyed the armed autonomy of the Wa and every trace of their indigenous framework of remembrance that the conquering forces could find. Yet, the resulting "enforced fading" was also largely embraced by many Wa people, particularly those who did not wish to return to the past. Many Wa individuals will also now, consequently, look in horror at how Chinese commercial tourism entrepreneurs appropriate and peddle kitsch versions of historical Wa head-hunting warfare paraphernalia, something which many see as deeply inauspicious (Fiskesjö 2015).

Wa History under Assault

The Chinese military and administrative takeover of the Wa lands in the 1950s (including later in the UWSA area) represented a wholesale assault on Wa institutions and culture. With foreign domination came the destruction of a self-ruled society, along with many of its attributes and tools related to self-reproduction and self-subsistence.

To take just one example, in the area where I conducted fieldwork, neither the institution nor the decorated house of the Wa ritual chief, the *o lang*, still exist, and there are only faint memories of both. It is the same with the log drums, which were the clan-sustained focal points of social life; these drum sites doubled as ritual and communication centers, while also serving as the end node of an aqueduct system that brought water into Wa villages. There are less-tangible examples of these impacts, including the sharply diminished authority of Wa interpretations of their own past. Today, all that seems to remain of independent Wa society is the invisible social scaffolding of the clan system—effectively the most basic system of social reproduction.

From my perspective, I was surprised by the defeatist attitude I often found among people I met during fieldwork. However, I slowly came to appreciate that this atmosphere could be partly due to a particularly abrupt break with the past that occurred here. In 1958, the Chinese authorities, after governing the area for years without abolishing indigenous institutions, suddenly ordered the confiscation of Wa people's firearms. A small war broke out as a result, with the Chinese military killing some locals. Their weapons were eventually confiscated, and many Wa people were forced to flee to Burma as refugees. For those who remained, the social and political institutions of the Wa were demolished and supplanted with an arrangement of Communist party secretaries holding veto powers over appointed village chiefs.

A similar trajectory of the Wa's waning independence played out in other areas conquered by China—perhaps most dramatically in Tibet. There, after the initial conquest, the initially peaceful Communist military occupation eventually turned into a campaign of attacking and demolishing indigenous institutions. The same seems to have happened across China, yet I am unaware of any scholarship that jointly examines this synchronized late-1950s Chinese policy shift. In the Wa area, as elsewhere, decades of brutal domination of local populations followed, and it was only in the 1980s that people were once again given a few years of respite: they were again permitted to brew the indispensable rice beer and revive small house sacrifices, among other customarily valued practices (but community rituals and Wa political institutions remain forbidden).

As I learned in the 1990s and 2000s, when I did the bulk of my fieldwork, old myths were still remembered and told with pride. Yet society was divided over reviving any community rituals, which many felt would be taboo. In one instance, when a young woman suffered severe epilepsy, it was widely blamed on her taking part, years earlier, in a Chinese-arranged filmed performance of the pulling home of a (fake) new log drum—even though she was but one of the girls in Wa dress who accompanied the drum.

Some older people even held that the destruction of their old society, along with the onset of the current "Chinese era," had descended on the community as punishment, due to the community's own faulty service to the gods. This self-blame, if considered as an expression of a crushing psychology of defeat, seems akin to the "learned helplessness" discussed by Robert Dentan in his famous book on the Semai of Malaysia (2008). Dentan asserted that the persistent slave raiding and other violence experienced by the Semai led many to resign themselves to such suffering, much like victims of domestic violence may do.[7]

There is also another factor in the mix, which also works against the revival of disrupted traditions—which typically "grow" and change organically and are perhaps not easily revived on command. It became clear to me during my fieldwork that some older Wa people actively chose to refrain from teaching indigenous historical knowledge to younger generations. On the one hand, as mentioned, some elders felt it was useless in the new situation (i.e., the era of defeat) to engage in certain traditions. At the same time, this also resulted from a specific social practice of rejecting knowledge sharing, in which some elders actively aim to preserve (and not share) their knowledge to use as a social resource when needed (Valeri 1994). Compared with younger, stronger people, elders possess few other advantages than their role as sources of knowledge about the past; they therefore share it sparingly.

This practice of knowledge preservation is exacerbated by what was often, and sometimes still remains, a prideful competition among such elders for legitimacy, prestige, and authority. I was sometimes told by interlocutors that other people were useless, and that I should confine my interviews to them only (which I did not; instead, drawing on diplomatic skills learned while in my country's foreign service, I tried to remain on good terms with everyone, including with elders hoarding the past as a scarce and valuable resource).

Even in such a situation, knowledge sharing, such as the wording of key prayers deemed efficacious, was still taking place. But it occurred informally and only in limited circumstances. Again, I was initially naïve about this: I had imagined that people would be eager to pass on their traditions and see them survive, much like languages on the verge of extinction are revived by targeted efforts. But my imagination rested on the incorrect assumption that people necessarily conceptualized "tradition" and "heritage" this way—which many Wa elders did not.

Actually, it has probably been the same way through much of world history for writingless cultures and subcultures: when the scaffoldings that support a group's memories and traditions are toppled by some overwhelming force or process, their identity and very existence will erode along with these foundations. In this situation of direct dominance, James Scott (2009) has argued that writingless societies in these borderlands may even have deliberately avoided writing as a way to remain partially "illegible" to encroaching state powers.

Here, "might makes right"—as reflected in the Chinese state's efforts to erase the Wa completely, including the indigenous Wa conceptions of history. These efforts are powerfully enacted in several aspects of life. Above all, schooling is the primary "weapon." In former Wa country, schools use only Chinese and are oriented by a Chinese world view, which grants the central stage of history to the "civilized" Chinese and permits no corresponding space for purportedly "history-less" "minority" people. According to the predominant Chinese view, the Wa must eventually abandon their past and their identity and become Chinese instead. No space whatsoever is granted for any Wa perspectives on history in the Chinese-language schooling of Wa kids. Thus, even the bilingual teaching once pursued in some places has now been abandoned, along with the original Chinese investment in Chinese personnel learning the indigenous language of the nominally "autonomous" territories where they worked.

Importantly, the identity transformation performed in schools also pertains to names (Fiskesjö 2021). As described earlier, names are a core aspect of Wa identity. However, Chinese state policy shifted decisively in 1958 from a more conciliatory to a more imposing approach to their conquests. The wholesale assignment of Chinese names started in earnest at this time, including the replacement of Wa surnames with ones mainly derived from Han Chinese. These surnames have been imposed on every Wa person in Chinese territory, whose imposed surname might now read Zhang, Wei, Li, Chen, Yang, Xiao, Tian, or Zhao (representing the most commonly used). The surname is followed in official documents either by an awkward transliteration of given Wa names (mostly for adults and others who never attended Chinese school) or a *ming* (given name) with typical, explicit Chinese meanings. These names are often assigned to Chinese-schooled Wa students by their teachers, giving them names such as Li Jianhua (Li Build China) or Chen Xueming (Chen Study Bright). In these cases, the Wa person would now have an entirely Chinese name on their identification. Moreover, since this name will be their label in any interactions with Chinese people, it takes on a quality of second identity for many Wa people, while for Sinicized Wa cadres in administrative towns, this name might even become their primary means of self-reference. The complete disuse of Wa naming conventions and the incumbent dissolution of Wa identity is already a distinct possibility; in practice, however, a person's identity will often be split in two in Wa-dominated rural areas, with one part legible to the state and the other not.

The faltering status of Wa identity has unfolded very similarly in the Wa state on the Burma side of the border. Because of heavy Chinese influence (in combination with the legacies of political fragmentation of Wa lands and the failure to promote the Wa alphabet), official publications are often issued in Chinese, place names are mentioned in Chinese rather than in Wa, and state leaders are publicly known primarily by their Chinese names, complete with *xing* and *ming* (Chinese-styled surnames and given names).

In the Wa state, the formatting of *difangzhi* (official gazetteers) has also worked to subvert Wa history. These official gazetteers are composed not only entirely in Chinese, with only tokenistic Wa subtitles, but also with reference to the model of Chinese publications, which must adhere to a specific Chinese version of history even when writing about local history. This version of history usually is focused on when and how certain places were incorporated under Chinese rule (a common feature of all such Chinese gazetteers), coupled with observations about natural resources, and so on. Importantly, these publications are all co-authored by heavily biased Chinese authors, pre-censored in China, and printed in China.

Such a situation is not conducive to the continuity of a distinctive Wa history. Yet this continuity still does find place, in some ways—despite the forced assimilation, and despite the overall demotion of the Wa language to an inferior vernacular in this region. On the one hand, the informal transmission of knowledge about the past persists in rural areas; on the other hand, however, much of this knowledge transmission is ultimately interrupted by commandeering cadres, schooling practices, and labor migration, which can take people away from their communities for many years. It does involve the remembering of local tales and versions of origin myths, even if in scattered forms—as I also heard them told.

In addition, there is a limited literature by Wa scholars and writers, including in China, where Chinese-educated Wa scholars have published writings on Wa folklore, mythology, and history (although history is often addressed indirectly and is typically referred to from a myth or folklore perspective). These publications are in Chinese, with some also published in the alternative Wa alphabet that was (unfortunately) introduced by the Chinese government to displace the original missionary-invented alphabet still used in the Wa state. There are also Wa writers in Burma and Thailand, especially in the northern Thai city of Chiang Mai, where Wa textbooks and other books for Wa populations living in Burma have long been produced. In recent years, these efforts have been aided by the Wa Dictionary Project, led by Justin Watkins and his colleagues at SOAS (2006), who compiled Wa texts, proverbs (Watkins 2013b), and other forms of information. This team also produced a substantial *Dictionary of Wa* (Watkins 2013a) with entries rendered in Wa, English, Burmese, and Chinese. Given all these resources, there are thus some possibilities that Wa intellectuals themselves may continue to formulate and write a new Wa history, and the Wa language might even find new outlets (Liu 2015).

Conclusions

As an anthropologist, I view history, culture, and politics as intertwined. Whether we consider spoken accounts, memories of the past, or printed sources of various kinds, or indeed the kind of monumental memorials without inscriptions that I have also mentioned, we always have to be mindful of the social context.

In my own ethnographic and historical research with the Wa, this has meant attending to the historical and situational context and motivations of interlocutors. I shall never forget the seemingly never-ending debates with interlocutors regarding my purpose as an ethnographer.

I did not understand the reason for these debates at first, but I later realized that such discussions were ongoing among my interlocutors even in my absence, and people were understandably suspicious that I may be hiding nefarious motives, not least since I arrived with the Chinese government's approval. While I stated my interests in Wa history and culture, perhaps any material I collected would be used against the Wa, as was the Chinese ethnography of the 1950s and 1960s—which mapped the societies in order to subdue them. Or maybe my research motivation was a cover for something else, perhaps a war to come. (I did say that I went to school in America, which has been known to bomb places, a point frequently repeated in Burmese state media by Burma's military rulers.)

People are justified to be suspicious of foreign researchers, and ethnographers can only adopt an attitude of acceptance and openness to any questions asked by interlocutors about oneself and one's purpose. (Not least in Wa country, where reciprocity is highly valued, meaning that a question asked will often provoke another in return.) The key point of ethnography is to try to understand another's perspective, which is necessarily a dialogic and dialectical effort: my striving to understand the Wa conception of their history and their relations with the outside world also helped me in everyday social interactions, and vice versa.

Ethnographers located in China, where the state narrative is superimposed on indigenous and local worldviews, must be acutely aware of the unavoidable entanglement of these two perspectives. In my account above, I may have oversimplified this point. It is not only a case of local accounts being overwhelmed by a particular state narrative (although this is certainly true in many cases, and it is certainly true for the Wa in this region); it is also about how different people take up this challenge. Of course, Wa intellectuals, and especially those who are Chinese-trained, can appreciate the biases and gaps in the state's version of history, and even if they may be seduced by and buy into the mantras of the official dogmas, while it may not be possible to publish critical, independent stances, they may still be able to develop a new indigenous discourse in some form.

Education is a dangerous thing. I recall chance meetings with Chinese-schooled Tibetan youths in Lhasa, who were fluent in Chinese, and who quizzed me (the European foreigner) about my view of Tibet's relations to China. They asked me about the tired Chinese notion that the historical Mongol imperial overlordship over Tibet meant that it was part of China during that part of history. "No, it didn't," they said, triumphantly.

The classic example is of course the British-schooled Indians, who turned against the British empire. As with Gandhi himself, who, when asked of his opinion of Western civilization, supposedly retorted, "It would be a good idea."

Chinese-trained Wa intellectuals may not have the same eloquence, but even more importantly, they are not allowed onto any stage where they might talk back to the empire in this way—in the language of the colonizer!

In a region like Wa country, where writing, publishing, and public speaking are firmly controlled by the Chinese state, Wa culture might have to continue as a vernacular subculture, necessarily subdued by the dominating Chinese versions and caricatures of Wa life. Wa culture and historical memory may also simply vanish altogether, as has happened to many other people who once existed inside what is now the Chinese empire.

As Uradyn Bulag has pointed out, Chinese state policy since 1950 has been "directed at destroying the possibility that non-Chinese national identity might have any political meaning, at destroying the minorities' capacity to think and engage in politics independently as sovereign ethnic groups" (Bulag 2010, 426). Indeed, the aims and effects of these policies also apply to the historical consciousness of these "minorities." And if we take the accelerated forced-assimilation campaign currently underway in Xinjiang (in effect now a genocide; cf. Fiskesjö 2023) as a signal of things to come, it is possible that such rapid and violent transformations may become new state policy in an increasingly nationalistic China bent on securing its "greatness" by way of formally abolishing the "minorities."

In the meantime, ethnographers who are able to go and navigate the precarious situations on the ground would do well to listen carefully to what locals have to say, and weigh these words carefully against other evidence of history that we can find. And yet, our interpretations remain solely ours, as the scholar's ultimate responsibility.

Notes

1. Kengtung, a Shan kingdom that has now been claimed by Burma, was once apparently itself Wa territory, only later conquered by the Shan. On regional history, including Kengtung, see Fiskesjö 2013b, 2021.

2. For comprehensive overviews of these and other sources, see Fiskesjö 2013a, 2021; on the use of such sources, see Lentz and Michaud, this volume.

3. Evans-Pritchard (1940, 6ff), as discussed by many others, including Fiskesjö (2010, 2021).

4. The widely used term "Wa State" is a carryover from British colonial usage, referring to an entity that is statelike but not recognized as fully sovereign (such as, for example, US "states"). This usage is informally continued in the Chinese term *Wa bang*; in Burma, the Wa state is known by the Burmese military junta regime as Special Region 2.

5. Future genetics studies may also bear out the prediction that the Wa of today indeed are derived from early immigrants into the region (as opposed to people like the Tai or Shan, and the Chinese and Burmese, who are all apparently later in-migrants).

6. Note that the autonomy of each Wa locality in the past was such that even the week would vary somewhat in length, in the local dialect of each area! The principles of naming remain the same, but the exact look would vary.

7. Due to their acquired peacefulness, the Semai have since often been misread as one of the "peaceful societies."

References

Bulag, Uradyn E. 2010. "Twentieth-Century China: Ethnic Assimilation and Intergroup Violence." In *Oxford Handbook of Genocide Studies*, edited by D. Bloxham and A. Dirk Moses, 426–444. Oxford: Oxford University Press.

Cardinal, Gil. 2008. *Totem: The Repatriation Collection*. Directed by Gil Cardinal. Ottawa: National Film Board of Canada.

Dentan, Robert K. 2008. *Overwhelming Terror: Love, Fear, Peace, and Violence among Semai of Malaysia*. Lanham, MD: Rowman & Littlefield.

Evans-Pritchard, E. E. 1940. *The Nuer: A Description of the Modes of Livelihood and Political Institutions of a Nilotic People*. Oxford: Oxford University Press.

Fiskesjö, Magnus. 2000. "The Fate of Sacrifice and the Making of Wa History." PhD diss., University of Chicago.

———. 2009. "The Autonomy of Naming: Kinship, Power, and Ethnonymy in the Wa Lands of the Southeast Asia–China Frontiers." In *Personal Names in Asia: History, Culture and Identity*, edited by C. Macdonald and Y. Zheng, 150–174. Singapore: Singapore University Press.

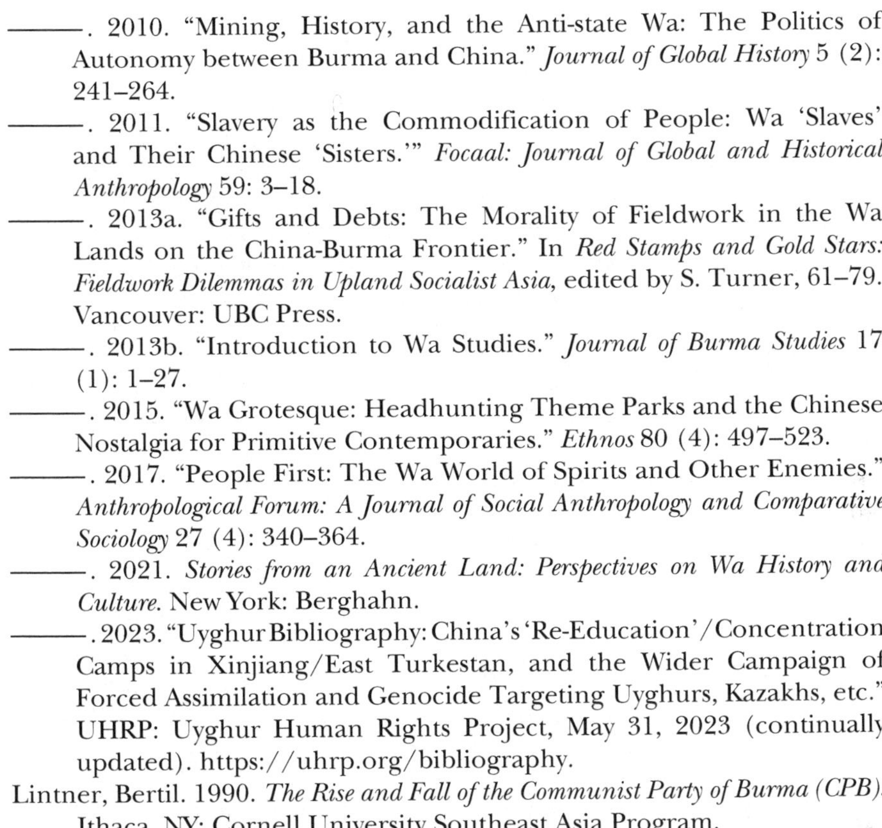

———. 2010. "Mining, History, and the Anti-state Wa: The Politics of Autonomy between Burma and China." *Journal of Global History* 5 (2): 241–264.

———. 2011. "Slavery as the Commodification of People: Wa 'Slaves' and Their Chinese 'Sisters.'" *Focaal: Journal of Global and Historical Anthropology* 59: 3–18.

———. 2013a. "Gifts and Debts: The Morality of Fieldwork in the Wa Lands on the China-Burma Frontier." In *Red Stamps and Gold Stars: Fieldwork Dilemmas in Upland Socialist Asia*, edited by S. Turner, 61–79. Vancouver: UBC Press.

———. 2013b. "Introduction to Wa Studies." *Journal of Burma Studies* 17 (1): 1–27.

———. 2015. "Wa Grotesque: Headhunting Theme Parks and the Chinese Nostalgia for Primitive Contemporaries." *Ethnos* 80 (4): 497–523.

———. 2017. "People First: The Wa World of Spirits and Other Enemies." *Anthropological Forum: A Journal of Social Anthropology and Comparative Sociology* 27 (4): 340–364.

———. 2021. *Stories from an Ancient Land: Perspectives on Wa History and Culture.* New York: Berghahn.

———. 2023. "Uyghur Bibliography: China's 'Re-Education'/Concentration Camps in Xinjiang/East Turkestan, and the Wider Campaign of Forced Assimilation and Genocide Targeting Uyghurs, Kazakhs, etc." UHRP: Uyghur Human Rights Project, May 31, 2023 (continually updated). https://uhrp.org/bibliography.

Lintner, Bertil. 1990. *The Rise and Fall of the Communist Party of Burma (CPB).* Ithaca, NY: Cornell University Southeast Asia Program.

———. 2021. *The Wa of Myanmar and China's Quest for Global Dominance.* Bangkok: Silkworm Books.

Liu, Tzu-kai. 2015. "Minority Youth, Mobile Phones, and Language Use: Wa Migrant Workers' Engagements with Networked Sociality and Mobile Communication in Urban China." *Asian Ethnicity* 16 (3): 334–352.

Proschan, Frank. 2001. "Peoples of the Gourd: Imagined Ethnicities in Highland Southeast Asia." *Journal of Asian Studies* 60 (4): 999–1032.

Scott, James C. 2009. *The Art of Not Being Governed: An Anarchist History of Upland Southeast Asia.* New Haven, CT: Yale University Press.

Valeri, Valerio. 1994. "'Our Ancestors Spoke Little': Knowledge and Social Forms in Huaulu." In *Halmahera and Beyond: Social Science Research in the Moluccas*, edited by L. E. Visser, 195–211. Leiden: KITLV Press.

———. 2001. "Wild Victims: Hunting as Sacrifice and Sacrifice as Hunting in Huaulu." In *Fragments from Forests and Libraries: A Collection of Essays by Valerio Valeri*, edited by J. Hoskins, 249–288. Durham, NC: Carolina Academic Press.

Wang Ming-ke. 2006. *Yingxiong zuxian yu dixiong minzu: Genji lishi de wenben yu qingjing* (Hero ancestors and brother nationalities: The texts and contexts of primordial histories). Taipei: Yunchen.

Watkins, Justin. 2013a. *Dictionary of Wa: With Translations into English, Burmese, and Chinese = Phuk lai toe: Dee bleeh lox Vax lox Hawx—lox Man—lox Enggalang = Pug lai doui: Ndee nbleeih loux Vax loux Hox—loux Man—loux Eing Ga Lang.* Leiden: Brill.

———. 2013b. "A Themed Selection of Wa Proverbs and Sayings." *Journal of Burma Studies* 17 (1): 29–60.

Watkins, Justin, et al. 2006. SOAS Wa Dictionary Project (including "A Bibliography of Materials in or about Wa Language and Culture"). Art and Humanities Research Council, accessed October 27, 2023. http://www.humancomp.org/wadict.

Yin, Shaoting. *People and Forests: Yunnan Swidden Agriculture in Human-Ecological Perspective.* Translated by Magnus Fiskesjö. Kunming: Yunnan Education Publishing House, 2001.

CHAPTER 4

On the Rim of Hollowness

Crafting Historical Anthropology in the Lao Highlands

Pierre Petit

I WAS TRAINED AS AN ANTHROPOLOGIST and Africanist in Belgium. My research was mostly based in the Democratic Republic of the Congo, which was still named Zaire when I completed my PhD at the Université libre de Bruxelles in 1993. It is partly by chance and partly due to the deep aspiration to begin something new that I started research in Laos in 2003. The change was not as radical as it might appear, however. Many research interests and concerns that I had developed in the Congo were maintained and matured in Laos and eventually found their way into my book *History, Memory, and Territorial Cults in the Highlands of Laos* (Petit 2020). Taking a reflexive stance, I discuss the practicalities of that research in the present chapter.

My Africanist background made me sensitive to the challenges of historical anthropology. In 1961, Jan Vansina, a Belgian historian who conducted fieldwork in the Congo in the 1950s, published *De la tradition orale: Essai de méthode historique.* This seminal book was translated into English in 1965 and provided the basis of a later book, *Oral Tradition as History* (1985), where the author refined his methodological framework. Vansina was certainly not the first scholar to study history in a context where written sources are scarce and where orality is the main vector of knowledge on the past. However, he was the first one to elaborate a critical method to use such oral sources. The "oral traditions" at the core of Vansina's method are "verbal messages which are reported statements from the past beyond the present generation" (Vansina 1985, 27). This definition differentiates oral traditions from other oral sources, including testimonies from direct witnesses (which represent the primary source of what is usually called "oral history"), because "there must be transmission by word of mouth over at least a generation" (28). Vansina argued that oral traditions conserve relevant historical information for historians, but that the latter must critically look for alterations along their chain of transmission.

Although Vansina's ideas have been contested, the use of oral traditions has repeatedly been debated by scholars focusing on Sub-Saharan Africa, notably in the journal *History in Africa,* which was established in 1974 by its first editor, David Henige, who was much engaged in this field of research (Doortmont 2011). This scholarly interest has an explanation: in Sub-Saharan Africa, oral traditions have been a major source of information on the precolonial past, which was important for legitimizing the nascent postcolonial states and rooting them into a distant past. By comparison, the premodern states of continental Southeast Asia had developed writing systems and produced chronicles for centuries. These chronicles became the key source used by historians during the colonial period, and they remained the primary textual resource for newly independent Southeast Asian states in building their national narratives. Notably, these national histories have never included the narratives of populations whose historical traditions were oral, and such prejudice has also never been fully alleviated.[1] I do not mean to say that there is no scholarly interest in oral traditions in Southeast Asia,[2] but I do suggest that they have not gained as much momentum as they have in sub-Saharan Africa in the 1960s–1980s, and that they have rarely been considered beyond academic spheres.

When I started research among the Tai Vat of Laos, I was struck by scholars' scant attention toward oral traditions relating to the past, which certainly fueled my interest in them. Tai Vat narratives on history interest me particularly for what they reveal about the group's origins, the chronology of their migrations, their contact with other groups in the region, their former economic activities, their concrete relations with the French colonial administration, and their involvement in the Indochina Wars. I am also interested in the way oral traditions are strategically used and always reflect political positions.

Vansina's intellectual posture on oral tradition was not shared by all Africanists. I was trained in anthropology by Luc de Heusch, who vehemently challenged Vansina's positions.[3] De Heusch argued that in Central Africa, oral traditions about groups' origins have little to do with historical events; they convey more about patterns of thought, a line of analysis I followed during my early research in Congo (Petit 1996). Presently in Laos, I am sensitive to what the oral traditions of the Tai Vat divulge about their subjective relation to the state, their self-perception as a group, their moral assessment relating to other ethnic groups, their relationship with local spirits, as well as their collective appraisal of time and of mobility. I feel no contradiction when I claim affiliation to both of these eminent scholars: I owe to Vansina[4] my interest in the factuality of history, and I owe to de Heusch my attention to the subjective patterns that inform any narrative on the past. De Heusch is particularly useful when considering the earliest episodes of a group's historical traditions, which are often confined to myth, while Vansina is more relevant when considering periods closer to the present. The debate between the two postures remains theoretically inspiring.

Beyond this Africanist background, I am also more largely connected to the field of memory studies. This intellectual tradition stems from the works of Maurice Halbwachs (1925, [1950] 1997) on collective memory, and Pierre Nora's (1997) collection *Realms of Memory*; it remains very salient until the present (Berliner 2005, 2020). I was notably involved in research on the mnemonic use of Central African art objects (Roberts and Petit 1996), and on urban memory as it is transmitted using everyday objects (Petit 2001; Petit and Sizaire 2009). In my research among the Tai Vat, I have also been interested in the pragmatic dimensions of remembering, narrating, and transmitting history; in the situated and embodied contexts of its performance; and in the role of writing, objects, landscapes, and rituals in making history.

The Tai Vat of Houay Yong

I came to Laos in 2003. Until 2008, I conducted research in Thongnamy (ທົ່ງນາມີ), a multiethnic village in the center of the country (Petit 2006). Among the villagers was a group of Tai Vat (ໄທຫວາດ) families—the Tai Vat being a subsection of the Tai Dam or "Black Tai." I established strong relations with them. At the time, the ban on swidden agriculture was being strictly enforced by the Lao state (Goudineau 1997), and Thongnamy was mainly populated by highlanders who had resettled due to this policy. My research focused on mobilities (Petit 2008b). From 2009 onward, I became interested in the consequences of migration in the home villages of those who had resettled, and

I headed to Houay Yong (ຫ້ວຍຍອງ), the homeplace of the Tai Vat I had known in Thongnamy, to learn more. Houay Yong is in the province of Houaphan, a mountainous area that had been the cradle of the Lao revolution (Tappe 2013), which has since been experiencing a significant outmigration of its population (Petit 2017). Its ambiguous position of historic centrality and geographic remoteness is an important feature of the province.

Houay Yong is more precisely situated in the district of Muang Et. The latter shares its border with Vietnam and is close to the district of Yên Châu, the home of all Tai Vat in Vietnam. Muang Et is an ethnic patchwork. Among the seventy-eight villages of the district, four are primarily Tai Vat and three have a multiethnic population that includes Tai Vat households. The other ethnic groups living in the area are Lao, Tai Dam (Black Tai), Tai Dèng (Red Tai), Hmong, Iou Mièn (Yao), Khmou, and Singmoun. This diversity is partly due to the wars triggered by the Chinese flag armies, who settled the area that is now the north of Vietnam and Laos, between the late 1860s and 1870s (Davis 2017). When their region was invaded by the Yellow Flags, some Tai Vat fled and resettled in the valley of the Houay Yong stream, a tributary of the River Nam Ma. This migration happened in 1872 or soon after, which I have deduced based on oral and written sources (Petit 2020, 69–75). The Houay Yong valley was already settled by other groups, but the Tai Vat population flourished during the colonial period and progressively took leadership of the area. In 1952 and 1953, the violence of the First Indochina War (1946–1954) in Northwest Vietnam pushed many more Tai Vat out of Yên Châu. They headed—again—to Laos, forming a second wave of Tai Vat migration into the Houay Yong valley. During the Second Indochina War (1955–1975), Houay Yong was on the Lao communist government's side and was fortunately spared from direct confrontation.

Laos has partly transitioned toward a market economy since the 1975 communist revolution, although the political regime has not changed. Presently, the 530 inhabitants of the village make their living from farming activities (paddy rice cultivation at the bottom of the valley, cash crop cultivation on the mountain slopes, cattle breeding, and so on). Since 2000, however, the village has been progressively depopulating, due first to the resettlement of families to Thongnamy, and second to the massive numbers of youth migrating to the capital, Vientiane, a trend that has continued strongly until the present (Petit 2017).

Fieldwork was carried out in collaboration with the National University of Laos. During my eight research stays, I was accompanied by one or two junior colleagues from the Faculty of Social Sciences, who acted as research assistants. Conversations were conducted in Lao and/or in Tai Vat/Tai Dam languages. One of my research assistants was Tai Dam and another was Tai Dèng, both from close areas in the north of Houaphan. This cultural and linguistic proximity facilitated communication, in all senses of the term. I have myself an intermediate level of understanding of Lao, which I used more for controlling the translation than for conducting interviews. We lived in the village and shared everyday experiences with our hosts (Petit 2020, 18–28).

How History Came to Me

I did not intend to be involved in serious historical research at first. I was interested in history only as a background for understanding the migration and the recent social changes of Houay Yong. However, my hosts turned out to be quite interested in history. When I started my research, I was quickly directed to Thaaboun, an elderly man who was presented as the head expert of the village's history. The research on that topic quickly captivated me; it was like a game of patience, or a puzzle, with a general pattern appearing as its parts were assembled little by little. I enjoyed this progressive and cumulative aspect of this research. What I was told in a particular village would echo what I was told in another place and/or what I discovered in a published or unpublished source. While such historical information did not always converge, I felt confident that my work could eventually result in a chronology of the main events that had occurred in the region since the mid-nineteenth century. By comparison, my research on mobilities and their consequences was interesting, of course, but the heuristic challenge rested mostly on interpretation, as the facts themselves were easily established (Petit 2015).

The local history was replete with enigmas that teased my curiosity. For example, the Tai Vat were not the first inhabitants of the Houay Yong valley: they were preceded by Tai Soi (ໄຕໂຊຍ), who were Buddhist (the Tai Vat worship only spirits). Their presence is evidenced by a temple that has disappeared in the last decades, an old cemetery, and Buddha statues that had been discovered in caves of nearby mountains. The last Tai Soi left the village in 1945 or 1946, in obscure circumstances (see below). Such a mysterious history stimulated my curiosity, a feeling I shared with my colleague Oliver Tappe, who did ethnohistorical research close to the home territory of the Tai Soi in Houaphan Province. We enthusiastically shared hypotheses about the presence of the Tai Soi in the Muang Et area, and he provided archives that turned out to be very helpful. Curiosity, discovery, and exchanges with other scholars have been central in my enthusiasm to engage in research.

By the end of my sixth stay in 2017, I began to feel the (academic) urge to write a monograph. I had a large, integrated manuscript where information had been compiled since the start of my stays, but it was too large, with too many topics to be published in a book format. I discussed publishing options with my two main research assistants, Amphone Vongsouphanh and Sommay Singthong, and we concluded that the chapters on history and on territorial cults[5] could be selected for a first publication. This choice was motivated by three factors: explaining history and territorial cults provides a much-needed context before addressing other topics regarding the Tai Vat and Houay Yong, history and territorial cults are locally valued areas of knowledge, and neither topic appeared to be politically sensitive in comparison with subjects more closely related to the policies of the government, such as land use or migration. This last concern was important, especially because I initially intended to publish a shorter Lao version of the book. Any publication involving the National University—especially those written in the national language—should avoid questioning state policies, leading to (self-)censorship (Petit 2013a).

Drafting began in January 2018, based on the material accumulated during the first six research stays. In August, I proceeded to the Archives Nationales d'Outre-Mer (ANOM), in Aix-en-Provence (France), where colonial archives from French Indochina had been gathered and stored. I spent six working days in the archives and photographed hundreds of documents, as I did not have time to analyze them on site. From November to December 2018, I carried out a seventh stay in Houay Yong to fill information gaps. The monograph was published one year later (Petit 2020).

Orality and History

My research on history has faced methodological and epistemological challenges. I will first discuss my way of dealing with oral sources. A distinction should be drawn here between biographical or eyewitness accounts, on the one hand, and oral traditions (passed from generation to generation), on the other, as argued by Vansina (see above). Biographical accounts are often rich in original and detailed information. For example, an elderly man, Thoongsôm, described to me his surprise when he observed, as a child, Japanese soldiers using plates and tableware during the 1945 invasion—a way of eating he had never seen before. Other eyewitness accounts include the often dramatic narratives of the families who left their homes in Vietnam to resettle in Laos in 1952 or 1953 (Petit 2020, 103–107). Many people can provide accurate details on their own (or on their family's) history. But with oral traditions relating to a more distant past, information becomes scarce, sketchy, and more unreliable. This is the hallmark of historical research, which is constrained by the hollows and lacunae of information. As argued by Yvan Jablonka: "History [. . .] crimps the void. It listens to a silence, it ruminates a disappearance, it looks for what is missing. [. . .] The historian can only establish earnestly a few facts: he does not experience the confidence of fiction or the optimism of factuality. In the historiography of the void, writing is the rim of hollowness" (Jablonka 2014, 241–243). When I tried to elicit oral information on the distant past, I often had the feeling of facing the hollowness described by Jablonka. This specific regime of knowledge, so different from what I experienced during ethnographic interviews on nonhistorical topics, seems related to two main factors: the limited circulation of oral traditions and their relative fragmentariness.

Few people are knowledgeable about the distant past in Houay Yong. Rural societies are often described as dense memory milieus. For example, according to Halbwachs (1925, 142), elders have free time and hence play an important role in the transmission of memory to younger generations. This is not the case at all in Houay Yong (or in the other villages in the valley), at least regarding oral traditions. The transmission of historical memory does not take place vertically between generations as Halbwachs describes, but horizontally between men who have reached social seniority. History, *pavat* (ປະຫວັດ), in the sense of a chronicle of the events that made a mark on the past, is a valued and sensible object of knowledge. Only a few male adults and elders were deemed to be legitimate interlocutors on the (distant) past: these are the *phou gnai* (ຜູ້ໃຫຍ່), literally the "important persons"—that is, adult or elder men who hold (or have held) responsibilities as political authorities or as senior members of first-settler lineages. However, we also worked with the youth and women, and we repeatedly tried to access history from their viewpoints as well. When we interviewed these latter groups, they claimed to be incompetent on such issues. Did they really lack knowledge about their history? Did they self-censor their knowledge because they did not consider themselves to be legitimate interlocutors? The question remains unanswered, but I would provisionally choose the first option, based on the practicalities of the transmission of oral history.[6]

In 2011, during a festive meal in Houay Yong, I attended a discussion where five senior males exchanged comments on the foundation of a neighboring village. Everyone spoke, and the conversation ran in all directions, proceeding by juxtapositions rather than by contradictory assertions. Everyone was eager to show off his capacity to take part in the exchange (Petit 2020, 56–60). This example illustrates very well the circulation of historical knowledge in an unsolicited context. The storytelling happened during one of the many festive events that punctuate village life, and where people are separated by gender, age, and status. Oral traditions are hence performed, updated, and transmitted in a small circle of male elites. Women, junior men, or men who have not been endowed with social responsibilities simply do not access the information and would certainly refrain from taking the floor among those respected elites. Access to history is consequently not a common good, but it is instead the privilege of a few.

This unequal access to historical knowledge had consequences for my positionality during the research. According to local standards, my own status as a male university professor in his forties/fifties, who is also married and a father, made me particularly fit to engage in these exchanges of lore. My colleagues and I were progressively co-opted by the elites of the village, who had some interest in presenting a version of history that legitimized the present order. Our own interest in historical topics probably also reinforced, at the village level, the social status of those we contacted to learn about the local past.

The second factor explaining the "hollowness" of a history based on oral traditions is its "sketchiness." The narratives that were reported to me were usually fragmentary: they mentioned a few places, a few names, and a few events, in a time amounting to two to five minutes. They tended to comprise the following: our ancestors fled Vietnam; they first settled here, then in a second place; they came into contact with such a group; this group and that group founded the village X and Y; the successive heads were A, B, C; and so on. But once the story had been told, our questions on detail were answered very briefly, and our interlocutors often simply professed their lack of knowledge: "I do not remember" (*bo chu* ບໍ່ຈື່); "I don't know" (*bo hou* ບໍ່ຮູ້). In some cases, this led to discomfort and nervous laughter.

The low level of precision of oral traditions could be related to their selective character. The episodes are organized along a simple narrative focused on what is relevant in the present time. Elements that are remembered by a generation can disappear with the next one if their content has lost relevance or has become embarrassing. For example, no one in Houay Yong remembers anything about the former political structures of Yên Châu, the home of their forefathers in Vietnam, which was a component of the Confederation of Twelve Tai Principalities (Sipsong Chu Tai). It is not surprising that such information has been forgotten, as it lost its pertinence once the villagers integrated into the polities of Houaphan in Laos. As argued by Halbwachs (1925, [1950] 1997), memory is shaped by collective representations and the stakes of the present; it is definitely not a resurgence from the past.

The two limits of oral traditions that I have evoked generate frustration. But the researcher, at first largely ignorant about local histories, quickly acquires a fair historiographical competence through interviews and written sources—especially regarding the oldest episodes of regional histories that are often unknown by local populations. This asymmetry reverses the usual situation of the ethnographic interview, where the informant prevails over the researcher in terms of local knowledge.

When researchers have more information than their interlocutors, new challenges arise. During interviews, ethnographers usually refrain from suggesting anything they know, for fear of imposing a frame of knowledge "from the outside." If so, how can ethnographers launch discussions and generate new questions when their interlocutors apparently know little on a particular topic? How can the former ensure the latter do not experience uneasiness or shame if the limits of their knowledge become conspicuous?

These methodological considerations pave the way for discussing our implicit epistemologies when conducting historical anthropology, as noted in the introduction of this book. In my view, historical anthropology typically aims at understanding the past according to an emic perspective. It reveals what people have considered relevant about their past. It is a subjective discourse riveted to the present, or an "ethno-history," in the sense of a recollection of the past narrated and interpreted by people from a specific group, according to their own cultural frames (Carmack 1972). Working in an ethnohistorical perspective means analyzing the local knowledge, conceptions, and representations that a group has developed regarding their past. The ethnohistorical researcher should theoretically be satisfied with whatever version of history was elicited, regardless of whether it was informationally dense or even factually relevant. But when endorsing the more usual posture of a historian concerned with the factuality of events, their chronology, and historical validity, frustration inevitably emerges because the researcher realizes the extent of what is unreachable due to the limits of local memory. The rim of hollowness may cause dizziness, especially when starting a research project.

Veiling and Unveiling

Historical episodes can also be remembered but voluntarily silenced or strategically reshaped according to the aspirations and anxieties of the narrators. History has to do with legitimacy, hence its strategic use by narrators.

This appeared clearly when I investigated the successive waves of settlement in the valley. Our informants all acknowledged that the Tai Vat were not the first settlers of the place; they were preceded by the Tai Soi, who originated from Muang Soi, a polity located farther east in the province. The presence of Tai Soi far from their home region was not clearly explained by my interlocutors.[7] They professed that over time, many had moved back into their home region while the Tai Vat grew in number. The last families moved away in 1945 or 1946, soon after the retreat of the Japanese armies that had invaded French Indochina.

The voluntary departure of the Tai Soi always disturbed me. Our interlocutors argued that Tai Soi were eager to go back home, or that they had become discouraged facing the industrious way of the Tai Vat who prospered in the valley. I was then told that Tai Soi had been requested to leave the valley after an administrative decision, following a dispute between the Tai Vat and the Tai Soi regarding the choice of the village chief. The head of the district eventually decided in favor of the Tai Vat, based on their diligence for work, even though the Tai Soi had built and owned the paddy fields of the valley. This explanation is disturbing in a social context where paddy rice cultivation and the status of first settlers are both highly valued.

I mentioned this story several times during interviews for it seemed elusive. Eventually, in December 2018, I was given another explanation. It was the early morning, and the village head was conversing in front of his house with the two other authorities of the village. I had good relations with the three men, and I casually asked a few questions about historical topics. During the discussion that ensued, the deputy chief pointed to the story of the Tai Soi. In fact, he said, the Tai Vat had bribed the district authorities to secure their support in the dispute that eventually led to the departure of the last Tai Soi. He followed this statement with a short burst of laughter, and the discussion proceeded on to other topics. His two colleagues did not react; they did not confirm nor deny his narrative (Petit 2020, 99–100).

This vignette is reminiscent of the notion of a hidden transcript (Scott 1990): sensible information can be shared inside a group but remain protected from investigations by dominant outsiders. The version that was disclosed by the deputy chief goes beyond the consensual narrative about the Tai Vat settling among other people and living in harmony with them—the trope of multiethnic harmony is highly valued in public discourses in Laos. Nonetheless, this narrative does not fully undermine the legitimacy of their presence, for industriousness is a core value for the Tai Vat, and cunning is valued within the group's intimacy.

Why does a group keep secrets for some events and not others? Why and how is a secret eventually unveiled? In the present case, I was already in my seventh stay in the village and our team had built trust with many villagers, including the three men involved in the discussion. Our interlocutors had certainly realized that we were dubious about the explanations provided until then about the Tai Soi's departure. Many decades had elapsed since the event, and the protagonists were all dead; secrecy had become less and less crucial in the self-representation of the village community. The context of the discussion also facilitated the following revelation: it was not an individual disclosure since the discussion was collective, involving the three leading authorities of the village. Their collegial presence, and the absence of any refutation from the two who did not talk about the event, substantiates the assertion of my main interlocutor. Could I publish this information or not? More broadly, can researchers reveal local secrets in their writings? The criteria I had in mind was whether this exposure could harm the local society (American Anthropological Association 2009). As the audience of my book—written in English—was international rather than local; as the events took place long ago and involved people who had all disappeared; as the tactic used by the Tai Vat (i.e., bribery) has been so common over the history of humankind; and as there is no ongoing dispute with the Tai Soi, whose descendants' place of residence is not even known, I felt that uncovering this assertion in my book would not jeopardize the villagers. However, if I were to publish a Lao version of the book, I would certainly contact my informants again to discuss the consequences of disclosing the episode in this way. I would also suggest mentioning it along with other versions that I was told.[8]

The French Colonial Past in the Local Memory

I expected that I would learn sound information on the French colonial period during fieldwork. This expectation was partly nourished by my experience in rural Congo; at the time (1988–1996), everyone above forty had direct experiences of the Belgian colonial period. Although colonial history was not at the center of my research, it was often referred to by my interlocutors. However, the context turned out to be different in Laos during my research in the 2010s. Interviews about the colonial period and its institutions generated shallow answers, and the topic did not often surface during unprompted discussions either. People mostly remembered taxes, military conscription, and forced labor, but I never heard anything about the administrative system, health care structures, education, and communication. I never heard the name of any Frenchman. I was surprised by such vague reminiscences.

A first explanation for the scarcity of commentary relates to the generational gap. Contrary to what I had experienced in the Congo, few people in Houay Yong had direct experiences of the colonial period. As the latter ended in 1953, when the French were expelled from the region, only elders in their seventies or eighties could provide firsthand information.

A second explanation is political. The paucity of commentary is a consequence of the regime's control over the past. In Laos as in Vietnam, the Communist Party's legitimacy largely rests on the narrative of the "liberation war" (Tappe 2013). Here, the national ideology unequivocally condemns all that is connected to the previous colonial presence, including the prerevolutionary social structures, described as "feudal," along the national understanding of Marxist-Leninism.

In the socialist countries of the region, the condemnation of the colonial order went hand in hand with punitive measures, especially during the war and the period that immediately followed. I have already mentioned that many Tai Vat fled from the area of Yên Châu in 1952 and 1953 to settle in Houay Yong. But after the 1954 ceasefire, most families did not return to Vietnam. Interviewees explained that the refugees enjoyed better living conditions in Houay Yong. The Vietnamese authorities eventually accepted that population shift, but they joined with the Lao authorities to identify refugees who had "committed offenses," that is, those who had collaborated with the French. The latter were repatriated to Vietnam, and no one heard more about them (Petit 2020, 105–107). On the Laotian side, the measures were apparently less severe. In the villages of the Houay Yong valley, I met former soldiers who had fought under the French flag, and all of them had been well integrated into village society. For the sake of discretion, I never enquired if they had faced any problems due to their past military affiliation.

Archival Work

To better understand how villagers relate to the colonial past, a detour to the archives was needed. In August 2018, I spent one week at the Archives Nationales d'Outre-Mer (ANOM) in Aix-en-Provence, an institution whose main assignment is to centralize archival fonds left by the former French colonial administrations. The documents related to Laos are easy to access and very informative on various issues. I became familiar with the archives related to Houaphan Province, especially those concerning Muang Et and Xieng Kho Districts, on which Houay Yong successively depended over time. Unfortunately, among the roughly three thousand pages that I consulted, I was able to spot only one mention of Houay Yong. In a tax-related document, the name of the village appears on a list of gun owners dated to 1902 (Petit 2020, 87–89). This does not mean that the name of Houay Yong will never appear in archives. The taxonomy of archives at ANOM is complex, and I certainly missed some relevant manuscripts. Other archive centers in France, Laos, or Vietnam could shelter information about Houay Yong as well.

Although frustrating, this archival research was rewarding for other reasons. I learned a lot about of the colonial system at large: administrative norms; taxes and forced labor; health, economic, and demographic data; local political systems; laws and courts; and the often-tense relationships between the officers of the colonial apparatus. The archives, together with the colonial literature (including the diary of Auguste Pavie [1919], who traveled through the region in 1888), were also decisive in providing the chronology from the 1870s onward—a dimension that was lacking in the oral traditions.

Among the Tai Vat, genealogy provides the main reference for sequencing time, which differs from chronological systems like the Chinese or Gregorian calendars. Genealogy supports a very specific relation to history. The best chronological approximation that I was given about the foundation of the Tai Vat villages in the valley came from a man in his seventies, who told me that the events he recounted took place during the time of his grandfather's grandfather (Petit 2020, 63). Without the archives and published sources, I would never have been able to date the events reported in oral sources. Conversely, without oral sources, nothing would be known about the Houay Yong valley, the settlement of the Tai Vat, or the former presence of the Tai Soi.

Archival work was also instrumental in designing questions for fieldwork. Some topics hardly emerged during my first interviews, such as the historical economy of the region. The archives contained precise data on forest products gathered in the area and on long-distance trade since the 1890s. The casual descriptions of these diverse subjects provided entry points for interviews and questions to help revive conversations. This was the case for raw shellac, a kind of resin that was long gathered in the region. Shellac was mentioned very briefly during my first interviews, but thanks to what I read in the archives and old colonial journals, I was able to ask precise questions about that important trade product. I also had a similar experience with trade roads; once the flow of conversation was opened with information from the archives, my interlocutors became more engaged, describing the armed guards who used to escort caravans, the alternative roads that could be used, the range of products exchanged, and so on. All these elements went beyond what I could learn from the archives themselves (Petit 2020, 94–97). The discussion above represents a clear example of a synergy of data sources highlighted in the introduction of this book.

Archives also helped me understand why the colonial system was not vividly remembered among villagers. The generational gap and the regime's anticolonial ideology are surely explanatory factors, as I argued in the previous section. But the shallowness of the local memory is also a consequence of the limited presence of the French colonial apparatus in the highlands of Laos. I mentioned that Houay Yong appeared only once in the administrative archives that I had consulted. Broadly speaking, the archives demonstrate that colonial officers rarely ventured beyond the main communication axes and usually had only secondhand knowledge about what was happening in the hinterlands. The French presence in Houaphan has always been very limited: before the First Indochina War, there had never been more than a dozen Frenchmen residing in the province. Therefore, the inhabitants of remote villages like Houay Yong had very little contact with the colonial administration. They had a practical knowledge of the lower tiers of the apparatus—the canton and the district, ruled by Lao elites involved in the indirect rule of the colony—but they had only a vague understanding of the higher levels of the system. The short and pithy responses from villagers to my questions about the colonial system mirror the ignorance and neglect of the colonial administration toward the hinterland, at least in this area (Petit 2020, 87–91).

Oral Memory and Writing

Until now, I have characterized historical memory in the region as oral. This statement should be nuanced. Houaphan has been part of the Lane Xang kingdom for centuries, as evidenced by territorial charts dating back to the middle of the sixteenth century. These charts have since been taken by the Siamese army when they left Laos in 1893, and they are now kept in Bangkok (Lorrillard 2021). In the ANOM archives, I found manuscripts in Lao script dating back to the late nineteenth and early twentieth centuries (Petit 2020, 53–56). However, apart from the list of gun owners mentioned above, I have never been able to find archives about Houay Yong or the nearby area. Obviously, the district and provincial administrations of the present regime must have conserved some documents, but because Houaphan is "the cradle of the Lao revolution," it is still considered a strategic zone, and I preferred not to arouse suspicion by requesting access to information that would have probably been denied anyway.

Although local history is mostly transmitted orally, this process is sometimes supported by written documents. Thoongsôm, mentioned above, who was the village head from the early 1970s to the early 1990s, keeps manuscripts in Tai Dam script (mostly prayers for funerals) and some handwritten notes in Lao that he keeps as a memory aid. For example, during an interview, he picked up a small notebook and read a page where he had listed the different spirits addressed in a disappeared land ritual. More recently, in January 2020, I learned that the past director of the primary school of Houay Yong, himself a descendant of the first-settler families, had written a text about the history of the village. He showed me the text, filling two pages in a schoolbook. He explained that it was the transcription of the history of the village narrated in 2001 by Thaabun, the local historian who I was directed to when I started my research. Significantly, the manuscript did not mention the migration from Yên Châu under the pressure of the Yellow Flags, the settlement in Houay Yong, or any of the other events that followed. The text was a genealogy of the founders' descendants: a list of names connected by family relationships, like "A had children K, L, M. M was the father of O and P," and so on. The historical events reported in the oral tradition had wholly disappeared. Yet, this genealogy was important for the schoolmaster, especially since he expressed his desire to become "master of the shirt," that is, the person in charge of the rituals addressed (in reverse genealogical order) to the late "masters of the shirt" and the other spirits protecting the village (Petit 2020, 116–144). This illustrates, once again, the importance of genealogy in the way local villagers relate to history.

In sum, when my interlocutors referenced written documents, which happened thrice, these notes were never a narrative, but they were instead a list, or a checklist, of spirits, chiefs, and/or lineage members. This does not mean that the owners of these manuscripts were not able to convey the events or the rituals connected to these lists. It simply demonstrates that the vernacular writing practices do not aim to transcribe oral lore, but rather strive to support it, which leaves room for (re)interpretation.

Until now, no local figure has written a book about the history of the region as has been done elsewhere in Laos, with the intent to produce an edifying chronicle of the glory of the Party (High 2021). But with more and more people accessing higher education and university, the area will eventually have its local historian, who will write a story that is presumably very different from the current oral traditions.

Writing and Ethics

It remains to be seen what effects, if any, my book could have on the society that hosted me. Beyond academic networks, scientific publications do not take place in a vacuum. This ethical issue raises questions about the consequences of my research—a good penultimate point before my conclusion.

A preliminary remark must be made on literacy in Laos. Even though a large majority of the population can read, few people read books. I have never seen a bookshelf in a private house since I started working in Laos in 2003, in cities or in the countryside. I cannot recall speaking about a novel or a monograph with an enthusiastic Lao reader either. Conversely, I remember the shame of a Lao colleague who could not name any Lao author of fiction when casually asked by foreigners. Of course, some people must own and read books, but they are a small minority. This idea tempers concerns that a book on history might become an authoritative reference delegitimizing oral traditions and adversely affecting their transmission. James Scott, in chapter 6½ of *The Art of Not Being Governed* (2009), argues that literacy solidifies oral traditions. However, a book on history can have effects only if some people, such as local bureaucrats and educators, relay its contents. The conditions for this are not easily met in the uplands of Laos, at least currently.

A second concern relates to statements in a book that could be condemned as politically wrong by authorities, which could endanger research participants at the origin of the information. Here again, the generally low levels of literacy in Laos (especially for anything written in English or French) diminishes the risk of this danger. Nonetheless, some bureaucrats might be committed to scanning the content of a book with this aim in mind, and English language literacy will probably improve in Laos in the future. This is the reason why I anonymized potentially sensitive comments in the book. I did not, however, anonymize the identity of all informants, which is increasingly recommended in social science research. I discussed the issue of participant anonymity with my research assistants and with villagers, and we concluded that mentioning people's names was the best way to acknowledge their collaboration in the research. Including participants' names also highlighted how dependent our team has been on those people who were kind enough to share their knowledge and spend time with us.

The positive aspects of sharing publications and other research by-products (such as archives) become obvious when considering the deontological charts of anthropology that have been issued since 1949 (Fluehr-Lobban 1998; American Anthropological Association 2009). I have provided archival documents and (selected) interview recordings to students from the National University, to arouse vocations among young researchers of this university, while I have also initiated an Erasmus+ exchange program and a PhD supervision in this view. I offered my book to the local authorities and, of course, to some villagers. The latter cannot read English, but the mere fact that a book has been dedicated to the history of their region satisfies many villagers and strengthens their self-perception. In a country where the Lao have the political and cultural hegemony (Petit 2008a), producing history from the standpoint of a minority group questions the very notions of center and periphery. The interest we displayed during the eight research stays induced reflexivity among villagers about their history, their culture, and their society. An old-style house was erected in the village in February 2020 to support the traditions and material culture of the Tai Vat (Stolz and Petit 2020); has our research contributed to the creation of a sense of heritage among villagers?

Conclusion and Perspectives

The aim of this chapter was to reflexively highlight how I have involved myself in writing a village's microhistory while attaching my research to a larger project of historical anthropology. Crossbreeding oral sources with archival research triggers an epistemological reflection about scale in human sciences. As argued by the historian Jacques Revel (1996), a specific event or phenomenon can be better understood if observed on different scales, varying from micro to macro perspectives.

I delineated the specificity of historical research by comparing it with a more present-oriented anthropology. Throughout three decades of field research in various places, ethnographic interviews have always struck me in their capacity to produce fine-grained and extensive information. The challenge, then, is usually not about producing enough information, but rather to cope with its overabundance. When dealing with historical data, however, the situation turned out to be very different. Here, information is scant, contradictory, and sometimes utterly missing. Anthropological history has an informational regime that is characterized by lacunae and hollows, whether in fieldwork or in archival research. In the valley of Houay Yong, information sometimes remained invisible without my hosts intending to hide such information, as the context did not make it salient, or because I simply did not ask the right questions. The dearth of information sometimes resulted from people's unawareness on a certain topic, because some were not involved in the transmission of historical knowledge, or because memory has faded over time. Further, information can be intentionally silenced or disguised for various reasons. Explaining the selective remembrance of the past, the unequal distribution of historical information in a population, or the complexities of secrecy is a fascinating challenge. As for the archives they turned out to be profuse with data that I had not anticipated, but also strikingly silent on those I was expecting to find. This contrasted regime of information led me to reconsider my implicit epistemology of research.

The mix of archival and oral research is stimulating and yields sound results. Archives provide a chronological and factual basis for the interpretation of oral history, and oral sources provide a revealing glimpse into the "ethno-history"—that is, an emic history—of a group. I have also considered the interplay between orality and written culture in the present day, for the highlands can no longer be characterized as hosting oral societies. More research into vernacular written cultures in this region should be a priority for the future.

As for the feedback of the researchers' written production on the host societies, it should be considered with care, for ethical reasons. The consequences of "doing history" about our hosts' societies are anything but trivial.

Notes

1. In Sub-Saharan Africa, there was also an imbalance in national narratives, but it did not rest on the literate/nonliterate divide. Here, recollections of precolonial kingdoms and large polities have usually been favored by national historiographies, to the detriment of societies on their margins and stateless societies.

2. Regarding Laos, for example, see Archaimbault (1973, 1991), Lemoine (2014), Evrard (2011), Bouté (2018), Tappe and Badenoch (2021), and my own research. My argument concerns the field of oral

traditions, not oral history—based on personal memories and often taking place in urban contexts—which is much more developed in the region (Lim, Morrison, and Guan 1998; Loh, Dobbs, and Koh 2013).

3. About the work of de Heusch and his controversy with Vansina, see Petit (2013b) and Adler (2015).

4. I am also indebted to two late historians: my professor Pierre Salmon and my colleague and friend Hugues Legros, with whom I conducted ethnohistorical fieldwork in 1991. This article is heartily dedicated to the memory of the latter. For their work, see Salmon (2007) and Legros (1996).

5. Territorial cults have a strong link with history, as they address collective ancestors and local spirits.

6. In January 2020, two female students from the National University were integrated into the research team. They were supposed to interview women about history, but this failed for different reasons, notably their young age and the fact that men joined the conversation as soon as the topic of history was raised. A new strategy is still needed.

7. Based on written and oral sources, I argue that their presence in Muang Et District is related to a conflict dating back to the early 1830s in Muang Soi (Petit 2020: 75–79).

8. The publication of a Lao version of the book would raise other concerns, such as the role of the Vietnamese army in the "liberation" of Houaphan Province. The Lao official account stresses the role of the Lao revolutionaries, but the oral and written evidence at hand points to the important role of the Vietnamese army in the decimation of French troops in April 1953 (Petit 2020, 103).

References

American Anthropological Association. 2009. "Code of Ethics of the American Anthropological Association (approved February 2009)." https://www.americananthro.org.

Adler, Alfred. 2015. "Anthropologie et histoire." *L'Homme* 213: 119–146.

Archaimbault, Charles. 1973. *Structures religieuses lao (mythes et rites).* Vientiane: Vithagna.

———. 1991. *Le sacrifice du buffle à S'ieng Khwang (Laos).* Paris: École française d'Extrême-Orient.

Berliner, David. 2005. "The Abuses of Memory: Reflections on the Memory Boom in Anthropology." *Anthropological Quarterly* 78 (1): 197–211.

————. 2020. *Losing Culture. Nostalgia, Heritage, and Our Accelerated Times.* New Brunswick, NJ: Rutgers University Press.

Bouté, Vanina. 2018. *Mirroring Power: Ethnogenesis and Integration among the Phunoy of Northern Laos.* Chiang Mai: Silkworm Books.

Carmack, Robert M. 1972. "Ethnohistory: A Review of Its Development, Definitions, Methods, and Aims." *Annual Review of Anthropology* 1: 227–246.

Davis, Bradley C. 2017. *Imperial Bandits: Outlaws and Rebels in the China-Vietnam Borderlands.* Seattle: Washington University Press.

Doortmont, Michel R. 2011. "Making History in Africa: David Henige and the Quest for Method in African History." *History in Africa* 38: 7–20.

Evrard, Olivier. 2011. "Les ruines, les sauvages et la princesse: Patrimoine et oralité à Vieng Phou Kha, Laos." *Aséanie* 27: 67–99.

Fluehr-Lobban, Carolyn. 1998. "Ethics." In *Handbook of Methods in Cultural Anthropology,* edited by H. Russell Bernard, 173–202. Walnut Creek, CA: Altamira Press.

Goudineau, Yves, ed. 1997. *Resettlement and Social Characteristics of New Villages: Basic Needs for Resettled Communities in the Lao PDR.* Vientiane: UNDP.

Halbwachs, Maurice. 1925. *Les cadres sociaux de la mémoire.* Paris: Alcan.

————. (1950) 1997. *La mémoire collective, édition critique établie par Gérard Namer.* Paris: Albin Michel.

High, Holly. 2021. *Projectland: Life in a Lao Socialist Model Village.* Honolulu: University of Hawai'i Press.

Jablonka, Ivan. 2014. *L'histoire est une littérature contemporaine: Manifeste pour les sciences sociales.* Paris: Seuil.

Legros, Hugues. 1996. *Chasseurs d'ivoire: Une histoire du royaume yeke du Shaba (Zaïre).* Brussels: Éditions de l'Université de Bruxelles.

Lemoine, Jacques. 2014. "Charles Archaimbault et son œuvre." In *Boudhas, Nagas et lieux de mémoire en R.D.P. Lao: Essais à la mémoire de Charles Archaimbault,* edited by J. Lemoine and B. Formoso, 151–182. Bangkok: OI Publishing.

Lim Pui Huen, James H. Morrison, and Kwa Chong Guan, eds. 1998. *Oral History in Southeast Asia: Theory and Method.* Singapore: National Archives of Singapore.

Loh, Kah Seng, Stephen Dobbs, and Ernst Koh, eds. 2013. *Oral History in Southeast Asia: Memories and Fragments.* New York: Palgrave Macmillan.

Lorrillard, Michel. 2021. "Du pouvoir central aux marges territoriales: Corpus anciens sur l'espace lao et l'histoire des hautes terres." *Péninsule* 83 (2): 41–90.

Nora, Pierre. 1997. *Les lieux de mémoire.* 3 vols. Paris: Gallimard.

Pavie, Auguste. 1919. *Mission Pavie Indo-Chine, 1879–1895, Géographie et voyages. VII, Journal de marche (1888–1889), Événements du Siam (1888–1889).* Paris: Leroux.

Petit, Pierre. 1996. "'Les charmes du roi sont les esprits des morts': Les fondements de la royauté sacrée chez les Luba du Zaïre." *Africa* 66 (3): 349–366.

———. 2001. "Introduction: De mémoire citadine." In *Mémoires de Lubumbashi: Images, objets, paroles; Ukumbusho (souvenir)*, edited by V. Sizaire, 1–7. Paris: L'Harmattan.

———. 2006. "Migrations, ethnicité et nouveaux villages au Laos. L'implantation des Hmong, Tai Dam et Khmou à Thongnamy (province de Bolikhamsay)." *Aséanie* 18: 15–45.

———. 2008a. "Les politiques culturelles et la question des minorités en RDP Laos." *Bulletin des séances de l'Académie royale des sciences d'outre-mer* 54 (4): 477–499.

———. 2008b. "Rethinking Internal Migrations in Lao PDR: The Resettlement Process under Micro-analysis." *Anthropological Forum* 18 (2): 117–138.

———. 2013a. "The Backstage of Ethnography as Ethnography of the State: Coping with Officials in the Lao People's Democratic Republic." In *Red Stamps and Gold Stars: Fieldwork in Upland Socialist Asia*, edited by S. Turner, 143–164. Vancouver: UBC Press.

———. 2013b. "Luc de Heusch, anthropologue et cinéaste (1927–2012)." *Journal des africanistes* 83 (1): 295–301.

———. 2015. "Mobility and Stability in a Tai Vat Village (Laos)." *Asia Pacific Journal of Anthropology* 16 (4): 410–423.

———. 2017. "L'exode rural au Laos: Mobilité, jeunesse et parenté à Houay Yong (province de Houaphan)." *Bulletin des séances de l'Académie royale des sciences d'outre-mer* 63 (1): 49–69.

———. 2020. *History, Memory, and Territorial Cults in the Highlands of Laos: The Past Inside the Present.* London: Routledge.

Petit, Pierre, and Violaine Sizaire. 2009. "Ce que disent les objets: réflexion sur la mémoire populaire à Lubumbashi." In *Images, mémoires et savoirs: Une histoire en partage avec Bogumil Koss Jewsiewicki*, edited by I. Ndaywel é Nziem and E. Mudimbe-Boyi, 155–176. Paris: Karthala.

Revel, Jacques. 1996. "Présentation." In *Jeux d'échelles: La micro-analyse à l'expérience*, directed by J. Revel, 7–14. Paris: Le Seuil-Gallimard.

Roberts, Allen F., and Pierre Petit. 1996. "Peripheral Visions." In *Memory: Luba Art and the Making of History*, edited by M. Nooter Roberts and A. F. Roberts, 211–243. New York: Museum for African Arts.

Salmon, Pierre. 2007. *Nouvelle Introduction à l'histoire de l'Afrique.* Paris: L'Harmattan.

Scott, James C. 1990. *Domination and the Arts of Resistance: Hidden Transcripts.* New Haven, CT: Yale University Press.

———. 2009. *The Art of Not Being Governed: An Anarchist History of Upland Southeast Asia.* New Haven, CT: Yale University Press.

Stolz, Rosalie, and Pierre Petit. 2020. "Emerging Public Spaces in Rural Laos." *Civilisations* 69: 171–196.

Tappe, Oliver. 2013. "Faces and Facets of the *Kantosou Kou Xat*: The Lao 'National Liberation Struggle' in State Commemoration and Historiography." *Asian Studies Review* 37 (4): 433–450.

Tappe, Oliver, and Nathan Badenoch. 2021. "Neither Tai, Lao, nor Kha: Language, Myth, Histories and the Position of the Phong in Huaphan." Japan-ASEAN Transdisciplinary Studies Working Paper Series (TDWPS) 12. Kyoto: Center for Southeast Asian Studies (Kyoto University).

Vansina, Jan. 1961. *De la tradition orale: Essai de méthode historique.* Tervuren: Musée royal de l'Afrique centrale.

———. 1965. *Oral Tradition: A Study in Historical Methodology.* London: Aldine Transaction.

———. 1985. *Oral Tradition as History.* London: James Currey.

CHAPTER 5

Crossing Oral History and Ethnography

*How Does an Anthropologist Look into the
Past in a Postrevolutionary Province?*

Vanina Bouté

HOW DO WE STUDY THE HISTORY of local societies for which there are
no or few archives? The situation becomes more complicated in the case
of the local societies of Laos, as there are very few historical documents
concerning the kingdom of Luang Prabang (Laos) into which these
societies were integrated during the modern period. How then can the
history of these local societies be traced, and from which sources? What
does the conjunction of history and anthropology allow in the case of
continental Southeast Asia?

When I started my doctoral research in 1999, I had only sparse and
vague information about the Phounoy, gathered from the few existing
documents and articles. Settled in the most northern province of Laos,
the Phounoy, a group of about thirty-five thousand Tibeto-Burman
language-speaking people, were among the few highlanders in Laos to
have adopted Theravada Buddhism over the past centuries. Henri Roux
(1924) described their society as highly structured; they had a vast territory, subdivided into clan territories. The Phounoy had prestigious
leaders, and despite their allegiance to the king of Luang Prabang, they
had some autonomy. Still, according to Roux, the Buddhism they practiced was similar to that of the Tai Lue, but they also performed rituals
dedicated to the spirits of the house, the village, and the territory.

When I began my fieldwork in Phounoy villages, I was struck by the
gap between such few articles and the reality I was facing: the clan territories were a thing of the past, young people were unaware of their clan
membership, the existence of spirits was fiercely denied and thought to
be nonsense, and so on. Mostly located in the mountains, the villages

appeared desolate, having lost half of their population within a few years. The last inhabitants denigrated their lifestyles and dreamt of living in the lowlands and cities as Lao people did. So, I started my work by trying to answer the questions I was asking myself: Why and how had this population been radically transformed between the beginning of the twentieth century (as the French military had described it) and when I encountered this group, and why did people seem to reject their past so strongly?

Understanding these changes, or rather measuring these changes by looking for their roots and/or revealing their mechanisms required an interest in the history of the group. The use of history seemed all the more obvious to me because of my initial training as an Americanist. For these area studies, many French anthropologists emphasized the need to look back at the past in order to understand the contemporary societies in which they worked. I was then able to "test" this approach on a different geographical area, for which, to my knowledge, no similar approach had been carried out.[1]

I have shown elsewhere the main results of this research (Bouté 2011, 2018). For the purposes of this book, I would rather go behind the scenes to show the methods I used to reconstruct the history of an "ethnic minority" in a context—which more broadly pertains to continental Southeast Asia—where written sources are scarce and access to the terrain is difficult.

I will start from the observation that written sources are rare among local societies in continental Southeast Asia. Sometimes contradictory, and often delivering only scraps of information, written sources require continual fieldwork. Second, I wish to show that research on history in the field also depends on the relationship that the state where the investigations are carried out has with the past. Moreover, the situation becomes more complicated in an authoritarian context, when the state and some people—depending on the relationship they have with the authorities—choose to silence that past. Finally, I will come back to the problems of collecting data on the past from villagers.

Continental Southeast Asia: Scarce Written Sources and Discrepancies with the Present

To consider the history of a population is first of all, in my opinion, to look back at all the writings—archives, secondary sources, and scientific writings—produced about a given region. One of my first observations at the beginning of my research on Laos was the conspicuous gap in scientific production between the Andean world and continental Southeast Asia (and Laos in particular). While on the Bolivian Andes alone the literature produced was impressive and had provided me with a solid foundation on which to build and orient my research, academic work on Laos (a country almost comparable in size and demography to Bolivia) was very scarce.

The first elements of ethnological literature on the populations of continental Southeast Asia appeared with the establishment of Western colonial administrations, at the beginning of the nineteenth century for Burma (under British administration) and at the end of the nineteenth century for Vietnam, Cambodia, and Laos (united within French Indochina). Even if they were produced as much by soldiers and administrators as by researchers, some of these documents testify to a real effort to get to know the so-called mountain populations. In addition to specific monographs or articles on certain societies, there are also collections of notes as well as linguistic and/or ethnographic records on groups of populations located in mountainous areas who are now at the crossroads of several countries.

But these initial works—limited in quantity and of unequal scientific quality—were not followed by real ethnographic research. During the colonial period, the work carried out by the École française d'Extrême-Orient was essentially of an archaeological or epigraphic nature. Yves Goudineau (2022) notes that in southern Laos, for example, no real village monographs appeared before the 1960s. There is, therefore, a small amount of ethnographic research on the populations of continental Southeast Asia, which essentially emerged between the end of the nineteenth century and the first two decades of the twentieth century, and then dried up in the 1930s until the outbreak of World War II. Research was not resumed until the 1960s for some countries in continental Southeast Asia (except for Vietnam and Burma, which closed its borders in 1962). Ethnological research on continental Southeast Asia has thus accumulated a considerable backlog: almost half a century has elapsed between the first ethnographic materials collected by members of the colonial administration and the first monographs on social anthropology devoted to mountain or minority populations in continental Southeast Asia.

The 1960s and 1970s saw the reemergence of a proliferation of work carried out in the field. This time, the fieldwork was conducted by ethnologists who were members of research institutions (this is especially true for Laos and Cambodia, while Vietnam was already caught up in the war), but nothing was done for the province of Phongsaly, which, from 1954, came under the command of the revolutionary forces of the Pathet Lao and forbade foreigners. After one or two decades of research, wars broke out, and the countries of ex-Indochina closed themselves off to all research: Vietnam in the mid-1950s, then Burma in 1962, followed by Laos and Cambodia in 1975. It was only in the mid-1990s that the first ethnological surveys resumed in Laos, and I began my investigations in 1999.

So I found very little work that mentioned the population—the Phounoy—with whom I intended to conduct field surveys. Here, I would like to return to the nature of these sources in order to show how the fragmentation of their content can finally have a heuristic value.

1. Colonial Sources: The Confusion of Names

Delving into the rare existing written sources on the history of minority populations in Laos requires research into archives and printed texts from the colonial period. I also worked from different translations of the royal chronicles of Luang Prabang and those of the surrounding kingdoms in order to reconstruct the possible contexts of Phounoy-speaking populations before the formation of the French protectorate of Laos. But it was evident that local populations were notably absent from these texts, which were mainly devoted to the ruling elites, as George Condominas (1990, 30) noticed before me: "Whether from Chinese historical records or Thai epigraphic texts, or even the *nithan* and *phongsavadan*, chronicles and annals in Pali and in northern Thai, the essential character of their sources has imposed on historians research which essentially traces factual history: determination of places and dates, establishment of the sequence of dynasties, biographies of kings and war-chiefs. [. . .] The people however are hardly mentioned." A first prerequisite—and a handicap perhaps for other researchers—is therefore being able to find these colonial archives and to read French.

By studying the works written by French soldiers, explorers, and doctors who traveled to the north of Laos at the end of the nineteenth century and in the first half of the twentieth century, we sometimes find—in the absence of detailed sociological or ethnological analyses—valuable information on the Phounoy as well as on the administrative functioning of what was to become the Fifth Military Territory (present-day Phongsaly Province) and, more widely, of northern Laos.[2] The most detailed one is an article by Roux (1924), which provides in-depth information on the Phounoy: a history of the population; their political organization; religious practices; descriptions of agricultural practices, tools, houses, and so on. This article is therefore a unique source on the Phounoy.

With the exception of Roux's article, looking for traces of the Phounoy in these various writings means sifting through, dissecting, and reading hundreds of pages of accounts, often of war expeditions (such as the accounts of a repression against the Hô [Chinese pirates] in the Phongsaly region in 1915–1916 by Eugène Guillemet [1921]). Such descriptions are preceded by the impressions of the European author on the "savages" (*Kha*), the dirty conditions of houses, the pusillanimity of villagers, the walks through the forest as well as the rudimentary lodging and unsophisticated cuisine. It also means getting acquainted with maps and trying to find the names of villages and their locations, such as in the *Atlas de l'Indochine* (1920). One can find one's way around thanks to the names of the rivers (Nam Té, Nam Lèng, and especially Nam Ou in the study area), while one also discovers unknown village names. After returning to the field, this information led to lengthy questions, ultimately revealing that the villages—often said to be two hundred to three hundred years old—have frequently changed names, and that there is a different name for each current village, which was given before the "liberation" of the country in 1975.

So, you basically have to know what to ask to get the right answers. And at first, we know nothing. During my first stays, I would never have thought to ask about the successive names of the village of Thongpi. As I cross-checked the maps from different eras (those from 1920, Aymé's from 1930, and those that could be found at the Geographical Services offices in Vientiane at the end of the 1990s, which had been drawn up by the French in the 1950s), I discovered successive generations of names for the same set of villages. I went back to Phongsaly and then asked the villagers to scroll backward through the names of their village: And in the 1970s? What about before? The village where I was based for my research was thus integrated into the Taseng Cardamome (a kind of canton) in the 1970s, and had been named Taseng Phanya Soulinya before 1954. However, this name that does not appear in the writings of the colonial administration at the beginning of the century, which only mentions a Taseng Phongsaly that encompasses the different cantons. After renaming the territories of the Phanya,[3] the villages were then renamed in the 1960s. The old ones, which were commonly the names of the founding chiefs (preceded by the Lao title of *sèn*), were considered to be traces of the former royal regime that needed to be eradicated. All the villages were thus given several successive names, which the inhabitants still used alternately to designate them (which added to my confusion). Thongpi was called Ban Soulinya, Say was formerly Sélou (but also called Thaonong by Roux), Phongsaly was called Sensili, and so on. Finally, there were mentions of village names or names of "cantons" (*taseng*) that no longer existed and of which no one had preserved the memory.

Another concern was the transcription of names: names of people, names of "ethnic groups," names of villages, and other toponyms. No two authors or maps used the same transcription. I have written elsewhere (Bouté 2010) about the multiple spellings and appellations given to the Phounoy (referred to as Kha Pay, Phay-Pounoi, Khas Phou-Noi, while also called Ong Hyao, Lao Seng, Phongset, etc.). For a long time, I asked the people of Phongsaly where the Kha Phay were (whose literature referred to them sometimes as the Phounoy, and sometimes as a group living nearby), and searched in vain for the Ong Hyao, which no one had heard of. It was the same for toponyms. The difficulty was then in finding a sufficient number of indications and maps to be sure that two phonetically close spellings corresponded to one and the same place (and not two different ones).

The question of ethnonyms in Asia was raised, among others, in the book edited by Christian Culas and François Robinne (2010). Culas (2010, 13) pointed out that that "the main difficulty will be to find, behind the categories and conceptions of the majority group with a written tradition and a normed history, the traces of the minority group's social practices and representations." In my own case study, the proliferation of names had a direct effect on the research method, which comprised the creation of files listing the different names of the same locality for each type of toponym, trying to identify the number of occurrences, and trying to pinpoint their location, and so on. But the proliferation of names also, above all, had a heuristic value (Bouté 2010). What may appear to be obscurities, misspellings, and nonsensical changes ultimately revealed "successive layers" of a population's history.

Different names for the same place actually corresponded to different administrative and political structures of the territory, for which no explanation could be found in historical sources and which the inhabitants could not explain. For instance, Lefèvre-Pontalis (1898) named this group of populations "Kha Phay," while distinguishing the inhabitants of the Muang Phounoy, which he initially called the "Kha Phay of Müang Phounoy," who he then referred to a few pages later as the "Kha Phay Phounoy." This term was progressively employed by other military personnel, then simplified, and at the beginning of the twentieth century, the "Kha Phay Phou Noy" (Guillemet and O'Kelly 1916) were simply called "Kha Phounoy" (Roux 1924), then "the Phounoy" (Aymé 1930). This illustrates how the name previously attributed by the Tai populations (first the king of Luang Prabang, then the Tai Lue chiefs) to a territory inhabited by small groups with a particular status eventually became the ethnonym of the inhabitants of this locality used by colonial administrators. *Kha* and *Phay* are two generic terms to designate populations as either servile (*Kha*) or a slightly less pejorative status (*Phay*). Here, the study of ethnonyms and their evolution makes it possible to follow the relational processes between centers of power and the Phounoy. As Hjorleifur Jonsson (2002) observed in northern Thailand, ethnic identities in the precolonial context must be understood as indices of rank and status above all. They remain fundamentally linked to a local context, which explains why culturally closely related populations may be known by different names, depending on the political power on which they depend (Jonsson 2002) or on the progressive local construction of their own power (Bouté 2011).

This need to understand, sort, and organize the diversity of appellations was the first step of my research (Bouté 2005, 2011). This step also enabled me to understand the geopolitical position of the Phongsaly region when the Phounoy claimed to have settled there in the second half of the eighteenth century. It is thus by cross-checking several sources that I managed to gradually reconstitute a first physiognomy of this territory. Politically, Muang-U territories in the north were attached to the Tai Lue realm of Sipsong Panna; the principalities of Sipsong Panna and Sipsong Chau Tai were in the east and west; and in the south, the *muang* of Boun Nua, Boun Tai, and Khoua were part of the kingdom of Luang Prabang. In the center, an area with no clear political claim remained, occupied by the Phounoy and Austroasiatic speakers (mainly Khmou).[4] (See map 2.)

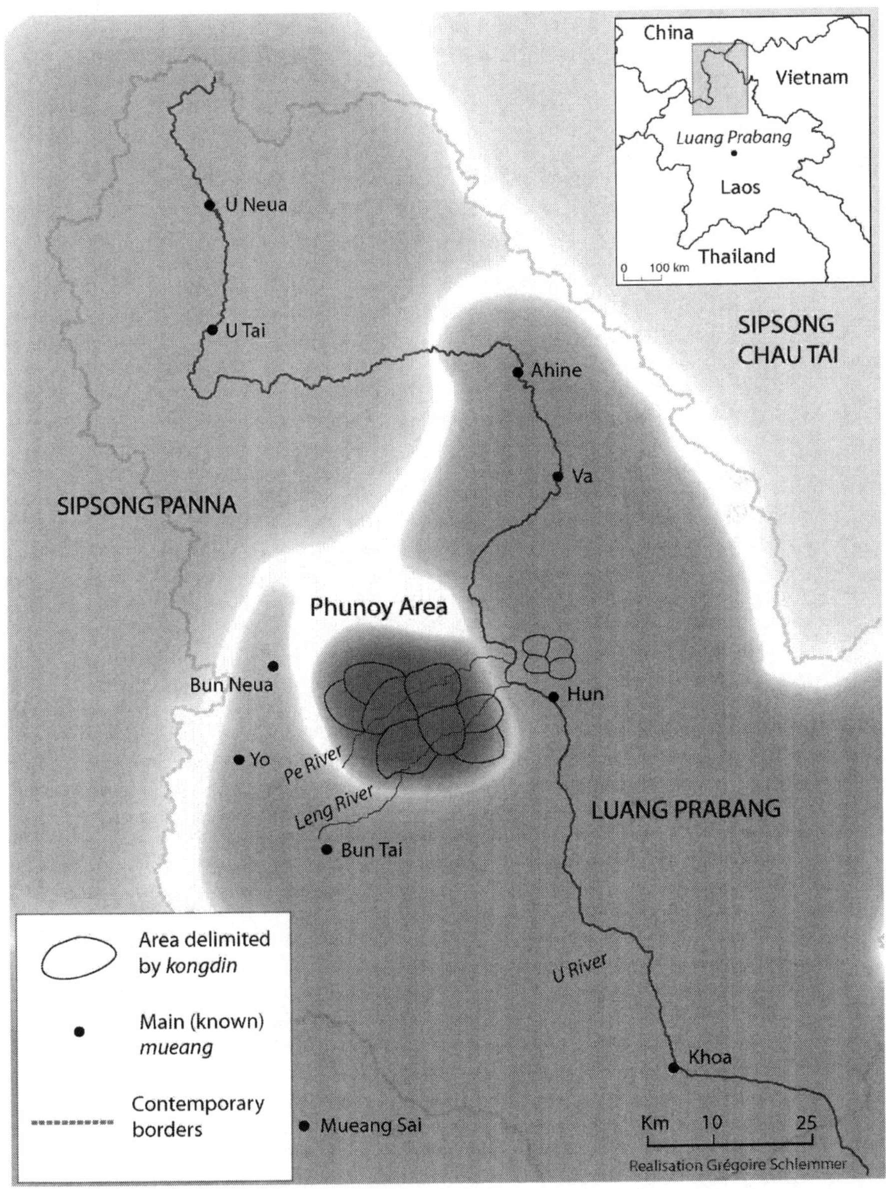

Map 2. The Phounoy territory, its *muang,* and its domains circa 1750. © G. Schlemmer.

2. Snippets That Shed Light on the Field and Vice Versa

In one of the hundreds of pages devoted to the marches of the rifle battalions—with long descriptions of the forests, leeches, exhausted mules, and tired porters—one will sometimes find little gems that revive the investigation in the field. An excerpt from Guillemet and K. O'Kelly (1916, 198) exemplifies one of these gems: "The court of Luang Prabang considered them to be the border guards of the kingdom and as such, always treated them in a special way, as a small state. Their leaders are the natural intermediaries between them and the King's officials."

It was the first mention of the Phounoy as border guards I found. No Phounoy had ever mentioned it to me before. So, I went through all the literature I could find on the subject. A few brief, rather vague mentions appeared. Roux (1924, 452) mentioned quickly: "Finally, it should be noted that before the arrival of the French in the Territory, the King of Luang-Prabang had entrusted the P'u-Noi with the guarding of the borders. It is probable that they had deserved this choice by showing courage at least in front of people belonging to races known to them." Pierre Lefèvre-Pontalis or Paul Néis did not talk about it, nor did Georges Aymé—who, however, devoted a substantial amount of his monograph on the Fifth Territory to the problems of border markers. Neither did Henri Cheyrou-Lagrèze in the 1920s, or Martial Doze, one of the last Frenchmen in the region in the early 1950s. It is therefore with very little information that I returned to Phongsaly with new questions about this Phounoy past of border guards.

In the town of Phongsaly—in which 80 percent of the population is Phounoy—officials from the provincial Department of Culture had assembled a collection of Phounoy oral histories in the mid-1990s, and now this was their official version. In fact, this history was engraved on a stone wall at the top of the province's only tourist site, and it was also published as a small cartoon booklet by the NGO Education sans frontières and distributed to children (see figure 5.1); this version was being repeated by everyone. In the villages, the inhabitants did not tell me about it when I asked them about the history of the Phounoy, except when I specifically asked them about their past as border guards. At first, they did not necessarily say more, and had little memory of guarding the borders for the kingdom of Luang Prabang.

On the other hand, many stories emerged around "border books" (*pum saidèng*), which later became more commonly known as "books of the earth" (*kongdin*) and proved to be the most fruitful sources. People waxed lyrical about the handing over of the books by the king of Luang Prabang, about the drawing of the borders (specific to a group of several villages) around their village, and about the ritual use of these books up to the present. For example, I was told:

> It was during the time of the Phanya Soulinya that the books were given out; before that, we don't know. We remember that since the time of the Phanya. The Phanya was given the books and it was he who then divided up the land and distributed the books among the clans.

> In the old days, when Pavie came to live here, it was the time of the Phanya. In the beginning, there were two: Souline and Soulinya; Soulinya was the most important one. At that time, the king gave each clan a book.

I also heard other narratives that had to be cross-checked, and, above all, collected in greater numbers to support these few pieces of information as much as possible.

I no longer had recourse in colonial literature, where no one had ever mentioned the existence of these books, nor the exact drawing of the borders, nor even the organization that presided over the division (and which one?) of the territory and its attribution to the Phounoy. Henri Deydier, a researcher who had come to explore the region in the early 1950s with the specific aim of finding original manuscripts, had not noticed anything when he concluded: "I have no illusions about the manuscripts he [the monk] must have, because in fact it's always the same list of titles that comes up. Just enough for the daily life of the pagoda, that is to say a few classical prayers" (1954, 57).

Starting with this colonial literature and learning more information about the past in the field—the existence of written documents sent by the king of Luang Prabang—it was then from the field to the texts that I set out again. Specifically investigating these documents, I tried to gather as much information as possible about them (e.g., Which village had them? What territory did they delineate?), going to each village that was supposed to have received them, and then photographing these documents. Most of the other books (*kongdin*) that the Phounoy kept in their memory cannot be found today because they disappeared in village fires, or their owners disposed of them due to very strict

Figure 5.1. Phounoy migration to Phongsaly as recounted in the cartoon booklet by UNESCO (Education sans frontière 1996, 3). The text roughly says: "The Phounoy came on foot from Mongolia and went to China; they were cattle breeders. They crossed many places, settled in one place and built houses. Then, there were wars between ethnic groups. The Phounoy then left and settled in the south of China." © V. Bouté.

prohibitions on their possession. According to these restrictions, people could only touch the book during the ritual dedicated to it, honor it on Buddhist holidays, and pay homage to the book during New Year's ceremonies (Bouté 2011). It is possible, however, to get an idea of the area covered by all the books given to the Phounoy, for although the elders noted that none of them were able to read the books anymore, the limits and attributions of a territory to a clan remained perfectly known. Indeed, the Phounoy attributed a ritual function to these books. In the event of war or violent or accidental death, the boundaries of the territory where the problem had occurred had to be recited by the *kongdin* owner. These rituals took place—depending on the area—until the 2000s. A book's homage ceremony was also organized on the occasion of the Buddhist New Year (*Pimai*) celebrations; this event took place regularly in the village of Thongpi until 2006, when the village disappeared.[5] It is also in this village—as well as with one of its former inhabitants, living in the town of Phongsaly—that four books and several royal ordinances were photographed (see figure 5.2). Thanks to a collaboration with Khampeng Kettavong, a historian at the Lao Academy of Social Sciences, and Khamsi Kinouanchanh (ÉFEO-Vientiane), I was able to translate these documents, written in Tham Lu and Old Lao, into modern Lao and then into French.[6] But the data they contain—particularly those relating to the drawing of borders—can again only be understood in light of fieldwork. Although the toponyms contained in this book do not appear on the geographical maps of the region, they were still in use

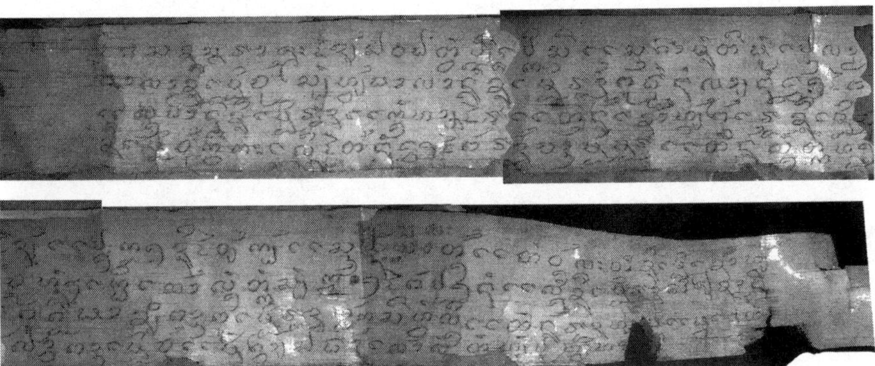

Figure 5.2. "Book" *(kongdin)* script held by the Lava clan among the Phounoy, 1750. © V. Bouté.

by my interlocutors at the beginning of the 2000s. Similarly, I would not
have been able to establish the identity of the original owners if I had
not previously carried out intensive surveys among the Phounoy on clan
names, the territorial divisions that prevailed, and the systems of alli-
ances between clans, among other topics.

I hope I have shown here the necessary comparisons between texts
and fieldwork. But there is a more field-specific dimension that I would
like to address as well, which is the difficulty of investigating the past in
the context of Laos in the 2000s.

Investigating the Colonial Period in an Authoritarian Context

Laos had been closed to foreign researchers since the new Pathet Lao
regime came to power in 1975, and when I arrived in 1999, few researchers with the status of anthropologist had done extended fieldwork.
Although the country had opened up a little to research projects conducted by Western researchers since the 1990s, the state did not abandon the desire to closely monitor these activities. First of all, I had to
gather a large number of authorizations duly marked with a red stamp,
along with research authorization from the Ministry of Information and
Culture, which took me six months to obtain. Next, I had to have this
paper stamped and apply again for authorization from the provincial
cultural services, then from Phongsaly district, and then from the province's police services.

I made my first visits to the villages armed with official papers and
red stamps from the administration. Authorities from the ministry first
endeavored to find one of their members to accompany me, but fortunately, none of them wanted to go to a remote province so far from
the capital and as difficult to access as was—particularly at the time—
Phongsaly.[7] They were especially discouraged by the meager per diem
that I could offer as compensation. Upon my arrival in Phongsaly, the
provincial Department of Culture also made a point of having one of
its members continually accompany me throughout my stay. The first
investigations were disastrous: my chaperone did not let me speak
directly to the villagers, wrote down all my questions in a notebook,
chose to translate those that seemed to suit him, and gave answers that
had little to do with those of the peasants. I modified my itinerary and
chose to go to the villages farthest from the roads, hoping to tire my
companion with long walks on steep slopes. Indeed, back in the town

of Phongsaly, he felt that I could now carry out my investigations alone. I was nevertheless faced with two difficulties: the state's mistrust of foreigners and its intent to keep quiet about the past, and the integration of these norms by the villagers.

1. The Impossible Investigation of the Royal and Colonial Past in a Revolutionary Province

Collecting information about the past, when that very past was described as counterrevolutionary, was very difficult at the beginning of my interviews, and I was still unaware whether the information I was collecting was incomplete because of the faulty memory of my interlocutors or because there was a conscious wish to conceal certain things from me. Indeed, provincial authorities at that time were still disseminating messages warning villagers to beware of Western tourists who ventured into districts without authorization, portraying them as potential troublemakers and hawkers of decadent morals. Thus, after one year of living in the province, I thought it was possible to attend New Year celebrations in a village and deliberately neglected to show my official papers. At nightfall, I was duly expelled from the village by a few zealous representatives of the Party and found refuge in an old hut built on wasteland. I got out of this situation relatively well—I learned later from the director of the Department of Culture of the province, who was very amused, that a tourist lost in an ethnic Hô village had been seized by the villagers and brought back triumphantly to the province's police station, trussed up like prize game with his arms and feet attached to a pole.

The situation was not specific to Phongsaly but to Laos in general. One year later, in 2000, two other French PhD students were expelled from the neighboring province of Oudomxay, under the false pretext of proselytizing. However, it turned out to be more acute in Phongsaly, reputed, like Houaphan Province, to be one of the two early revolutionary provinces that held even "harder" lines in terms of political ideology than the rest of the country.[8] This was probably true. I remember the first assistant who came with me to Thongpi, a young Lao man named Song from the ethnic Lao village of Ban Keun in Vientiane Province. He stayed in Thongpi for only a month, horrified by the living conditions in the village. Song liked to recount life in his Lao village, and he spoke to me freely about the small rite performed by the village "priest" (*chaocham*) to the guardian spirit of his village before his departure so that he would be protected during his journey. In the same year, when presenting a picture of Phounoy villagers to the provincial and district authorities, an anthropologist consulted by a local NGO in Phongsaly District mentioned the existence of *chaocham* in the Phounoy villages. This resulted in a general outcry, with the authorities protesting with indignation about the impossibility that such a superstitious ritual function could still exist in Phounoy villages, the members of which were Buddhists and good revolutionaries.[9]

In my meetings with the various authorities of the province, I therefore avoided mentioning my interest in the past—the royal past, then the colonial past—to avoid my potential eviction from the province. What was valid in 1999 and 2000 seems to still apply today. For example, in 2014, I was asked by a former deputy of the province, who had been commissioned by the governor of Phongsaly Province, to write a "History of Phongsaly Province" on the occasion of the sixtieth anniversary of the "liberation of the province" in 1954. He notably asked me for help in writing the chapter on the precolonial and colonial period. We worked together for days on this manuscript, but it is—at the time of this writing—still dormant in the censorship services of the national editions. My interviewer, whom I asked two years ago about the delay in publication, told me, somewhat embarrassed, that he had been told that all information on the colonial past should be rigorously checked by the censorship services.

2. In the Village: Police Investigation and Suspicion of Espionage

The situation was not necessarily easier in the village. Some elders, who had known the French and always believed that they were "eager to regain Phongsaly," saw me as a possible agent in their service. Other villagers, because of my authorizations stamped in red, thought I was sent by the Lao government. The family with whom I lived kept saying: "Beware of spies in the village." Old Sangfa, who lived in the house next door, told me: "Game has to be hidden because of spies in the village." "Maiseng tells you he has forgotten everything of the past? It's not true," my host Thitpan explained. "He is just afraid that you will repeat this to the government and that it will clamp down on us." Opium, the size of fields, and the number of buffaloes are hidden to pay less taxes, as are the village's past and "unorthodox" religious practices. Everything had to be hidden, as everything was likely to be reported to the authorities. Here, the suspicion of espionage appeared to play the same role as accusations of witchcraft elsewhere.

I was therefore confronted with several problems when conducting inquiries related to my different topics of research. Questions concerning the past proved to be the most difficult to tackle. Described as the border guards of the kingdom of Luang Prabang, and then as the favorite group of the French who settled in the region, the Phounoy now claimed to have been the most ardent supporters of the Pathet Lao since their arrival in the province. They therefore did not intend to return to a past or to practices that the state had described as archaic and profoundly antirevolutionary. Certainly, some aspects of their own history were quite unknown to most of the Phounoy under forty years of age. But for others, how should one describe the heavy silence of embarrassment, the awkward attempts to change the topic, and the immediate withdrawal into an icy silence of the people I interviewed? Always anxious to grab some clues left by my interlocutors during a conversation, I remembered more than once Michel Leiris's (1934, 221) bitter assessment: "Why does the ethnographic inquiry so often resemble a police investigation?"

My host—with whom the village council had decided that I could reside—proved to be the fiercest opponent of the past. As the past for him was before the 1960s (and therefore before the communists took power at the provincial level), everything I wanted to know about what had happened before (including administrative organization, the role of the Phanya, etc.) was described as a web of absurdities and retrograde periods that did not even deserve to be remembered. In the long run, I found other people in the village who were more lenient. As for my "antitraditionalist" host, I consoled myself by wondering about the reasons that could motivate him to make such assertions and by trying to understand where this attitude came from.[10] This general atmosphere of mistrust and suspicion left a lasting impression on me, at least subconsciously. When I was writing my thesis in France, two years after my first fieldwork visit in Phongsaly, I had nightmares about refusing to speak or, on the contrary, about the trouble I had caused by having spoken too much. My field notebooks are filled with notes about these dreams—stories of denunciation, spies, and arrests—that illustrate the fear my interlocutors had conveyed to me.

Doing History in the Field with Whom? A Fragmented Memory

Working on the past was not easy. Initially, I started to work in the present tense, but ultimately, it was the past that I needed to draw on to understand a shift, changes, snatches of discourse, or conflicts that could only make sense through the knowledge of a "before." I was faced with several problems, including a memory unequally shared by all on the aspects that interested me, as well as different—often even contradictory—memories on the part of my interlocutors.

1. Memories of the Past: A Memory Unequally Shared by All?

One of the difficulties that can arise for both historians and anthropologists relates to the place and status to be accorded to elements of discourse and especially to those who produce them. As Étienne Anheim (2012, 404) noted, one should proceed not with a factual and positive hierarchy of the informants but with a "sociological" hierarchy. Each individual, while having equal intellectual interest in the eyes of the researcher, does not necessarily have equal competence and equal effectiveness in social description.

Conducting my interviews initially in Lao, but assisted by an interpreter who repeated my questions if my listeners did not understand them well,[11] I first questioned the family circle, which often directed me to this or that elder through the phrase "him, he knows." They were always relatively old people (described as such by villagers—i.e., men over fifty years of age). One can think of anthropologists' assumptions—which would be shared here by their informants—that only men, particularly older men, possess and master knowledge. But this turned out to be true regarding local history. On various occasions, I also went to see those who were not described as persons of knowledge, whether it was because they were the only ones there in the village on a day when everyone else had gone to the fields, or because we had started to discuss an activity of the moment (e.g., the elder used to cut bamboo strips to make a basket). In all these interactions, and in the event that there was some degree of sympathy on both sides, I generally encountered two types of responses. Either the elder was thinking about my question but could not remember anything I was interested in, or he perhaps wanted to please me and told me that he "knew." In the latter case, he would tell me about events and places that would turn out to be uncorroborated by any of the dozens of other people I had met before and that would also not correspond to what I had read. Such information was often full of contradictions itself (which I did not realize until I reread my notes afterward). Of some of these elders, who have no form of "knowledge," it is frequently said in Laos that they are "elders who are just there, who are useless" (*photao you la la*). Others were not necessarily in this category; the villagers could recognize their skills, as was the case with old Photao Si, a former teacher who had taught French. But for the past in general, the historical memory of the village, and political history, he was not one of the "elders who know" (*photao thi hou*).

The same was true of women, including older women, whom no one ever described to me as "women of knowledge." For a long time, I was unable to communicate with them. It took me a long time to master Lao, and I never learned Phounoy fluently enough to conduct an entire interview in this language. Only from 2005 did I start going to villages with a young Phounoy individual who served as an interpreter and who helped conduct the interviews entirely in Phounoy. This is when I gained access to the knowledge of older women, who generally do not speak Lao. Of course, they had memories of the past (of celebrations of their youth, of meeting their husbands, etc.), but not of events that interested me, for several reasons that are not specific to the Phounoy. First of all, in the eyes of the villagers themselves, women—recognized as central for village life and the organization of important festive events—are not at the heart of political interactions, which remain a male affair. Knowing the name of this or that famous chief, the conflictual relations between this or that village, or the genealogy of a famous Phanya is therefore not a form of knowledge that is communicated to them. And the women themselves sufficiently integrate this type of representation so that they do not—at least that is what they told me—retain or know about ancient events, such as the migratory history of the Phounoy, their relations with their neighbors, the Tai Lue, or the kingdom of Luang Prabang.

There were actually only a handful of people left in the village of Thongpi who were recommended to me as "people who know." This was not a lot, but it was already much more than in most of the other villages I visited. There were two reasons for this lack of elders. First, the forty or so Phounoy villages were already depopulating in 1999, and the families of notables had left the villages before the others.[12] Second, the village of Thongpi, formerly known as Ban Phanya Soulinya, had been an important village as the place of residence of the Phanya, which in turn controlled several villages. The village was then a hub for political and religious authorities, where a certain number of descendants of important lineages still lived. This very small number of "people who know" quickly involved several things: conducting interviews (several with the same person) with each person designated as a "knowledgeable person" in Thongpi village. In order to fill in the gaps, I multiplied the sources by meeting people in as many villages as possible. I also traveled to places where villagers were migrating to, including the town of Phongsaly and the district capitals of Boun Nua and Boun Tai, inhabited mainly by Tai Lue, who could have a complementary or contradictory vision of the events I was told about. I went even to other provinces, such as Oudomxay or Vientiane, to meet former inhabitants of Phongsaly. Looking for new people seemed easy enough on the surface, with the same names coming up again and again in conversations: "You should go and see so-and-so; he is the descendant of Sènphongsimun and lives in the lowlands in the district of Boun Nua"; "Bounthong is a man of knowledge; he has gone to live in Vientiane to join his son. You will be able to find him there."

Once you have identified people to talk to, there is always the difficulty of going to meet people who do not know you initially. At the first meeting, people were distrustful, for some legitimate reasons that I explained earlier. I was careful to mention that it was "so-and-so" who sent me, but I was always told during my first interaction "I don't have the time." During the day, everyone would go to the fields, and no one would be available for interviews. If I went to work in the fields of the family where I lived, I would subsequently change my routine and work in the neighbors' fields all day, helping them to "save" time for an interview that we would have at the end of the day when we returned to the village. People understood this type of exchange and accepted it immediately. The major disadvantage of this method, which I applauded myself for initiating, was that I was too exhausted after a day spent weeding in the sun to carry out the interview. I would collapse in a corner of my host's house to rest my back or to sleep. After one or two months, I felt less tired and was able to conduct interviews.

But you do not exhaust someone's memory in one to two hours, and those who have conducted interviews know that it is difficult to keep someone's attention for a long time, especially when they are called upon to do all sorts of tasks: feed the pigs, go see the buffaloes, fetch water, go to the forge to repair a tool, visit a neighbor to discuss family problems, etc. Yet, my host would always take out a small bottle of rice wine to welcome me, and I would take out a packet of cigarettes. Smoking and drinking punctuated the interview, stretching our conversation until the end of the little bottle and until my rekindling of a new cigarette could no longer hold my host's attention, as they were called away for a more urgent task. I would go away, or I would be invited to dinner and talk time with the whole family on very different topics. In moments of vacation, on some morning when I was going nowhere, I reread my notes, often finding that the information given by so-and-so was quite different from that of someone else. I was then compelled to schedule a second interview and start the whole process all over again.

2. Elaborating History from the Present: Snippets, Fragments, Contradictory Discourses

The difficulty in trying to develop a collection of discourses was that they were about past events—not current practices—that could leave a mark only on the memory of each individual. Like all memories, those of my interlocutors were sometimes incomplete or forgotten, or the facts were reconstructed differently in the light of the present.

I have innumerable examples of the contradictions that most characterized the answers about the past that I obtained from my interlocutors. Here are two of them. The first example relates to what I was trying to find out about how the clans used to function. Until the early 1960s, clan organization had been very important in Phounoy society, but it had gradually disappeared, and all that remained were lineages without any particular names. One of the people who had been recommended to me as an "elder of knowledge" had told me: "In the time of the king, one had to marry into the same clan, but now not." Interested, I took note of the information, and the next day I asked the village chief's father about it. He replied: "No, no, before, we could not marry within the same clan." Alu and Thitpan, two other interviewees questioned separately, confirmed this assertion: "No, two people from the same clan could not intermarry." I thought I had the right information until a monk told me a month later: "Two people from the same clan could marry each other as long as it was after the third generation." In order to verify this simple information—"Were the clans endogamous or exogamous?"—I had to interview a total of thirty to forty people and visit as many villages as possible in the surrounding area until I was sure, in view of the large number of answers, that the first assertion was false (and the second correct).

The second example relates to the *kongdin* documents, once given by the king to the Phounoy. I said earlier that in the village where I lived, there were still two descendants of the people who had received these "books" (i.e., two copies). But the situation was complicated by the fact that—on this point everyone agreed—there had once been four copies: the king had given each clan two copies. As believed by the Phounoy—and according to the ritual use that was later made of the books—one of these copies was considered to be "male" and the other "female." Then began (for me) a hellish investigation to find out who had which copy, who was from which clan (there were two of them, the Lawa and the Phoutin), and who had the male and the female copy. The two descendants living in the village were an old widow (who had inherited the document from her husband) and a cheerful alcoholic, neither of whom knew whether the manuscript in their possession was the "male" or the "female" copy. The manuscripts in question could not (then) be consulted because no one knew how to read them, and the rituals bringing the two manuscripts together (the male copy being placed at the bottom of the altar, the female at the top) had not been performed since the 1960s. In addition, the owner of the third copy had left to live in Phongsaly city, and the fourth copy had disappeared in a village fire in the 1970s. Was the specimen in Phongsaly city the male or female specimen of the Phoutin clan? Each of my interlocutors was convinced that they had the right answer, except that none of them agreed: "The male book is the Phoutin's of Khampèng"; "Khampèng has the female book of the Lawa." "No, the female book of the Lawa is the one that was burnt in the fire." Making numerous syntheses and drawing up summary tables, I spent a lot of time on this question, before abandoning it altogether as no one could establish which copy was "male" or "female" anymore. In the end, through interviews and cross-checking data, I accumulated a certain amount of knowledge about the past from all the people interviewed, and therefore with this aura of prestige (or knowing), I was no longer met with the silent hostility that was so prevalent in the early days of my fieldwork. This knowledge could be useful to me: as my interlocutor could see that I "knew," he could go into more specific details that he would never have entrusted to me otherwise, and that his family would discover when he told me his story.

This knowledge may otherwise have created new writings on history among some of the Party officials in Phongsaly, especially one whom I shall call Phouvong here. An eminent Party member and head of the provincial Department of Culture at the time, Phouvong was Phounoy, like most of the province's officials. In the mid-1990s, he had initiated several activities to make his ethnic group better known and to restore its image, particularly among the capital's officials. Self-taught and patient, Phouvong had collected a few stories about the origin of the Phounoy and two or three customs of the past (including on the construction of the houses, on marriage, and on costumes). At his instigation and with the support of UNESCO funding, the "Official History of the Phounoy" was written on a large stone plate erected at the entrance of the main tourist site, Mount Phou Fa. Phouvong often questioned me about my research when I had to report on my activities to the Department of Culture. He was particularly interested in the Phounoy's history, even though he always took pleasure in trying to contradict me by showing that only his version was the right one. One day, I incidentally mentioned the books (*kongdin*); Phouvong's amazement was matched only by his disbelief. He tried to convince me that I was wrong, saying that it could not exist since he had never heard of it. He finally summoned two elders in order to thwart me, he hoped, with their denial. The elders quietly confirmed that there had always been *kongdin* in the Phounoy territory, perhaps ten or so in all, even though many had disappeared. Two days later, Phouvong came back to see me triumphantly: he "knew all about *kongdin*" and "had wanted to test me," he said. He knew "exactly what it was: an engraved elephant bone" (the *kongdin* are inscriptions on palm leaves). I could not change his mind. And so, the version of the little Lao book he is preparing today on the history of the Phounoy is about to officially record the history of a single *kongdin* throughout the territory, engraved on elephant bone.

Conclusion

In this chapter, I focused on the problems involved in building up the corpus of research material: secondary sources, archives, and data from the field. I tried to highlight the process of making an academic work centered on past events, for which observation—a key method in social science work—could not be carried out by the researcher.

The meeting of history and anthropology is indispensable for several reasons. With the exception of some research, anthropological studies of highland societies in continental Southeast Asia still make too little use of history. Several historians have already warned against the lack of history among the highlanders. Christian Daniels (2013), editor of a special issue of the journal *Southeast Asian Studies* devoted to this question, pleads for an in-depth study of the role of mountain dwellers in the formation of societies on the plains. For the historian, this study is essential to get access to a complete vision of the history of continental Southeast Asia.

In fact, combining anthropology and history in the studies of mountain populations in Southeast Asia allows us to take a new look at the relations between the regional power centers and highlanders. In particular, this meeting relativizes the essentialist vision of the relations between centers of power and the outlying populations as being necessarily antagonistic—a reproach that has been addressed both by historians and social anthropologists to the work of James Scott (2009). As Daniels (2013, 7) noted: "Another obvious shortcoming is that while purporting to narrate history, Scott fails to document the chronological changes that took place in the societies of individual or multiple upland ethnic groups; in other words, there is remarkably little 'history.'" The precise study of local ethnographies and histories effectively invalidates Scott's general hypothesis, as Jonsson (2002), Nathan Badenoch and Tomita Shinsuke (2013), and Oliver Tappe (2019) demonstrated. My own research (Bouté 2011) shows that a number of highland societies must be regarded as "internal margins," with perhaps various forms of autonomy, in a sphere of state-owned formations within which they have long practiced various types of transactions. This does not exclude participation in regional networks (commercial or intercultural) or other forms of exchange with neighboring ethnic minorities.

In order to reconstruct these local stories, one must read written sources and cross-reference them with oral narratives collected in the field. For mainland Southeast Asia and southwest China, this can be illustrated through the works mentioned above but also through other works by anthropologists advocating for the use of a historical approach to reveal local interethnic dynamics or relations between the state and the populations within its reach. This can be done through oral narratives (Evrard 2022; Gros 2011; Turner, Bonnin, and Michaud 2015), through reading colonial archives (Tappe 2019), or by crossing oral histories with colonial sources and/or written vernacular sources (Bouté 2018; Lentz 2019; Petit 2020).

In this regard, "making history" requires paying particular attention to local stories, mostly oral, but it must also lead to a heuristic rereading of written sources. As Simona Cerutti argued: "Sources themselves are actions whose meaning should be reconstructed" (Gronda et al. 2016, 2). Badenoch and Shinsuke (2013, 35) thus stressed the need to counterbalance the vision offered by the written sources emanating from the centers of power: "The need for recognition of uplanders' agency in history has been mentioned with increasing frequency [. . .], but local narratives demonstrating the historical dynamism of this agency are still critical for unloading the baggage of state-written history." Based on the case of the Mien of southern China and northern Thailand, Cushman and Jonsson (2020) demonstrate how official texts produced by kingdoms and empires tended to give an antagonistic vision of the relations between the center and periphery. Tappe (2019, 20) shared this observation for the region of northeastern Laos on the Vietnamese border: "The idea of an essential upland-lowland divide, exemplified by the developmental state, was shaped by both colonial and socialist discourses." For my part (Bouté 2011), I have shown how the diversity of appellations in northern Laos should not be interpreted as a confusion of certain external actors (such as royal power, then colonial power), but should be rather understood as an indication of the progressive transformation of a social status granted to a set of populations.

In the same way as written sources, oral narratives need to be collected from diverse and contradictory sources and cross-referenced with each other. If not, they are likely to be only a version of the facts of some actors. In the case of the Phounoy, these actors are often the descendants of the most powerful local lineages and, within them, those of the elderly men. This vision needs to be put into perspective with those of neighboring populations, which, depending on their own social status and the dialectical relationship maintained with the dominant regional powers, may prove to be very different. In this way, the analysis of the transformations of Phounoy society is not only a means of retracing the history of "local societies" but also a way of shedding light on the history of the more global societies among which they found themselves. Thus, the history of the Phounoy and the changes to their territory, their practices, and their understanding of political or ritual power, authority, and even identity can be understood as a broader contribution to understanding the complex processes by which some "marginal" societies in the confines of Southeast Asia have gradually come to integrate with lowland state societies, thereby also participating in the process of their formation.

Notes

1. With the exception of Rosaldo's ethnohistorical work on the Ilongots in the Philippines (1980). The work carried out otherwise up to that point remains mostly monographic, or approaches phenomena of social change as one-off phenomena resulting from the unilateral action of state policies, development actions, or tourism, eradicating any approaches related to social dynamics.

2. A few pages by Néis (1885) and especially by Lefèvre-Pontalis (1902) are notably devoted to the Phounoy. From the early twentieth century until the 1950s, the documents relating to the Phounoy or to Phongsaly Province are more numerous, mainly due to the establishment of military posts in the region. See Guillemet and O'Kelly (1916–1917), Cheyrou-Lagreze (1921), Aymé (1930), and Mordant (1934).

3. "Phanya" was a title of nobility awarded by the court of the king of Luang Prabang at the time of the Great Oath (oath of loyalty sworn to the king each year by all the heads of the kingdom). Tai dignitaries frequently bore titles, but they were rarely bestowed upon non-Tai populations.

4. Roux (1924, 453) and Doze (1955, 34) noted that this territory had been called the "Middle Land" (Muang Khang) by the ethnic Lao because of its location in the center of several *muang* inhabited by Tai or Lao populations. This term, designating the territory occupied by the Phounoy, is also mentioned in some royal edicts which were given to them in the nineteenth century.

5. For more information on these ritual ceremonies, the powers attributed to the *kongdin,* and the clan's territories, see Bouté (2011, 79–82, 127–142).

6. On the content of these documents, see Bouté (2015).

7. In 1999, it took two days by bus to reach the town of Oudomxay from Vientiane. From there, one more day of travel by truck was necessary to reach the town of Phongsaly. From Phongsaly, there was still a seven-hour walk to get to the village where I had chosen to stay, and on average, four to five hours of walking was necessary to reach other villages. During the rainy season, these times lengthen considerably, and it was sometimes impossible to travel to the villages (or to leave) because of flooded rivers.

8. Following the Geneva Agreements in 1954, it was decided that the Pathet Lao units would be consolidated in Phongsaly and Houaphan Provinces.

9. Personal communication with Ducourtieux, head of the local NGO Projet de Développement de la Province de Phongsaly, October 2000.

10. It turned out that his grandfather was a ritual officiant, and the revolutionary forces had ordered monks from the capital to burn his ritual accessories, cut his hair—the seat of his power—and more generally to eradicate this type of belief among the Phounoy villagers.

11. Indeed, I wanted to be as autonomous as possible in my interviews—talking to people without the presence of a third party as soon as possible. I followed the advice given by Condominas (1965; see chapter 18, devoted to the problems posed by the presence of an interpreter—loss of time, dependence on the interpreter, distancing oneself from the interlocutors, etc.), which François Bizot (in charge in 1999 of the ÉFEO Centre in Vientiane) had also reminded me of, insisting on being alone while doing fieldwork: "If you have an interpreter, people will forget that you are there with them and will look and speak only to an interpreter." So I carried out my fieldwork accompanied by Bouangeun, an interpreter, during the first five months. It was only when I was familiar with the region and its inhabitants that I conducted my inquiries alone, directly in Lao (most Phounoy understand and speak Lao; for some interviews conducted with elderly people who did not speak this language, I worked with a Phounoy interpreter).

12. I explain the reasons for these migratory phenomena in Bouté (2005).

References

Anheim, Étienne. 2012. "L'historien au pays des merveilles? Histoire et anthropologie au début du xx1ᵉ siècle." *L'Homme* 203–204: 399–427.

Atlas de l'Indochine. 1920. Hanoi: Service géographique de l'Indochine.

Aymé, Georges. 1930. *Monographie du Vᵉ territoire militaire.* Hanoi: Imprimerie d'Extrême-Orient.

Badenoch, Nathan, and Tomita Shinsuke. 2013. "Mountain People in the *Muang:* Creation and Governance of a Tai Polity in Northern Laos." *Southeast Asian Studies* 2: 29–67.

Bouté, Vanina. 2005. "Des gardiens des confins aux bâtisseurs des plaines: Parcours d'une population tibéto-birmane du Nord Laos." *Moussons* 8: 35–60.

———. 2010. "Names and Territoriality among the Phounoy: How the State Creates Ethnic Group (Lao PDR)." In *Inter-Ethnic Dynamics in Asia: Considering the Other through Ethnonyms, Territories, and Rituals,* edited by C. Culas and F. Robinne, 79–99. London: Routledge.

———. 2011. *En miroir du pouvoir: Les Phounoy du Nord Laos; Ethnogenèse et dynamiques d'intégration.* Paris: École française d'Extrême-Orient.

———. 2015. "An Ethnohistory of Highland Societies in Laos." *Journal of Lao Studies* 2: 54–76.

———. 2018. *Mirroring Power: Ethnogenesis and Integration among the Phounoy of Northern Laos.* Chiang Mai: Silkworm Books.

Cheyrou-Lagrèze, Henri. 1921. *Esquisses laotiennes.* Rochefort: Imprimerie Norbertine.

Condominas, George. 1965. *L'exotique est quotidien: Sar Luk, Vietnam Central.* Paris: Plon.

———. 1990. *From Lawa to Mon, from Saa' to Thai: Historical and Anthropological Aspects of Southeast Asian Social Spaces.* Occasional Paper of the Department of Anthropology, Research School of Pacific Studies. Canberra: Australian National University.

Culas, Christian. 2010. "The Ethnonyms of the Hmong in Vietnam: Short History (1856–1924) and Practical Epistemology." In *Interethnic Dynamics in Asia: Ethnic Relationships through Ethnonyms, Territories, and Rituals*, edited by C. Culas and F. Robinne, 13–42. London: Routledge.

Culas, Christian, and François Robinne, eds. 2010. *Interethnic Dynamics in Asia. Ethnic Relationships through Ethnonyms, Territories, and Rituals.* London: Routledge.

Cushman, Richard D., and Hjorleifur R. Jonsson. 2020. "Mosquito-Relish Diplomacy: *Emperor Ping's Charter* and Hill-Valley Dynamics between China and Thailand." *Journal of the Siam Society* 108 (2): 87–121.

Daniels, Christian. 2013. "Introduction: Upland Peoples in the Making of History in Northern Continental Southeast Asia." *Southeast Asian Studies* 2 (1): 5–27.

Deydier, Henri. 1954. *Lokapala.* Paris: Plon.

Doze, Martial. 1955. "Romancero Kha." *Tropiques* 379: 33–40.

Education sans frontière. 1996. ບັນກາດງບພິເສດສຳລັບແຂວງຜົ້ສາວິ Cartoon booklets, special about Lao provinces. Vientiane: Ministry of Education/UNDP.

Evrard, Olivier. 2022. "The Ruins, the 'Savages,' and the Princess: Myths, Migrations, and Belonging in Viang Phu Kha, Laos." In *From Tribalism to Nationalism: The Anthropological Turn; a Tribute to Grant Evans*, edited by Y. Goudineau and V. Bouté, 160–191. Copenhagen: NIAS Press.

Goudineau, Yves. 2022. "The Anthropology of Southern Laos and the Origin of the Kantu Issue." In *From Tribalism to Nationalism: The Anthropological Turn; a Tribute to Grant Evans*, edited by Y. Goudineau and V. Bouté, 131–165. Copenhagen: NIAS Press.

Gronda, Roberto, Tullio Viola, Yves Cohen, and Simona Cerutti. 2016. "Histoires Pragmatiques." *European Journal of Pragmatism and American Philosophy* 8 (2). http://journals.openedition.org/ejpap/654.

Gros, Stéphane. 2011. "Economic Marginalization and Social Identity among the Drung People of Northwest Yunnan." In *Moving Mountains: Livelihoods and Identities in Highland China, Vietnam, and Laos,* edited by J. Michaud and T. Forsyth, 28–49. Vancouver: University of British Columbia Press.

Guillemet, Eugène. 1921. *Sur les sentiers laotiens.* Hanoi: Imprimerie d'Extrême-Orient.

Guillemet, Eugène, and K. O'Kelly. 1916–1917. "En colonne dans le Haut-Laos." *Revue Indochinoise* 9/10: 169–228; 11/12: 329–405; 1/2: 9–86; 3/4: 187–276.

Jonsson, Hjorleifur. 2002. *Mien Relations: Mountain People and State Control in Thailand.* Ithaca, NY: Cornell University Press.

Lefèvre-Pontalis, Pierre. 1902. *Voyages dans le Haut-Laos et sur les frontières de la Chine et de Birmanie.* Paris: Ernest Leroux.

Leiris, Michel. 1934. *L'Afrique fantôme.* Paris: Gallimard.

Lentz, Christian C. 2019. *Contested Territory: Dien Bien Phu and the Making of Northwest Vietnam.* New Haven, CT: Yale University Press.

Mordant, Ct. 1934. "Monographie du Ve territoire militaire (Phongsaly)." *Extrême Asie* 82: 545–552.

Néis, Paul. 1885. "Voyage dans le Haut Laos." *Le Tour du Monde,* no. 1303, July 1, 1–80.

Petit, Pierre. 2020. *History, Memory, and the Territorial Cults in the Highlands of Laos: The Past Inside the Present.* London: Routledge.

Rosaldo, Renato. 1980. *Ilongo Headhunting (1883–1974): A Study in Society and History.* Stanford, CA: Stanford University Press.

Roux, Henri. 1924. "Deux tribus de la région de Phongsali." *Bulletin de l'Ecole française d'Extrême-Orient* 24: 445–500.

Scott, James. 2009. *The Art of Not Being Governed: An Anarchist History of Upland Southeast Asia.* New Haven, CT: Yale University Press.

Tappe, Oliver. 2019. "Towards a Historical Anthropology of Upland Laos." *Highlander* 1 (1): 19–25.

Turner, Sarah, Christine Bonnin, and Jean Michaud. 2015. *Frontier Livelihoods: Hmong in the Sino-Vietnamese Borderlands.* Seattle: University of Washington Press.

CHAPTER 6

Harnessing History

*The Synergy of Oral and Written Historical Accounts
in the Production of Anthropological Knowledge
(Yunnan, China)*

Sylvie Beaud

DURING FIELDWORK, THE ETHNOGRAPHER in China is often caught
between different types of historical discourses as well as various traces
of memory scattered everywhere, all of which could hold potential use-
fulness. The number of documents and research productions on the
history of China can be overwhelming. Oral testimonies of the informants, archives, interviews with local historians or civil servants, stelae,
ritual, and theatrical practices, among others, all provide different
pieces of the historical puzzle(s) of the investigated topic. If history,
writ large, is a discourse on the past, then we can make the two following statements: (1) it can be found anywhere in the field (in buildings,
in people's memory, in archives, in practices, etc.), and (2) we need to
distinguish between various modalities and uses of discourses on the
past by different actors. How do informants speak about history, and
when/how do they refer to it? How do we, anthropologists, make use of
these historical accounts? How do these accounts "dialogue" between
themselves, and with our academic writing?

In the present chapter, I shall look back at the research I conducted
among Han people in Yunnan during the years of my doctoral studies (2005–2012). During that period, I gathered as much material as
possible in a journey that took me from hiking in the field in search
of stelae and landmarks, to libraries in Paris, Hong Kong, and Tokyo,
and through several bureaus of specialists in China and abroad. Several
years after completing the field research and various academic outputs,
I have examined and reflected upon that singular experience of making

use of history (viewed as records of the past) while not being a trained historian. So, this chapter represents a personal testimony, more practical than theoretical, yet hopefully helpful in nurturing self-reflection among my peers.

I did not initially plan to explore the local historical records and even less to attempt to reconstitute past events myself. However, it became unavoidable as the informants themselves were referring to history in multiple ways. The ensuing situation made me an "incidental historian" as detailed in the present volume's introduction (issue 2). I adopted a posture that I consider typical of anthropology, that is, starting from the informants' discourses and exploring the past backward to make sense of it. This approach can be reminiscent of the "regressive method" theorized in general history, and notably supported by Marc Bloch (1931, 1964). The regressive method has been criticized due to its risks of creating an artificial continuum of permanent traits and anachronisms. For these reasons, this method remained a minor trend in history. In anthropology, however, looking back at a particular past is often necessary to understand a contemporary situation, although historical knowledge does not constitute a goal in most cases.[1]

Reflecting on the use of history in anthropological research implies a distinction between its various usages in the field: Who is referring to history, and how? What are (or could be) their interests in doing so? What purpose are they serving? No matter what discourse is at stake, whether historical or otherwise, it is always "situated." In a political environment where people's words are closely watched, one should also consider the potential risks to informants from overtly reviving the past. In the case of China, talking about history, whether past events or the way these events are officially treated, can be highly sensitive, and I met some people reluctant to enter such kinds of conversations. For instance, someone speaking of the Guan Suo Opera (the ritual I was investigating) would recall an event and deny it straight after to remain in the orthodoxy. A villager told me, after watching a performance ordered by the local government on a cultural festival in Yangzong in 2002: "Everything you saw today is Han [i.e., from the Han ethnic people], but the Guan Suo Opera is actually a superstition." As we were having this talk while walking in the street, he was clearly concerned about being heard, and he felt the urge to clarify that he did not personally believe in the masked opera ritual.[2]

In the process of researching, understanding, and writing history, the case study I was involved in showed some specificities that conditioned my fieldwork. The Guan Suo Opera (Guan Suo Xi 关索戏) was a seasonal activity; it normally took place once a year at the Chinese New Year, in Yangzong township (a valley located about thirty-five kilometers east of Kunming, the capital of Yunnan Province; see figure 6.1). It was

Figure 6.1. The Guan Suo Opera marching at the lantern festival. © S. Beaud.

played by men of Xiaotun village. They performed rituals to exorcize pestilences in a drama that partly consisted of acting out the battles of generals of the Three Kingdoms (ca. 220–280 CE), a story widely spread through popular literature. The seasonal frequency of the Guan Suo Opera made salient the irregular performances that happened to be scheduled outside of the ritual period. It helped me see the change occurring in front of my eyes by both observing the troupe's unusual activities and the actors' reactions to them. Actors frequently offered comparisons about an (often idealized) past situation: "It was better before," or "Things were not regular this time." These common statements, sometimes taking the forms of projections into the future, such as "We are going to be famous from now on," or "We may make money with this extra activity in the future," could be put into perspective and compared with my own past observations and other descriptions available in published sources (see Hong 1992; Liu Xiaojin 1997; Ueda 2003; among others).

Over the course of my fieldwork, I identified several groups of informants and several ways in which history was used. I then had to make various use of history myself as a researcher, following the hint provided by the fieldwork data. Mirroring the chronology of my research, in this chapter, I first explain who my informants were, what sources I looked for, and how I navigated through them. Second, I draw upon my encounters with local civil servants and publications about the Guan Suo Opera to show how I was led to reflect on the recent history of the political discourse surrounding the opera. Third, I introduce the historical references embodied by the main characters and the literary content of the opera as well as other relevant traces of memory inscribed in the valley. These literary and topographical data constituted a layer of references to conceptualize the past that intertwined with other layers, jointly creating a multifaceted picture of local history. Fourth, I look at the actors' discourses and show how they led me to research in various directions about the local population's past. This investigation toward the past enabled me to uncover the underlying cultural representations and conception of time. With a better understanding of the local past, I later reflect upon the continuity of that history in the present. Over the course of the years I spent in Yangzong, I indeed witnessed several events that soon appeared as "history in the making," since they had a strong impact on the actors' practices, discourses, and expectations.

In this chapter, which takes the form of a self-reflexive investigation on a journey into anthropological research, I thus argue that history was in the service of anthropology: it proved effective not only in deepening my analyses (by adding a vertical dimension to the horizontal—present-time—research) but also in uncovering a way of thinking. By doing so, this chapter shall also shed light on the interplay of oral and written information.

Sources, Access, and Method: Pulling Out All the Stops

Who were my "informants"? As I followed the Guan Suo Opera troupe anywhere it was invited to perform, its twenty-five members soon became my most regular informants, though not all of them with the same closeness. As mentioned above, only men were allowed to play in the masked opera. I was thus led to interact mainly with men in that context.[3] I also interviewed women whenever I could, especially in the village, but they hardly knew anything about the Guan Suo Opera or refused to tell me about it. Since the ritual authority of the Guan Suo Opera was exclusively in the hands of men, I assumed that even knowledgeable women would not dare to publicly show their own understanding of the opera. Apart from more targeted interviews, I considered any daily conversation with anyone as a source of information. The fact that I spent a long time in the field made it possible to informally talk with villagers instead of setting up proper interviews that may have seemed too formal. Adopting the posture of using all available means, I still followed the few journalists (all men) who came to Yangzong, witnessing and recording all their formal interviews. In sum, most people with whom I discussed the Guan Suo Opera, whether in the field or otherwise, were men, except for my main interlocutor in the county's cultural affairs office, who was a woman. Among women, I should also mention Liu Xiaojin, who directed the documentary *Mask* (1997) on the Guan Suo Opera, whom I interviewed once in 2006. Overall, my most regular informants were the villagers of the whole Yangzong township.

When villagers were not available, I took the chance to visit museums, meet with specialists, and travel abroad. Notably, I went to Tokyo, where I was lucky enough to secure an appointment with a specialist on masked drama, who was one of the first researchers to have conducted field research in the Chinese countryside. These interviews did not specifically focus on the Guan Suo Opera's history, but I benefitted from this person's advice and reading recommendations. Upon my return from Tokyo, some officials and civil servants from the local governments seemed eager to interact with me, while I was rather reluctant (it shall become clear why below). After several dinners and a lot of alcohol, we finally got to know each other a little. They turned out to be quite welcoming, and I had frequent conversations with some of them, especially those directly in charge of the organization of the Guan Suo Opera at the cultural affairs office. Some of those officers, as well as some researchers I met over the course of my research, generously offered me copies of books they had written or considered relevant for my study.

Apart from the informants' discourses, which took daily dedication and patience to gather, the first written sources I had at my disposal were two books on the Guan Suo Opera that I found at the bookstore in Chengjiang, published by the local government (Hong 1992; Liu Ticao 1997). The content of these two books provided an overview of the Guan Suo Opera, including some historical aspects.[4] I regularly visited the bookstore and the county library, both of which were distributing these publications by the local government. In contrast, the bigger bookstores in the provincial capital boasted many kinds of recently published books, but they had hardly any local publications. Beyond books, I was also searching for archives and gazetteers. On a trip abroad, I took the chance to visit the library of Hong Kong University, which possessed a copy of the oldest Chengjiang gazetteer I knew of, dated 1719.[5] The documents were consultable only on microfilm, and while I was allowed to print them (which was quite expensive), I had to zoom closely and could only print a fragment of the page on A4-sized paper. The prints piled up and the order became jumbled, so these gazetteers turned out to be unexploitable. I was more fortunate with a second gazetteer, dating from the Daoguang era (1821–1851), which I photographed at the county library in Chengjiang. During the later years of my doctoral studies, I was able to find a great amount of bibliographically valuable resources, many of which are historical and include copies of old documents, from the rich collections of libraries in Paris and Tokyo.[6]

Concerning my methodology, except for academic publications, I have treated all these discourses, documents, and data as primary sources. I also chose to conduct my entire research in the field "casually": I introduced myself as a student and chose to not request official permission to conduct my research, since the region was not closed to foreigners. This was motivated by my first experience in 2002 when, on my very first trip to Chengjiang, I requested an appointment with county government officials and asked for permission to go to Yangzong township, over which the county held authority (see map 3). In Yangzong, I realized that I had approached this process in the wrong way, as I should have first requested authorization from the lowest governmental level (Yangzong township) before going to the county government. Indeed, I soon found out that the recommendation letter I was kindly given was

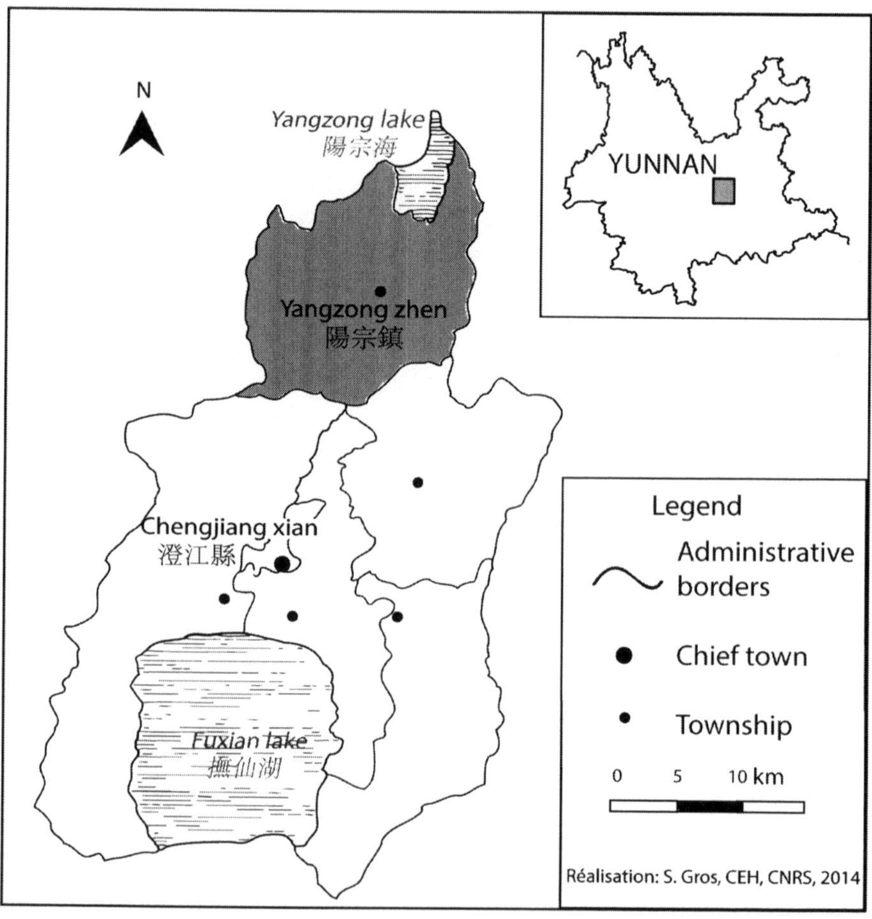

Map 3. Yangzong township, Chengjiang district, in Yunnan. © S. Beaud and S. Gros.

forcing people under that authority to accommodate me in ways that I did not agree with, including taking out the opera masks even if it was not appropriate according to the ritual procedure. So, on my following trips, I limited official procedures to the mandatory police registration.

I truly wished to "pull out all the stops" to gather the maximum quantity of data from the field on any and all topics, even if some—such as my carelessness with the microfilm prints of the Kangxi gazetteer—proved to be unusable or not directly related to my research purpose. To sum up, I consulted many interlocutors and traveled to several locations, while combining diverse kinds of data sources—from folk almanacs bought at the weekly market in Yangzong to interviews with renowned specialists abroad—and treating them with similar consideration.

Investigating the Official Production and Use of History: The Power of Labels

In building the argumentation of my doctoral dissertation, I chose to start with the external discourses on the Guan Suo Opera before analyzing the internal discourses. This decision was guided by the fact that the dominant discourse was emanating from government officials, as a result of the Chinese history in the twentieth century. The masked opera, like most ritual activities at that time, was indeed banned as a superstitious ritual and interrupted during the Cultural Revolution (officially 1966–1976). The local publications mention about twelve years of interruption, but it is possible that the interruption started earlier and that the expression "Cultural Revolution" in the actors' discourses serves as a symbol rather than a strict historical period. The masks were destroyed, and the scripts burned to ashes. The troupe became active again in the 1980s with the "reform and opening" policy instigated by Mao's successor, Deng Xiaoping. Local governments then faced the challenge of rehabilitating and legitimizing activities that were, until then, considered to be "opposed to both socialist political order and atheist ideology" of the state (Li Lan 2010, 1). To do so, officials and researchers jointly achieved a conceptual reinterpretation by requalifying such activities in cultural terms. In the case of masked operas, two key notions came into play: "*nuo* opera" (*nuoxi* 傩戏) and "living fossil" (*huo huashi* 活化石) (Li Lan 2010; Beaud 2012a). The term *nuoxi*, sometimes translated as "exorcistic opera," has been used in any publication on revived rituals making use of masks. *Xi* is still a common word for opera today, but *nuo* is noted by a very ancient and rare character. Those who worked on rehabilitating these activities adopted an exegetical approach that meant finding the oldest known occurrence of the character. They agreed that it was to be found in the *Zhou* ritual (*Zhouli* 周礼), dating from the second century BCE. Here, *nuo* referred to ancient rites called Big *Nuo* (*Da Nuo* 大傩), conducted at the royal court by a ritual master wearing a mask, consisting of expelling pestilences at the turn of winter.

Following this initial mention in subsequent texts, these officials retraced a unilinear history of the term. That history was then assimilated into the history of masked ritual practices and eventually extended to any masked ritual activities through the transformation of the notion of *nuo* into *nuo* opera (*nuoxi*), *nuo* dances (*nuowu* 傩舞), *nuo* customs (*nuosu* 傩俗), *nuo* arts (*nuoyi* 傩艺), and ultimately *nuo* culture (*nuo wenhua* 傩文化). This was done regardless of potential changes to the content of the character (the *signified,* in Saussure's [(1916) 1995] terms) over the centuries. Within the modern *nuo* culture system, there was also a subcategory called "military drama" (*nuowu* 傩武). Considered to have been brought to the southwest of China by soldiers sent from central China to pacify the "Barbarians" (nowadays, ethnic minorities), the Guan Suo Opera was often described in publications as a *nuo* opera of the martial category (*wu*).[7]

Corollary to the requalification of all the masked activities into *nuo* operas, the officials still faced the challenge of making those formerly "feudal" practices into activities that could fit the state's Marxist ideology. The politically favored concept of "living fossil" achieved this goal. In the case of *nuo* dramas, these should be understood as a living practice that is rooted in an ancient past, with such a long history that it has become a part of culture. In the 1980s, it soon became recurrent in publications related to the restart of the masked operas that they "provide evidence for the evolutionary theory of society" (Li 2010, 21). The Guan Suo Opera itself was officially labeled a "living fossil of drama" (*xiju de huo huashi* 戏剧的活化石) during an international conference that took place in Chengjiang county in 1994. That process eventually paved the way to its recognition as intangible cultural heritage in 2011 (see below), providing a strong argument to request support from the government. Placing all the masked practices under the single label of *nuo* culture and viewing them as "cultural fossils" also served the nationalist purposes of the political agendas at the time (Li 2010).

From this example, we can see how the Chinese authorities produced the history of masked operas at the end of the twentieth century and provided an unilinear evolutionist version that fit the political orthodoxy (see the current volume's introduction, issue 8). In doing so, and following the general trend of official macro-history, the interruption of the twentieth century became insignificant. Moreover, the officers were also led to rewrite the plays in order to replace the scripts. As analyzed by Sabine Trebinjac (2000, 2008) in the case of the production of Uyghur music, this led to a phenomenon of not only writing history, but also creating a national tradition.

From a historical anthropologist's point of view, however, the history of the Guan Suo Opera could not be written without considering the twentieth century's interruption. There was a "before" and an "after" to that rupture, and the "before" became almost impossible to know in full detail once the artifacts were destroyed and most of the contemporary witnesses gone. Instead of trying to reconstitute the past of the practice, I therefore turned to investigate the characters and the performed stories. Who was Guan Suo, the main character of the eponymous opera?

Reading Landscape History: Traces of History in Literary Texts, Toponyms, and Stelae

My research led me to consider Guan Suo as a social hero and a cultural emblem for the population. As a civilizing hero of China's southwest, he united descendants of exogenous soldiers and indigenous people and was also a protective god of their territory (Beaud 2017, chap. 4).

I first looked at the plays themselves. I compared the official texts of the Guan Suo Opera (in Liu Ticao 1997) to my own transcriptions of the actors' performances. I used the texts in two ways: one was to highlight the similarities and differences with the published version, and the second was to fill in the blanks of the oral version when parts were missing, even though I was aware that it might have been rewritten and rearranged by the cultural officers. However, the plays did not provide much detail on the Guan Suo Opera characters' biography. I then turned to ancient historical accounts, notably the *Chronicles of the Three Kingdoms* (*Sanguozhi* 三国志 [3rd century] 2002), but I soon found that the existence of Guan Suo himself was far from clear. I searched for literary sources and historical studies.[8] Even in related literature, I had to dig into the historical evolution of the tales themselves to grasp the complexity and the evanescence of the character.

Guan Suo was mainly known thanks to a chantefable, the *Biography of Hua Guan Suo* (*Hua Guan Suo zhuan* 花关索传), excavated from a grave near Shanghai in 1967 (Oman King 1989). He was not a historical figure, in contrast to his supposed father, the famous Guan Yu (d. 219 CE). In the current version of the *Romance of the Three Kingdoms* (Luo 2005), Guan Suo was described as a general who had been sent as the vanguard to Yunnan during the Campaign to Pacify the Southern Barbarians, led by Zhuge Liang in 225 CE. This campaign was historically accurate (though Guan Suo's involvement was not). According to the villagers in Xiaotun, Guan Suo established his camp at the location of their village. Even if this information belonged to the realm of myth rather than history in the narrow sense, traces of the character across southwest of China nevertheless exist in the region's topography: these are mainly found in the names of places, such as "townships" (Guan Suo *zhen*), "mountain ridges" (Guan Suo *ling*), and "temples" (Guan Suo *miao*).

The foundation of at least some of these temples seems strongly connected to the implementation of garrisons at the beginning of the Ming dynasty (1368–1644). According to Anne McLaren, a specialist in Chinese vernacular literature, the cult of Guan Suo was encouraged by the Ming central government in order to legitimate its authority in the region by reminding the local people of the old conquest by Zhuge Liang (McLaren 1998). References to the military campaigns under Zhu Yuanzhang (1328–1398), the Ming dynasty's founder, were often presented as the main source of the Yunnanese (Han) population. As a corollary of these campaigns, a local scholar writing a history of the Yangzong population said that a tombstone from the Yang lineage (members of which still live in the township capital) attests to the transport of the Ma family into what was to become the Domain of the Ma (Mazhuang), a village located close to Xiaotun (reported in Yang 2004, 237). That campaign was also mentioned in the local gazetteer (*Daqing Daoguang Chengjiang fu zhi*, Book 3, n.p.). I searched for the stele in the surroundings of Mazhuang village, but I could not find it. However, a stele now installed inside the temple that hosts the Guan Suo Opera did mention the Ma family and a claim of ownership of land near the temple (transcribed in Hong 1992, 121–122; French translation in Beaud 2012b, 490–491).

Yet, the use of toponyms has been twofold. Many informants, including scholars, tended to refer to toponyms as proof of the existence of Guan Suo. However, it was very likely that, even if the place names preexisted, the explanation that made them fit within this history might have been created a posteriori. Observing the systematic adequacy between history and toponyms, Katō Sango, a teacher sent to Okinawa in 1899, wrote: "Traces of manipulation are obvious: it is very likely that it is not the historical facts that generated the toponyms, but rather the toponyms that created the facts" (Katō 1906, 14). Thus naming, or at least explaining the names, provided a base for a later cult or reappropriation.

Villagers in Yangzong and local scholars alike also resorted to toponyms to explain the mixed origins of the township; in a pattern that was often seen in Yunnan, the population in Yangzong resulted from intermarriages between indigenous people (who now mostly belong to the Yi national minority and are still represented in the surrounding valleys) and soldiers coming from the central regions of China (registered as Han). They argued that the names of the villages in Yangzong reflect this history. The area was said to be traditionally composed of eighteen villages, among which eight still bore a military unit name, including the character camp (*ying* 营) or garrison (*tun* 屯). Xiaotun itself literally means "the small garrison," and its ancient name was said to have been the Vanguard Camp (Xianfengying), in reference to an initial military establishment that the informants directly associated with Guan Suo, the general of the Vanguard (see map 4). The other villages were defined as "natural" villages (*zirancun* 自然村).

Based on these scattered traces of history supported by other arguments, I came to the conclusion that Guan Suo was a tutelary figure and cultural emblem that federated the ethnically diverse populations of the eighteen villages through a common territorial cult (Beaud 2017). Here again, it should be noted that I resorted to a sort of history of the landscape, writ large, which did not follow a predetermined posture but rather arose because I was encouraged to consider these aspects by the informants' discourses.

Making Sense of the Informants' Discourses on the Past: A Nonlinear Conception of Time

Contrary to the official linear history of the *nuoxi* applied to the Guan Suo Opera in the publications, the actors expressed different

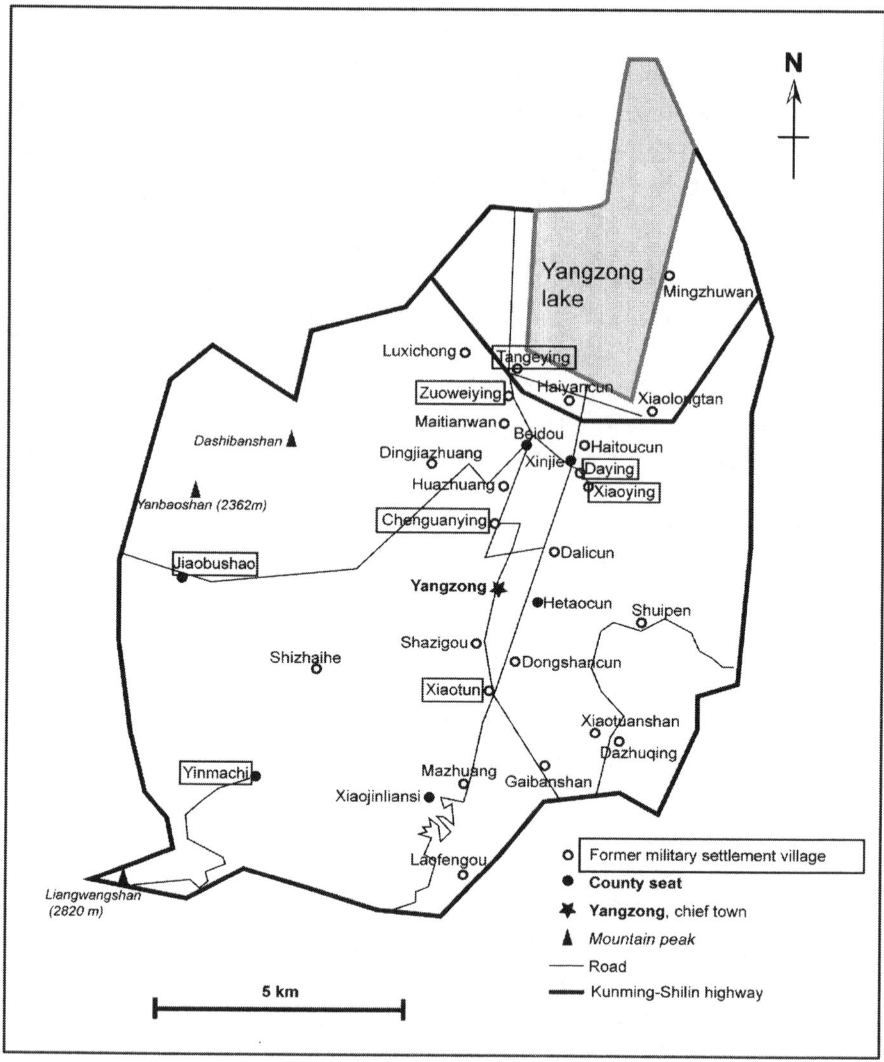

Map 4. Map of Yangzong township showing ancient military establishments and natural villages. © S. Beaud.

perspectives on the ritual opera's origins. First, I had to acknowledge that there were several versions of the opera's history among the villagers, and that the way they referred to history seemed somewhat confusing at first glance. My task thus consisted of following the hints provided by each discourse in order to make sense of it. This enabled me not only to combine the different versions into a tentative dating of its origins but also to understand their underlying conception of time. That said, rather than reconstituting the history of the Guan Suo Opera, I focused on the sociological configuration that gave rise to the masked ritual, on the one hand, and to the way informants were expressing and transmitting it, on the other hand.

In Xiaotun village, it was common to hear the following notion: "The Guan Suo Opera dates back to the Three Kingdoms, three hundred years ago" (although the Three Kingdoms corresponds to the third century CE, more than 1,700 years ago). Yet the respondents who juxtaposed these periods were not totally ignorant of the chronology of imperial history. How was it that they seemed to be mixing time up in this way? My research started with the findings of Chinese researchers, many of whom suggested that the Guan Suo Opera took shape during the Daoguang era (1821–1851). As mentioned above, they also agreed on the idea that the Guan Suo Opera had been brought to the region by garrison soldiers. The major difference between that research and my own investigation was that their main informant was a man from the Gong lineage (hereafter Mr. Gong), who died in 2001 at the age of ninety-two. Since my first visit was in 2002, I was unable to meet him. Thus, I had to rely on secondhand sources regarding his knowledge. I used several kinds of data, including studies written by local researchers, the works of Chinese and foreign historians, and, above all, various discourses circulating in Xiaotun village. Previous research did not place much weight on the points of view of members from other lineages, mainly because Mr. Gong was the eldest actor and the one who had rewritten all the plays from memory in the 1980s. His scripts had constituted a precious base for the officers in charge of documenting and rehabilitating the Guan Suo Opera, and his testimonies naturally became their dominant point of focus. Nonetheless, the voices of the other villagers were also worth considering. The particular history of the three lineages that were involved in the opera provided an alternate view of its origins and reflected the diversity of the local population.

The Gong account quoted in the *Guan Suo Opera gazetteer* (Hong 1992, 81) argued that the Guan Suo Opera, whose main purpose was to exorcise pestilences, had been taught to the villagers in a village called Datun, located outside of the Yangzong valley, in order to help rid them of recurring plagues. However, the testimony was not precise regarding historical dates; it first mentioned that Xianfengying village (now Xiaotun) was created by Guan Suo when he established his vanguard camp there during the Campaign to Pacify the Southern Barbarians in 225 CE. The camp was used again for military purposes during the Qing dynasty more than a thousand years later, when the central authority sent troops to stop a rebellion (known as the Panthay Rebellion, 1856–1873). At this point, the garrison's name was changed to Xiaotun, which remains today.[9] Regarding the epidemic outbursts, the testimony only said: "At the beginning of the Qing dynasty, some families from the Gong lineage moved to [Yangzong valley]," and that, "*Later on*, there was an outburst of epidemics that none of the usual treatments [i.e., medical and ritual] could eradicate" (Hong 1992, 81, emphasis added).

Apart from the Gong lineage's account, there was a "Li account," mainly embodied by the retired actor currently in charge of the opera. His discourse was less elaborate than the Gong one. He simply said that his ancestors played the Guan Suo Opera and shared it with him. It started with his great-great-grandfather from Liushuwan. The reference to migrations coming from the Liushuwan area (in Nanjing), which was widespread all over Yunnan, corresponded to the contingencies of military campaigns led by the Ming dynasty's founder, introduced above. This account thus corroborated the official version of a militaristic ritual practice brought by soldiers.

Contrastively, members of the Zhou lineage provided minimal discourse on their lineage's origins; they simply stated that they were from "here" (i.e., Yangzong valley). In Xiaotun, as in Yangzong in general, almost all the villagers identified themselves as Han, but some of them claimed that their ancestors belonged to populations that were now categorized as "minority nationalities." They did not necessarily refer to the same ethnic group, and in fact, it was very likely that various groups occupied the valley over time. Nonetheless, the main discourse among the Zhou argued that their ancestors were Yi, who later became Han as the result of intermarriage. In any case, the Zhou discourse did not provide any information on the Guan Suo Opera's origins, as it only referred to the origins of the lineage.

By combining the information gathered from the testimonies of informants, official local gazetteers, studies on Yunnan's demography (Cartier 1979; Lee 1982a, 1982b), the history of the bubonic plague in the nineteenth century (Benedict 1996), and military history (Atwill

2005; Di Cosmo 2006; Giersch 2006), I could draw the hypothesis that the Guan Suo Opera may have emerged at the end of the Panthay Rebellion, when a second peak of the plague devastated the region in the Tongzhi era (probably around 1872–1873; Beaud 2016).

This corresponded to the Gong account, as he connected the name of Xiaotun to the rebellion and the reactivation of its military function. The notion of "reactivation" was indeed central and helped me understand the way people talked about the past. As analyzed by McLaren (1998), the new military settlers reproduced, even though under different conditions, the establishment of the garrison troops who had arrived under the previous dynasty. It was not surprising, then, that people talked about the second wave of military implementation using the terms of the previous one, which was itself often reduced to its emblematic scheme of soldiers and migrants from Nanjing. In the discourse of the Xiaotun villagers, these models were conceptualized in the terms of Guan Suo's mythic role as a vanguard general during Zhuge Liang's campaign, who also established his camp in their village. Thus, one pacification campaign was conceptualized in reference to a previous one. Migration and military colonization were put in the same terms. The diachronic references encased one another like nested boxes and tended to give the impression of being synchronically associated. Thus, the iterative process mentioned in the present volume's introduction (issue 3) of exploring archives and historical studies from the actors' discourses provided a more precise date and clear context that shed light on the origins of the masked opera. It also highlighted the Yangzong people's way of thinking about the past (ethnohistory; issue 4 of the introduction). Here, the more recent period of history (Qing) was being conceptualized in the terms of an older period (Ming), which was itself conceptualized in terms of an older one, and so on, ultimately resulting in a symbolic reference to the Three Kingdoms period.

Influencing Historical Narratives: The Researcher's Responsibility and External Factors

Clarifying the sociopolitical context in which the Guan Suo Opera started in the nineteenth century has been a crucial step in understanding its original purpose and the ritual organization of the valley. However, it only partly explained what was at stake in the masked activity at the time of my research. When I arrived to Yangzong in 2005, I was immediately informed of a rumor about how the internationally famous movie director Zhang Yimou was supposed to come to the region to shoot the Guan Suo Opera. It later turned out that Zhang Yimou had indeed shot a movie in Yunnan involving a masked opera. But, contrary to the rumor, he did not go to Yangzong and did not feature the Guan Suo Opera itself. The movie, called *Riding Alone for Thousands of Miles* (Zhang 2005; hereafter *Riding Alone*), nonetheless had a direct and great impact in Yangzong as we shall see.

A few days after my arrival, a journalist came to film the Guan Suo Opera, but this initially had nothing to do with the abovementioned movie; it was a documentary project, ordered by the local government for archival purposes. The documentary took a while to be edited, and by the time the journalist submitted his initial version, the movie *Riding Alone* had been released and the local government was aware of my own long-term presence in the region. The journalist was consequently asked to change the script in order to include those two elements. So, instead of being a factual archive about the regular activities of the Guan Suo Opera, the documentary was retitled *In Search of the Guan Suo Opera*, and it told the story of Boliere, a French anthropologist, who had watched the movie *Riding Alone* and decided to take a trip in search of the Guan Suo Opera.[10] This is how I became a part of the local history myself, on terms that I could not chose.

However, that was the smallest impact that Zhang's *Riding Alone* had locally. As he did in several previous films, he had recruited nonprofessional actors to play the roles of the local characters. One of them was Li Jiamin, a regular farmer from Chengjiang county. As I was taken to visit him for the purpose of the new version of the documentary, I took the chance to interview him. I found out that he had discovered the existence of the Guan Suo Opera thanks to his involvement in *Riding Alone*. He met the eldest actor of the Guan Suo Opera, learned a part of the play, and had even made plans to "develop" it—plans that the actors in Xiaotun were totally unaware of. Yet, his ideas had not materialized by the time I left the region a year later.

However, another local nonprofessional involved in *Riding Alone* was working for a travel agency in Kunming. Similar to Li Jiamin, he became interested in the Guan Suo Opera due to his participation in the movie and sensed its potential for tourism development. He contacted the head of Xiaotun village and established a contract regulating on-demand performances for tourists that his agency would take on tour. As far as I know, he brought in one group of tourists in 2006.

These two self-established potential promoters were not the only ones to show interest in the Guan Suo Opera. A locally influential journalist in Chengjiang also took advantage of the international movie to promote the Guan Suo Opera. He became active on the internet in 2005 by creating a personal blog, and he later created another one entirely devoted to the Guan Suo Opera.[11] He notably wrote an article titled "What Was the Opera Performed in Zhang Yimou's *Riding Alone for Thousands of Miles?* The Guan Suo Opera of Chengjiang."[12] The fact that the Guan Suo Opera was not actually part of the movie seemed secondary, with the article introducing the rich cultural heritage of Chengjiang county, the ruins of an antique city (estimated to be from the third century CE) sunk under the Fuxian Lake's waters, the fossils discovered on Mount Maotian outside of Chengjiang city (dating to about 500 million years ago), and the Guan Suo Opera, the "living fossil" of *nuo* culture.

Among other important events that affected the history of the Guan Suo Opera, there was a study written by an officer in charge of tourism resources at the provincial level, which was also made public thanks to the same blog. The study was nothing more than a project of touristic exploitation of the masked opera. It applied the well-known UNESCO lexicon by labeling the Guan Suo Opera an "intangible cultural heritage" and seemed almost directly addressed to the state council in charge of national heritage classification. Following one another, these events gradually built a path to the final recognition of the Guan Suo Opera as national intangible cultural heritage in 2011 (Beaud 2015).[13] Currently, the potential for tourism-based business emphasized in the abovementioned study appears to be increasingly achievable, with the implementation of an ecotourism development project spanning over twenty years (2010–2030). According to this plan, Yangzong township and its Guan Suo Opera will stand as the cultural center of the area, while neighboring townships will be exploited according to their own resources (economic, environmental, etc.).

History in the making was thus almost palpable in the discussions that were going on when I arrived to Yangzong in the very beginning of 2005. Only a certain length of field investigation could provide an understanding of what was happening and the impact of events. Even though the Guan Suo Opera was performed during only one month around the Chinese New Year, I remained in the region throughout the year, and I was able to witness some unexpected events that impacted the actors quite strongly, not only in their performances but in their mentality as well. My subsequent historical study consisted of drawing connections between scattered facts, establishing causal relationships between events, and historicizing facts that, while in the field, I could only see synchronically.

Conclusion

One of the keys of my field research was its long-time horizon. Five years spanned from my first fieldwork in Yangzong in 2002 to the last Chinese New Year I spent there in 2007. This allowed me to see important changes that were taking place while keeping a certain continuity.

Historical research, in the narrow sense, helped me navigate through the path paved by the informants in order to make sense of their discourses, analyze their practices, and explain their underlying cultural representations. I not only figured out how the local society was producing history, but I also found out that various local actors would tell various histories, and that they did not share the same conception of the past. On the one hand, the production of a unilinear history through selected records of past events by government officers and researchers, responding to a political agenda, reflected the necessity of tracing historical continuity and a cultural tradition. On the other hand, the villagers' nonlinear history uncovered a circular model of symbolic references that enabled them to conceptualize a past event using the terms of a previous one.

Even though ethnic policies have fluctuated over the decades of the People's Republic of China, minority nationalities have generally benefited from "advantages" that made minority status sought out, especially in the period between the two censuses of 1982 and 1990 (Gladney 1994; 2004, 22–23). Yangzong's population, however, did not make this choice and conversely claim their Han ethnicity. By doing so, they related themselves to a military ancestry that attached them to the Chinese empire, the locus of power. Thanks to a historical perspective, I was able to understand the ways in which the figure of Guan Suo and the Guan Suo Opera were crucial to this population, not just because they were unique to the region but because they held a people's history and the item (cultural emblem, protective god) to which they placed the value of their existence. In the national context, in which Yunnanese remote peasants had barely any part to play, the Guan Suo Opera constituted a key organizational instrument of a local microcosm rooted in a past social and ritual organization that still persists today. Through the symbolic identification of a conquering hero representing the central authority, they could assert their legitimacy on a given territory.

The present chapter also shows that the ritual masked opera's history was still in the making, with new factors at stake, mainly related to provincial economic development based on tourism. And, eventually, Boliere's "epic of another kind" (i.e., the archival documentary), no matter how anecdotal it might seem, reminds us that the anthropologist always impacts the local society they are conducting research on, and their presence affects the course of history as much as any other factor.

Although resorting to history became a determining part of my doctoral research, it was not a matter of reconstituting the past of the locality or the population per se. I was rather in search of historical explanations to shed light on a few specific points raised by informants. Written information and historical studies were then harnessed to serve an anthropological demonstration. I did not think it was necessary to reconstitute the formative evolution of the Guan Suo Opera, but I had to figure out the sociological context in which it probably took shape in order to understand its current social and ritual importance. Similarly, my tentative dating of the origins of the Guan Suo Opera was not decisive in terms of date, but the investigation itself provided an understanding of the way in which actors viewed and transmitted the memory of its origins.

For this purpose, I had to rely heavily on historians' studies considering that each string I pulled was leading to a full-length research project, as the articles and books published by qualified historians attested. So, I combined firsthand data with the history drawn by historians. The published studies provided a global view and tendency on a particular point. For instance, in order to understand what was at stake when the Guan Suo Opera might have been created, I relied on Carol Benedict's research on the history of the bubonic plague in the nineteenth century, which started in Yunnan (Benedict 1996). I could then correlate the general tendency of the epidemics unfolding throughout the province, as analyzed by Benedict, with the local gazetteer, which mentioned such outbreaks at a higher degree of temporal precision for Chengjiang county than Benedict's account. The local archives enabled me to confirm that the general threads described in historical studies applied to the area. In other words, cross-checking historical academic studies with local archives allowed me to move between scales and obtain finer information. The notion of scale in geography implies a form of hierarchy, and we know, at least since Louis Dumont's study ([1967] 1979), that the latter implies categories that are interconnected and interdependent. The recognition of the Guan Suo Opera as national intangible heritage clearly illustrated the variation in scale of the investigated events as well as their interconnection.

I concede that there might be a certain vanity in trying to weave a coherent fabric out of scattered fragments of heterogenous nature; one even may call it "savage" history. However, I realized that historians were similarly confronted with the heterogeneity of information, and they also had to sew patchworks. If history is anywhere, a researcher's access to it is in fact widely subject to the hazards of fieldwork. Thus, our use of history is conjunctural and necessarily dependent on its relevance to the investigated topic. Then, the specificity of an anthropological approach may consist of considering every piece of information as a primary source—equally questioned and equally valued—while the full consideration of the notion of scale constitutes the condition that facilitates synergy between oral and written sources.

Notes

1. The objectives differ nonetheless because the regressive method implies a double movement, from the present toward the past and then back to the present again, in order to reconstitute the way an A (past) situation led to a B (current) situation. Whereas in anthropology, the past is sought out as a reference point, sometimes as a symbol only. It is a matter of figuring out historical references that still make sense in the present; thus, the second movement of the regressive method does not seem compulsory.

2. This claim to be Han was a leitmotif in the villagers' discourse during my first fieldwork: the Yangzong people were challenged on their ethnicity on several occasions and explicitly asserted their Han ethnicity. Yunnan is famous for its ethnic diversity (holding twenty-five of the fifty-five officially recognized "national minorities" [*shaoshu minzu* 少数民族]), but the Han, the ethnic Chinese, still make up about two-thirds of the province's population. In that context, I was led to question how and why, in order to prove their "Hanness," the Yangzong people were resorting to the cultural traits that distinguished them the most from other Han (such as the ladies'

embroidered clothes, which looked typically "ethnic" and very similar to the ones of the neighboring Yi national minority, as well as their unique ritual masked opera; see Beaud 2003, 2017).

3. Being a woman investigating a men's practice initially made a few actors uncomfortable. I was eventually accepted as an observer after I promised to neither request to perform myself nor steal their secrets to recreate a Guan Suo Opera in my country. I later learned that the exclusion of women may also relate to notions of purity, but I have never been rejected for that reason, at least not openly. As analyzed by S. Trebinjac (1995) on her own experience among the Uyghurs, I probably similarly benefitted from the fact that I was seen as a foreigner and a researcher before being seen as a woman.

4. Hereafter, I will refer to these two reference books as "the publications" or "the local publications."

5. The local gazetteers (*difanzhi* 地方志) constitute official accounts of all the important events that happened in a set area during a set period of time. They are regularly rewritten (officially "sorted," *zhengli* 整理) and extended by civil servants. The habit of writing such gazetteers is still practiced: the latest version of the Yunnan provincial gazetteers was released in 2020.

6. I was an "invited foreign researcher" at the Institute for Advanced Studies on Asia of the University of Tokyo, and I was also a research assistant in the Global COE Program on Chinese theatre project, hosted by the Tsubouchi Theatre Museum of Waseda University. Between 2010 and 2012, these positions afforded me with full access to the immense collections of their respective libraries.

7. See Gu (1989), Hong (1992), Jin (1995), Qiu (1994), and Chen (1998), among others.

8. Mainly the works of Gail King (1985, 1987; Oman King 1989) on the story of Hua Guan Suo, and of Anne McLaren (1985, 1998) on Ming chantefables in general.

9. The Rebellion, named from the Birman term "Panthay" (see Atwill [2005, 10] for its etymology and implications), opposed local ethnic groups as well as some Han Chinese, under the guidance of Hui (Muslim) leaders, to the Qing imperial regime. It soon resembled a civil war and radically changed Yunnanese society (Giersch 2006, 217–218).

10. Boliere (i.e., myself) was the way my Chinese name, Bu Yali, has been transcribed in the English subtitles of the documentary.

11. "*Yangzong hai* 阳宗海," Sina (*Xinlang boke*), accessed November 7, 2023, http://blog.sina.com.cn/chengjiangjiangyanbin.

12. "'*Qianli zou dan qi' shi shenme xi: Chengjiang Guan Suo xi* 千里走单骑是什么喜：澄江关索戏." The article, which was an opinion piece posted by the author on the Xinhua news agency's forum (January 8, 2006), has been removed from the Xinhua website, but a reference to that text and its basic content regarding the Guan Suo Opera can be found on the China Radio International website: http://news.cri.cn/gb/9223/2006/01/10/1266@855618.htm.

13. See the description of the Guan Suo Opera on the Chinese ICH website: http://www.ihchina.cn/Article/Index/detail?id=13565.

References

Atwill, David G. 2005. *The Chinese Sultanate: Islam, Ethnicity, and the Panthay Rebellion in Southwest China, 1856–1873*. Stanford, CA: Stanford University Press.

Beaud, Sylvie. 2003. "De l'habit au costume: Une forme de revendication identitaire des Hans de Yangzong (Yunnan)?" Master's thesis, Université Paris X Nanterre.

———. 2012a. "Un 'fossile vivant' de la culture *nuo* nationale: Réflexion sur la désignation de *nuoxi* appliquée au *Guan Suo xi*." *Études chinoises* 31 (1): 95–108.

———. 2012b. "Masques en parade: Étude d'une ethnicité à la jonction du politique et du rituel, l'exemple du Théâtre de Guan Suo (Yunnan, Chine)." PhD diss., Université Paris Ouest Nanterre.

———. 2015. "La fabrique d'un patrimoine chinois: De production culturelle nationale à tradition théâtrale locale." *Ebisu* 52: 291–321.

———. 2016. "How the North Tried to Pacify the South through Ritual Practices: On the Origins of the Guan Suo Opera in the Nineteenth Century." In *Imperial China and Its Southern Neighbors*, edited by Victor Mair, 316–337. Singapore: ISEAS.

———. 2017. *Masques en parade: Ethnicité et enjeux de pouvoir dans le Sud-Ouest de la Chine*. Nanterre: Presses universitaires de Paris Ouest.

Benedict, Carol. 1996. *Bubonic Plague in Nineteenth-Century China*. Stanford, CA: Stanford University Press.

Bloch, Marc. 1931. *Les caractères originaux de l'histoire rurale française*. Oslo: H. Aschehoug.

———. 1964. *Apologie pour l'histoire ou Métier d'historien*. Paris: Armand Colin.

Cartier, Michel. 1979. "La croissance démographique chinoise du XVIIIe siècle et l'enregistrement des Pao-chia." *Annales de démographie historique*, 9–28.

Chen Tianyou 陈天佑. 1998. "Guan Suo xi: Dianxing de xiquxing nuoxi 关索戏:典型的戏曲性傩戏" (The Guan Suo Opera: A typical case of Nuo opera influenced by Scenic Opera). In Yunnan minzu yishu yanjiusuo 云南民族艺术研究所 (Research Institute on Ethnic Arts in Yunnan) and Yuxi diqu xingshu wenhuaju 玉溪地区行署文化局 (Yuxi Cultural Affairs Office) (dir.). *Yunnan nuoxi nuo wenhua lunji* 云南傩戏傩文化论集 (Collection on Yunnan Nuo Opera and Nuo Culture), 144–160. Kunming: Yunnan minzu chubanshe.

Daqing Daoguang Chengjiangfu zhi 大清道光澂江府志 (Local gazetteers of Chengjiang Prefecture compiled during the Daoguang era of the Qing dynasty). 1821–1851. 15 manuscript books. N.p.

Di Cosmo, Nicola. 2006. *The Diary of a Manchu Soldier in Seventeenth-Century China, "My Service in the Army,"* by Dzengsěo, with introduction, translation and notes by Nicola Di Cosmo. London: Routledge.

Dumont, Louis. (1967) 1979. *Homo hierarchicus: Essai sur le système des castes.* Paris: Gallimard.

Giersch, Patterson C. 2006. *Asian Borderlands: The Transformation of Qing China's Yunnan Frontier.* Cambridge, MA: Harvard University Press.

Gladney, Dru C. 1994. "Representing Nationality in China: Refiguring Majority/Minority Identities." *Journal of Asian Studies* 53 (1): 92–123.

———. 2004. *Dislocating China: Muslims, Minorities, and Other Subaltern Subjects.* Chicago: University of Chicago Press.

Gu Feng 顾峰. 1989. "Yizhi dute er yi you de nuoxi: Guan Suo xi 一支独特而移有的傩戏——关索戏" (A peculiar and changing Nuoxi: The Guan Suo Opera). In Guizhousheng minzu shiwu weiyuanhui wenjiaochu 贵州省民族事务委员会文教处 (dir.). *Zhongguo nuo wenhua lunwen xuan* 中国傩文化论文选 (Collection on Chinese Nuo culture), 265–280. Guiyang: Guizhou minzu chubanshe.

Hong Jiazhi 洪嘉智, dir. 1992. *Guan Suo xi zhi* 关索戏志 (The Guan Suo Opera gazetteer). Beijing: Wenhua yishu chubanshe ("Zhongguo xiqu zhi Yunnan juan congshu").

Jin Chong 金重. 1995. *Shen ren jiaocuo de yishu. Xinan minjian xiju yu zongjiao* 神人交错的艺术——西南民间戏剧与宗教 (A Drama of Men and Gods—Folk Dramas and Religions in Southwest China). Kunming: Yunnan jiaoyu chubanshe ("Xinan yanjiu shuxi").

Katō Sango 加藤三吾. 1906. *Ryūkyū no kenkyū* 琉球の研究 (Research on the Ryukyu), 3 vols. Sasebo 佐世保 (no publishing house mentioned).

King, Gail. 1985. "Discovery and Restoration of the Texts in the Ming Chenghua Collection." *Ming Studies* 20: 21–34.

———. 1987. "A Few Textual Notes regarding Guan Suo and the Sanguo Yanyi." *Chinese Literature: Essays, Articles, Reviews* 9 (1–2): 89–92.

Lee, James. 1982a. "Food Supply and Population Growth in Southwest China, 1250–1850." *Journal of Asian Studies* 4 (4): 711–746

———. 1982b. "The Legacy of Immigration in Southwest China, 1250–1850." *Annales de démographie historique*: 279–304.

Li, Lan. 2010. "The Changing Role of the Popular Religion of Nuo (傩) in Modern Chinese Politics." *Modern Asian Studies* 44 (2): 1–23.

Liu Ticao 刘体操, dir. 1997. *Guan Suo xi* 关索戏 [The Guan Suo Opera]. Kunming: Yunnan xinwen chubanshe ("Nuoxi di er ji").

Liu Xiaojin. 1997. *Mask: Field Research on a Folk Performance*. Documentary film. Kunming: Yunnan TV.

Luo Guanzhong 罗贯中. 2005. *Sanguo yanyi* 三國演義 (Romance of the Three Kingdoms). Beijing: Renmin wenxue chubanshe.

McLaren, Anne E. 1985. "Chantefables and the Textual Evolution of the San-kuo-chih yen-i." *T'oung Pao* 71 (4/5): 145–227.

———. 1998. *Chinese Popular Culture and Ming Chantefables*. Leiden: Brill.

Oman King, Gail. 1989. *The Story of Hua Guan Suo—Hua Guan Suo Zhuan* 花關索傳. Tempe: Arizona State University Center for Asian Studies.

Qiu Kunliang 邱坤良. 1994. "Guan Suo yishi yu Guan Suo xiju: Yi Yunnan Chengjiang Xiaotun 'wan Guan Suo' weili 關索儀式與關索戲劇——以雲南澂江小屯"玩關索"為例" [The Guan Suo ritual and the Guan Suo Opera in Xiaotun village, Chengjiang district, Yunnan province: The case study of "Playing Guan Suo"]. *Minjian xinyang yu Zhongguo wenhua guiji huilun wenji, Taibei, 1993 nian 4 yue* 民間信仰與中國文化國際會論文集, 臺北, 1993 年4月 [Proceedings of the International Conference on Chinese Culture and Popular Beliefs, Taipei, April 1993], 2 vols., 587–620. Taipei: Hanxue yanjiu zhongxin yinxing.

Sanguozhi 三国志 (Chronicles of the Three Kingdoms). (3rd century) 2002. Compiled by Chen Shou, 3 vols. Beijing: Tuanjie chubanshe ("Zhongguo gudian mingshu wenku").

Saussure, Ferdinand de. (1916) 1995. *Cours de linguistique générale*. Paris: Payot.

Trebinjac, Sabine. 1995. "Femme, seule et venue d'ailleurs: Trois atouts d'un ethnomusicologue au Turkestan chinois." *Cahiers d'ethnomusicologie* 8: 59–68.

———. 2000. *Le Pouvoir en chantant: L'art de fabriquer une musique chinoise*. Nanterre: Société d'ethnologie.

———. 2008. *Le Pouvoir en chantant: Une affaire d'État . . . impérial*. Nanterre: Société d'ethnologie.

Ueda, Nozomu 上田 望. 2003. "Unnan Kan Saku gi to sono shuhen 雲南關索戲とその周辺" (The Guan Suo Opera of Yunnan and its environment). *Kanazawa daigaku Chūgoku gogaku Chūgoku bungaku kyoshitsu kiyō* 金沢大学中国語学中国文学教室紀要 (Kanazawa University's Bulletin of the Laboratory for Chinese language and literature) (6): 69–97.

Yang Yingkang 杨应康. 2004. *Chengjiang fengwu zhi* 澄江风物志 (Chengjiang scenery gazetteer). Kunming: Yunnan renmin chubanshe.

Zhang Yimou. 2005. *Riding Alone for Thousands of Miles* (千里走单骑 *Qian li zou dan qi*). Zhang Yimou Studio, Toho Company Ltd., Sony Pictures Classics.

CHAPTER 7

Making History While Being in History

The Histories of the Qiang and Rma

Wang Ming-ke

THE QIANG ARE A CHINESE ETHNIC MINORITY with a population of approximately 310,000 living along the eastern fringes of the Qinghai-Tibetan Plateau in western Sichuan. Despite their being a minority of minorities,[1] scholars believe that their history can be traced back as early as the Shang dynasty (sixteenth through eleventh centuries BCE) or even earlier, and that their descendants now live among the Han, Tibetans, Yi, and ten other ethnic minorities in the southwestern part of China.

My work on the Qiang started about thirty years ago. I began by deconstructing the history of the ancient Qiang against the then dominant approaches in Chinese scholarship. I argued that, between the Shang and Han dynasties (sixteenth century BCE to third century CE), the ethnic label "Qiang" as recorded in old Chinese sources was an exonym used by "the people of the Central Plains" (*zhongguoren;* a term that later became a synonym with "Chinese") to signify some alienated tribes of sheep-herders in the western part of the Sinosphere. During this period, Qiang was not a self-ascribed ethnonym, but was rather a superimposed category, and the history of the Qiang was recounted through the eyes of proto-Chinese authors who viewed these tribes as "western others." Chineseness, as an ethnic entity, was yet to come into being, and "Qiang" was nothing but a reflection of this othering process. "Qiang" denoted the westernmost ethnic boundary as demarcated by the earliest inhabitants of the Central Plains (*zhongyuan,* or "China proper"), who have defined themselves since the eighth century BCE as "Huaxia"—the progenitors of today's Han. As more and more lands and tribes were incorporated into the kingdoms and empires of the Central Plains, this boundary shifted farther westward until the Eastern Han dynasty (25–220 CE), when it ultimately reached the eastern edge of the Qinghai-Tibetan Plateau (Wang Ming-ke 1992).

Given these assumptions, a question needs to be asked: How should we make sense of the existence of a group of people in western Sichuan that now self-identifies, and is also seen by others, as Qiang? Searching for an answer to such question, I made my first field visit to the Qiang areas of the upper Min River valley in 1994. Just a few days after my arrival, locals told me that they had never heard about the "Qiang" people and had never thought of themselves as such until they were so categorized by Chinese officials in the 1950s and after. These mountain dwellers tended to call themselves Rma—an autonym whose pronunciation varies from one area to another—and it was not until the 1970s and 1980s that they started to equate it with Qiang. Elders still remembered that, in the past, Rma represented the people who lived within a group of "fortress villages" in a small valley or part of the valley.

Following my research interests in ethnic identity and historical memory, new questions arose. Who were the Rma? What memory supports their identity? How did the Rma "acquire" a new memory and eventually become Qiang? What are the processes that underlie this shift? From 1995 to 2003, I explored all these questions through fieldwork among the Qiang of the upper Min River and Jian River valleys. The result of these fieldwork visits is a crucial part of my book *The Qiang between the Han and the Tibetans*, which was published in 2003.

The focus of this chapter is not the knowledge I have gathered through multiple field and archive inquiries regarding the Qiang, but rather the methodology and epistemology being used in the process of data collection and analysis as well as a series of ethical self-reflections on my own work with this ethnic group. This chapter is divided into five sections. The first two sections introduce my fieldwork methodology, where I explain (1) how I conducted these visits, (2) why I adopted a multisited strategy, and (3) what kinds of information I collected throughout. The third section elucidates how I analyze Qiang history and the history of other frontier peoples found in ancient Chinese texts. In the fourth and fifth sections, I offer some epistemological and ethical reflections on the knowledge thereby produced from these analyses. I then conclude the chapter by elaborating on my own positionality.

Multisited Ethnography

In 1994, a friend introduced me to some Qiang folks. I was so lucky to have been granted that opportunity to meet them. Most of them were intellectuals affiliated with the Weizhou Normal School of Wenchuan. At that time, they were all involved in a large project that sought to promote the standardization of the Qiang language and its romanized writing system (pinyin) through the compilation of a Qiang dictionary.[2] Over the years, I saw them enthusiastically investigating, collecting, and fostering Qiang language and culture. They were so proud of being Qiang, as they believed and learned through the national history of China that the Qiang are a small but old minority group acknowledged as the "ancestor" of Tibetan, Yi, and even Han Chinese people.[3]

Between 1995 and 2003, I made eight field trips—one or two months per trip—to the upper Min River valleys and Beichuan in Mianyang (see map 5), and together with my local friends, I investigated the Qiang and their Tibetan neighbors. The villages we visited were either my friends' own native villages or the villages of their acquaintances and students.

All our field visits took place during the summer or winter school breaks. When I arrived in Wenchuan, the administrative center of all Qiang areas, I often found that my Qiang friends were busy meeting

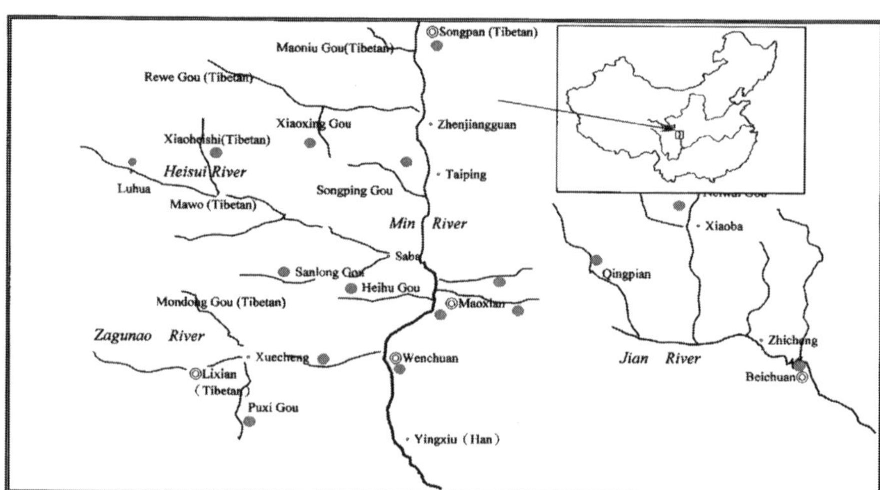

Map 5. Sketch map of Qiang areas in China, with fieldwork locations indicated in gray. © Wang Ming-ke.

about the Qiang dictionary. If such was the case, I had to find accommodation in a school classroom or at the closest hotel for a few days, while taking advantage of the situation to listen to their discussions and chat with them before, during, or after their daily meetings. Their discussions primarily revolved around how to properly pronounce or define a term in the Qiang language. This was very difficult and contestable work. The reason for this difficulty is that all local Qiang dialects share common phonology and grammar, but the native languages (or dialects) of different localities (i.e., a village cluster or valley) are mutually unintelligible, and the people of a given locality tend to believe that their native language is the most standard one. For the same reason, Sichuanese Mandarin has become the de facto lingua franca for everyday conversation between Qiang folks from different areas. For the Qiang people in Beichuan and other Sinicized Qiang counties, Sichuanese has become or is gradually becoming their mother tongue.[4] I could easily grasp the meaning of what they said when I communicated in the Sichuanese dialect not only with my Qiang friends but also with other Qiang people I met.

My field experience in Qiang townships—in Wenchuan, Maoxian, Songpan, Lixian, and Beichuan counties—was somewhat different than the one I had gained in Qiang mountain villages. While hanging around the towns, I was surrounded by Qiang intellectuals who worked in local schools or government departments. They told me about the history and culture of their own people. Most of them repeated what I had already learned from the works of established Chinese historians and ethnologists. Among these conversations, I heard the story of Great Emperor Yu, the founding father of the legendary Xia dynasty, who according to Chinese sources was born in the "western Qiang" (*xiqiang*) region, and therefore is commemorated by almost all the people from the above towns as a Qiang hero and ancestor. No one actually knows where the Great Yu's birthplace is, but this seemed to be a topic of much debate and competition between townships, as people tried to demonstrate the central role of a place and its people in all Qiang areas through "history."[5]

One of the harshest yet truly most enjoyable moments that I had over all these years of intensive fieldwork occurred when I ventured deep into the valleys and climbed up to the top of a mountain to visit a village. Villages are located on high mountain slopes at elevations of hundreds or a thousand or more meters above the valley's stream, taking about one to four hours or even more to reach from the base of the mountain. A fortress-village is made up of thirty to eighty households, and two to five villages form a village cluster. Several villages or village clusters within a small valley along the mountain stream form a wider social network. The most outstanding feature of these villages is their impressive defense towers built out of stone (see figure 7.1). Many of these towers can exceed a hundred feet in height, and most of them—with exception to those being erected after 2000 for tourism development purposes—were built at least eighty years ago.

We were distinguished guests in each of the villages we visited. This was because my Qiang companions were teachers at the Weizhou Normal School, teachers of local village teachers, or teachers of the hosts' children. My status as a scholar coming from Taiwan was also fairly helpful. Villagers were especially curious about Taiwan and Taiwanese people, and sometimes they had more questions for me than I had for them.

We stayed in a village for about four to seven days, then we moved to another village in the upper streams of the same or another valley. We went back to visit these villages again in the same year or within the following years. I thus became an old friend to many of the village hosts

Figure 7.1. Stone towers of the Ergeami village at Heihugou, Maoxian County, western Sichuan. © Wang Ming-ke.

in a relatively short period of time. I did not plan to engage in multisited ethnography, nor did I plan to do such long-term fieldwork. This happened due to the nature of my inquiries and the answers I received. There were two practical reasons for me to constantly move from one site to another. First, while villagers were very busy with their daily activities, they were still eager to show us their greatest hospitality; this made us feel that we should not stay too long in one place. Second, I was just a visitor from Taiwan; I might have caused trouble to my hosts if I had stayed in the same village for more than four or five days. According to official regulations, visitors should register at the local security bureau, which was usually very far from the villages I was visiting. So if I stayed only for a few days, my host did not need to bother to apply for a formal registration for me.

Most importantly, however, I adopted this field strategy for two other reasons. First, the focal points of my investigation were Rma identity and related emic history(ies), along with the concomitant changes that took place from the 1920s to 1990s—that is, approximately a generation before and after the Chinese Communist Revolution of 1949. In this respect, I discovered that not only did some of the physical and cultural features of these mountain dwellers differ considerably from one place to another, but also that Rma from different places retained different emic histories, which explains how village-based communities (people of the same village, a village cluster, or an entire valley) came into being. A multisited approach was therefore necessary to collect oral information and other ethnographic data from villages in different areas and with very diverse sociocultural backgrounds. Second, my interest in Qiang ethnic identity and historical memory has been influenced by the following streams of research: (1) the notion that history has many voices (Ritchie 2003; P. Thompson [1978] 1988) and voices speak from the bottom up (E. P. Thompson 1994); (2) collective or social memory and its relation to social identity and distinction (Halbwachs [1942] 1992); (3) experimental psychology (Bartlett 1932); (4) so-called structural amnesia, which suggests a discrepancy in the intergenerational transmission of memory(ies) from fathers to sons (Gulliver 1955); and most notably, (5) anthropological theories on ethnicity, ethnic change, and historical memory (van den Berghe 1981; Smith 1986; Tonkin, McDonald, and Chapman 1989; Roosens 1989) that followed the publication of Fredrik Barth's edited volume *Ethnic Groups and Boundaries* (1969). These findings were meaningful to my research questions. They led me to opt for a multisited strategy and gather data from people of different valleys, genders, ages, religious beliefs, and levels of education.

Altogether, I visited nearly a dozen Qiang mountain valleys. Those where I stayed longer and returned more frequently are Aixigou in Songpan, Neiwaigou in Beichuan, and Yonghegou in Maoxian. From both a geographical and cultural point of view, these villages lie, respectively, on the most Tibetanized Rma valley in the west, the most Sinicized one in the east, and in the valley in between. These locations are also the homelands of three of my best Qiang friends. I selected these field sites to make a comparison between Rma village-based communities in all Qiang-populated areas. In terms of cultural, linguistic, and physical similarities, the inhabitants of these villages fall along a spectrum with the most Tibetanized of Songpan on one end and the most Sinicized of Beichuan on the other.

Data Collection in the Field: What, How, and Why?

I used two methods to collect data while in the field. The first method was ethnographic observation, in which I gathered data directly from what I saw and heard in the field and through conversations with my local hosts. I kept notes of all conversations I had, relying primarily on my memory. I wrote them down every day before going to sleep, and I further reorganized them as soon as I returned to Taiwan. The thus obtained information about (1) the natural environment and man-made territorial boundaries; (2) subsistence strategies; (3) social grouping, identity, and distinction; and (4) cultural representations. Taken together, these data have given me a general understanding of the human ecology of the area.

Influenced by the abovementioned streams of research—including Pierre Bourdieu's ([1979] 1984) concept of habitus and his insights on the biases that may blur the researcher's gaze (Bourdieu and Wacquant 1992) as well as the postmodern critique of rationality and objectivity—I began to doubt the field knowledge that I gained from my own sensory experience and memory. Therefore, I applied a second method, tape recording, to supplement what I learned through field observation.

Most of the information that I collected through tape-recorded interviews comprised local stories, legends, and "histories" (*zegvea*).[6] Throughout these interviews, utmost consideration was given to the orator's personal feelings, opinions, and interpretations as well as to other people's engagements in conversations over such stories, legends, and histories. Of all the tape-recoded materials, the most significant were "histories." In order to record histories, I asked my hosts a very simple question: How did it come about that the people (or your ancestors) settled down here? The "people" in this question range from their family, their village, their village cluster, and up to the Qiang "nationality" (*minzu*). I gathered histories from Qiang people with very diverse backgrounds in terms of region, family, gender, age, and education. After coming back from my fieldwork visits, I converted these materials into a written form, typing them word by word. I value these data as very important "representations of reality," a crucial idea that I borrow from Bourdieu ([1979] 1984). I consider them as oral or textual representations of the social reality of a given village, village cluster, or mountain valley where the orators have been immersed. The relationship between these histories and their corresponding realities is best illustrated by Paul Ricoeur's notion of "historicity." As Ricoeur (1981, 274) put it, the term "signifies the fundamental and radical fact that we make history, that we are immersed in history, [and] that we are historical beings." In the following pages, I will explain how I integrate the histories drawn from these oral recordings with the ethnographic data gathered from the field. I will take Aixigou, a small valley in Songpan, as an example.

Aixigou, simply translated as "the valley of Aixi," belongs to the main river valley of Xiaoxinggou and lies between Rewugou (Tibetan) to the west and Daerbiangou (Qiang) to the east. During my fieldwork years, there were three villages in the valley, with a total population of about 150. These villages shared and protected all natural resources in the valley. They strictly distinguished each village's territory from that of their neighbors and competed for resources (e.g., yak pasture and medicinal herbs) in the high mountain slopes around the valley where village boundaries were unclear. The following three passages are word-by-word transcriptions of oral histories collected in 1996 from interviews conducted in Aixigou (Village 1 and Village 2).

> In the earliest days there was no one here. Three brothers came. The eldest was a cripple. One brother settled here [Village 2], and the youngest went to village 1. The eldest said: "I would like to live here [Village 3] so that I can enjoy more sunshine." This is why Village 3 is exposed to sunshine earlier in the morning [than we are]. The youngest was afraid [to be left alone]. His brother [the

one who settled in Village 2] said: "You can be buried at our village after you die." So all the deceased of Village 1 were buried here.

At the very beginning, three brothers came here. Originally there was no one here. Three brothers came from the lowlands. No, it was not three brothers [actually]; it was nine brothers. Nine brothers occupied this land. Three of them came to this valley [Aixigou]. Two lived together in the valley of Daerbian, and two settled in the main river valley of Rewu.

There were seven brothers: One in Heishui, one in Songpinggou, one in Hungtu, one in Xiaoxing, one in Maoniugou, one in Songpan, and one in Zenjiangguan.

These records show that the villagers of Aixigou signify their current spatial and social connections with their neighbors by recalling the "histories" of their common ancestral brothers (see map 6). The "history" narrated in Case 1 sheds light on the primordial ties between the folks

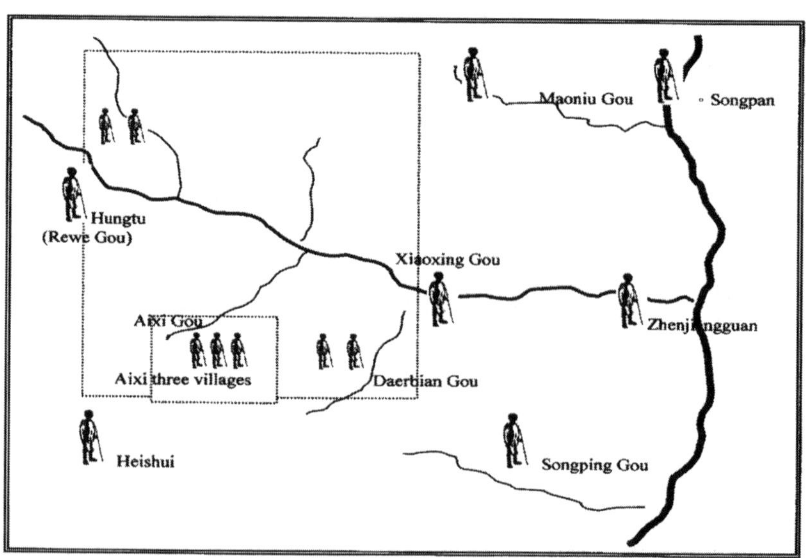

Map 6. Sketch map of the locations of ancestral brothers as reported in the oral accounts of Aixi villagers. (Source: Wang Ming-ke 2003, 224)

of each village (descendants of an individual brother), and on the ties between all people in the three villages (descendants of the three brothers). Case 2 tells the "history" of nine brothers (actually those mentioned are only seven) and links Aixi villagers with those of the neighboring Rewu and Daerbian valleys in a network of fraternal relationships. The "history of seven ancestral brothers" shown in Case 3 situates the people of Xiaoxinggou (Aixi villagers included) within a far wider regional context that encompasses six other major localities in the modern-day counties of Songpan, Heishui, and Maoxian.[7]

As I have suggested elsewhere, stories of ancestral brotherhood can be viewed as a kind of history (historical memory and narrative), or its prototype, within which primordial ties among people unfold in a very direct and simple way. The memory of ancestral brothers binds together people of different clans, villages, village clusters, and valleys who are simultaneously socially equal, distinctive, economically intertwined, and rivalrous. Leaving aside the patriarchal ideology that supports the narrative of each story, it can be noticed that the metaphors of "brothers" are threefold: unification, distinction, and confrontation. They indicate the people of a region who co-own, share, and compete for local resources. Informed by such histories, people learn to interact with others in varying spatial and social contexts, and to protect their own boundaries while simultaneously respecting those of others. The daily activities of most people, especially those directed to basic subsistence, are regulated by and rooted in their understanding of "history." In other words, the "histories" that people made up and took to be true are representations of the reality they lived in. As histories are internalized in people's minds, they give shape to and reinforce the way people experience the world around them. I have argued that histories of ancestral brothers are the products of a specific cultural mentality toward history (or the past in general)—that is, the "historical mentality of ancestral brothers," as I named it. This mentality grows and gets nourishment from the ground of a specific human ecology—one of a small and clearly delimited territory where internal cooperation, scarce-resource allocation, social distinctions, competition, and at times confrontation mold people's interactions with one another (Wang Ming-ke 2003).

Moreover, there are noteworthy symbolic cultural markers, like women's traditional clothing and religious beliefs in mountain deities, that also function as representations of reality. Qiang women's clothes are distinctive and colorful, and women wear them on a daily basis, while men's dress does not differ from that of local Han Chinese men. Head kerchiefs and aprons are made in varied styles and embroidery patterns. Women used to wear them as a distinguishing marker of their own village, village cluster, or valley. Differences in women's clothing between neighboring groups are tiny but critical for locals in that they like to joke about or criticize the women's clothes of their neighbors, near or far.

As for the worship of mountain deities, the boundary between different settlements and groups of people is further reinforced through religious beliefs and social practices. Each village has its own mountain deity, as does each village cluster. The significance of Qiang beliefs in mountain deities is clearly illustrated—maybe clearer than any academic study has ever done—by the interpretation of a Qiang elderly man who once said to me: "Mountain deities protect our boundaries. There are far and near boundaries; there are big and small mountain deities." All these cultures—female dress customs, mountain deity beliefs, and the historical mentality of ancestral brothers—are structured practices. They give shape to representations that support people's social reality (i.e., human ecology and group boundaries).

Human ecology and related cultures correspond with the people's Rma identity and community life, which had existed in the first half of the twentieth century but were disappearing during my fieldwork years. As I have been told by many middle-aged or older Qiang people in the 1990s, the autonym Rma was used to represent only the people of their own valley or part of the valley, from which the Tshep (lit. the "barbarians who settled upstream") and the Erh (the Han Chinese downstream) were both excluded. Therefore, the villagers who called themselves Rma were also identified by the people upstream as the Han (Erh), and by those downstream as barbarians (Tshep).

Between 1994 and 2003, I observed that the human ecology behind the cult of sacred mountains, women's dress, and other cultural traits was still extant, although it had experienced a gradual decline. Younger generations started to cast doubt on their own culture. They no longer regarded the "mythical" history of their ancestral brothers as "true" and stopped worshipping mountain deities. One of the practical reasons for that was the increased competition over high-priced medicinal herbs (i.e., *Cordyceps*) that grew on mountain peaks. People tended to ignore or even deny traditional village boundaries. It is against this backdrop of social change, as I myself have witnessed over the years, that the Rma ultimately became the Qiang.

Doing Fieldwork in Archives

After 2003, I endeavored to reinterpret the role of the Qiang in China's national history in light of my own readings of locally obtained data on the Rma and their oral accounts. I started a new research project that aimed to provide a new understanding of heroic histories recorded in Chinese archive materials and of the human ecology hidden therein. In that project, I used the same multisited approach and method of analysis of representation to explore the relationship between these histories and the reality they represent. This is what I call "doing fieldwork in archives." Here, the relationship between representation and reality becomes one between text and context. The result of such an endeavor has been a book about the development of historical memories and China's human ecology through time (Wang Ming-ke 2006). If my 2003 book on the Qiang or Rma is a work that, in anthropological jargon, "makes the strange familiar," then my 2006 book can be seen as one "making the familiar strange."

What follows are a few excerpts from this book in which I analyze four historical narratives of ancestral heroes written by Chinese historians of the early imperial era (second century BCE to fifth century CE). Among them, the history of a Qiang legendary ancestor called Wuyiyuanjian is the main focus of my analysis, not only because it is in line with the above themes but also because from the standpoint of ancient and modern Chinese, it is one of the most important historical memories that keep shaping the images of people living in the Qinghai-Tibetan Plateau.

These narratives are drawn from the primary sources summarized below and concern the whole of China.

1. In the northwest of China

Based on the "History of the Later Han" (*Hou Han Shu*) compiled by Fan Ye in the fifth century CE, Wuyiyuanjian, a Rong slave of the Qin Kingdom, fled to the Qiang lands of the upper Yellow River valley. Because of his ability to work miracles, he was worshipped by locals as a godly king. He taught people farming and hunting. He and his descendants ruled the Qiang ever since.

2. In the northeast

According to the "History of the Former Han" (*Han Shu*) compiled by Ban Gu (32–92 CE), after the collapse of the Shang

Dynasty (1600–1046 BCE), a royal Shang prince called Jizi, who was also the uncle of the last Shang king, fled to Chaoxian (around today's Manchuria and North Korea). He taught agriculture, silkworm-rearing, and the established standards of social propriety to the indigenes of Chaoxian, and they thus made him their king.

3. In the southeast

In the "Records of the Grand Historian" (*Shi Ji*) by Sima Qian (ca. 145–86 BCE), it is recorded that Taibo, prince of Zhou (1050–771 BCE), fled to the lands of Wu in the lower Yangtze River valley, and yielded the royal throne to his youngest brother. Admiring Taibo's noble sentiment and behavior, the Wu indigenes made him their king.

4. In the southwest

As specified by Sima Qian, at the end of the Warring States period (475–221 BCE), Zhuang Qiao, a general of the Chu Kingdom in the middle Yangtze River valley, was sent to conquer the Dian Kingdom in today's central Yunnan. Upon victory, Zhuang's motherland was destroyed by the army of the Qin Kingdom. Thus, he remained among the Dian people and became their king. (See map 7.)

Reading these textual narratives against each other is like shifting the focus of observation from one field site to another. The selected histories written by ancient Chinese historians are therefore no different from those represented and conveyed orally to me by my Qiang hosts. Like the histories of Qiang ancestral brothers, the four histories given above are built upon common narrative structures and systems of signs. There are two main structural layers in these histories. The first layer represents the historical mentality of ancestral heroes, which corresponds to the highly centralized and stratified human ecology of imperial China. The second one is the hero-fleeing-to-the-frontier plot, whereby a "loser hero" flees to a faraway land and is worshipped as a king by locals. In both layers, there are multiple signs that convey the values and emotions of Chinese compilers. They are found within each text and can be grouped into two categories: (1) signs of polity (i.e.,

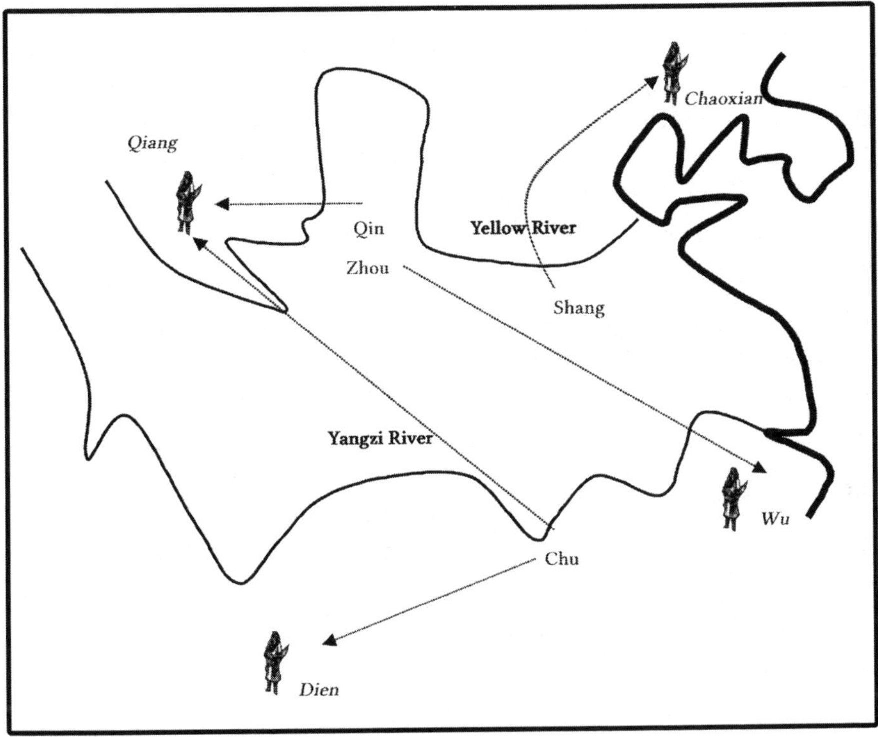

Map 7. Sketch map of the directions where the frustrated heroes fled as reported in Chinese ancient texts. © Wang Ming-ke.

the Shang, Zhou, Chu, and Qin states) and (2) signs of social distinction (i.e., a prince, general, or slave of barbarian origins). The Shang and Zhou polities were at the center of an idealized Sinosphere—the "Central Kingdom" or "Central Plain"—while Chu and Qin were at the periphery of it. The prince was a noble, the general ranked lower in terms of social status, and the slave obviously lived at the margins of society. This means that in the eyes of ancient Chinese authors the people of Wu and Chaoxian were the most civilized, so they imagined that the ruling families of these people were the offspring of noble heroes who had fled from China. The Qiang of the upper Yellow River valley, on the contrary, epitomized the most alienated "other."

Taken as a whole, these histories and their variability are representation(s) of a social reality at different levels. At the first and most fundamental level, the reality they attest to is the highly centralized and strictly stratified human ecology of the Central Kingdom. At the second level, the reality revealed is the political hegemony of such a kingdom, its imperial projections over peripheral lands and people, and the ethnocentric stance of Chinese authors. Finally, the reality at the third level is the cultural imaginary, degree of emotionality, and political intention of these authors when they depict the barbarian "others" as a peripheral "us."

If we read these historical texts independently, the signs found in their respective narrative structure(s) go largely unnoticed. But when we put them together and compare them carefully, their nature as structured social memory becomes evident. These texts are collective social memories, coded by their authors' identities and positionalities as well as by the social realities in which the authors lived. Therefore, the nature of my study on these histories is not so much about investigating "historical facts" as represented in the texts but rather about decoding the "historical reality" (or context) from these texts.

Let me return now to the themes of Qiang history in Chinese archives. The *History of the Later Han*'s chapter "Record of the Western Qiang," which contains the story of Wuyiyuanjian, is definitely the most important record on the ancient Qiang. Besides Wuyiyuanjian, there are two other heroic histories recorded in this chapter. The first one is about Sanmiao, an evil tribal chief who belonged to a subbranch of the ancient Jiang clan. After being defeated by Emperor Shun, founder of the legendary Yu dynasty in the Central Plains, Sanmiao was exiled to the Qiang lands in the upper Yellow River valley in the northeastern part of the Qinghai-Tibetan Plateau. He and his followers were the very people who originally populated these lands. The second one is about another tribal leader called Ong, who was the grandson of Wuyiyuanjian. Out of fear of the Qin's military forces, Ong and his tribe moved to the south. His men and their descendants scattered around the southwestern part of the plateau, thereby losing contact with the Qiang of the upper Yellow River valley. These two narratives, like that of Wuyiyuanjian, follow the same hero-fleeing-to-the-frontier plot. One can notice that all of them reflect the author of the "Record of the Western Qiang" and his contemporaries' views and emotions and the imagination of the people living in the Qinghai-Tibetan Plateau. The first one, by establishing that the Qiang of the upper Yellow River valley are the descendants of a defeated rival of Emperor Shun, is meant to signify the inferior nature of the Qiang. The second one further speculates on the inferior nature of a tribe who dwelled in the southwestern and the inland areas of the plateau, and is described as a side branch of the main stem of the Qiang living in the upper Yellow River valley.

Notably, although the ethnonym "Qiang" has appeared in Chinese sources for over three thousand years, and while many peripheral people have been labeled as Qiang, the most extensive compilation on "the history of the Qiang" was done by Chinese scholars only on two historical occasions involving China's western boundary. The first one took place during the fifth century and brought about the compilation of the aforementioned "Record of the Western Qiang." At this time, the westward expansion of the Chinese empire had already reached its ecological and political limits. The writing and compilation of this historical document served to either shape or justify the newly fixed ethnic and political boundaries of western China. With this in mind, I treat the story of the Qiang's founding ancestor Wuyiyuanjian as a sign of discrimination and exclusion of the people beyond such boundaries.

The second time was almost 1,500 years later, in the first half of the twentieth century, when modern nationalism was on the rise and Chinese historians developed a renewed interest in the Qiang. It is in this context of historical revisionism that many works on the history of the Qiang have been published as a complement to "the history of the Chinese nation." In these publications (Lin 1936; Lu 1934; Wang Tonglin 1934), the Qiang-Jiang connections become the new focus of attention. Wuyiyuanjian was now a stigmatized symbol of ethnic exclusiveness, while the legendary Sanmiao and ancient Jiang clan were both elevated as the true heroic ancestors of the Qiang. Many prominent Chinese historians have contributed to this process of modern historical (re)construction. Among them are Zhang Taiyan (1919), Gu Jiegang (1962), and Fu Sinian (1930). In their books and articles, the Qiang are described as an ancient and once very powerful ethnic group who, after being repeatedly defeated by the emperors of China and Tibetan kings, fled in all directions and intermingled with the Tibetans, Yi, and ten other minority groups scattered around southwest China. In contrast to previously compiled official histories of the Qiang, which functioned as a marker of exclusion, this (re)branded version of Qiang history became a blueprint of ethnic inclusiveness. Such a characteristic is revealed especially in the way the Jiang clan is glorified—the Jiang were the descendants of the legendary Emperor Yan, who is described in China's ancient documents as the brother or defeated rival of the Yellow Emperor, believed to be the ancestor of the Han or Chinese nation and a staunch ally of the Zhou Kingdom during its conquest battle against the Shang. Eventually, the so-called barbarians of past Chinese dynasties were therefore turned into national minorities, and this became the new social reality.

The foregoing are just a few cases that help explain how I do "fieldwork in archives" by adopting the same methodologies that were used in my fieldwork among the Qiang. Not unlike the latter, where the objects of observation are the social representations of Qiang villagers, the objects of observation in my "archival fieldworks" are the textual representations of Chinese authors of ancient and modern times. The realities revealed through these representations do not pertain to the Rma or Qiang minority but rather to ancient or modern China, with the people of the Qinghai-Tibetan Plateau being a marginal part.

Epistemological (Self-)Reflections

What are the historical facts and social realities that I have gained so far? What is the rationale that informs the way I do fieldwork and archival research on the Qiang? How do I ascertain the authenticity of facts and realities?

To address the first question, I draw on Ricoeur (1981), who maintains that in most European languages, the term "history" has two meanings: what really happens and the narrative of events. It is the same in Chinese, where "history" (*lishi*) can refer to both meanings. As for the first meaning, I argue that there are two bases for narratives about what happened or existed in the past. In other words, narratives about the past are based on one or the other, or sometimes a mixture of (1) a series of events, material artifacts, artificial construction(s), thoughts, and/ or everyday activities of an individual or group of persons and (2) the social reality in which people lived as well as all contemporary events, artifacts, people's activities, and historical narratives (either in written or oral forms) that merely count as representations of such reality.

Given these readings of "history" and "what happened in the past," it is clear that the focus of my study is not "facts that happened in the past." I do not argue for the historical facts of certain heroes or wars in which these heroes fought or were involved, nor do I seek evidence regarding the events that led some legendary brothers to establish themselves in places where their alleged descendants live today. My foremost concern is to explore the "reality" of what either existed in the first half of the twentieth century (in the case of the Rma), or in the period from the Shang to fifth century CE (in the case of ancient and imperial China). As I have postulated in the preceding sections with examples from both Qiang and Chinese narratives, "the reality" can *reveal itself* in representations of varied forms. Among them, the histories that people narrate, write, and believe in are what really matters. This is because those who "make history" are simultaneously immersed in a social reality that is paradoxically both regulated and affected by the histories they have made.

The goal of my textual analysis is to disclose the relationship between representation (text) and reality (context). The meaning of these two terms, and the relationship between them, is perfectly illustrated by Bourdieu's ([1979] 1984, 482) most celebrated wording, "the reality of representation and the representation of reality." In my previous works, I have suggested that the reality in which people live is always a matter of structure, or levels of structure when the reality being dealt with is that of a complex society. Likewise, people's minds are also articulated in levels of structure that mold their social representations and can consequently reinforce a given reality. If one takes the reality of imperial China as an example, there are at least three structural levels that can be discerned. The first and most fundamental one is the human ecology of imperial China. As already anticipated, this is exemplified by a highly centralized and hierarchically stratified society that is built on internal exploitation and external expansion or defense. The second is the imperial polity and its system of dynastic rulership. The third is the ethnocentric ideology of the ruling elites and intellectuals (including history compilers or authors).

Alongside these structures, there are three other structures that shape the representations of reality. These are (1) the historical mentality of ancestral heroes, (2) the genre of official dynastic history, and (3) the hero-fleeing-to-the-frontier narrative plot. When seen in light of these multiple structures of representation, the four selected narratives examined in the previous section undoubtedly reinforce the reality of imperial China—its fundamental human ecology, its dynastic polity, and the inherent ethnocentrism of its people.

Bourdieu-inspired approaches to the study of representation and reality, the analysis of people's mental or cultural structures that frame their perception of reality, and the method of multisited ethnography can be best illustrated by the metaphor of a "hand lens." When one observes an object (i.e., a social reality or historical fact) through such a lens (i.e., structure in the form of a bias, ideology, or mentality), what one perceives in one's mind is a twisted image (i.e., representation) of the observed object. To better understand the nature of an object, one can move the lens toward another object, compare the way the image of these two objects changes on the surface of the lens, and determine the rule that governs the variation in size or shape of the image. If one understands how the lens works—that is, how it twists people's perceptions of objects—one would be able to gain more knowledge of the object under the lens.

Let us assume now that the way we move the lens to observe different objects, or to observe an object from multiple angles, represents the methodology of multisited ethnography, while the objects are the social reality or historical facts under study. It is clear that there is no absolute knowledge of such reality or facts, because these, like any object, are always placed under the lens at some distance from the observer. Even when one observes them by moving the lens, the knowledge that one can acquire about them is always indirect and speculative. In other words, one has learned more about the lens than the objects themselves. Nevertheless, I believe that this specific type of knowledge—the awareness of one's own mentality, schema, biases, ideology, genre, habitus, and any other "structure" that twists one's mind and the process of observation—can deepen the understanding of a social reality or historical fact. If one ignores the existence of the lens between the observer and the object being observed, one will keep seeing and thinking about representations as if they are realities.

An Ethical Reflection on My Work about the Qiang

One night during a field survey, I joined some elderly villagers who sat on a yak felt and chatted around the fireplace. They were talking about the hostilities that once existed between villages of neighboring valleys, causing an endless cycle of communal violence and vendettas that lasted until the 1950s. Then, an old man mocked himself and said, "It is because, in the past, we did not know that we are an 'ethnic minority' (*minzu*)." His words often return to me, especially when I write about Qiang history and the social reality they lived in decades ago. If it is true that people are satisfied with what they have today and are proud of their history and

Qiang identity, for what reason and in what positionality am I to deconstruct their Qiang identity and the knowledge behind it?

Life in the past was not a rose garden. The Qiang's villages and houses represent the past, reflecting the harshness and perilousness that this people had experienced. Villages are built on high mountain locations for defense purposes. The aforementioned stone towers are a prominent landmark of old villages, and houses are closely attached to one another, leaving only a very narrow walkway in between them. Every house has small windows and thick outer walls with small holes for shooting. These features are the best illustration of how fear and violence were part of people's daily lives.

After the Communist Revolution and the subsequent state-led program of ethnic classification that solidified minority identities (Mullaney 2011), people started to bear the "fruits of revolution." Local bullies were punished or permanently removed, and any form of ethnic discrimination has been prohibited ever since. Young people from remote villages or poor families had been recruited, educated, and later became local officials and party cadres. The economic advantages of being an ethnic minority came in 1990s and after. Large sums of government money flowed into Qiang and other minority-populated areas of the country to subsidize economic development programs.

Notwithstanding the rising living standards, the present is also not a rose garden. For many Qiang, being a minority in contemporary China means occupying a peripheral position economically, politically, and ideologically. The economic boom witnessed since the 1990s did not come without contradictions. The economic gap between this minority region and the country's prosperous provinces has grown larger and larger. Among the costs of achieving full electricity access was the cutting down of forests that had been carried out on a large scale during the 1980–1990s. This, together with mass road-building projects, which caused immense damage to the fragile environment, resulted in the severe floods in the middle and lower reaches of the Yangtze River in 1998. Then, to protect the geological stability of the upper Yangtze River valley, a new policy named "restoring farmland into forests" was decreed in 1999. Qiang villagers have been unable to practice terraced cultivation on their mountain slopes ever since. With the exception of a very few who have succeeded in private businesses or have built their own professional careers, the majority of Qiang people have either relied on local tourism or relocated to faraway cities along the coast in southeast

China, where they sell their labor as factory workers (Bian 2017). Ethnic tourism, for which the people's "indigenous ecology"—often a synonym for "backwardness"—has become a commercial product that tourists seek, hence reinforcing the inferior status of local people, both culturally and socially. This image of ethnicity has been fostered by a rigid academic concept of "culture," which conceives of ethnic minorities or indigenes as "people living within culture" as opposed to "modern citizens" who place themselves at the edges of history.

The harmful effects of such rigid academic and social images can be better illustrated by an event that occurred in the summer of 2008, right after the devastating earthquake here. The Qiang, who lost one-tenth of their entire population because of the earthquake, suddenly came under the spotlight. At this very tense moment, geologists, geophysicists, and social workers all warned about the urgent environmental danger faced by villagers in Dragon-Creek Valley (Longxigou)—a densely populated valley around Wenchuan. Therefore, the government relocated about two thousand Qiang people from their mountain settlements down to terraced lowlands along the Min River valley. For the following two months, these earthquake refugees lived in tents and waited until an official decision was made. One option was to resettle them elsewhere in Sichuan, away from their original homes. Social scientists, historians in particular, raised another warning against the resettlement plan. Their concern was that if the refugees were to be resettled far away, they would lose their Qiang identity, native language, and culture. This concern was shared by many Qiang intellectuals and local leaders. Unable to tolerate the summer heat and government's hesitation, villagers eventually moved back to their mountain settlements. This made me question the kind of knowledge that we, as scholars of the social sciences and humanities, produce through our works. Can academic knowledge really help people? What is its practical value? It also makes me think about how much frustration and suffering people might have experienced in the name of "preserving and protecting minority cultures and identities." Should academic knowledge be held responsible for this?

After the publication of my book in 2003, I sent a copy of it to each of my Qiang friends. I put a note in each copy to explain why my views on Qiang history and culture might differ from those of other Chinese scholars. I told my friends that the "history" that they should be proud of is not that of "the people who had been defeated and whose descendants are now scattered among China's many minority groups," but rather the history of ancestral brothers that their Rma ancestors believed in. Their brotherly histories could tell the Han Chinese, who see themselves as the carriers of a great history and civilization, or tell people in the so-called civilized world that there is a society that they are not familiar with. In such a society, there are no established and outsiders, no conquerors, and no conquered, since everyone is the descendant of an ancient brotherhood. Therefore, the Han Chinese and anyone else in the "civilized world" should develop a reflexive understanding of their own heroic history and accept that the reality of any hierarchical distinction between the established and outsiders, the conquerors and conquered, is nothing but the product of historical memories, for better or worse.

Concluding Remarks

Together with the Qiang, my books from 2003 and 2006 also deconstruct the history in which Han Chinese believed. Thus a similar reflection also occurred to me: based on what reason and in what positionality should I deconstruct the history they believed? I will draw on my personal history to address such a question. While I am in mainland China, I am a Taiwanese individual, which in the mindset of Chinese people stands for "marginal Chinese." While in Taiwan, I am a marginal Taiwanese individual, or so-called mainlander, because my father came from the mainland to Taiwan in 1949. As the two regions are bound by very close yet hostile ties, my identity cannot but shift between the two of them. It is precisely this condition of "dual marginality" that made me develop a keen interest in ethnic studies, and above all in the relationship between ethnicity and historical memories. This has pushed me to constantly (re)examine my own positionality and identity. Having said that, I consider the contents of my books not deconstructive in the postmodern sense of the term. They are actually shaped by my own reflexive understanding of what "being Chinese" and "making Chinese history" implies. Such reflection is obviously rooted in the personal views, perceptions, and thoughts of a scholar who is culturally and emotionally attached to mainland China and Taiwan, which ergo reminds himself of his own marginality.

Moreover, in response to my readers' queries, I published *Rethinking History and Reflexive Historiography* in 2015, where I outlined the methodologies used in my previous works and their epistemological significance. On the flyleaf of the book, I describe the scene of a pond in the countryside that is reproduced here in its entirety to elucidate what, as I see it, an ideal study on history might be.

> When we are sitting beside a small pond on a summer night, we hear diverse croaky voices made by frogs of different sorts. Eventually our attention is attracted by the loudest and most steady among all frog-voices. All of a sudden, in our minds, feeble frog-voices gradually become "silent" and unheard. Those voices being heard are the "authoritative history," whilst the unheard ones are the "peripheral history or narrative." This metaphor implies that our understanding of "history" lies in listening to the many contending voices and the synergies between them. It is through "listening" that the hidden scene of the ecology of the pond, within which the frogs play an important role, can be disclosed.

Notes

1. At present, the Qiang population totals 312,981 people (National Bureau of Statistics of China 2021, tab. 2-22). Compared to other minorities, such as the Tibetans (6,282,187) and Yi (9,830,327), the Qiang's status as a minority of minorities is self-evident.

2. The Weizhou Normal School was built to train elementary school teachers who work in local minority villages. The Ethnic Affairs Commission has many branches all over the country at the provincial and county levels.

3. For an ethnographic account on the genesis of these minorities with particular reference to the Yi of southern Sichuan (Nuosu) and other Qiangic-speaking groups, see Harrell (2001).

4. This tendency is more obvious among the young people in all the Qiang-populated counties, as I was once told by a Qiang teenager: "It is strange that we can speak Sichuanese without learning it, but for speaking our own language, we need to learn."

5. A similar case comes from Gyalrong Tibetans of Danba County, Garzê Tibetan Autonomous Prefecture, who have selectively borrowed historical narratives on the "eastern queendom" (*dong nüguo*) of Chinese sources to promote their own ethnic identity. On this topic, see Tenzin (2014).

6. There is no counterpart to the concept of "history" in the Qiang language. The nearest term for "history" is *zegvea,* the meaning of which is closer to the English "long ago" or "the past," as the notion of "long long ago" is expressed as *zegvea zegvea.*

7. In his work on the oral histories of Tai Vat villagers in Laos, Pierre Petit has expounded that narrating history is a men's prerogative (Petit 2020, 56–69). This is also true for the Qiang, in that men are much more interested in and knowledgeable about history than women. However, this depends on the close link between "history" and people's daily lives. If one, for example, looks at the three oral accounts on the ancestral brothers given above, it is easy to see that the first one—the history of three brothers as portrayed in the daily experiences of Aixi villagers—was commonly known and narrated by people of different ages and sex. The second, the history of nine brothers, was known and told only by a few men because it was regarded as less relevant to the social reality of the villagers. The third, connecting the Aixi to the wider cultural region, was reported by just one man who had lived in the town for many years.

References

Barth, Fredrik, ed. 1969. *Ethnic Groups and Boundaries.* London: George Allen & Unwin.

Bartlett, Frederick. 1932. *Remembering: A Study in Experimental and Social Psychology.* London: Cambridge University Press.

Bian, Simei. 2017. "Mountains, Gods and Modernity: Resilience and Adaptations in the Sino-Tibetan Borderland of Northwest Sichuan." PhD diss., University of Oslo.

Bourdieu, Pierre. (1979) 1984. *Distinction: A Social Critique of the Judgement of Taste.* Trans. by Richard Nice. London: Routledge & Kegan Paul.

Bourdieu, Pierre, and Loïc Wacquant. 1992. *An Invitation to Reflexive Sociology.* Chicago: University of Chicago Press.

Fu Sinian 傅斯年. 1930. "Jiang Yuan 姜源" (The origins of the Jiang clan). *Bulletin of History and Philology* 中央研究院歷史語言研究所集刊 2 (1): 130–135.

Gu Jiegang 顧頡剛. 1962. *Siyue yu Wuyue* 四嶽與五嶽 (Four mountains and five peaks). Beijing: Zhonghua Press.

Gulliver, Philip H. 1955. *The Family Herds: A Study of Two Pastoral Tribes in East Africa, the Jie, and Turkana.* London: Routledge & Kegan Paul.

Halbwachs, Maurice. (1942) 1992. *On Collective Memory.* Translated by Lewis A. Coser. Chicago: University of Chicago Press.

Harrell, Stevan. 2001. *Ways of Being Ethnic in Southwest China.* Seattle: University of Washington Press.

Lin, Hueixiang 林惠祥. 1936. *Zhongguo Minzu Shi* 中國民族史 (The history of the Chinese nation). Shanghai: Shangwu Yinshuguan.

Lu, Simian 呂思勉. 1934. *Zhongguo Minzu Shi* 中國民族史 (The history of the Chinese nation). Shanghai: Shijie Shuju.

Mullaney, Thomas. 2011. *Coming to Terms with the Nation: Ethnic Classification in Modern China.* Berkeley: University of California Press.

National Bureau of Statistics of China. 2021. *Zhongguo tongji nianjian 2021* 中國統計年鑒 2021 (China statistical yearbook 2020). http://www.stats.gov.cn/tjsj/ndsj/2021/indexch.htm.

Petit, Pierre. 2020. *History, Memory, and Territorial Cults in the Highlands of Laos.* London: Routledge.

Ricoeur, Paul. 1981. "The Narrative Function." In *Hermeneutics and the Human Sciences: Essays on Language, Action and Interpretation.* Cambridge: Cambridge University Press.

Ritchie, Donald A. 2003. *Doing Oral History.* Oxford: Oxford University Press.

Roosens, Eugeen E. 1989. *Creating Ethnicity: The Process of Ethnogenesis.* London: Sage Publications.

Smith, Anthony D. 1986. *The Ethnic Origins of Nations.* New York: Basil Blackwell.

Tenzin, Jinba. 2014. *In the Land of the Eastern Queendom: The Politics of Gender and Ethnicity on the Sino-Tibetan Border.* Seattle: University of Washington Press.

Thompson, Edward Palmer. 1994. *Making History: Writings on History and Culture.* New York: New Press.

Thompson, Paul. (1978) 1988. *The Voice of the Past: Oral History.* Oxford: Oxford University Press.

Tonkin, Elizabeth, Maryon McDonald, and Malcom Chapman, eds. 1989. *History and Ethnicity.* London: Routledge.

Van den Berghe, Pierre L. 1981. *The Ethnic Phenomenon.* New York: Elsevier.

Wang Ming-ke 王明珂. 1992. "The Ch'iang of Ancient China through the Han Dynasty: Ecological Frontiers and Ethnic Boundaries." PhD diss., Harvard University.

———. 2003. *The Qiang between the Han and the Tibetans: A Historical Anthropological Study on a Chinese Border* 羌在漢藏之間:一個華夏邊緣的歷史人類學研究. Taipei: Lien-ching Press.

———. 2006. *Heroic Ancestors and Brotherly Nationalities: Text and Context of Primordial Histories* 英雄祖先與弟兄民族:根基歷史的文本與情境. Taipei: Yun-chen Press.

———. 2015. *Rethinking History and Reflexive Historiography* 反思史學與史學反思. Taipei: Yun-chen Press.

Wang Tonglin 王桐齡. 1934. *Zhongguo Minzu Shi* 中國民族史 (The history of the Chinese nation). Beiping: Wenhua Xueshe.

Zhang Taiyan. (1919) 1924. "Xu Zhongxing 序種姓" (An introduction to the Chinese race). *Jian Lun* 檢論. Shanghai: Shanghai Gushu Liutongchu.

CHAPTER 8

The Vietnam War

Insights from the Lao Borderlands

Vatthana Pholsena

THIS PAPER IS A reflection on my research journey seeking to gain new insights into the history of the Vietnam War in border regions in Laos.[1] My choice of such locations and the people who inhabit these areas was guided by the idea that a historical investigation of the conflict in "peripheral" areas could contribute to the production of an alternative history to that focused on nation-states and major urban centers and, hence, the writing of a much-needed multicentered history of the Vietnam War in mainland Southeast Asia. Less is known about what happened in these areas and the lived experiences of their inhabitants, most of whom belong to ethnic minority groups. Yet, these areas were often of crucial strategic significance and their inhabitants were equally, if not more, impacted by war violence.[2]

What needs to be analyzed are not only the "big" events, but also their anthropological dimensions, that is, how people have lived them and what they think about them today. The use of the life history and life story methods, in particular, have been important in my research. I follow here Geyla Frank's (1995, 145) distinction between life histories and life stories, namely "Life histories focused mostly on diachronic change within anthropology's traditional paradigm of naturalism or realism; research on life stories, on the other hand, [. . .] focuses on the strategies speakers use to fashion coherence from the disparate and potentially contradictory experiences of their lives." In other words, life histories seek to capture the complex course of an individual's life through his or her retrospective account. The life story method focuses on memory processes, as personal narratives reconstruct the realities as experienced in their own specific ways. I will discuss these two approaches to oral sources that are both utilized—complemented by written materials whenever possible—in my research.

I shall draw on my several years of investigation into the experiences of the Vietnam War in the upland areas of central and southern Laos. This geographical space constituted a strategic center and logistics base area, and was the location of the Democratic Republic of Vietnam (DRV) army's transportation network during the conflict, famously known as the Ho Chi Minh Trail (HCMT). The first two sections of this chapter cover my research on both combatant and civilian experiences of the Vietnam War in the east of two provinces in central and southern Laos (respectively, Savannakhet and Sekong Provinces). The objective was not only to collect "stories" of the war—although this constituted the first step—but also and above all to look for connections in peoples' narratives with historical change. Indeed, at the core of oral history lies the awareness that personal experience is part of history, and it is through individual narratives that oral history finds, in Alessandro Portelli's (1997, 6) words, "a connection between biography and history, between individual experience and the transformations of society." In the last part of my chapter, I look back on my investigation into the structural changes experienced by local societies in some of these eastern areas that were under communist control, and explain how I gradually added to an oral history project a reconstitution of a social history of the Vietnam War in these areas through an examination of state and social formation processes.

Historicity of Personal Experience: The Use of the Life Story Method

Until relatively recently, very few foreign researchers had succeeded in getting long-term access to the field in Laos. The situation began to slowly improve after the communist regime started to open up to foreign investors, tourists, and, to a lesser extent, NGOs, in the wake of economic liberalization in the early to mid 1990s. Nevertheless, bureaucratic obstacles and political surveillance were (and are) still prevalent in this authoritarian regime. As far as I was concerned, access to the field was furthermore complicated by the fact that I conducted research among members of ethnic minority groups inhabiting the upland areas of Laos, where government concerns for "national security" and suspicion toward foreign researchers are especially heightened. An experience commonly shared by foreign researchers is the convoluted path to getting fieldwork research permits and their tangled interactions with state bureaucracy and Party officials. I was no exception. At the start of my long-term doctoral fieldwork in Laos, after weeks of unsuccessful meetings in Vientiane and half-hearted promises of assistance from officials who in any case had no authority to issue research permits, my options were running out. It was a suggestion by the experienced anthropologist on Laos, the late Grant Evans, that eventually led me to approach the Lao Front for National Construction (LFNC),[3] the Lao Party-State's mass organization in charge of class, religious, and ethnic minority issues. I was initially skeptical and apprehensive about working with such a political and ideological institution. Had I heeded my doubts and concerns I would not have met Khambai Nyoundalat, then the head of the LFNC's Research Department on Ethnic Groups.

Born in the eastern district of Vilabuli in Savannakhet Province, he was of Brou Makong[4] origins and trained as an ethnologist in Vietnam and the former Soviet Union. Khambai granted me research permits on more than one occasion and accompanied me on a few research trips in Savannakhet, Saravan, and Sekong Provinces in the late 1990s and early 2000s. He generously introduced me to his acquaintances in the Lao administration as well as to his friends and relatives wherever we went. These contacts would prove to be of significant help in my research endeavors during my subsequent field trips to these provinces on my own or with an assistant from the mid to late 2000s. In short, Khambai was the patron who facilitated my access to my field sites. I believe that the reasons why he chose to help me were because he genuinely enjoyed doing fieldwork[5]—he was an insatiably curious and tenacious researcher—and also because I was a young French female PhD student with Lao origins who must have appeared harmless, possibly naïve, and definitely exotic to him.[6]

A couple of years after completing my doctoral studies, Khambai and I participated in a research project funded by the Toyota Foundation, which aimed to collect the life stories of former revolutionaries noted for their "heroic" actions during the Vietnam War in three southern provinces, namely, Sekong, Savannakhet, and Saravan. I was interested in these revolutionary fighters for what their narratives revealed about their historical roles and their own understanding of historical events. The setting of the interviews was not ideal, though. We interviewed the informants as a team of three or more (on one occasion, a female lecturer from the National University of Laos came to the field with us), which may have been intimidating to some interviewees. Khambai was a former high-ranking official—he had retired by then—although his congeniality and cultural know-how greatly helped to mitigate the hierarchy between him (and his fellow researchers) and the interviewees. His linguistic skills (he could speak the languages of various southern minority groups, including his own, as well as Vietnamese) and his ethnicity and intimate knowledge of local cultures often enabled him to create an atmosphere of conviviality and trust in the houses and villages we visited (rice alcohol helped, too), even though we could never completely erase the social distance between us and our informants.

Khambai's line of questioning reflected a particular understanding of Lao anticolonial history.[7] He set off our 2004 interview with Manivanh, a well-known revolutionary figure in Savannakhet of Katang ethnicity, in this manner: "To begin with, tell us why you joined the Issala [the pioneering Lao nationalist movement]. Why? For what reasons? For family reasons? Because you were beaten?" With these questions, Manivanh began to unfold the story of her revolutionary life: "I would like to tell you my story."[8] The informant, a celebrated communist cadre, was used to visits from officials and journalists and telling about her revolutionary life. Autobiographies have been an essential element of communist movements, as a tool for their leaders to know and control the private and public opinions of their cadres and for the latter to apply self-criticism and demonstrate their allegiance to the Party (Pennetier and Pudal 1996). In Laos, the autobiography is called *sivapavat*, which is in the form of a questionnaire for Party cadres who internalize its wording and structure to tell their "story." So, the veteran did not need prompting from Khambai (or anyone else). Manivanh came from a materially poor background, was recruited as a young girl, went through the wartime educational apparatus and ideological circuit, and became a cadre within the revolutionary movement. What persuaded her to join the struggle, as she told us, was also the prospect—exceptional in those circumstances—of going to school, studying, and escaping her current way of life. As she narrated, "Then, in 1962, I left [the village]. My uncle and brother came to take me. At that point, I knew I wanted to leave. Because first, I was full of hatred, I hated the enemy! And secondly, I wanted to study, I especially wanted to study. At that time, I even didn't know to read [Lao]. I could only speak it. I sacrificed [*sala*] myself.

I left the family, the village, around June 20, 1962. I joined the mobilizing group in the province of Muang Phin. I followed my uncle and my brother." In her exemplary narration, she never mentioned her personal suffering, though the harshness of her life during the war was perceptible in her account. Nevertheless, she never expressed anything other than ordeals that she shared with her revolutionary comrades as a group. As an interesting comparison, when writing about war veterans and resistance fighters during World War II in Italy, Portelli (1981, 103) noted that "often, these individuals are wholly absorbed by the totality of the historical event of which they were [a] part, and their account assumes the cadences and wording of *epic*" (emphasis in original). By these narratives of self, people are expressing the desire to impose an order, to form a "whole" out of "constituent parts" (that is, events), and thus to retain a sense of their life—past and present—that is coherent and meaningful (J. Bruner 1991, 8).

At the end of her interview, Manivanh modestly expressed her contentment and gratitude toward the state for her house and her monthly war veteran pension. The rationale underlying Manivanh's narrative concurs with comments made by Sophie Quinn-Judge (2001, 269) on the lives of early Vietnamese women revolutionaries: "For the generation of women who began the revolution in Vietnam, the traditional virtues of stoicism and self-sacrifice were the ones that dominated their lives." Though she never said it, Manivanh lived an exceptional life for a woman of her background and origins by breaking from her group's cultural and social norms to embrace the anticolonial cause and the itinerant life of a communist militant, enduring sacrifices that she also wanted to remember as a result of her choice.

When I went back to Savannakhet on my own a few years later in 2008, I chose a different approach (namely, the one-to-one interview), as I wanted to explore new acts of telling a life story as the sole attentive listener. In company of Khambai and other Lao researchers, I had sensed that my ambiguous status had been, as anthropologist Judith Okely (1996, 32) observed in her fieldwork, that of "[a member] of an alien 'race'"—that is, in my case, neither Lao nor *farang* (the Lao word used to refer to Westerners).[9] On my own I felt that I would be freer in my efforts to change people's perceptions of my "strangeness." Yet, the most I achieved in these efforts was to appear as a female Lao/Asian *farang*, although my gender and relatively young age (I was then in my thirties) helped to lessen my racial "other-ness."

I would be introduced to informants by an acquaintance who was a local resident. That was how I met Khamla, a former communist agent of Brou ethnic origins. I interviewed her twice alone in her house in the town of Savannakhet. She was affable, often laughed during the interviews, and spoke her mind. Our conversations each time lasted around two hours and covered a diverse range of topics, not exclusively related to her revolutionary life. Her account was not always linear; I would let it drift, then after a little while I would refocus the interview that I had planned with the emphasis on a few key topics. For instance, Khamla spoke spontaneously of "unrevolutionary" behaviors; unlike Manivanh, who was a "National Hero" (*vilasôn hèng sat*), she may have felt less compelled to maintain a "coherent" narrative. For example, every household under the Communists' supervision had to pay a "rice tax" (*khao phasi*)—although it was strictly forbidden to use this "counterrevolutionary" (*patikan*) term during the war—which in official language, or political phraseology, was known as "rice to help the nation" (*khao souay sat*). The quantity to be donated depended on each household's productive capacity. Every year, a cadre was tasked with assessing and monitoring the quantity of rice "paid" by each household. But the seemingly well-calibrated policy did not always run as smoothly as this and at times faced some (passive) resistance. "It happened that households, the richer ones, would lie to us and would declare a lower quantity," recalled Khamla. "But neighbors would come and tell us the truth. We of course also carried out our own checks among households."

Khamla remained a ground-level cadre, her desire to be "better educated," she said, remaining unfulfilled: "I never went anywhere. The Central Level (*khantheung*) never sent me anywhere, neither in the north [of Laos] nor to Vietnam;[10] only some training of one month or two here and there. I learned everything by myself and with the help of friends and comrades." She kept being assigned to the same task—liaising between the Party and populations of her own ethnic background in her native province. In a sense, she never grew out of her ascribed "ethnic" role, because she was never given the opportunity to do so. Yet, she strove to learn with the support of her community, as she, a young female minority militant, endeavored to move above her ascribed social and gender positions through her own efforts in spite of the communist hierarchy's indifference.

Khamla was aware that she could have expected a better outcome from her years of devotion to the revolutionary cause. "My friends and colleagues keep saying that I'm stupid," she told me, sounding rather upset, during one of our conversations. "They think I could have asked for more with my revolutionary background. But I'm not stupid, I'm intelligent, I helped to liberate the country! I live in a state house, and I'm not asking for anything else."[11] Khamla then mentioned that she had never married or had children, and said this was "fine" with her and she was at peace with it. Marital status and, especially, childlessness are often mentioned in interviews with female guerrillas as a fate that befell many of them because a family life was incompatible with the duties of war (Khoo 2004; Lanzona 2009).

Portelli (1981, 97–98) noted that the "distinguishing factor" of oral sources from written documents was their "form" namely, the tone, the volume, intonation, and rhythm of speech. Such traits are "the emotional function, the narrator's participation in the story, the way the story affects the narrator." Expressions of pride and defiance tinged with sadness in Khamla's voice were richer in meaning than the factual accounts in lengthy memoirs penned by Lao revolutionary leaders. Oral sources "tell us not just what people did," Portelli (1981, 99–100) wrote, "but what they wanted to do, what they believed they were doing, what they now think they did." In essence, the narrator's subjectivity plays an integral role in the reconstitution of her past. In her own way, Khamla's narrative as a minority woman revolutionary shifted between personal and historical experiences, private and public statements, or, to use Portelli's (1997, 6) words, "performance-oriented narratives" and "theme-oriented testimonies."

The historian observes that oral history is about focusing on the no-man's-land that lies between what happened and what is inside the witnesses' minds (Portelli 2009). In other words, there are "inevitable gaps between reality, experience and expressions" (E. Bruner 1986, 7). Narrative is a way of making sense of experience. Narrators can create a coherent narrative, even for disordered or unhappy experiences. However, there are some experiences that are far more difficult to translate into narrative. The use of oral sources among groups that are not widely represented in official history is frequently associated with a militant approach, that is, giving voice to those who have never been asked to voice their views, hence creating the risk of "succumbing to a non-productive fascination" (Peschanski 1992, 2); in other words, to revive a past rather than explain it. A tension exists between, on the one hand, the evocative mode (an impulse to seize the "pulse of the living" and, on the other, the analytical mode (a contradictory impulse to follow "science and scientific method" (Hardy 2003, 21). How to resolve this tension? The answer is with rigor and methodology: to make the context (i.e., technical conditions) of the interview more explicit, to enable readers to judge for themselves the reliability of the sources, to provide counterexamples, and to supplement with written sources. We, the scholars, provide the necessary elements to explain the context and should let the readers judge by themselves. In other words, we should let individuals also express views that are sometimes ambiguous, sometimes contradictory.[12]

War and Social Change: The Use of the Life History Approach

To my regret, I never interviewed Khambai Nyoundalath. He would not let me (or, to my knowledge, anyone else). Nonetheless, during our many conversations, he shared memories of his childhood and schooling in Vietnam. He was recruited in his teenage years by Vietnamese soldiers who were mobilizing rural populations in eastern Laos—as early as the late 1940s in some upland areas located near the Vietnamese border. Khambai, as a child, regularly brought food prepared by inhabitants of his village to those soldiers who camped during the day in the forest to avoid being found by enemy patrols or denounced by villagers who were hostile to communist infiltration. It was during one of those trips that a group of Vietnamese soldiers offered him "the chance to study in Vietnam before returning to help his country." He left his village in 1959 at the age of thirteen, not knowing that it would be some fifteen years before his return to Laos.

During my doctoral research, I developed an interest in people who shared Khambai's trajectory. Thus, from the late 1990s, I started to search for and interview those who had been more or less willingly recruited as children by communist forces in areas penetrated or controlled by the latter and sent to study in northern Vietnam or northeastern Laos between the late 1950s and the early 1970s (Pholsena 2017b). The Communists' objective was to educate and to train these children to become the vanguard citizens and servants of the new socialist state. I was intrigued by this population of young people and wanted to learn more about their memories and experiences of a unique wartime education system and to what extent they had been shaped by it. In short, I wanted to study the revolutionary project from within and from an everyday life perspective.[13] I met some of these former students through a mutual acquaintance, others in the field, and others still by chance encounter. In sum, I gathered a corpus of oral materials over the next ten years or so.

I quickly realized, however, that this would not be a study of an age cohort. Ages varied significantly among these individuals, the oldest being born in the aftermath of World War II and the youngest in the early 1960s. My methodological approach drew instead on the concept of generation, as developed by Karl Mannheim (1952). His generational theory emphasized the importance of shared experience over the biological definition of generations. Generations are more likely to arise in times of comprehensive social change and instability, such as during wars, revolutions, and crises. Mannheim stated: "[W]e shall therefore speak of a generation as an actuality only where a concrete bond is created between members of a generation by their being exposed to the social and intellectual symptoms of a process of dynamic destabilization" (303). Mannheim's concept of generation put clear emphasis on the collective experience of historical events in a specific biographical phase and the way a collective arranges its experience.

Although not fully aware of it at the time I started collecting these biographical lives, I was attempting to reconstitute a facet of the social history of the Indochina Wars through this investigation. These revolutionary students could not be defined as a homogenous group along age group, ethnic, or geographical lines. In addition, they followed different paths at the end of their studies: some went back to their provinces to resume a farming life; others were recruited into the state administration (or left a few years later to work in the private sector or become self-employed). A few did extremely well and today belong to the ruling political class and sit on the Party's Central Committee or even in the Politburo, the Lao Communist Party's most powerful political organ. Only their childhood and adolescence in revolutionary schools define them as a social group sharing a distinct historical experience. When these students left their homes and villages, they broke away from a way of life ruled by specific cultural and social norms. They traveled within the same geographical and ideological space framed by revolutionary structures between eastern Laos and northern Vietnam. These young boys and girls came from different provinces and various ethnic backgrounds but shared similar experiences of mobility, rupture, and change during a specific period of time. As such, they formed a distinct generation.

Even so, this generation of revolutionaries was not simply structured by unique institutions and events; its members also assigned meanings to such processes and responded in different ways to the proto-state apparatus's efforts to transform and to homogenize them as living subjects and as a category. Working through their life histories helped me to understand how they internalized and negotiated values and ideals of discipline, hard work, putting the collective before oneself, and social egalitarianism—taught by a wartime education system that was determined to turn them into exemplary citizens of the new socialist state. Phèt's life course is one of the diverse range of illustrations of this process that I collected.[14] She was an ethnic Triang businesswoman and lived in Vientiane. I had known her since the late 1990s and one evening had a lengthy conversation—lasting nearly four hours—with her at her house. The interview was somewhat impromptu—I had not requested it, but she knew I was interested in individuals with her profile, and that evening she decided she wanted to share her memories with me. What follows is a concise presentation of her life history.

Phèt was born in the mid-1950s into an impoverished peasant family in Sekong Province. She was recruited by Lao revolutionaries to go and study in northern Vietnam in 1967. She learned the Lao language in a boarding school for Lao pupils set up in Phú Thọ Province. Her days followed a strict routine alternating between classes (in Lao and Vietnamese) and physical activities. She especially enjoyed singing lessons, where she "could chant Vietnamese revolutionary songs endlessly." It was no ordinary schooling, though: US bombing interrupted her classes on several occasions. She remembered digging trenches with her classmates around the school and running to them during air raid alerts. Phèt was eventually sent back to Laos in 1972. She pursued her studies in Viang Xai, in Houaphan Province (where the Lao Communist Party's headquarters were established), and upon her graduation was sent to work in the Ministry of Agriculture. She liked then to take notes at each meeting, "otherwise how to remember everything that is said and then to be able to pass it on and to explain it to other people?" In general, Phèt "liked to study, write, and read."

After leaving the civil service a decade later, Phèt remained an active citizen; at the time of our interview in 2007, she was the head of the local Lao Women's Union branch and her urban village's Party secretary as well as a member of the war veterans' committee. She told me: "Someone who had never worked could not do this job. It takes organization, discipline, knowing what office hours are." She pointedly added that these civic works gained her "respect" (*khaolôp*) and "honor" (*kiat*), whereas presumably her current career as a saleswoman did not, or not to such an extent. Her social identity as a (former) civil servant educated in the communist educational system still deeply informed her behavior and sense of self even after she became a capitalist entrepreneur.

Although collective education did not have the same impact on all children (bitter memories and flight were not uncommon) and some ethnic minority groups benefitted more from it than others, communist ethnic policy in the countryside of eastern Laos during the war offered the path to social mobility to many people of diverse ethnic origins and often humble socioeconomic backgrounds, and thereby contributed to their integration into society and the new socialist state after the seizure of power by the Communists in 1975. Wars and revolutions par excellence bring about the kind of disruption that changes political orders and social relations. I align myself with the claim by anthropologist Stephen Lubkemann (2008, 1), according to which, "[R]ather than treating war as an 'event' that suspends all social processes, anthropologists should study the realization and transformation of social relations and cultural practices throughout conflict, investigating war as a transformative social condition and not simply as a political struggle conducted through organized violence."

I had the chance to meet the revolutionary cadre that recruited Phèt (i.e., her uncle). The study of his biographical life helped me to further understand the kind of social change that occurred in the uplands of Laos and, especially, the rise of a new citizenry during the war. Loung ("Uncle") Nyone, like his niece and recruit, Phèt, was an active member of the new social class born out of the struggle between "old regime" and "revolutionary" forces in the upland areas of Laos. He played an important role in the expansion of the communist movement and nascent administration in Sekong. He had been the province's first head of the Education Department and in charge of enrolling children during the war. I was introduced by Phèt's brother-in-law, who worked in the provincial cultural department, and recorded lengthy interviews (the first one in the company of Phèt's brother-in-law, thereafter on my own) over several visits at Loung Nyone's house in Lamam, Sekong's capital, in 2011 and 2012.

Loung Nyone was born in Ban Dakbong in Dakchung, the province's southeastern district bordering Vietnam. As he told me, his ancestors used to live in Vietnam and fled to Laos in order "to hide from the French." However, when they reached the other side of the mountains, they were unable to escape colonial rule; as a result, his eldest brother was forcibly enrolled as "the French's coolie" to work on road construction. Loung Nyone was too young to be recruited as forced labor; he joined the Communist movement instead. In the aftermath of World War II, his village was among the first in the district to be infiltrated by the Communists: "We were the first to leave," he claimed, "first in joining the revolution, first in getting into the literacy campaign, before all the other villages." The Communists found in Loung Nyone an individual who was predisposed to change. Growing up in a family that "had nothing," he wanted "to study and to learn." He himself became a teacher after the 1954 Geneva Accords. In the following years his trajectory shadowed that of thousands of other communist recruits.

During the war years, he implemented an intensive period of "mobilization" (*ladôm*), drafting children into the revolutionary movement: "If you stay with your fathers and mothers, your life will never change, you'll stay ignorant." He was persuasive (in his view) because he himself "sacrificed" his family, "left" his village and "moved around"; in brief, he had paid a high personal cost for the cause of the revolution. In reality, only poor households agreed to let their offspring depart, owing to their destitute situation. It happened that some children left without their parents' consent. "For that, I was accused of being a bad person." But Loung Nyone did not express any regret during our conversations, as he firmly believed that parents were ill informed of the benefits of education: "They were ignorant," he said bluntly, and added "for me, my principle is that if you have no education, if you can't read, you can't understand, you can't do anything." Loung Nyone believed in the morality of his ideas and actions.

Not only did Loung Nyone believe in personal development and emancipation through formal education, he fiercely campaigned during the war to lift the people of his home and neighboring districts out of what he called the "slavery system" (*labôp khathat*):

It is I who abolished the rites and customs. At each violent death (*tai houng*), the whole family used to give up everything, house, cattle. Everything! They went into the forest for a year. Then after

one year they were allowed to build a house on the edge of the village, and after two or three months they were allowed to go back
in the village. No more taboo! (*Bo hai khalam!*) I imposed an end
to the taboos in ten villages, to the point of making my mother
cry. [. . .] The taboos harmed the economy, the villages' production. [Faced with the elders' opposition] we explained the reasons, they didn't understand. But we didn't force them. [. . .] My
mother cried and lamented: "That, we cannot, that we cannot
either. We cannot do anything." We followed the way of solidarity
(*néo thang samakhi*). The disputes and conflicts were over, because
we followed the path of the Party-State.

Neither his mother's tears nor the elders' resistance made Loung
Nyone flinch. He soldiered on, applying the "political theory" (*thitsadi
kanmuang*) he learned during his two-year studies in Hanoi in 1964
and 1965. His resolve undeniably grew out of his ideological training,
yet his own personal experience might also have motivated his aver-
sion to certain of his people's customs: "We kept killing one another,
like my father's brothers [. . .] by ignorance, because of backward customs. [. . .] We killed people to pour their blood on the land so that we
could obtain a good harvest." He thus welcomed the decision by the
Communists when they "ordered an end to these disputes, to intervil-
lage wars and interclan massacres."

Loung Nyone acquired an education and new knowledge, became
modern, and turned his back on and fought against some of what he
perceived as his people's regressive and harmful traditions (though
often at great cost to people's cultures and livelihoods). Armed with a
deep belief in his revolutionary task, he also strove to enlighten—as he
saw it—children of ethnic minority origins (even against their parents'
will); in brief, he became an active citizen and a committed leader in
the new revolutionary, then socialist, state. In a sense, Loung Nyone's
citizenship goes back to Aristotle's definition of the concept, which was
that citizenship is less a matter of legal contract than of political action
(Leydet 2017).

Yet, he maintained his ethnicity. He could speak fluently (and sing
in) Triang language. He married three of his four daughters—all to
ethnic Lao men—according to "Triang rituals" because "the weddings
were organized in [his] house."[15] He still owed money at the time of
our conversations for the purchase of two cows and one buffalo on the

occasion of his youngest daughter's marriage.[16] During one interview, he expressed a request to "be buried beside his wife" and a wish to have his funeral follow Triang rites. In a way, as he became a loyal citizen of the new State of Laos, Loung Nyone discovered for himself a different way of being Triang.

Longue Durée and Social-Anthropological Perspectives

I continued to explore the social dimensions of war when my fieldwork in the eastern regions of Savannakhet Province followed a new track in the form of research on the Lao-Vietnamese borderlands in the early 2010s. During my investigation into combatants' and civilians' experiences of the conflict, I became intrigued by a puzzling fact. I collected statistical data on civil servants, including teachers, in Sepon District, and found that a disproportionate number (over 50 percent) of administration and school personnel belonged to one ethnic group (the Phouthai), despite the fact that this group constituted barely 30 percent of the population. The Brou (a highland people found on both sides of the Lao-Vietnamese border)—who formed the large majority in this district—contributed only 10 percent of the teachers, despite having been recruited in larger numbers than the Phouthai (a sedentary ethnic group settled in the plains and the foothills of Sepon) by the revolutionaries in pursuit of their state-building project.

I drew on a combination of materials to find out the cause of this imbalance. I interviewed some fifty teachers of Phouthai and Brou ethnic origins, who were trained during and/or in the aftermath of the Vietnam War, in Sepon in 2010. In addition to oral sources and fieldwork materials, I studied French colonial archives. Indeed, to attribute the emergence in Sepon of a state structure in the aftermath of the Communists' victory solely to the revolutionary movement was to overlook two important interdependent factors, namely, the spatial organization that pre-dated the birth of modern nation-states and the social and political dynamics that ran through it.

In the seventeenth century (according to village chronicles), in exchange for their support, the king of Vientiane assigned the Phouthai of eastern Savannakhet to rule over the territories of "*Muong*[17] Tchépone, *Muong* Vang, *Muong* Phong, and *Muong* Champhone," covering a relatively large zone of present-day Savannakhet Province.[18] The relationship between the king of Vientiane and Phouthai "notables" or "district chiefs" (*chao muang*) followed the same ruling arrangement found elsewhere in Southeast Asia whereby a central and distant ruler passed on his authority to local chiefs in return for keeping more remote regions within his kingdom's orbit.[19] Subsequently, the Phouthai *muang* were conveniently used as a buffer zone by the kingdom of Siam and the Viêt state in the aftermath of their confrontation in the mid nineteenth century, a state of affairs that lasted until the arrival of the French in the late nineteenth century.[20]

French colonial rulers did not make substantial changes to the boundaries of the preexisting Phouthai *muang*. On the contrary, they reinforced at least some of these administrative units in the first half of the twentieth century by locating minor military-administrative bases and schools at their center. The nascent Lao Communist party subsequently relied on these proto-state structures and the people they produced to launch its process of political and social transformation in the Sepon border region and beyond (Pholsena 2018).

During my interviews with teachers in Sepon, especially those of Phouthai ethnicity, one name in particular often came up. Born in Ban Nayôm (in the present-day district of Vilabouli) in the early 1940s, Ajarn ("Professor") Bouasone was a Phouthai teacher and recruiting agent in Sepon during the war. I met him in 2010 at the large compound he had built a few kilometers away from Savannakhet town, where he let his son run a restaurant and a complex of bungalows. His village was among the few to have had a primary school in the colonial era. In 1961—"the Liberation year"—he obtained his qualification as a primary school teacher and was recruited as a traveling instructor by the Lao Communists. He was very active from the mid 1960s to the late 1970s, enrolling many children (most of whom were Phouthai) in the revolutionary movement. He proudly listed for me individuals among his former students who were now "important people" (*phounyai*),[21] that is, influential people. He himself was formerly the deputy director of the provincial cultural department.

The life history of such "revolutionary teachers," supplemented with archival sources, helped me to understand the significance of the bridging role (between the French and the communist regimes) performed by some Phouthai. Bouasone belonged to an "in-between generation," educated in the colonial school system only to serve a revolutionary movement less than a decade later. In an area where the process of state formation was still uneven, individuals—such as Bouasone—who were mobilized by and served the new political authority during the war in the "liberated" zones were able to influence, at the micro level and within their limited capacity, the composition of the state and its hierarchy to the benefit of fellow members of their ethnic group, resulting in their enhanced social mobility in Sepon.

Historian Katherine Bowie (2018, 873) writes: "Oral histories can do more than 'fill in the gaps.' By bringing in new voices, they can bring us closer to history as it actually happened. They also have the power to challenge prevailing historical paradigms, thereby making history that much more accurate and more democratic." Although it had a huge impact on their minds and bodies, the Vietnam War did not reduce Phouthai (and Brou) populations to being solely passive victims of violence, which is how peoples who lived in these strategic border areas during the conflict have been commonly portrayed—as simply being in the wrong place at the wrong time.[22] Rather, these peoples were also actors in the multilayered history of the region. The Phouthai and the Brou participated in different ways, either voluntarily or unwillingly, in a process of mutual appropriation involving external powers and local actors. During the Indochina Wars, significant numbers of Phouthai and Brou people contributed to the construction of the revolutionary state (through education and/or the army). In turn, the Phouthai benefitted from social mobility, forming an elite that emerged in the aftermath of the war as a new social class of leading civil servants in Sepon.

In contrast, members of the postwar Brou elite have attained a different kind of social status. Thanks in part to their long-practiced mobility,[23] cross-border kinship relationships, and linguistic skills (Lao and Vietnamese) as well as to their accumulation during and after the war of social and political capital, they hold the position of brokers for the contemporary Lao and Vietnamese states in this borderland area.[24] They are able to cross ethnic borders, that is, to communicate and to forge links with members of other ethnic groups (including Lao and Vietnamese state officials), drawing their authority and legitimacy from knowledge, skills, and practices, some of which were acquired outside their group during the war while others have been transmitted and learned over generations within their community (Pholsena 2017a).

Without underestimating their impacts, wars cannot account for *all* changes. Social historian Natalie Z. Davis's (1981, 274) incisive remarks on the contribution of anthropology to historical research come to mind: "Markets do not always drive out gifts, centers do not always eliminate particular localities, and history does not always replace myth. Anthropology can widen the possibilities, can help us take off our blinders, and give us a new place from which to view the past and discover the strange and surprising in the familiar landscape of historical texts." When central powers impose (or try to impose) their rule on—from their perspective—peripheral areas such as borderlands, they do not operate on "empty" territory but, to the contrary, must negotiate with preexisting social categories and relationships of authority and power which, far from dissolving with the penetration of the modern state and the imposition of territorial borders, adjust to the new context.

Concluding Remarks

In my research journey into the Vietnam War in the borderlands of central and southern Laos, I endeavored to learn more about and understand better the complex interactions between individual experience and historical change, identity, and social transformation. When the narrative allowed it, I would strive to make Portelli's (1997, 6) connection "between biography and history, between individual experience and the transformation of society."[25] Improperly contextualized, stories of ordinary people about their past stand in danger of remaining just that: stories. To become something more, life stories have to be situated in the wider world of complex social processes that give them greater meaning (Behar 1990, 227). When Khamla spoke bitterly of her friends' dismissive remarks, this both reflected her view on her personal situation and was also her comment on the experience of a minority female combatant. The emotions felt and expressed by Khamla in that interview were as much triggered by her friends' insensitive attitude as by her reflection on lost opportunities promised by the revolution, compounded by the awareness that she was an actor in that history.

I used the life history approach to confront what Medick (1987, 76) has identified as "A fundamental methodological difficulty [in social history research] [that is,] how is it possible to comprehend and to present the dual constitution of historical processes [. . .] the complex interdependence of encompassing structures and the agency of 'subjects'?" I tussled with this question during my investigation into the social history of the war and revolution. In the end, in the same way that I did not consider these men and women as passive subjects of social engineering, I did not view the revolutionary state as only a military-bureaucratic organization. It also existed through cultural and social practices, which were internalized to varying degrees and reproduced in various ways by its "subjects." Indeed, between those who returned to their villages at the end of the war, weary of "a lifetime of war," and those who were "happy to live with the State, in the hands of the State, with the Party-State," little was shared except the—yet unique—experiences and memories of the revolutionary educational system (Pholsena 2017b, 128).

In parallel, with the aid of social anthropology perspectives, I explored a perplexing legacy of the war and the revolution in the borderland district of Sepon. I relied on a combination of materials and methods to carry out this research, as I needed a diversity of data and methods to grasp the issue: archival sources and oral traditions to attain a critical *longue durée* perspective, statistical data to obtain a view of parts of the state, and life histories to enrich archival sources and to put individuals and groups back into the history of the region. A closer look into the structures of power and social relations before the modern period in this small (yet culturally and linguistically diverse) area contributed to my understanding of the roots of the present-day social hierarchy between the Phouthai—who dominate the local administrative and political apparatus—and the Brou—who despite their lower social position are nonetheless more competent in negotiating with state regimes across the Lao-Vietnamese border. "History," as Sherry Ortner (1984, 159) reminds us, "is not simply something that happens to people, but something they make."

Notes

1. I would like to thank Jean Michaud, Pierre Petit, and Sarah Turner for their insightful comments. All views and errors are mine.

2. The deadliest period of the Second Indochina War (1964–1975) for the local populations began in the mid-1960s with the process of "escalation" as the United States poured in aid to support the Republic of Vietnam (RVN) in the south of Vietnam. The insurgent communist movement in South Vietnam was supplied with men and materials from the DRV along the Ho Chi Minh Trail, a network of interlocking foot paths, roads, and rivers that was set up by the DRV army to circumvent the Demilitarized Zone (DMZ) dividing the north from the south of Vietnam. By mid-1964, the US administration was convinced that sustained bombing attacks directed against the HCMT in Laos and at key targets in the north of Vietnam might stop communist supplies flowing into the south of Vietnam from the north

and thus give the RVN time to stabilize politically and gradually gain control of its provinces. In December 1964, the US Air Force launched airstrikes throughout eastern Laos, expanding in April 1965 to a day-and-night air campaign that lasted for nine years. As a result, Laos became the most heavily bombed country per capita in history.

3. This mass organization is now called the Lao Front for National Development.

4. The Mon-Khmer speaking Brou Makong peoples were estimated to account for 2.5 percent of the total population in Laos in 2015—that is, 163,285 people (Lao Statistics Bureau 2015, 121).

5. I know few high-ranking officials who would agree to travel on a passenger bus with a student.

6. My family left Laos in the aftermath of the 1975 communist takeover when I was a toddler, and until the start of my fieldwork, I had spent virtually my entire life in France.

7. History must be "correct" in Laos—that is, it must legitimize the leadership's rule and, as always in the case of communist states, must also follow the single party-state's vision. The state printing press continues to churn out memoirs of Party leaders and histories of Laos as well as of "heroic" provinces (those that fought the toughest battles against the "enemy" and subsequently suffered the most, for example, Houaphan and Xieng Khouang in the north, or Saravan/Sekong in the south), all of which follow the same underlying pattern: the celebration of the party-state's righteous guidance that led to the liberation of the Lao people from "colonial tyranny" (the French) and then the "imperialist forces" (the Americans) thirty years ago (though amid the political rhetoric, valuable historical information can also be found).

8. A more expanded version of the life stories of Manivanh and Khamla can be found in my book chapter titled "'Minority' Women and the Revolution in the Highlands of Laos: Two Narratives" (Pholsena 2013).

9. In addition, I do not have apparently "typical" Lao facial traits (whatever these might be), as I have been told many times in Laos, which probably deepened my "alien-ness."

10. The Lao Communist movement's headquarters were located in Houaphan Province (formerly called Sam Neua), in northeastern Laos. Many Lao revolutionary cadres were sent during and after the war to the DRV for political and ideological training.

11. The government sold houses located in downtown Savannakhet (some of which had been abandoned by their owners, who fled the country

in the aftermath of the Pathet Lao's victory) to highly deserving war veterans at a low price.

12. See, for example, Pholsena (2010).

13. My reflection on this issue was stimulated by social history works on former Central and Eastern European communist regimes and societies; see, for instance, Kott (2001) and Christian and Droit (2005).

14. I use a pseudonym.

15. His eldest daughter's wedding followed the rituals of her husband's religion (Buddhism) as they got married in Saravane, Sekong's neighboring province.

16. According to Loung Nyone's ideological beliefs, indebtedness should disqualify a Triang wedding as a "wasteful and nonproductive" tradition. His personal support of a Triang wedding for his daughter, however, clearly shows that gaps exist between ideology and its practice, even among the most committed political citizens.

17. The term *muang* (sometimes written *Muong*) historically refers to the highly variable political and geographic entity based on a hierarchical sociopolitical structure dominated by the Tai. Tai peoples are the speakers of the languages in the Tai branch of the Tai-Kadai language family. They are spread throughout southwestern China and mainland Southeast Asia, with some inhabiting parts of northeast India.

18. These village chronicles were in the possession of the Phouthai chiefs of "Muang Tchépone" and "Muang Vang," according to M. Damprun (1904, 61–62), a colonial administrator in Savannakhet who drew on these chronicles to write the history of the province.

19. See, for example, Bouté (2011), Davis (2011), Le Failler (2011), and Tappe (2015).

20. Following the uprising of Chao Anu (the last king of Vientiane, 1805–1828) against Bangkok in 1827 and his subsequent defeat, Siam launched raids into Lao territories on the eastern bank of the Mekong as well as into the western and central parts of the Plain of Jars (in the present-day province of Xieng Khouang in northeastern Laos). The Siamese army's incursions accelerated the (formal) incorporation into the Vietnamese administration of the border areas along the Annamite Chain, including most of present-day Savannakhet Province, except for the westernmost districts located along the Mekong (Nguyễn 1997, 158, 161–162).

21. A Lao term that literally means "important people."

22. See Hickey (1982), Christie (1996), and Salemink (2003).

23. For centuries, the highland peoples have been moving back and forth across political boundaries between "Laos"and "Vietnam," fleeing warfare, looking for land, avoiding taxes, escaping from harsh living conditions, or seeking a better livelihood, or simply for trading and visiting relatives (see Vargyas 2000).

24. Many Brou served in the Pathet Lao military forces and the People's Army of Vietnam, for example.

25. Indeed, I had to accept at times that not everyone had something meaningful to say and not all discourses yielded insights into the contexts and processes of which they were a part.

References

Behar, Ruth. 1990. "Rage and Redemption: Reading the Life Story of a Mexican Marketing Woman." *Feminist Studies* 16 (2): 223–258.

Bouté, Vanina. 2011. *En miroir du pouvoir: Les Phounoy du Nord Laos; Ethnogenèse et dynamiques d'intégration*. Paris: École française d'Extrême-Orient.

Bowie, Katherine A. 2018. "Palimpsets of the Past: Oral History and the Art of Pointillism." *Journal of Asian Studies* 77 (4): 855–877.

Bruner, Edward M. 1986. "Experience and Its Expressions." In *The Anthropology of Experience*, edited by V. W. Turner and E. M. Bruner, 3–30. Urbana: University of Illinois Press.

Bruner, Jérôme. 1991. "The Narrative Construction of Reality." *Critical Inquiry* 18 (1): 1–21.

Christian, Michel, and Emmanuel Droit. 2005. "Écrire l'histoire du communisme: L'histoire sociale de la RDA et de la Pologne et en France." *Genèse* 61: 118–133.

Christie, Clive J. 1996. *A Modern History of Southeast Asia: Decolonization, Nationalism, and Separatism*. London: I. B. Tauris Publishers.

Damprun, M. 1904. "Monographie de la province de Savannakhet (Laos Français)." *Bulletin de la Société des études indochinoises* 47: 19–71.

Davis, Bradley C. 2011. "Black Flag Rumors and the Black River Basin: Powerbrokers and the State in the Tonkin-China Borderlands." *Journal of Vietnamese Studies* 6 (2): 16–41.

Davis, Natalie Z. 1981. "Anthropology and History in the 1980s." *Journal of Interdisciplinary History* 12 (2): 267–275.

Frank, Geyla. 1995. "Anthropology and Individual Lives: The Story of the Life History and the History of the Life Story." Review of *Life Stories: The Creation of Coherence*, by Charlotte Linde; and *Storied Lives: The Cultural Politics of Self-Understanding*, by George C. Rosenwald and Richard L. Ochberg. *American Anthropologist* 97 (1): 145–148.

Hardy, Andrew. 2003. *Red Hills: Migrants and the State in the Highlands of Vietnam*. Honolulu: University of Hawai'i Press.

Hickey, Gerald Cannon. 1982. *Free in the Forest: Ethnohistory of the Vietnamese Central Highlands 1954–1976*. New Haven, CT: Yale University Press.

Khoo, Agnes. 2004. *Life as the River Flows: Women in the Malayan Anti-colonial Struggle*. Kuala Lumpur: Strategic Information and Research Development Centre (SIRD).

Kott, Sophie. 2001. *Le Communisme au quotidien: Les entreprises d'Etat dans la société est-allemande*. Paris: Belin.

Lanzona, Vina A. 2009. *Amazons of the Huk Rebellion: Gender, Sex, and Revolution in the Philippines*. Madison: University of Wisconsin Press.

Lao Statistics Bureau. 2015. *The 4th Population and Housing Census (PHC) 2015*. Vientiane: Ministry of Planning and Investment.

Le Failler, Philippe. 2011. "The Đèo Family of Lai Châu: Traditional Power and Unconventional Practices." *Journal of Vietnamese Studies* 6 (2): 42–67.

Leydet, Dominique. 2017. "Citizenship." In *The Stanford Encyclopedia of Philosophy (Fall 2017 Edition)*, edited by E. N. Zalta. https://plato.stanford.edu/archives/fall2017/entries/citizenship.

Lubkemann, Stephen C. 2008. *Culture in Chaos: An Anthropology of the Social Condition in War*. Chicago: University of Chicago Press.

Mannheim, Karl. 1952. "The Problem of Generations." In *Essays on the Sociology of Knowledge,* edited by P. Kecskemeti, 276–320. London: Routledge & Kegan Paul.

Medick, Hans. 1987. "'Missionaries in the Rowboat'? Ethnological Ways of Knowing as a Challenge to Social History." *Comparative Studies in Society and History* 29 (1): 76–98.

Nguyễn, Thế Anh. 1997. "Les conflits frontaliers entre le Viêt Nam et le Siam à propos du Laos au XIXe siècle." *Vietnam Review* 2: 154–172.

Okely, Judith. 1996. *Own and Other Cultures*. London: Routledge.

Ortner, Sherry. 1984. "Theory in Anthropology since the Sixties." *Comparative Studies in Society and History* 26 (1): 126–166.

Pennetier, Claude, and Bernard Pudal. 1996. "Écrire son autobiographie (les autobiographies communists d'institution, 1931–1939)." *Genèses* 23: 53–75.

Peschanski, Denis. 1992. "Les effets pervers." *Les Cahiers de l'IHTP* 21. http://ihtp2004-siteihtp2004.ihtp.cnrs.fr/spip.php?article231.

Pholsena, Vatthana. 2010. "Life under Bombing in Southeastern Laos (1964–1973): Through the Accounts of Survivors in Sepon." *European Journal of East Asian Studies* 9 (2): 267–290.

———. 2013. "'Minority' Women and the Revolution in the Highlands of Laos: Two Narratives." In *Women in Southeast Asian Nationalist*

Movements, edited by S. Blackburn and H. Ting, 198–225. Singapore: NUS Press.

———. 2017a. "Politics of Cross-Border Living in Southern Laos–Central Vietnam." In *Ethnic and Religious Identities and Integration in Southeast Asia,* edited by K. Gin Ooi and V. Grabowsky, 31–55. Chiang Mai: Silkworm Press.

———. 2017b. "War Generation: Youth Mobilization and Socialization in Revolutionary Laos." In *Changing Lives in Laos,* edited by V. Bouté and V. Pholsena, 109–134. Singapore: NUS Press.

———. 2018. "State Formation, Social Hierarchies, and Ethnic Dynamics: A Case from Upland Laos." *Ethnic and Racial Studies* 41 (7): 1294–1311.

Portelli, Alessandro. 1981. "The Peculiarities of Oral History." *History Workshop Journal* 12 (1): 96–107.

———. 1997. *The Battle of Valle Giulia: Oral History and the Art of Dialogue.* Madison: University of Wisconsin Press.

———. 2009. "Life after 30: Reflecting on 30 Years of the History Workshop." Johannesburg. Unpublished paper.

Quinn-Judge, Sophie. 2001. "Women in the Early Vietnamese Communist Movement: Sex, Lies, and Liberation." *South East Asia Research* 9 (3): 245–269.

Salemink, Oscar. 2003. *The Ethnography of Vietnam's Central Highlanders: A Historical Contextualisation, 1850–1990.* London: Routledge Curzon.

Tappe, Oliver. 2015. "A Frontier in the Frontier: Sociopolitical Dynamics and Colonial Administration in the Lao-Vietnamese Borderlands." *Asia Pacific Journal of Anthropology* 16 (4): 368–387.

Vargyas, Gábor. 2000. *A la recherche des Brou perdus, population montagnarde du Centre Indochinois.* Paris: Etudes Orientales/Olizane.

CHAPTER 9

Gathering Life Stories and Oral Traditions among the Na of Southwest China

Pascale-Marie Milan

DOING ANTHROPOLOGICAL RESEARCH with the Na people (Mosuo 摩梭 in Mandarin) comes with methodological challenges not only specific to the historical, sociocultural, and political contexts of China but also the anthropological knowledge we have of this ethnic group. Dealing with their identity means entering into a debate involving not only local history but also the history of the Chinese nation and the history of humankind (Harrell 2001, 216). Famous for their extreme matrilineal and matrilocal systems, the Na are one of the most ethnographically studied ethnic groups and have been popularized incorrectly in anthropological literature as *a society without fathers or husbands* (Cai 1997). Their most spectacular attributes have been a sexual custom where men visit women at night, an organization of relations between relatives in which the role of the maternal uncle replaces that of the biological father, and a transmission of property and filiation by women, among others. In the eyes of Chinese officials, the Na people are routinely depicted as a primitive and backward matriarchal society, a judgment fitting the ideologically evolutionist discourse on "minority nationalities" (*shaoshu minzu* 少数民族) within China (Yan and Song 1983; Zhan et al. 1980). The end result is a community seen as stable and almost immutable that glides through history sheltered from any influences, cultural contacts, or social changes—a portrait only made more blatant in this time of China's domestic tourist expansion.

Since the start of the political and economic liberalization of the late 1970s, tourism has become one of the main strategic tools used in China to "advance" remote regions and ethnic minorities living in southwest China. The 2000 Go West Campaign[1] carried with it a touristic strategy "coded in a modernist assimilationist state-oriented discourse" (Swain 2011, 177; see also Goodman 2002). Tourism expansion was part of an extensive market-oriented reshaping (Walsh 2005; Mattison 2010; Blumenfield 2014; Blumenfield et al. 2018; Milan 2019).

During the late 1990s, Lugu Lake, straddling the border between Sichuan and Yunnan (map 8), where a substantial part of the Na population lives, became a favorite destination for Chinese middle-class vacationers. Thousands started arriving by bus for two or three days to gaze at this beautiful "mountain and water landscape" (*shanshui* 山水), expecting a journey "to a simple and ancient self" (McKhann 2001, 36). As one of many consequences of this "friendly invasion," daily life for the hosts has taken two markedly strategic directions. Onstage, the Na people have come to publicly perform a version of self—conforming to Chinese narratives focused on their uniqueness—namely as a matriarchal society of titillatingly "loose women." Backstage, however, the Na congregate and work to instrumentalize the outside discourse on their identity with the aim of adjusting it to their own agenda and carving out a better place for themselves in the modernist politics of the state. Studying social change for my doctoral dissertation, one of the first things I observed about the Na was these surprisingly different perspectives than those given in previous anthropological studies. A challenge no doubt, but also an opportunity for a young scholar to assert a distinct voice. Accordingly, this chapter deals with the methodological questions I faced and the ethical choices I had to make during my eleven months of fieldwork between 2012 and 2014. Detailing the onstage and backstage narratives will first help to convey the issues at stake. I will argue for an emic account of indigenous conceptualizations of ordinary life, life narratives, and memories by framing these against the Chinese hegemonic discourse on history, but also against some earlier anthropological investigations as well.[2] In doing so, I will discuss how my positionality allowed me to access the backstage, particularly in connection with the tourism industry. Finally, I will show how the Na categorize and conceptualize history, and I will advocate for a pluralism of voices to account for a micro-history from below.

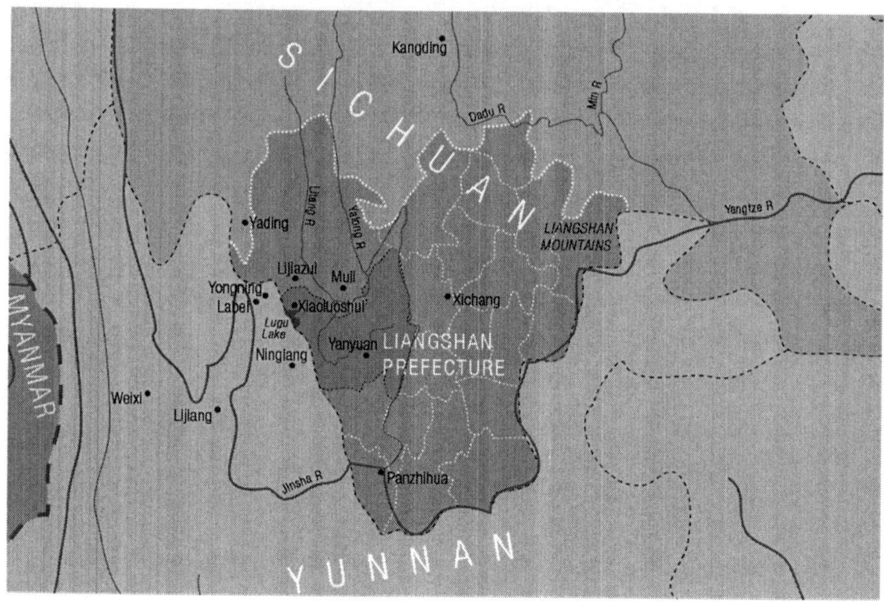

Map 8. Lugu Lake and the region inhabited by the Na and the two villages of ethnographic investigation, Lijiazui and Xiaoluoshui. (Source: P.-M. Milan 2016, 30; Design: H. Da Silva; © P.-M. Milan)

Onstage versus Backstage: A Touristic Effect

Tourism in Lugu Lake started in the 1990s and has steadily expanded since. Its development has relied on selling Na culture as a local renewable resource of sorts. Top-down state labeling carefully directed the Chinese urban market to focus on a fantastical take on matriarchy that paints the Na as living fossils, while on the ground, their exotic—and eroticized—gendered practices were put at the core of the sale of their culture (Walsh 2005). Of particular interest was the Na visiting system, by which men visit women at night to have intercourse, called *séssé* in the Na language (Narua)[3] and *zouhun* (走婚) in Mandarin. Tourists can also visit the "bridge of *zouhun*" (*zouhun qiao* 走婚桥), a bridge allegedly built, say the guides, by a Na lover to join his partners for the night. One can also find "*zouhun* rice alcohol" (*zouhun jiu* 走婚酒) and, in some food stalls, advertisements for sexual titillation by indicating the possibility for visiting (*zouhun*) opportunities (fig. 9.1).

Women are thought to be "freely available for sex, to whom present lovers have no future commitments, or of a land where women rule" (Walsh 2005, 450). These representations are embedded in a complex representational space endowed with the aura of a country composed of "women/ daughters" (*Nü'er guo* 女儿国), with hypothetical links to the historical Female Kingdom (Nü Guo 女国) in the fantasy novel by Wu Cheng'en, *The Journey to the West* (*Xi You Ji* 西游记) (Walsh 2005, 464–465). Others, such as Bai Hua's novel *The Remote Country of Women*,[4] feature an impossible love between a Han man and a Mosuo woman, a story that recasts the nature-culture divide and portrays the

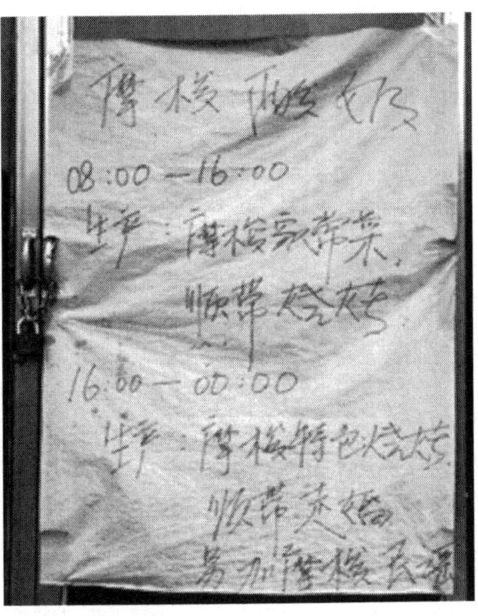

Figure 9.1. Front of a barbecue restaurant. It's written that *zouhun* is possible between 16:00 and 00:00 to lure the tourists (*shundai zouhun* 顺带 走婚). Lige, June 2011. © P.-M. Milan.

Na through their purity of feeling and innocence compared to the calculating and jealous Han (Harrell 2001, 251). To complete the picture of idyllic love, the work of the indigenous scholar Lamu Gatusa on Na folk stories, songs, and poetry has nurtured a romantic picture of men traveling on long-distance trading expeditions to the point that they "reenter the imaginary of the Mosuo as adventurers and seducers" (Walsh 2005, 466).

Such commodification of ethnic identity in China has routinely turned landscape, personhood, performance, and artifacts into something authentic and consequently, both tourists and Na engage in "mythical realities of the 'exotic others' [. . .] relationally constructed between the tourist and the toured, dictated by market forces, or defined by dominant cultural tropes and reaction to them" (Swain 2011, 174–175). The Na, who are not blind to the hegemonic discourse on their identity, engage in its commodification to fit the tourist gaze. Eager to transform both their economic and social conditions and to reverse the stigma of being "backward" (*luohou* 落后) and "primitive" (*yuanshi* 原始), to which state categorization and popular representations confine them, many consent to play into what tourists seek (see also Adams 1996).

Agency has enforced the compartmentalization of social and cultural visibility between onstage and backstage scenes (Walsh 2005; Milan 2019). Onstage, Na agents perform their identity through folk songs, discourse on the veracity of the sexual custom, the lack of fathers, etc. For tourists, these confirm Na "authenticity," and they feel that they are experiencing time travel with a living fossil society due to the supposed matriarchy of the Na. These speeches contrast sharply with backstage behavior or narratives. According to James C. Scott's understanding of subaltern mentality, "the open interaction between subordinates and those who dominate" are public transcripts (J. C. Scott 1992, 2). That is to say that the Na, who are considered to be at the bottom of the evolutionist ideology that shapes the Chinese conception of alterity, use conventional patterns of speech—i.e., folk songs, anthropological official discourse—for tourists who are mainly Han or urban Chinese. However, "discourse that takes place 'offstage,' beyond direct observation by powerholders" (J. C. Scott 1992, 4), is totally different. Here, Na agents calculate that the extra income can improve their "quality" (*suzhi* 素质) and help them climb the evolutionist scale to enter the same time period that the Han tourists live in (Milan 2012, 2013).

This strategic divide in the representation of self has entailed major challenges for me. Gathering meaningful ethnographic knowledge therefore became a methodological quandary, because if public transcripts (J. C. Scott 1992, 2006), enforced by metanarratives, are relatively easy to follow, the hidden transcript is much trickier to access. I will return to this problem later in this chapter.

Fitting In

Ethnographic work is constrained in China by the political dimension of research, political restrictions on certain subjects, limited access to data, regions closed to foreign researchers, and/or control of researchers' movements (Thurston and Pasternak 1983; Pieke 2000; Heimer and Thøgersen 2006; Hansen 2006; Bamo et al. 2011, Turner 2010, 2013b; J. Michaud 2013). In this context, reflexivity and flexibility can considerably improve one's immersion in the field (Turner 2010, 2013a).

Positionality helps to situate knowledge (Abu-Lughod 1991; Joan Scott 1991; Haraway 2007; Turner and Delisle this volume). This notion has been specifically conceptualized by feminist geographers (Rose 1997; Madge 1993; Sultana 2007). In research, this concept refers to the *position*, made of essentialist and reified images often shared culturally, that is assigned to a researcher and the *positioning* that a researcher undertakes by negotiating and adjusting to local categories in order to find their place. Awareness about one's positionality permits a reflexive reading of the self or multiple selves (Rose 1997; Madge 1993; Sultana 2007). Race, ethnicity, nationality, age, gender, economic and social status, sexuality, level of education, and even language skills and social class are all distinctive signs that the researcher must question to understand the way they are perceived locally (Madge 1993; Sultana 2007) as well as how they will perceive the local reality.

It can also include philosophical perspectives and ways of viewing the world, political leanings, and specific combinations of these, such as having the same gender and sense of humor as the informants but being very different in terms of ethnicity and social class. (Turner 2010, 126).

The local circulation of images of the Other via the internet and television or live through tourism made me seemingly fit into broad, essentialized categories: Western woman, tourist, student. During my first stay at Lugu Lake in 2007 in a village boasting tourist facilities, I was immediately directed to the most expensive guest house, where the owner also spoke fluent English. The bus driver's hasty conclusion that I was "just traveling" determined the economic categorization into which I was assigned, which undoubtedly emanated from my appearance. Because of my skin color and my light-colored eyes, I reflected the advertisements extolling the beauty of white skin. As soon as I presented myself as French, there was also a romantic cliché,[5] which was then added to the tenacious fantasy associated with loose sexuality. At the beginning of my fieldwork, despite my attempts to escape it, I remained confined to the tourist category. Reflecting on my situation, I saw how much Na people's representations reflected above all imaginings of social, cultural, and economic distinctions—much the same as the locals' own images were in the mind of Han tourists. We shared that.

To wiggle myself out of these categories, I moved to a less touristic settlement where the "head of one house" (*ddabu*) offered me to settle permanently. Yet, other stereotypes arose. The temporality of my ethnographic work did not overlap well with their time frame. Because of their tourism-oriented livelihoods, the household members had neither the time nor the inclination to answer the questions of this anthropologist, whose research seemed rather pointless. Even the term "anthropology" (*renleixue* 人类学) did not make any sense to them. I also did not want, however, to declare myself as an "ethnologist" (*minzuxue jia* 民族学家), because even though many scholars have conducted research in the area, I felt a level of distrust, which was certainly due to the historically political intentions that scholarly state agents had in the past (see Cai 1997). At most, I could be a student of culture and traditions eager to know more. To circumvent obstacles, it seemed opportune to deploy subtle strategies, tricks, and negotiations according to the position assigned to me and the positioning I wanted to have in order to access the depths of the hidden transcript.

Being a "single woman from elsewhere," to use Sabine Trebinjac's words (1995), was the element of an "atypical intrusion." My status and behavior were uncommon in the Lugu Lake communities and even among Na women. In a way, a foreign female ethnologist can be perceived of as "asexual," because I differed so much from local stereotypes (Trebinjac 1995; Smith 2006). But my age (in my thirties) and the fact that I did not yet have children were two signs that made Na women assume I could not bear a child, which did not help my integration into the community. The body, the ethnologist's "first [. . .] instrument" (Mauss 1934, 10), is fully engaged in the field (Conquergood 1991; Wacquant 1989).

Copying Joanne Smith's (2006) strategy among the Uyghurs, I nevertheless tried to blend into the local categories of gender as much as possible. I made myself useful, I contributed regularly to ordinary tasks, I cooked, I welcomed tourists into Na houses, and so on. With time and in spite of all the rest, this proactive strategy allowed me to build strong links with family members, villagers, and tour guides (fig. 9.2). I was even allowed to present myself under my hosting house name, which facilitated my integration into a network of relationships. I then negotiated my presence in a household of another nontouristic village (see next section). My hosts no longer considered me as a guest (*hinbbae*), allowing me to grasp and enter their daily lives and the components of their kinship including their reciprocity system (Milan 2016, 2019, 2021). Taking root in two Na houses opened the door to systems of kin and neighbors and to spending time in other related houses. I became so involved in this social network that, as Jean-Guy Goulet (2011, 117–120) put it, I had "the possibility of entering or believing in the world of the people [met] on the ground." And, as a woman positioned in this matrilineal society, women's voices concerning past narratives have become more audible. Indeed, past narratives paradoxically privilege the "men who know" too often (see also Fiskejö and Petit this volume).

Over the previous fifteen months, I had learned the Na language, having realized that this would go a long way in giving me (at least some) access into the hidden transcript. This strategy has significantly changed the direction of my fieldwork. I could reply that I am a "woman of the Na language" (*nya narua gunia niq*) instead of "that white woman over there."[6] Thanks to this new proximity, I was thereafter invited to Na houses—even if sometimes only for a fleeting encounter. In the remote village where women over forty had only vague notions of Chinese, they enjoyed conversing and teaching me more Narua. My interlocutors always took time to translate their speeches if they could, although they often felt it was meaningless. I was then able to manage daily conversation, but I was still limited when it came to following a conversation. The Na language has a particularity in which the tones and certain phoneme

Figure 9.2. Celebration of the author's birthday with the hosting family. The Na people are not used to celebrating their birthdays. Xiaoluoshui, July 2011. © P.-M. Milan.

agreements change from one sentence to another. Narua can indeed differ between villages and even between speakers of the same village. Faced with the disparity of the transcriptions, in-depth ethnolinguistic work would come to fill the oscillating anthropological interpretations and feed the rather recent linguistic studies (Lidz 2010; Dobbs and Yan 2018; A. Michaud 2018a, 2018b).

Methods

To pave the way for my potential research in the second location (the nontouristic village), I first visited with a Na man from a touristic village in order to assess the possibilities. This man, with whom I had already established a good relationship, told me that he knew people in this village from a particular household—let us call it A. The links he had with this household, however, were soon revealed to be in the realm of economic subordination, as was often the case between houses in touristic and nontouristic villages. His mother had employed a young girl from this household to handle tourist services. Consequently, even though he was helpful with interviewing house members about local traditions, I felt this location would not work, and I chose to live with another household instead. A few months later, when I thought that I had become sufficiently integrated into this village's life, I went back to A household to gently inquire about the feasibility of collecting songs from them, which they happily agreed to. Folk songs take many forms of oral tradition, including legends, tales, and myths, and they represent testimonies of the past enshrined in oral tradition. Sung in Na language, they offer a glimpse into their worldview, and these songs are particularly interesting in my case when referring to women. As I had done with many other households, I expressly asked this *ddabu* in Na language to share songs about the past. She readily accepted, and to my surprise, she launched into the following song:

> *O ne le jo a zu jo*—no translation available[7]
> *Mao zhu xi ne fanshen ni*—毛主席（让我们）翻身了[8]—Chairman
>   Mao emancipated [us].
> *aha bbala ma da ami*—[recurring narrative of songs]
> *Ba la ya aha a li li*—[recurring narrative of songs]
> *Mao zhu xi ne fan shen ni*—毛主席（让我们）翻身了—Chairman
>   Mao emancipated [us].

O kuo nimi tu nigu—He is like the sun to me.
aha bbala ma daa mi—[recurring narrative of songs]
Ba la ya aha a li li—[recurring narrative of songs]
Ama mo jo ta jo ke—没有妈妈—I don't have a mother.
Mao zhu xi la a ma ni—毛主席就是妈妈—Chairman Mao is
   [my] mother.
aha bbala ma da ami—[recurring narrative of songs]
Ba la ya aha a li li—[recurring narrative of songs]

Narua is a language prone to metaphor. There are various singing styles, but songs are usually performed between two singers or more so as to become a gentle joust. While many songs are well known to all, improvisation is a central element of performances. The one I had just heard blended praises to Mao Zedong with a traditional song, clearly suggesting that Mao had replaced the most important figure in Na worldview: the mother.

This song is exemplary of storytelling linked to the context of enunciation, for which the official discourse, the public transcript, has been playing an important part since the start of tourism expansion. Even though Mao is generally well liked by Na people because, as say they, he freed them from feudal servitude, an analysis of situated speech clearly suggests that this rendition tells more about the perception that the *ddabu* had of me than about Na history. With household A, I had not negotiated my position or participated in daily work. Caught in another web of relations, my positionality changed (Rose 1997; Turner and Delisle this volume). I felt mistrust on their part and thought of Trebinjac's (2000) work in Xinjiang documenting the alterations of folk songs to frame minority people as national subjects. Yet, Na songs are representative of indigenous beliefs and customs to the point that they are part of their consciousness of belonging to one another. This alteration by the *ddabu* singer underlines the extent to which some among the Na, as with other Chinese minority nationalities, either have allowed or even welcomed the dominant discourse into their own repertoire. Of course, their adoption of this discourse could also represent a front, a public transcript to mitigate the possible adverse effects of a meddling foreign ethnologist. This kind of distrust also appeared in the tourist context for other reasons.

One day in June 2012, while I was staying in Lugu Lake at a friend's house, I asked to record her thoughts on tourism and its connections to her own life story. By then, I knew she had married a man from

Guangzhou the year before, who first came to the lake as a tourist; nonetheless, as befits a "good" Na woman mindful of the official line, she said that she was practicing the sexual custom of men visiting women at night. As I quickly realized, this was a telling example of the bias automatically induced by the presence of a recording machine and, we could even add, by conversing in Chinese. Dominated subjects such as the Na, and Na women in particular, have no interest in publicly confronting the Chinese metanarrative that allows them to take advantage of tourism. Learning from this lesson in practicing infrapolitics among dominated societies, I thereafter conducted my interviews without a recorder. Conversations flowed more freely, and people seemed to be more outspoken about their lives and feelings. Interruptions often occurred, but these were accepted, as our chats might simply start on one day and end on another. With friendship as a method, "conversation, everyday involvement, compassion, generosity, and vulnerability" were part of ethnographic work (Tillman-Healy 2003, 735; Lentz, Turner and Delisle, Vargyas, Wang, this volume). I learned that this level of informality allowed me to collect fragments of subordinate discourse and, on occasion, enter the hidden transcript.

During evening dance performances for tourists, young Na girls were often harassed by disrespectful male guests asking if they practiced the visiting system and if there was a way they could take advantage of it. In reaction to such unwanted interactions, the girls had taken to mumbling in their language the term *makrajua*, equivalent to English slang for "shutting someone up," while simultaneously beaming a broad smile. Crossing the language barrier helped me tremendously in reaching a more in-depth understanding of the field through local voices. I had initially conducted most of my discussions in Putonghua, but, when possible, I prioritized gathering materials in their language, especially regarding oral traditions. I remembered how people were later surprised to hear me speaking their language, not to mention that I could present myself with my hosting house's name.

Linguistic skills helped me avoid simplistic or out-of-context interpretations. Together with a clear conscience of my own positionality, it made it possible to consider "the successive places and roles attributed to the observer, as well as the rhetorical strategies of the informants" (Bensa 2006, 34). This reflexivity enabled me to understand the power relations of tourism and more clearly distinguish between the public and hidden transcripts. These latter allowed for discerning the public roles played by the powerful and powerless and the mocking, vengeful tone displayed offstage (J. C. Scott 1992).

Fragments of Ama's Life Story and Accounts: Looking into Past Narratives

Let me bring Ama into this discussion. I collected her story in fragments, but whatever fragments she told me, her stories were meant to teach me more about the social environment and the Na people's worldview. For instance, telling me about her youth, Ama highlighted profound differences between the Na and the Nuosu. She might detail how the Na dressed differently from the Nuosu, who wore black felt cloaks and belts of cartridges, and how the Na were careful to not be confused with the Nuosu (see also Blumenfield 2014). Her accounts were never dated, however. She was only referring to her age, her family members that were alive, and to certain events without naming them. Knowing her astrological sign and elements of her story, I understood that she was talking about the "democratic reforms" (*minzhu gaige* 民主改革) period implemented across China's southwest in 1956–1957. Ama explained to me another time that she had been living in Luoshui, on the Lugu Lake shore, and relayed the harshness of life and the scarcity of food here. Such difficulties originated when villagers had to feed the Yongning/ Tusi/Chinese troops (she used these terms interchangeably). When recounting this story, she also contrasted the Nuosu with the Tibetan/ Lama people, whom they used to welcome into their home. In this way, she was in fact expressing how much the Na's tradition and ethnicity related more to the Tibetan people than to the Nuosu.

At the age of sixteen, following the death of her mother, Ama moved from Luoshui to her sister's house close to Yongning. Unexpectedly, she told me that her mother was *boa* (Pumi), even though she was normally referred to as Na or Mosuo. She then moved to the village of Xiaoluoshui when the "lord" (*sipi*) of Yongning gave land to drive out the Han and Naxi who had settled there earlier. The Naxi moved to Dazui, the neighboring village, because of the magnanimity of the rulers of Muli toward the Naxi. Ama then married a *Naxi daba*[9] "ritual specialist" of this village, but she did not go to live with him. Bringing together the elements she told me, I asked her if she was Na: *"No Na anié?" "*Yes, of course," she said. My question just did not correspond to her fluid categories nor to the official Chinese ones and even less to those of Western anthropologists.

This story raises important questions about ethnicity and social organization; for instance, the Na are matrilineal and the Pumi, patrilineal. This, however, is consistent with the adaptability of ethnicity described in southwest China by Western scholars (McKhann 1998; Harrell 2001; Gros 2014). When settling in a Na village, migrants were sharing in daily life, which bounded them together with cultural values, so that the "inside" (*awo*) has the power to incorporate the "outside" (*apo*). This dichotomy of Na cosmogony offers a glimpse into the everyday processes driving identity, ethnicity, and kinship issues.

Life stories share some conventional patterns of speech with oral traditions. When telling stories about the past, whether they are personal or collective memories, the Na use formulas highlighting the way they conceptualize the past. Ama, like others, was always using the term *eshae* or sometimes *eyi eshae* to refer to life stories, proverbs, tales, traditions, and even mythical narratives. Intertwining elements of (oral) "traditions" (*ddeelo*) and "narratives of the past" (*eshae khua*), she said that she was "telling stories (of the olden days)" (*eshae khua*). *Eshae* specifically refers to a bygone past and *eyi eshae* to an even more distant past, but these terms are used interchangeably. These rhetorical formulas were often punctuated by sentences like "this is how we say" or "my mother or grandmother told me the story like that." While expressing the power of memory the Na have developed, past accounts all bind historical material with the present day, conveying past actions and beliefs in the same way. As James C. Scott (2009, 230–231) argued, "Because oral traditions survive only through retelling, they accumulate interpretations as they are transmitted. Each telling forcibly reflects current interests, current power relations, and current views of neighboring societies and kin groups." Like Ama had told me that "telling stories about the past is useful today," many Na people also expressed to me how recounting these narratives represents a way to educate and remember "the moral and social teachings of the community" (Gatusa 2021), and to comment on social changes and continuities.

Life stories, including historical events, can become oral traditions because the rhetorical forms and terms people use to refer to both blur the distinction between the recent and very distant past. Although differences between myths, oral traditions, and life stories can be established through anthropological work—and myths are clearly tied to *daba* rituals—the retelling movements of Na oral transmission amounts to a mythologizing process. Notwithstanding their tremendous diversity, oral traditions share recognizable elements of social organization with life stories, such as why people get married or how they settle and "divide houses" (*zitu*). Whatever the stories are, they include the socio-spatial environment and remarkably, they follow a mythological template by borrowing some elements like a flood, mountains (seen as deities), sky (seen as a divine house of a mythical heroine), food shortages, and so on.

However, as acts of situated speech emanating from different informational processes, these accounts were changing due to environmental differences between villages. So, people were largely telling the same stories, not to mention their tendency to mix genres. I was a little baffled. Their way of referring to the past did not fit my classification schema. The Na case clearly blurred the distinction that Jan Vansina (1985) made between oral tradition and oral history. The former would correspond to accounts that are not contemporary with the informants and that were transmitted by word of mouth before their birth. The latter would consist of eyewitness accounts of more contemporary events. However, the plurality of voices made it possible to learn another insight about the past—a localized, embodied one that is linked to the present-day.

As noted above, Ama's accounts were never dated. Only the temporal fragments such as her age, family members, and so on that she slipped into her story allowed me to track the account. All the life stories I collected were conveyed similarly, as were the oral traditions too. Both resemble a genealogical thought regime, shared by many ethnic groups throughout the Sino-Tibetan borderlands (Gros 2014; Harrell 2011; Wellens 2012). Often orally transmitted, this regime is an important part of the Na people's lives that can be understood "in terms of kinship and a sacred geography (the souls of the deceased reverse the migratory routes to return to the land of the ancestors)" (fig 9.3) (Gros 2014, 85; see also Rock 1955; Mathieu 1998, 2003; McKhann 2003, 2012; Chen 2012). *Daba* specialists use this knowledge together with household members to lead rituals for which migration routes are needed (see Mathieu 1998; Chen 2012). Depending on lineage, household, and village, these migratory routes do not lead to the same ancestral land. How then can the Na be related to the ancient Qiang tribes, as suggested by the official metanarratives, if not to construct a history of common belonging for the nation-building process?

Unlike genealogical narratives, the historical ones used in the official discourse are dated and chronologically oriented. They suggest an "othering" process by fixing identity through time (see Wang, this volume). Through a shared interest for origins that the state has with

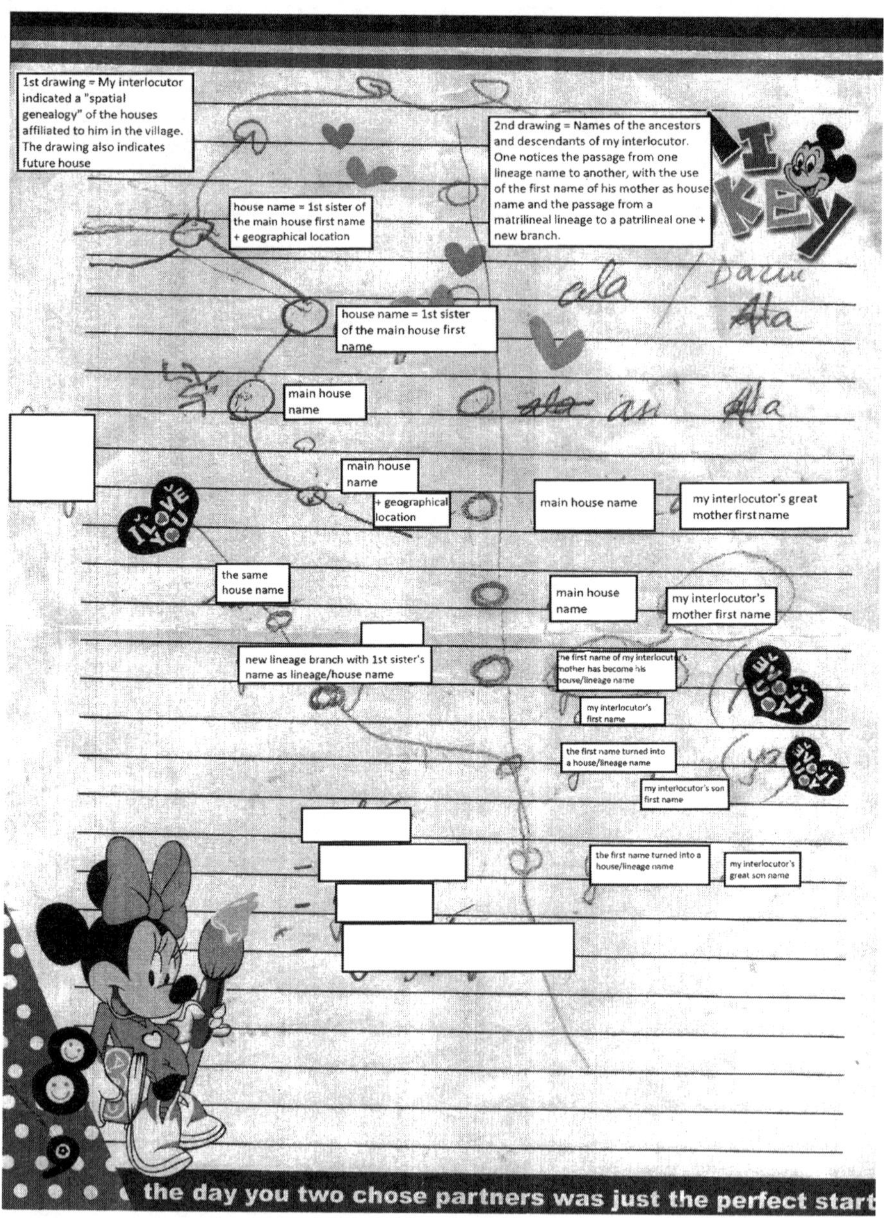

Figure 9.3. An unexpected drawing from an interlocutor presenting a "spatial genealogy" of the lineage's houses and a secondary lineage. My interlocutor wanted to explain the lineage and house name change. It is interesting to note that the lineage became patrilineal after the departure of the female ancestor from her native house. Notes are from the author (June 2014). Blanks and explanations are used to preserve anonymity. © P.-M. Milan.

minority groups, the Chinese government built a "unity of the past" that invokes a common ancestry and close historical ties to the nation (Gros 2014). For instance, the Na located in the Sichuan province are officially labeled as Mongol,[10] and many locals tell stories that connect this official discourse with their mythology (fig. 9.4) (see Harrell 2001, 216–

Figure 9.4. A Na interlocutor from Sichuan Province presenting a portrait of Nabuhra, "the uncle of all Na." This "ancestor" was indifferently identified as Kublai Khan or Genghis Khan by my interlocutors. A portrait was offered to all villagers by a Han tourism entrepreneur who regularly visited the village. Lijiazui, December 2012. © P.-M. Milan.

238; Wellens 2012, 315–316). The Na were either related to the ancient Female Kingdom or to the ancient Qiang—two versions of history that, in any case, incorporate local identities into the national discourse on China's origin and historical development. As Wang (1999, this volume) has noted, Qiang ethnic identity is a "superimposed category" resulting from distinct historical processes, which cannot be restricted to the current ethnic label. Understandably, researchers are very careful with any links made between the Tibeto-Burman language groups and the ancient Qiang (Mathieu 2003; Wellens 2012; Gros 2014).

Despite all my efforts to research how the Na deal with the past, I have not yet been able to feel how much history is embodied in their present life. Every Na individual knows their genealogy and thus knows how to identify ancestors. They perform this knowledge every day by feeding these ancestors on the fire where they cook. They feed the departed ones before they feed themselves, protecting them from evil spirits just as they protect themselves. Dealing with the Na's past may thus reflect E. Valentine Daniel's (1996, 50) distinction between myth and history, with the former encompassing a way of being and seeing and the latter representing only a way of seeing. I am acutely aware that the anthropological knowledge that I have produced is eminently situated, and that it reveals only a tiny part of Na worldview. At most, I can restore significant wording and motifs that allow me to capture fragments of the ways the Na conceptualize the past, report on the topics they discuss, grasp more important historical events intertwined with their personal and family histories, and perceive traces of an history of their own among the different types of narratives they use.

Nevertheless, all the stories they told me were the usual community teaching that allowed me to circumvent the touristic discourse depicting the Na as a matriarchal society without fathers or husbands and composed of idyllic lovers. While always considering my positionality, the details I recorded have widened my view of Na social organization and kinship. By participating in everyday life and listening to what people shared, I gathered nuanced narratives about Na kinship in their own language. For instance, people would talk more about their "house" (*awo*) and their belonging to it rather than to the "family" or "household" (*yidu*), which was previously recorded as the basic social unit (Zhan et al. 1980; Yan and Song 1983; Shih 2010). I was able to go further than Weng (1993) on the symbolic importance of the mother's house or Shih (2010) in highlighting the house (*awo*) rather than the *yidu* through everyday language (Milan 2016, 2021). I argue for the existence of various strategies, such as marriage or adoption, to continue the houses and thus the necessity to consider it as a rather efficient kinship group (see fig. 9.3) (Milan 2016, 2019, 2021).

However, one thing is certain: Chinese metanarratives used in tourism are increasingly intruding in everyday life. The Na's limited room to maneuver and the acceptance of tourism development is changing their self-perception, and their singular voices have become inaudible. Modernity and new livelihood opportunities call on the youngest Na to adopt new lifestyles and to express themselves in Chinese instead of Narua. In this context, advocating for a pragmatic approach that considers all versions of past stories—specific to localities and to speakers—would engender profound anthropological understandings and is of utmost necessity.

Conclusion

By reflecting on my positionality, I can clearly highlight how my informal approach for gathering life stories proved to be more than just an improved method for documenting the past accounts of an oral society without writing. Given the tourism situation and the historical paradigm characterizing the Na in China as primitive and backward, many Na individuals are cautious with public speech. The reflexivity I practiced to find a place from which I could research helped me access the backstage of tourism as well as the hidden transcripts untold in tourism interactions. Depending on the links I had developed with my interlocutors, the conditions and contexts of this narrative mattered. Speech is situated.

The Na people are dominated subjects caught in the race toward development and modernization, and their silenced stories matter. Even if they do not fit the researcher's usual categories, these stories, and the ways they are told, help paint canvases of meaning while also avoiding the oversimplification of Na social organization. Importantly, paying attention to local voices helps to recognize their agency instead of their inability and/or lack of opportunity to record their accounts of the past in writing; a local focus also acknowledges the Na as actors in their own lives (J. C. Scott 2009). Above all, attention to Na people's narratives allows one to recapture a past to which a collective or singular subjects belong. Lived experiences, including family/lineage lore, are not written down in historical records, but they help seize the (dis)continuity in history that the Na underwent. Further research would facilitate an understanding of history as marked, interspersed, and even dislocated by the tense environment of the Maoist era. Instead of turning them into characters of a nation-building process that promotes metanarratives about their past, I advocate for a pluralization of Na people's voices to build a microhistory that can (hopefully) account for their worldview.

Notes

1. China's western development program *(xibu dakaifa)* contains a variety of strategies to be implemented over a ten-year period.

2. My thesis takes issue with the idea of a society without fathers or husbands and draws on other more recent research that shows the Na's agency in tourism (Walsh 2001), facing media representations (Blumenfield 2010, 2014), and transformations due to economic growth (Mattison 2010), while also discussing work about kinship that highlights the household as a basic social unit (Shih 2010) and analyzing its symbolism (Weng 1993).

3. Unless specified, romanized *narua* terms are written according to the recent dictionary made by Alexis Michaud (2018a) and Roselle Dobbs and Xiong Yan's orthography system (2018).

4. *Yuanfang you yi ge nü'er guo* 远方有一个女儿国, translated into English in 1994.

5. France was associated with the term "romantic" (*langman* 浪漫).

6. They use the ungracious term *boshe*, referring to the white flesh of pigs, which is a historical formula similar to the Chinese one used to name a "foreigner" (*yangguizi* 洋鬼子).

7. The meaning of the terms used is too ambiguous, and I have no comment on the meaning. I therefore prefer not to translate this sentence.

8. Only some verses have been translated into Chinese. However, other translations are within my linguistic competence. When Na terms are sung, they are not written according to A. Michaud's (2018a) dictionary.

9. I refer to *daba* (also written *ddabe*) instead of *dongba*, since she told me that he was a *daba*. The *daba* are specialists in Na rituals, while the *dongba* are specialists in Naxi rituals. This blurring of conceptions is useful in understanding how ethnic boundaries are contingent and religious categories are confused.

10. In the Yunnan province they are officially a Naxi branch but identified since the 1980s as Mosuo ren (摩梭人).

References

Abu-Lughod, Lila, 1991. "Writing against Culture." In *Recapturing Anthropology: Working in the Present*, edited by R. G. Fox, 466–479. Santa Fe: School of American Research Press.

Adams, Vincanne, 1996. *Tigers of the Snow and Other Virtual Sherpas: An Ethnography of Himalayan Encounters*. Princeton, NJ: Princeton University Press.

Bamo Ayi, Stevan Harrell, and Ma Lunzy. 2011. *Fieldwork Connections: The Fabric of Ethnographic Collaboration in China and America*. Seattle: University of Washington Press.

Bensa, Alban. 2006. *La fin de l'exotisme: Essais d'anthropologie critique*. Toulouse: Anacharsis.

Blumenfield, Tami. 2010. "Scenes from Yongning: Media Creation in China's Na Villages." PhD diss., University of Washington.

———. 2014. "Resilience in Mountainous Southwest China: Adopting a Socio-ecological Approach to Community Change." *Cahiers d'Extrême-Asie* 23: 281–300.

Blumenfield, Tami, Chun-Yi Sum, Mary K. Shenk, and Siobhan M. Mattison. 2018. "Poverty Alleviation and Mobility in Southwest China: Examining Effects of Market Transition and State Policies in Mosuo Communities." *Urban Anthropology* 47 (3–4): 259–299.

Cai, Hua. 1997. *Une société sans père ni mari: Les Na de Chine*. Paris: Presses universitaires de France.

Chen, Jin. 2012. "Le rivile Na: Étude des chants et rituels des Daba (Sichuan et Yunnan, Chine)." PhD diss., EHESS.

Conquergood, Dwight. 1991. "Rethinking Ethnography: Towards a Critical Cultural Politics." *Communication Monographs* 58 (2): 179–194.

Daniel, E. Valentine 1996. *Charred Lullabies: Chapters in an Anthropography of Violence*. Princeton, NJ: Princeton University Press.

Dobbs, Roselle, and Xiong Yan. 2018. "Yongning Narua Orthography: Users' Guide and Developers' Notes." https://halshs.archives-ouvertes.fr /halshs-01956606.

Gatusa, Lamu. 2021. "Reflections on Mosuo Oral Lore." *Matrix* 2 (1), https://www.networkonculture.ca/activities/matrix/issues/vol2_iss1.

Goodman, David. 2002. "The Politics of the West: Equality, Nation-Building, and Colonization." *Provincial China* 7 (2): 127–150.

Goulet, Jean-Guy. 2011. "Trois manières d'être sur le terrain: Une brève histoire des conceptions de l'intersubjectivité." *Anthropologie et Sociétés* 35 (3): 107–125.

Gros, Stéphane. 2014. "Devenirs identitaires dans les confins sino-tibétains: Contextes et transformations." *Cahiers d'Extrême-Asie* 23: 63–102.

Hansen, Mette H. 2006. "In the Footsteps of the Communist Party: Dilemmas and Strategies." In *Doing Fieldwork in China,* edited by M. Heimer and S. Thøgersen, 81–95. Honolulu: University of Hawai'i Press.

Haraway, Donna. 2007. "Savoir situés: La question de la science dans le féminisme et le ÿ rivilege de la perspective partielle." In *Manifeste cyborg et autres essais,* edited by L. Allard, D. Gardey, and N. Magnan, 107–142. Paris: Exils Éditeur.

Harrell, Stevan, 2001. *Ways of Being Ethnic in Southwest China.* Seattle: University of Washington Press.

Heimer, Maria, and Stig Thøgersen, eds. 2006. *Doing Fieldwork in China.* Honolulu: University of Hawai'i Press.

Lidz, Liberty. 2010. "A Descriptive Grammar of Yongning Na (Mosuo)." PhD diss., University of Texas, Austin.

Madge, Clare. 1993. "Boundary Disputes: Comments on Sidaway (1992)." *Area* 25 (3): 294–299.

Mathieu, Christine. 1998. "The Moso Ddaba Religious Specialists." In *Naxi and Moso Ethnography: Kin, Rites, Pictographs,* edited by M. Oppitz and E. Hsu, 209–234. Zürich: Völkerkunde Museum.

———. 2003. *History and Anthropological Study of the Ancient Kingdoms of the Sino-Tibetan Borderland: Naxi and Mosuo.* Lewiston, NY: Edwin Mellen Press.

Mattison, Siobhan M. 2010. "Economic Impacts of Tourism and Erosion of the Visiting System among the Mosuo of Lugu Lake." *Asia Pacific Journal of Anthropology* 11 (2): 159–176.

Mauss, Marcel. 1934. "Les techniques du corps." *Journal de Psychologie* 32 (3/4). http://classiques.uqac.ca/classiques/mauss_marcel/socio_et_anthropo/6_Techniques_corps/Techniques_corps.html.

McKhann, Charles. 1998. "Naxi, Rerkua, Moso Meng: Kinship, Politics, and Ritual on the Yunnan-Sichuan Frontier." In *Naxi and Moso Ethnography: Kin, Rites, Pictographs,* edited by M. Oppitz and E. Hsu, 23–45. Zürich: Völkerkunde Museum.

———. 2001. "Tourisme de masse et identité sur les marches sino-tibétaine." *Anthropologie et société* 25 (2): 35–54.

———. 2003. "Sacred Trails: Genealogical Mapping and the Creation of Historical Space among the Naxi of Southwest China." *Histoire et Anthropologie Asies* 2: 29–47.

———. 2012. "Origin and Return: Genesis and the Souls of the Dead in Naxi Myth Ritual." In *Origins and Migrations in the Extended Eastern Himalayas,* edited by H. Toni and S. Blackburn, 275–298. Leiden: Brill.

Michaud, Alexis. 2018a. 摩梭-汉-英-法词典 [Na (Mosuo)-Chinese-English-French dictionary (Chinese version)]. https://shs.hal.science/halshs-01744420.

———. 2018b. *Tone in Yongning Na, Lexical Tones, and Morphology*. Berlin: Language Science Press.

Michaud, Jean. 2013. "Comrades of Minority Policy in China, Vietnam, and Laos." In *Red Stamps and Gold Stars: Fieldwork Dilemmas in Upland Socialist Asia*, edited by S. Turner, 22–39. Vancouver: UBC Press.

Milan, Pascale-Marie. 2012. "Contournement et instrumentalisation de l'identité culturelle Mosuo dans la rencontre touristique." *Via* 2. https://doi.org/10.4000/viatourism.1072.

———. 2013. "Festivité, performance et agencéité chez les Na de Chine: Du lien social à l'arène politique." *Cultures-Kairós* 2. http://revues.msh parisnord.org/cultureskairos/index.php?id=684.

———. 2016. *The Na of Lijiazui*. Genève: Somogy/Berbier-Mueller.

———. 2019. "Tourisme et changement social chez les Na de Chine: Étude comparée d'une coutume sexuelle; Le séssé." PhD diss., Lyon 2 University and Laval University.

———. 2021. "Entraide et réciprocité chez les Na de Chine: Une lecture de la socialité na et de la centralité des maisons dans l'organisation sociale." *Matrix* 2 (1). https://www.networkonculture.ca/activities /matrix/issues/vol2_iss1.

Pieke, Frank N. 2000. "Serendipity: Reflections on Fieldwork in China." In *Anthropologists in a Wider World: Essays on Field Research*, edited by P. Dresch, W. James, and D. Parkin, 129–150. New York: Berghahn Books.

Rock, Joseph, 1955. "The D'a Nv Funeral Ceremony with Special Reference to the Origin of Na-khi Weapons." *Anthropos* 50 (2): 1–31.

Rose, Gillian. 1997. "Situating Knowledges: Positionality, Reflexivities, and Other Tactics." *Progress in Human Geography* 21 (3): 305–320.

Scott, James C. 1992. *Domination and the Arts of Resistance: Hidden Transcript*. New Haven, CT: Yale University Press.

———. 2006. "Infra-politique des groupes subalternes." *Vacarme* 36: 25–29. https://doi.org/10.3917/vaca.036.0025.

———. 2009. *The Art of Not Being Governed: An Anarchist History of Upland Southeast Asia*. New Haven, CT: Yale University Press.

Scott, Joan. 1991. "The Evidence of Experience." *Critical Inquiry* 17 (4): 773–797.

Shih, Chuan-Kang. 2010. *Quest for Harmony: The Moso Traditions of Sexual Union and Family Life*. Stanford, CA: Stanford University Press.

Smith, Joanne N. 2006. "Research Report—Maintaining Margins: The Politics of Ethnographic Fieldwork in Chinese Central Asia." *China Journal* 56: 131–147.

Sultana, Farhana. 2007. "Reflexivity, Positionality, and Participatory Ethics: Negotiating Fieldwork Dilemmas in International Research." *ACME: An International Journal for Critical Geographies* 6 (3): 374–385.

Swain, Margaret Byrne. 2011. "Commoditized Ethnicity for Tourism Development in Yunnan." In *Moving Mountains: Ethnicity and Livelihoods in Highland China, Vietnam, and Laos,* edited by J. Michaud and T. Forsyth, 173–92. Vancouver: UBC Press.

Thurston, Anne F., and Burton Pasternak. 1983. *The Social Sciences and Fieldwork in China: Views from the Field.* Boulder, CO: Westview Press.

Tillmann-Healy, Lisa M. 2003. "Friendship as Method." *Qualitative Inquiry* 9: 729–749.

Trebinjac, Sabine. 1995. "Femme, seule et venue d'ailleurs: Trois atouts d'un ethnomusicologue au Turkestan chinois." *Cahiers d'ethnomusicologie* 8: 59–68. https://journals.openedition.org/ethnomusicologie/1128.

———. 2000. *Le Pouvoir en chantant.* Vol. 1, *L'art de fabriquer une musique chinoise.* Nanterre: Société d'ethnologie.

Turner, Sarah. 2010. "Challenges and Dilemmas: Fieldwork with Upland Minorities in Socialist Vietnam, Laos, and Southwest China." *Asia Pacific Viewpoint* 51 (2): 121–134.

———. 2013a. "Dilemmas and Detours: Fieldwork with Ethnic Minorities in Upland Southwest China, Vietnam, and Laos." In *Red Stamps and Gold Stars: Fieldwork Dilemmas in Upland Socialist Asia,* edited by S. Turner, pp. 1–21. Vancouver: UBC Press.

———, ed. 2013b. *Red Stamps and Gold Stars: Fieldwork Dilemmas in Upland Socialist Asia.* Vancouver: UBC Press.

Vansina, Jan. 1985. *Oral Tradition as History.* Madison: University of Wisconsin Press.

Wacquant, Loïc, 1989. "Corps et âme: Notes ethnographiques d'un apprenti-boxeur." *Actes de la recherche en sciences sociales* 80: 33–67.

Walsh, Eileen R. 2001. "The Mosuo—Beyond the Myths of Matriarchy: Gender Transformation and Economic Development." PhD diss., Temple University, Philadelphia.

———. 2005. "From Nu Guo to Nu'er Guo: Negotiating Desire in the Land of the Mosuo." *Modern China* 31 (4): 448–486.

Wang Ming-ke. 1999. "From the Qiang Barbarians to the Qiang Nationality: The Making of a New Chinese Boundary." In *Imagining China: Regional Division and National Unity,* edited by Huang Shu-min and Hsu Cheng-Kuang, 43–80. Taipei: Institute of Ethnology.

Wellens, Koen. 2012. "Migrating Brothers and Party State Discourses on Ethnic Origin in Southwest China." In *Origins and Migrations in the Extended Eastern Himalayas,* edited by H. Toni and S. Blackburn, 299–319. Leiden: Brill.

Weng, Naiqun, 1993. "The Mother House: The Symbolism and Practice of Gender among the Naze in Southwest China." PhD diss., University of Rochester.

Yan Ruxian and Zhaolin Song 严汝娴, 宋兆麟, eds. 1983. *Yongning Naxizu de Muxi zhi* 永宁纳西族的母系制 (The matrilineal system of the Yongning Naxi). Kunming: Yunnan renmin chubanshe.

Zhan Chengxu, Wang Chengquan, Li Jinchun, and Liu Longchu 詹承緒, 王承權, 李近春, 劉龍初, eds. 1980. *Yongning Naxizu de Azhuhun he Muxi Jiating* 永宁纳西族的阿注婚和母系家庭 (The Azhu marriage and the matrilineal family of Yongning Naxi). Shanghai: Shanghai renmin chubanshe.

CHAPTER 10

"I Never Knew My Dad Experienced That!"

Reflections on a Collaborative Oral History Project with Hmong Youth and Elders in Upland Northern Vietnam

Sarah Turner and Sarah Delisle

COAUTHOR SARAH DELISLE and a young ethnic minority Hmong man, Chen, sat down to reflect on an oral history they had just completed with Chen's grandfather in Sa Pa, northern Vietnam. Sarah Delisle asked Chen:

> SARAH DELISLE: When we spoke with your grandfather was there anything you learned that you didn't know before, about your family's past?

> CHEN: Yeah! I learned stories from what my grandfather shared with us. Like when he said he'd lived in China for many years and that his generation moved here from China, and then in Vietnam they had moved around and lived in different places before settling here. I never knew that or that my family came from China. I was surprised to learn that.

Completing fieldwork in the Socialist Republic of Vietnam with members of ethnic minority communities mixes professional, political, and private domains of life in complex ways. The country's socialist government has maintained a firm grip on political control across the country, and Vietnam has remained a single-party state despite economic reforms. Concurrently, state officials, especially those closer to the center of power in Hanoi, tend to regard ethnic minority communities living in the country's mountainous frontier regions as "backward" or "lazy" and in need of modernization (van de Walle and Gunewardena 2001; Koh 2002; Sowerwine 2004; Turner 2013b). In reality, these upland communities are often highly adaptive to policy changes, economic opportunities, and environmental changes, as they have been for generations. While these communities and the individuals and households within them are seldom in positions of political power or financial wealth, neither are they passive victims of such changing circumstances. This means that ethnic minority upland farmers frequently contest or negotiate "the rules" of the Vietnamese state, while being well aware of the importance and suppleness of culture, history, and social relations (Michaud 2012; Turner 2013a).

For outsiders wishing to work with such communities and learn more about their cultures, histories, livelihoods, and sociopolitical negotiations, gaining formal access is an ongoing challenge. To undertake officially authorized social science fieldwork in contemporary Vietnam, one must have the correct authorizations—or red stamps—from a range of different levels of state bureaucracy. Most frequently, obtaining such authorizations (with either official or unofficial fees) requires connections to either a state research institute or a Vietnamese university. At times, one can also gain such permissions via nongovernmental organizations (NGOs), although this can raise different concerns, as NGOs may have their own research agendas that they expect researchers to follow. Collaborative participatory research is even more difficult to implement than standard ethnographic approaches here, since government authorities remain cautious of those wanting to undertake long-term fieldwork, especially in upland ethnic minority communities (Mackenzie, Christensen, and Turner 2015).

In Vietnam, fifty-three groups of "national minorities" (*các dân tộc thiểu số*) have been officially recognized since 1979, and those living in the northern uplands numbered approximately 9.3 million, or 10 percent of the country's population at the time of the 2019 census (General Statistics Office, Vietnam 2020; Michaud 2022). A discourse of "selective cultural preservation" probably best categorizes the state's approach to these minority communities, with cultural performances, material culture, and tourist-focused goods seen as the elements of ethnic minority culture worthy of preservation (Ó Briain 2018). Simultaneously, "unsavory" practices, such as swidden agriculture or expenditures for shamanistic rituals, are strongly discouraged by the state, with upland ethnic minorities continuing to be poorly understood by many Kinh (the lowland majority) (McElwee 2004). The Hmong, the focus of this chapter, are one of these "minority" cultures and are a kinship-based society living primarily in the uplands of southwest China and the northern mountainous areas of Vietnam, Laos, Thailand, and Burma (Lee and Tapp 2010). Hmong livelihoods in this region are predominantly agricultural and semi-subsistence-based, with a core crop of rice or maize that is supplemented by small home gardens. Some Hmong households also engage in cash cropping, non-timber forest product collection and trade, or wage work for income (Turner, Bonnin, and Michaud 2015).

Apart from the Tai-speaking minority groups in Vietnam's northern uplands (e.g., Thái, Tày, and Nùng), most other societies in this region, including the Hmong, have not produced written archives. Without such self-produced, emic written histories, what is known by and shared with outsiders regarding the early histories of Hmong in Vietnam is relatively minimal. Moreover, Hmong culture and language are overwhelmingly embedded in oral tradition, with an historical absence of literacy (Lee and Tapp 2010; Michaud 2020). Hmong are one of the stateless, kinship-based societies that have no common writing system, with over 24 different scripts having been created for the language (Michaud 2020). Instead, Hmong "have a very developed oral tradition" that includes many rich origin stories, legends, and myths, as well as traditional botanical knowledge. Having been "passed down orally for generations," these oral traditions have shaped the vernacular production of their own history (Lee and Tapp 2010, 49, 47; see also Livo and Cha 1991; Nguanchoo et al. 2019). As Tapp (2003, 35) stresses: "An oral tradition has been vital to the transmission of Hmong culture and the maintenance of Hmong identity." Thao (2002) underscores that cross-generational knowledge transfer is central to this oral tradition, with knowledge being passed on to younger generations (see also Thao 2006).

It is in this context that, in 2013, with financial support from the National Geographic (US) Legacy Fund, we designed the Hmong Voices Project. This applied project emerged from discussions that the first author, Sarah Turner (hereafter Sarah T), had previously held with a long-time Hmong friend, Shu Tan, in Sa Pa town, Lào Cai province, about what an outsider could do to support Hmong culture in the area. Shu was concerned that local Hmong youth were increasingly unaware of their local family and community histories and traditional craft techniques. While oral tradition remains a core part of Hmong culture in these uplands, Shu noted that with more youth attending local boarding schools, and with growing access to the internet and mobile phones, their time spent with elders was decreasing, and opportunities to learn about the past were diminishing. Thus, the Hmong Voices Project was born. In collaboration with Sapa O'Chau, a Hmong-run social enterprise that Shu Tan and supporters had established in Sa Pa town, our project aimed to document oral histories and traditional knowledge in Hmong communities while bringing together youth and elders. The project was also a way for younger Hmong men and women to learn more about their heritage, by being a core part of the project.

Sapa O'Chau operates a boarding facility for ethnic minority youth attending local schools, while also providing extra tutoring (often by overseas volunteers) for these youth. It also runs a hotel and tourist café in Sa Pa town, and offers trekking and village homestay services for tourists. Collaboration with Sapa O'Chau was essential for this project, a partnership facilitated by strong relationships between Shu and the authors over a number of years. The first author, Sarah T, had completed ethnographic fieldwork with Hmong and other minority communities in Sa Pa District since 1999. She had also worked alongside Shu for a number of years to develop funding proposals for Sapa O'Chau, to help recruit overseas interns, and to organize an international advisory board. The second author, Sarah Delisle (hereafter Sarah D), had previously helped with the management of the advisory board, including running its virtual meetings for two years, and she had completed her master's thesis on ethnic minority livelihood changes in Sa Pa District.

In brief, for the Hmong Voices Project, we recruited eight young Hmong men and women trekking guides with basic or intermediate English comprehension and oral skills, and taught them the basics of interviewing elders in an oral history style (detailed below). The guides—or youth interviewers—then completed an oral history interview with someone of an older generation whom they already knew, such as an elder in their family or a long-time neighbor in their village. In these interviews about the changes that the elder had experienced in their lives, the elders reflected on and retold their personal experiences of changing political landscapes, their strategies for creating sustainable upland livelihoods, and the challenges of increasing market integration and shifting family structures. Each interview was taped and then reworked to make a continuous written story script (also detailed below). The story script was then returned to the elder for participant validation. These revised and participant-approved scripts were then recorded by the Hmong youth interviewers in English as oral history stories, so as to reach as broad an audience as possible (including members of the international Hmong diaspora who speak different dialects). The finished recordings are available on the Sapa O'Chau website.[1] While not the focus of this chapter, a second aim of the project was to record and archive traditional Hmong craft and musical techniques for younger generations to access. For this, we interviewed and filmed community members weaving hemp fabric, dyeing cloth with batik methods, designing Hmong jewelry and playing the *qeej*, a traditional Hmong woodwind instrument. These videos are also available on the Sapa O'Chau website, with the hope of retaining and spreading this traditional knowledge.

In this chapter, our aim is to critically reflect upon the oral history segment of this project, while detailing the collaborative process that we developed and highlighting the strengths and drawbacks of our approach. Next, we outline the five-step process we followed to try to create a "performance based collaborative form of writing" that involved Hmong elders and youth (Brooks 2005, 182). We then critically reflect on our positionalities regarding this process and on the positionalities and commentaries of the youth interviewers and elderly interviewees. We conclude by highlighting some of the political and ethical considerations raised when undertaking such a project with ethnic minority individuals in a socialist state.

While touching on many of the ten issues outlined by Pierre Petit and Jean Michaud in this book's introduction, we particularly focus on four of these elements in this chapter. These are number 1, "A 'Duty of Remembrance,'" with our applied project striving to support the transmission of historical knowledge; number 5, "A Gendered Access to the Past—and Writing about It," with our focus on writing about a gendered history, as well as gendered negotiations in the field; and number 9, "Reflexivity and Positionality in Authoritarian Situations," with discussions of how we navigated this context. Our concerns regarding the most ethically sound way to complete this project—number 10, "Ethics"—are woven into our discussions throughout this chapter.

Producing Historical Narratives in a Multistep Collaborative Process

Step 1. Recruiting Youth Interviewees and the Group Training Session

Youth involved with Sapa O'Chau who were eighteen years old or older were informed about the project by Shu, and those who were interested were invited to a training session. In total, eight trekking guides completed the training and participated in the project, with seven as interviewers and one helping with Hmong-to-English translation. These youth included three men and five women ranging in age from eighteen to thirty-one. Five had been involved in research projects prior to this oral history project, four having worked directly with Sarah D during her master's thesis research, so they had already developed a good rapport.

The initial training covered the basics of interviewing elders in an "oral history" style. Topics included ethical practices, such as gaining consent; how to build rapport; and different ways of asking questions. The discussions about ethical practices also centered on the importance of ensuring that the elder was aware of what would happen with their words and stories. Likewise, confidentiality was also stressed, with discussions focusing on the importance of keeping people's names and stories secret and not sharing these details with others. The youth interviewers were mindful of these concerns. For example, one interviewer, Chi, stated that she was apprehensive that other residents of her elder's village would find out about what the elder had said and perhaps not like it. When we reiterated that all elders would be given pseudonyms before their histories were published (as we have also done for the youth interviewers here), Chi's apprehension waned.

We asked the youth to think of older family members who they thought would be comfortable being interviewed. Some youth raised questions about which ages would characterize someone as an "elder," as some youth no longer had living grandparents. The group collectively agreed that even if someone was only in their sixties, they would have lived through a number of important events, such as the American War (as the Vietnam-America War is locally called), the peak and termination of socialist collectives, the rise of the market economy, and a number of other important changes in the area. Hence anyone in their sixties or older was deemed a possible elder participant.

Five youth interviewed family members, including parents, in-laws, and grandparents, while the remaining four interviews were conducted with long-time neighbors or family friends. Five youth collected the oral history of one elder each, and two youth collected two oral histories each, reaching a total of nine. Elders ranged in age from their early sixties to ninety-four and included five women and four men from five different communes in Sa Pa District (see table 1). The training was very interactive and included Sarah D and the youth taking turns asking and answering the oral history questions (e.g., "Can you tell me about yourself?" "Can you tell me about your family history?"). In this way, the youth were introduced to the oral history process while also helping validate the possible questions. For instance, they suggested a couple of word changes, including using the Hmong terms for "farm work" instead of "livelihoods," as they deemed this would be easier for elders to understand. Because the training session included the youth practicing interpreting the questions from English to Hmong, this was used to gauge each youth's comfort level with switching between the two languages. While some struggled with certain vocabulary, all the youth interviewers were keen to be involved in the project, so we agreed that one of the youth with proficient interpretation skills would assist with reviewing the recorded oral histories of others, if needed.

Through this training process, it became apparent that the youth already knew some aspects of how life had been in the past, especially about certain difficulties that older generations had faced. Many youth talked about their grandparents and parents not having enough reliable food sources previously, and turning to banana trees, ferns, or other gathered foods for sustenance. Others recalled being told how elders would walk to Lào Cai City (thirty-three kilometers away from Sa Pa town) to buy goods before there were well-stocked shops in Sa Pa town or in the villages. Considering the youths' prior knowledge, we highlighted the need to let the elder answer the question being posed, even if the youth thought they knew the answer.

Step 2. Initial Oral Histories

After the training, each youth met with Sarah D individually at the Sapa O'Chau headquarters to trek together to each elder's village. Before setting out, a pre-interview was completed with each youth covering information on their age, village, brief family history, their experiences as a trekking guide or research assistant, and so on. These were later supplemented with exit interviews as the project was ending, which included reflexive-focused questions. Here, we asked the youth interviewers whether they would describe their own life as easier or harder than the lives of those they interviewed, whether they learned anything about their family's history or the history of the area during the process, whether they thought the elder was intimidated during the interview or during participant validation, and so on. Details from those reflections are included below.

Table 10.1.   Details regarding Hmong youth interviewers and the elderly interviewees

Youth interviewer name (pseudonym)	Youth interviewer age	Youth interviewer gender	Interviewee's relation with youth interviewer	Interviewee age	Interviewee gender
Nhia	23	Man	Long-time neighbor	60s	Woman
Chen	19	Man	Grandfather	67	Man
			Long-time neighbor	60s	Woman
Kee	23	Man	Grandmother	80s	Woman
Chi	18	Woman	Brother's mother-in-law	67	Woman
Lan	27	Woman	Grandfather	90	Man
Tau	31	Woman	Sister's mother-in-law	94	Woman
			Father	77	Man
Hua	31	Woman	Long-time neighbor	61	Man
Kai	23	Woman	Helped with translation		

Upon arrival at the elder's home and after introducing the project and obtaining consent, Sarah D started the interview by asking a couple of basic questions regarding household composition, years lived in the village, and so on. Youth interviewers typically became more confident after watching these initial interactions, and Sarah D encouraged them to take the lead for the rest of the interactions. Overall, the topics covered included broad questions about the elder and their family, such as their age and the number of people in their family, including children and grandchildren, their parents' hamlet (if the elder was a married woman), their family history, and their livelihood activities. These were supplemented with questions about changes that the elder had experienced in their lifetime, changes in local livelihoods, and discussions of specific historical periods or events such as the 1979 China-Vietnam border war. Elders were also asked about the future and whether they had specific concerns with regard to their children or grandchildren, as well as the source of such concerns.

As with all interpretation activities, there were some common difficulties. For example, youth interviewers would sometimes reduce a several minutes-long response by an elder to just a couple of words in English. The content collected thus depended heavily on the skills of the specific youth who was directing and interpreting an interview. For instance, during one interview, Sarah D tried several times to reformulate a question in the hopes of gaining a more detailed response, but the youth interviewer continued to struggle to interpret the reworded question. Several times youth recommended that they avoid asking certain questions—such as about widowhood or politics—to protect the elder, which Sarah D immediately respected. When asked about these potentially unsettling questions post-interview, one youth interviewer replied that he did not want to ask about widowhood because he did not want to make the elder sad.

Managing the presence of other family members or listeners also proved challenging when they interjected with their own replies. At other times, interviews flowed very easily if the youth and elder were fully engaged in the process. One of these sessions ended with the elder "interviewing" Sarah D about her background and life story, as the youth interpreted. As Sarah D noted in her field journal afterward:

The visit went really well. Chi is a really good interviewer and it felt more like we were having a nice conversation than we were conducting an oral history interview. It was clear Chi enjoyed it because she was equally engaged in the process: she asked follow-up questions without prompting and seemed keen and interested throughout. [The elder] was also quite talkative which helped too! One of the nicest parts for me was at the end when I asked if [the elder] had any questions and she proceeded to ask me questions similar to those I asked her: "Was I poor like her when I was younger? How did I make money?" etc. It felt nice to be able to share like that and when we finished I felt less like we'd been interviewing her and more like we had simply been exchanging life stories. (Sarah D, field journal)

We had five cases in which the youth interviewer and elder participant were of the opposite sex, and we observed that this made little difference to building a strong rapport. Instead, prior familiarity between the two individuals appeared to be more important and helpful for ensuring rapport. We also noted that elder women were as interested and engaged in the conversations as elder men, and that they were able to give rich accounts of a broad range of themes, including topics beyond what are locally deemed as "women's topics." For example, elder women were similarly animated in their discussions of livelihood strategies, migration, and changes in the local environment as elder men were. We found this range of themes that women were comfortable discussing revealing, given that Hmong society is traditionally patriarchal, and hence it is often assumed that men should speak for the family. On the other hand, we were not that surprised at the women's range of knowledge, knowing that women pass down much information and many skills to younger generations regarding food crops, traditional medicines, specific shaman rituals, hemp and cloth production, embroidery, and so on.

Step 3. From Transcripts to Oral History Stories

Once the initial oral history was completed, the recording was transcribed by Sarah D. The original recordings ranged from one hour to ninety minutes but were not always easy to follow due to background noise (family members talking, sounds outside, children playing/yelling) and other on-the-ground realities. Sections of a recording when the youth had struggled to interpret or when the interpretation was unclear underwent a quality-check by Kai, a youth participant with advanced English skills. This check involved listening to short excerpts and checking them against the transcripts Sarah D had prepared. This was a valuable exercise as Kai indicated that each youth had done a very good job interpreting; overall, there were no major changes to make and only a few details to add.

Once this quality check was completed, the transcripts were reworked into coherent story scripts by Sarah T and Sarah D (see text box). One of the challenges of collecting and making these oral histories available was that in recounting their memories, elders often jumped back and forth chronologically, making the transcripts difficult to follow. In addition, as the youth interpreted and asked for clarifications, further digressions in timelines were produced. We therefore undertook a form of storytelling, mildly editing the transcripts into chronological order (Christensen 2012). To make a continuous script, which we hoped would be easier to understand, we also smoothed or "tidied" the transcriptions via "naturalized transcription," removing some features of spoken language such as "ums" and "ers" (see Bucholtz 2000; Henderson 2018). While we are cognizant that we were imposing a structure and modifying the original transcripts by undertaking these steps, this process nevertheless allowed us to "present findings in ways that *make sense*, that *speak to* and *speak with* the communities in which the research takes place" (Christensen 2012, 233; emphasis in original). The edited story script was then returned to the elder for participant validation.

Editing Process

In the process of creating these recorded oral history stories, we smoothed out wording that might have been confusing or misunderstood (~~strikethrough~~ or *italics* here) and we added details where appropriate that were told to us during the participant validation process (**bolded**). Moreover, a few words were changed because of pronunciation problems for the youth interviewer in the final recording in English. For example, *embroidery* was changed to *needlework* here.

Excerpt from Za's Edited Oral History Story

My name is Za. I'm almost 70 years old. I married my husband when I was 15 and moved to Cat Cat village from my parents' in Ta Phin village. My parents were farmers. We had a lot of rice paddy so we had enough food to eat. We had a big family. I had 2 brothers and 4 sisters. One of my sisters stayed in Ta Phin and three married and moved to Ma Cha village. Growing up I spent my time doing ~~embroidery~~ *needlework*, taking care of buffalo and taking care of my younger siblings. [...]

When I first came to Cat Cat village there were only 14 houses. There was lots of forest around the village and only a few rice paddies. Now there are more than 100 houses. That's too many. There's not enough land for so many people. For some families with less land, it's difficult to grow food. **My family had lots of land but when my sons got married we had to share it with them, so now it's little. We can't get more land now unless we want to buy more. Everywhere belongs to someone. Most people don't want to sell because without land they cannot grow food and they will be hungry.**

Now most of the forest in the village is gone and there are many rice paddies. Before, the soil was rich and we could plant crops. Now the soil is poor and we need to use chemical fertilizer or nothing grows. **Sometimes we don't have enough money to buy fertilizer. We need 800 kilograms per year. This costs about 6 million dong [~US$250]. We use our cardamom money to buy fertilizer. My son sometimes also works as a porter for treks to Fansipan and gets money from that.**

Step 4. Oral History Story Participant Validation

Participant validation or member checking is increasingly used as a tool for establishing credibility in qualitative research and for upholding the integrity of research findings. Results are returned to participants for them to determine and approve that the completed scripts accurately portray what the participants initially conveyed. Indeed, using this form of internal authentication is argued to act as a qualitative proxy for traditionally quantitative evaluations of rigor (Baxter and Eyles 1997;

Barbour 2003; Turner and Coen 2008). For these reasons, we wanted to take our oral history stories back to the elders so that they could confirm that the scripts accurately portrayed the information that they had provided. We also wanted to make sure that the elders were absolutely comfortable sharing the information contained within these oral history stories. This was especially important to us due to the fact that ethnic minority-state relations in Vietnam are such that minority individuals can be easily harassed or persecuted for speaking out against the state or for voicing opinions that are not considered positive regarding any (however vague) political topic (McElwee 2004; World Bank 2009).

Returning to elders with their edited story scripts proved to be extremely valuable as they took the opportunity to add further details or clarify certain elements. For example, during an initial interview, an elderly woman in Hau Thao village had provided few details about the China-Vietnam border war, but on the second visit, she elaborated that together with her husband and two children she had fled the village and stayed in the mountains for ten days, surviving on corn flour that they had carried with them. An elderly woman in Ta Van village added more details about her second husband and children, and about her worries for the future, including the bribes that they were expected to pay at the local hospital. After this participant validation step, the additional information and clarifications were worked into the story scripts. We also decided to add dates of key historical events so that the oral history stories were comprehensible to a broader audience.

Step 5. Youth Audio-Recording Their Oral History Interviews with Elders in English

> As Kai is practicing the script she suggests that I read a line and then she will repeat/read it after me. We try this for the first sentence and it goes quite well! Basically I start the recorder and press pause, read out a sentence and then unpause when Kai repeats. ("Wait for the beep!") It sounds a lot less like reading and more like someone is just speaking. Great! (Sarah D, field journal)

During the final stage of creating the oral history stories, each participant-validated script was recorded in English by the youth interviewer and then added to the Sapa O'Chau website. Members of the Hmong diaspora in the West are not necessarily able to easily understand the Hmong dialect spoken in northern Vietnam, and we hoped non-Hmong-speaking individuals might want to listen to these stories as well. This step was a learning opportunity for the youth interviewers since they were able to practice their English reading and pronunciation/enunciation skills—useful for their work as tourist guides. The initial idea was to have the youth read the story script, but some struggled and the resulting recording was stilted, which distracted from the elder's story. After several attempts, we decided that one of us would read one sentence of the story script at a time, and then the youth interviewer would repeat the sentence while being recorded. This worked well for all the youth involved.

While preparing the oral history scripts for the website, we created additional background information for the website to help contextualize the stories. We also spoke with Sapa O'Chau employees about where the Hmong Voices Project page could be placed for maximum visibility. The final location was not where we would have placed it necessarily (within the social enterprise's website tourism section), but we let Shu and Sapa O'Chau employees make that ultimate decision.

Discussion: Critical Reflections of Positionality and Power Relations

Positionality, or the recognition that "all knowledge is produced in specific contexts or circumstances and that these situated knowledges are marked by their origins" (Valentine 2002, 116) relates to all those involved in the research process, not just the researchers. In this case, we needed to be mindful of the impacts that the positionalities of the elder interviewees, youth interviewers, and ourselves would have on the research process and outcomes. One's positionality is inclusive of one's ethnicity, class, gender, age, sexuality, and (dis)ability (Hopkins 2007). It also incorporates life experiences, ways of viewing the world, and political leanings and positionings, with these characteristics being relational and never static (McDowell 1994). This means that we knew it would be impossible to fully grasp all the interactions at play during (and after) the Hmong Voices Project or their impacts on the processes and individuals involved. As G. Rose (1997) notes, the researcher's identity is fluid and changes in an iterative process (particularly in relation to research participants), and hence we needed to think in terms of "situated knowledges," "hybrid spaces of research," and "webbed connections" (Rose 1997, 308, 315, 317).

Two White Women Researchers "in the Field"

These positionalities and interactions were being played out in the borderlands of a socialist state with members of an ethnic minority community. This broader context had an important impact on how we undertook the project and on the relationships that developed at all levels. Having the support of Sapa O'Chau was critical, not only for creating a collaborative project but also pragmatically for gaining official permissions to gain access to the field. This field context heightened our awareness of our privileged positionalities as two Western-educated middle-class white women with the socioeconomic privilege to fly in and out of Vietnam when we wanted (albeit with the correct visas). Such mobility remains far beyond the financial means of many of our Hmong collaborators, never mind the bureaucratic red tape required for them to obtain a passport.

Despite the nearly impossible task of trying to understand the impacts of our positionalities across time and space, we attempted to remain critically reflexive throughout the project. To try to do so, we kept the following questions in mind: Were we providing enough space for authentic stories to be told? How were our positionalities and actions impacting the manner in which the youth and elders conducted themselves and interacted with each other? What should we and could we be doing differently?

While being mindful to not slip into reification, we observed that being women researchers facilitated fairly easy rapport with elder interviewees. However, the rapport between the elder interviewee and the youth seemed to be the most important determinant of how well the oral history progressed. Grandchildren seemed particularly at ease when interviewing their grandparents, and these sessions generally went smoothly. Chen explained regarding interviewing his grandfather: "I know him and he knows me for a long time, so it's easier to talk with him." Nonetheless, family dynamics could also create obstacles. In one instance, during a participant validation session, the elder started out very enthusiastically, indicating that he had "many more" stories to share. As the session progressed, the youth—his daughter—got frustrated that he kept retelling stories that had been covered in the first interview. Unfortunately, the youth told the elder that he did not need to keep retelling stories he had already shared, and the elder's responses became less expansive. Overall, however, the richest conversations about elders' lives occurred when the youth interviewers had known the elder for a long time.

Our "foreignness" placed us in a somewhat ambiguous gender role, allowing us to discuss certain topics with Hmong men that would not necessarily be the norm, such as duties and livelihood tasks seen as "men's work" (see also S. Scott, Miller, and Lloyd 2006). The presence of the youth, often a family member, also appeared to contribute to increasing the willingness of the elder to discuss such topics. This issue of trust was mentioned several times by youth in exit interviews. As youth interviewer Kee commented when asked whether he thought his grandmother was intimidated at all during the interview: "I can say she was not scared with us. She was confident because she knows I'm her grandchild." Similarly, when asked whether she thought it was easy for her mother-in-law to speak with us, Chi replied: "Yes, because we know each other already, so she trusts us and she can say anything she would like to say."

Our age placed us in certain and different categories as well. Here, Sarah D was older than most of the Hmong youth interviewers but close enough age-wise to be able to relate to them fairly well, while she was also significantly younger than our interviewees. On the other hand, Sarah T was clearly a generation older than the youth interviewers and a generation younger than the interviewees. Nonetheless, when Sarah T joined in participant validation trips and worked with the youth interviewers, it did not seem to change the dynamics very much. Familiarity with research team members, sometimes over a number of years, as well as multiple interactions during the Hmong Voices Project, appeared to have worked well to gain and maintain trust.

We were mindful not to be associated with any local state officials, as this would have very likely made both youth interviewers and elderly interviewees suspicious of our motives, resulting in a loss of rapport or trust. Indeed, possible government surveillance was brought up by one youth in her exit interview. When asked how she felt during the interviews and whether she felt scared or intimidated, Chi replied: "The questions were ok, but what I was scared of in the village was when we were speaking to the person, the government people would come and ask 'What are you doing here?' [. . .] It was very lucky that we didn't have any big camera with us, we had a very small recorder." The youth interviewers noted that they also felt more at ease knowing that Shu Tan from Sapa O'Chau had discussed the project with Mr. Cao, a local Hmong ex-policeman affiliated with Sapa O'Chau who has maintained strong connections to local communities and to higher-level officials in Sa Pa District. In the youths' opinions, these connections afforded project members and interviewees possible protection from harassment from other state officials.

Youth Interviewers' Reflexive Accounts

> SARAH D: So overall what would you say about your experience?

> TAU (young woman interviewer): I think it's a good thing to do this project and for me to be able to learn; to learn some more from the old people, to talk with you, and to practice my English.

The pre-interviews and exit interviews with youth interviewers provided valuable insights into their experiences of the research process. As our chapter title indicates, the exit interviews created an opportunity for the youth to reflect on what they had learned over the course of the project and highlighted the intergenerational and often intrafamilial knowledge transfers that had occurred. Regional history, especially the 1979 China-Vietnam border war, was a topic that many youth noted that they had learned more about. They also mentioned becoming more knowledgeable about different aspects of their family history, such as that their forbears emigrated from China, or about the local natural history, including changes that had occurred in the surrounding landscape and environment. The focus on the past also brought up many comparisons with the present.

Another question asked during exit interviews was how the youth thought their lives compared to the elders'. Overwhelmingly, youth indicated that their lives were easier than those of the elders they had interviewed. Whereas many elders reported needing to eat corn or cassava in the past when rice was in short supply, many of the youth indicated that the more stable food supply nowadays represented a significant difference with the past. Several reasons for this difference were given, including greater rice yields. As Tau explained: "Now we have more food so it's easier. [. . .] I work in the rice fields or the corn fields and we get more food so we have enough." Hua added that life was also easier because there were more shops to buy food if necessary. Increased economic opportunities were also cited as a reason for life becoming better. Lan stated: "I think life's easier now. It's easier to make money and we have enough food so we don't need to go into the forest to forage or carry wood to sell." Youth also cited greater educational opportunities as a positive change. Chen noted: "I think for me my life is better than my grandfather because I've been able to go to school and learn more things." Chi added that being able to learn to speak English provided more opportunities for work than her mother-in-law had experienced when she was young.

One of the more practical concerns raised by six of the youth interviewers in their exit interviews was the difficulty they had interpreting between Hmong and English. The youth specifically noted that they struggled to interpret words that did not seem to have an equivalent in the other language, and that they had difficulties "keeping up" with the elders when interpreting longer story segments. Yet, based on quality checks of the original oral history recordings and on feedback from Kai, who helped cross-check the transcripts, the youth did a commendable job. This was even more remarkable given the fact that this was the first time many had participated in such a project or had interpreted extensive dialogues on varied topics.

Concluding Thoughts: Retelling and Constructing Upland Histories

The Hmong Voices Project has provided insights into the history of this upland region that challenge the Vietnam state's preconceived narratives and discourses regarding this locale. State policies and literature continue to be overwhelmingly based on assumptions of primitivism, stagnation, and unproductivity regarding upland minority populations (Lieberman 2010). While there is a growing body of literature attempting to counter such interpretations of the lives and livelihoods of Hmong communities in Lào Cai province (e.g., Turner, Bonnin, and Michaud 2015; Delisle and Turner 2016; Bonnin 2018; Garber and Turner 2022), the Hmong Voices Project revealed a number of new findings, further illuminating historical and contemporary processes and relations. These included details about individual and household mobility patterns and resilience during the China-Vietnam border war, the historical use of forest products for household food security, and the impacts of rapid economic change in these communities. For example, we learned far more than previously documented about the role of opium in local live-lihoods when it was being promoted by the Vietnamese state prior to the early 1990s. We were also provided with important, nuanced details regarding the impacts of the China-Vietnam border war on local liveli-hoods, mobilities, and especially the emotional toll during that period of upheaval. We also learned about the local impacts, including con-cerns over land sales, of lowland to upland migration waves of Kinh migrants. These details have enriched work that we have published since the Hmong Voices Project (e.g., Turner and Oswin 2015; Michaud and Turner 2017; Turner 2022), and such details have been part of ongoing discussions with local social enterprise members, as well as with Vietnam-based academics and students. Of course, we need to be mindful that there were stories that were left out too, perhaps too painful to recall, considered irrelevant due to the rapid changes under way in the uplands, or deemed too political to discuss (cf. Creef 2000).

James C. Scott (2009, 230–231) notes: "Because oral traditions sur-vive only through retelling, they accumulate interpretations as they are transmitted. Each telling forcibly reflects current interests, current power relations, and current views of neighboring societies and kin groups." As shown above, these interpretations are further influenced by who they are told to, how they are then understood and—in our case—how they are then shaped into oral history stories. These stories of the elders involved in the Hmong Voices Project have been impacted yet again by the broader political context and the need to safeguard individuals and locales; they are socially constructed narratives with inevitable distortions and omissions. Yet, as Grele (1991, xvi) persua-sively argues, oral histories are recognized as having a key role in "get-ting a better history, a more critical history, a more conscious history which involves members of the public in [its] creation."

Our discussions above regarding positionality revolved around fairly immediate concerns about the impacts of gender, age, ethnicity, fam-ily positioning, and socioeconomic status of ourselves, the youth inter-viewers, and the elders involved. Yet such considerations often avoid uncomfortable debates regarding the rights of Global North researchers to undertake research in the Global South and the structurally unequal power relations, different agendas, and possible misinterpretations and representations that come with such research. There are critical schol-ars who would thus declare that it is best not to be subject to possible accusations of "appropriating and exploiting a powerful story for their own personal and professional ends" (Kohl and Farthing 2013, 91). We struggled with such concerns (and continue to do so), and yet we saw value in attempting to create accessible oral history stories for a broad audience to access. We hoped to support local Hmong individuals who had *asked us* for ways to safeguard the compelling stories of elders in their community, and we wanted to show solidarity with those with whom we work, "becoming closer while respecting the distance that remains" (Brabeck 2004, 52). Our commitment was to create a conduit for these stories to be told when they otherwise would not have been. Did we succeed? Probably not very well; the oral history stories continue to gain "hits" on the Sapa O'Chau website, more than eight years after they were uploaded, but they are not promoted in a very enticing manner. In hindsight, we probably should have also recorded them in *Hmong Leng*,[2] the local Hmong dialect, as well as in English, although at the time smartphones and internet access were not common in local communities. On the other hand, however, elders noted that they enjoyed the process and seemed proud of their final stories, intergenerational ties appeared to have been strengthened, and youth interviewers said that they would be keen to be involved in a similar project again, as Chi explained:

> SARAH D: Would you be interested in doing something like this again in the future?
>
> CHI: Yeah!
>
> SARAH D: Yeah?
>
> CHI: Yeah, I'm interested.
>
> SARAH D: Great!
>
> CHI: Because you ask questions and I can learn also.
>
> SARAH D: You learn things too?
>
> CHI: Yeah, you know, when you ask questions, the first person to understand [the answers] is me. I understand more than you. So I interpret to you.

Finally, by placing the final oral histories onto a website rather than working them into an academic article, it could be argued that we avoided the erasures and significant editing sometimes required by reviewers and journal conventions. The stories hence remain in a fairly "raw state" compared to if they had been analyzed for a typical academic publication. Clearly, they are still hybrid narratives, but they are also collaborative ones, striving to have minority voices heard.

Notes

1. "Hmong Voices," Sapa O'Chau, accessed October 30, 2023, http://sapaochau.org/sapa-trekking-and-homestay/hmong-voices.

2. Most Hmong in the Vietnamese uplands self-identify as Hmong Leng (also known as Green or Blue Hmong; Hmoob or Moob Leeg in the Romanized Popular Alphabet).

References

Barbour, R. 2003. "The Newfound Credibility of Qualitative Research? Tales of Technical Essentialism and Co-option." *Qualitative Health Research* 13: 1019–1027.

Baxter, J., and J. Eyles. 1997. "Evaluating Qualitative Research in Social Geography: Establishing 'Rigour' in Interview Analysis." *Transactions of the Institute of British Geographers* 22: 505–525.

Bonnin, C. 2018. "Cultivating Consumer Markets: Ethnic Minority Traders and the Refashioning of Cultural Commodities in the Sino-Vietnamese Border Uplands." In *Routledge Handbook of Asian Borderlands,* edited by A. Horstmann, M. Saxer, A. Rippa, 325–333. London: Routledge.

Brabeck, K. 2004. "Testimonio: Bridging Feminist and Participatory Action Research Principles to Create New Spaces of Collectivity." In *Traveling Companions: Feminism, Teaching, and Action Research,* edited by M. Brydon-Miller, P. Maguire, and A. Mclntyre, 41–54. Westport, CT: Praeger.

Brooks, L. M. 2005. "Testimonio's Poetics of Performance." *Comparative Literature Studies* 42 (2): 181–222.

Bucholtz, M. 2000. "The Politics of Transcription." *Journal of Pragmatics* 32: 1439–1465.

Christensen, J. 2012. "Telling Stories: Exploring Research Storytelling as a Meaningful Approach to Knowledge Mobilization with Indigenous Research Collaborators and Diverse Audiences in Community-Based Participatory Research." *Canadian Geographer* 56 (2): 231–242.

Creef, E. T. 2000. "Discovering My Mother as the Other in the *Saturday Evening Post.*" *Qualitative Inquiry* 6 (4): 443–455.

Delisle, S., and S. Turner. 2016. "'The Weather Is Like the Game We Play': Coping and Adaptation Strategies for Extreme Weather Events among Ethnic Minority Groups in Upland Northern Vietnam." *Asia Pacific Viewpoint* 57 (3): 351–364.

Garber, P., and S. Turner. 2023. "Entangled, Unraveled, and Reconfigured: Human-Animal Relations among Ethnic Minority Farmers and Water Buffalo in the Northern Uplands of Vietnam." *Environment and Planning E*, https://doi.org/10.1177/25148486231151808.

General Statistics Office, Vietnam. 2020. *The 2019 Vietnam Population and Housing Census: Completed Results*. Hanoi: Central Population and Housing Census Steering Committee.

Grele, R. J. 1991. *Envelopes of Sound: The Art of Oral History*, 2nd ed. New York: Greenwood.

Henderson, H. 2018. "Difficult Questions of Difficult Questions: The Role of the Researcher and Transcription Styles." *International Journal of Qualitative Studies in Education* 31 (2): 143–157.

Hopkins, P. E. 2007. "Global Events, National Politics, Local Lives: Young Muslim Men in Scotland." *Environment and Planning A* 39 (5): 1119–1133.

Koh, P. 2002. "Perception and Portrayal of Minorities in Vietnamese Communist Ethnology (1954–2001)." MA thesis, Department of History, National University of Singapore.

Kohl, B., and L. C. Farthing. 2013. "Navigating Narrative: The Antinomies of 'Mediated' Testimonios." *Journal of Latin American and Caribbean Anthropology* 18 (1): 90–107.

Lee, G. Y., and N. Tapp. 2010. *Culture and Customs of the Hmong*. Santa Barbara, CA: Greenwood.

Lieberman, V. 2010. "A Zone of Refuge in Southeast Asia? Reconceptualizing Interior Spaces." Review of *The Art of Not Being Governed: An Anarchist History of Upland Southeast Asia*, by James C. Scott. *Journal of Global History* 5 (2): 333–346.

Livo, N. J., and D. Cha. 1991. *Folk Stories of the Hmong: Peoples of Laos, Thailand, and Vietnam*. Westport, CT: Libraries Unlimited, Greenwood Publishing Group.

Mackenzie, C. A., J. Christensen, and S. Turner, 2015. "Advocating beyond the Academy: Dilemmas of Communicating Relevant Research Results." *Qualitative Research* 15 (1): 105–121.

McDowell, L. 1994. "The Transformation of Cultural Geography." In *Human Geography: Society, Space and Social Science*, edited by D. Gregory, R. Martin, and G. Smith, 146–173. London: Macmillan.

McElwee, P. 2004. "Becoming Socialist or Becoming Kinh? Government Policies for Ethnic Minorities in the Socialist Republic of Viet Nam." In *Civilizing the Margins: Southeast Asian Government Policies for the Development of Minorities*, edited by C. R. Duncan, 182–213. Ithaca, NY: Cornell University Press.

Michaud J. 2012. "Hmong Infrapolitics: A View from Vietnam." *Ethnic and Racial Studies* 35 (11): 1853–1873.

———. 2020. "The Art of Not Being Scripted So Much." *Current Anthropology* 61 (2): 240–263.

———. 2022. "Ethnography in the Northern Vietnamese Highlands." In *Routledge Handbook of Highland Asia,* edited by J. J. P. Wouters and M. T. Heneise, 430–450. London: Routledge.

Michaud, J., and S. Turner. 2017. "Reaching New Heights: State Legibility in Sa Pa, a Vietnam Hill Station." *Annals of Tourism Research* 66: 37–48.

Nguanchoo, V., P. Wangpakapattanawong, H. Balslev, and A. Inta. 2019. "Exotic Plants Used by the Hmong in Thailand." *Plants* 8 (1): 1–16.

Ó Briain, L. 2018. *Musical Minorities: The Sounds of Hmong Ethnicity in Northern Vietnam.* New York: Oxford University Press.

Rose, G. 1997. "Situating Knowledges: Positionality, Reflexivities, and Other Tactics." *Progress in Human Geography* 21 (3): 305–320.

Scott, James C. 2009. *The Art of Not Being Governed: An Anarchist History of Upland Southeast Asia.* New Haven, CT: Yale University Press.

Scott, S., F. Miller, and K. Lloyd. 2006. "Doing Fieldwork in Development Geography: Research Culture and Research Spaces in Vietnam." *Geographical Research* 44 (1): 28–40.

Sowerwine, J. C. 2004. "The Political Ecology of Yao (Dzao) Landscape Transformations: Territory, Gender, and Livelihood Politics in Highland Vietnam." PhD diss., Department of Wildlife Resource Sciences, University of California, Berkeley.

Tapp, N. 2003. *The Hmong of China: Context, Agency, and the Imaginary.* Leiden: Brill Academic Publishers.

Thao, Yer Jeff. 2002. "The Voices of Mong Elders: Ways of Knowing, Teaching, and Learning with an Oral Tradition." PhD diss., Claremont Graduate University, California.

———. 2006. *The Mong Oral Tradition: Cultural Memory in the Absence of Written Language.* Jefferson, NC: McFarland.

Turner, S. 2013a. "Dilemmas and Detours: Fieldwork with Ethnic Minorities in Upland Southwest China, Vietnam, and Laos." In *Red Stamps and Gold Stars: Fieldwork Dilemmas in Upland Socialist Asia,* edited by S. Turner, 1–21. Vancouver: University of British Columbia Press.

———. 2013b. "The Silenced Research Assistant Speaks Her Mind." In *Red Stamps and Gold Stars: Fieldwork Dilemmas in Upland Socialist Asia,* edited by S. Turner, 220–238. Vancouver: University of British Columbia Press.

———. 2022. "Slow Forms of Infrastructural Violence: The Case of Vietnam's Mountainous Northern Borderlands." *Geoforum* 133: 185–197.

Turner, S., C. Bonnin, and J. Michaud. 2015. *Frontier Livelihoods: Hmong in the Sino-Vietnamese Borderlands.* Seattle: University of Washington Press.

Turner, S., and S. E. Coen. 2008. "Member Checking in Human Geography: Interpreting Divergent Understandings of Performativity in a Student Space." *Area* 40 (2): 184–193.

Turner, S., and N. Oswin. 2015. "Itinerant Livelihoods: Street Vending-scapes and the Politics of Mobility in Upland Socialist Vietnam." *Singapore Journal of Tropical Geography* 36 (3): 394–410.

Valentine, G. 2002. "People Like Us: Negotiating Sameness and Difference in the Research Process." In *Feminist Geography in Practice: Research and Methods,* edited by P. Moss, 116–132. Oxford: Blackwell Publishers.

van de Walle, D., and D. Gunewardena. 2001. "Sources of Ethnic Inequality in Viet Nam." *Journal of Development Economics* 65: 177–207.

World Bank. 2009. *Country Social Analysis: Ethnicity and Development in Vietnam.* Washington, DC: World Bank.

CHAPTER 11

History of a Life History

*An Eastern Bloc European Anthropologist
in "Communist" Vietnam*

Gábor Vargyas

In 1989, during my last fieldwork visit among the Bru of Quảng Trị Province, Central Vietnam, I recorded an eighteen-hour-long life history of a widely informed, exceptional Bru man, covering *grosso modo* two-thirds of the twentieth century, from French colonization to the end of Vietnam War and the resumption of life around reunification. As the story was full of—then and ever since—touchy political and ideological details, I promised to refrain from publishing any of the recording during the last quarter century. In 2007, in the course of a new fieldwork period in Đắk Lắk Province among a Bru community who were resettled during the war, the exceptionally icy circumstances of my fieldwork convinced me to give up my hopes for the advent of a politically benign period in which the story might be welcome and end my reticence to publication. If I disclose some of the delicate details of my field research below, I do it in the hope that it will cause no harm to my Bru friends or any of the persons involved. Research in the social sciences under antidemocratic regimes always runs the risk of having political repercussions that may call into question the purpose of our research.

Hungary and Vietnam: Sociopolitical and Historical Contexts of the Fieldwork

Between 1985 and 1989, profiting of a situation I had only known the disadvantages of, i.e. having been born and lived thirty-seven years in a "communist" country, I conducted fieldwork among the Bru [. . .] of Central Vietnam. (Vargyas 2000, 9)

This is the first phrase of my book *A la recherche des Brous perdus . . .* (*In Search of the Lost Bru . . .*).[1] An Eastern Bloc European "communist"[2] researcher in a Southeast Asian "communist" country is surely a tickler for most of my readers, including fellow anthropologists! And yet the story is plain, albeit uncommon, and for different reasons not yet told. In what follows, I shall reflect upon this situation of being an "Eastern-European" anthropologist working in a Southeast Asian "brotherly" communist country, through the history and vicissitudes of an eighteen-hour-long Bru ethnohistory I recorded in 1989. Delineating some of the constraints and pressures I had (and still have) to cope with, just as the solutions and answers I gave to them, I shall present an "insider's" view of doing fieldwork in a "brotherly" communist country, raising some fundamental questions regarding (historical) anthropological fieldwork in totalitarian countries. Such questions relate to ideological suspicion and confidence, censorship and self-censorship, ethics and the dangers of disclosing information received, and especially personal relationships to our long-time local colleagues/partners/assistants—the power of friendship.

Before discussing these questions, a short historical-political reminder is needed to contextualize the Hungarian and Vietnamese periods of my two fieldwork visits from 1985 to 1989 and from 2006 to 2007. Hungary, the "merriest barrack in the Socialist lager/concentration camp" was an Eastern Bloc country between 1949 and 1989 due to the liberation/occupation of Hungary by Soviet troops in 1945. After forty years of direct Soviet interference, the Hungarian People's Republic ceased to exist in 1989 when, following Soviet "reconstruction" (*perestroika*), a democratic transformation took place and the (Third) Hungarian Republic was proclaimed. Soviet troops, stationed "provisionally" in Hungary since 1945, left the country soon afterward. My first fieldwork visit (a total of eighteen months between 1985 and 1989) in Quảng Trị Province occurred precisely during this period of "regime change." It started in socialist times, and socialism ended in Hungary on October 23, 1989, while I was still in Vietnam.

As for Vietnam, the end of the Vietnam War and reunification in 1976 brought about a general hardening of the lines. The years 1976–1989 were a period of exceptional hardship from every point of view—ideologically, politically, and economically alike—with complete political closedness, general hostility toward and/or phobia of foreigners (even to "brotherly" ones), state-controlled Five-Year Plans, collectivized agriculture, a "subsidy economy" (*bao cấp*) with its system of food tickets, famine in many parts of the country, hyperinflation of the Vietnamese national currency (*đồng*), and so on. All that I knew from history in Hungary and Eastern Europe was a living reality in Vietnam. The fruits of the Renovation Period (*Đổi Mới*), initiated officially in December 1986, were only to be felt later. Despite being "communist brothers," we belonged to two (partly) different worlds.

Vicissitudes to Reach the Field

My first fieldwork visit took place in this fraught context, with all its contingencies and constraints. Belonging to the same club of Soviet satellite states opened the doors of one of the most inaccessible ethnographic fields in the world at the time. The project was set up within the framework of a scientific cooperation between two "socialist brother" countries' research institutions, the Institutes of Ethnology of the Hungarian Academy of Sciences (HAS) and its Vietnamese counterpart, the Vietnamese Academy of Social Sciences (VASS). The aim of the investigation was a holistic cultural anthropological study of a relatively enclosed, self-sufficient "traditional" ethnic minority group (which happened to be the Bru) through long-term participatory research. Fieldwork was to be carried out by a joint Vietnamese-Hungarian research team. As part of the agreement, the Hungarian stakeholders were to receive several young Vietnamese ethnographers for six months in order to prepare them for modern fieldwork; the Vietnamese stakeholders were to cover the costs of the stay of the research team in the field and provide research permissions. After some vicissitudes, a young colleague then aged twenty-eight, Vũ Đình Lợi, was chosen as the Vietnamese member of the team. In 1986, he spent six months in Hungary.

However simple this approach might seem, it was full of unforeseen "unexploded ordnance" (UXO). First of all, with an interesting mixture of disdain and concern for Europeans, independent from the person in question, Vietnamese colleagues shared the general conviction that Europeans could not survive in conditions that *they* (i.e., the Vietnamese) considered "hard": in the "highlands" among "primitive" peoples. Vietnamese people maintain long-held negative stereotypes about "hill peoples" (*mọi*) as true "savages" who eat raw food (salads), live in trees (pile dwellings), and have tails like monkeys (loincloths). These prejudices and fears had been only partly overcome by Vietnamese ethnographers themselves, who, for numerous reasons, spent short periods in the field. Thus, ensuring the well-being and safety of esteemed foreign guests was considered to be a quasi-patriotic (and in the given circumstances, political) duty of the host country and host institution. Therefore, non-Vietnamese researchers ("brotherly" ones included) were not allowed to venture unaccompanied in "dangerous" places. In this way, Vietnamese had projected their own fears and prejudices by trying to protect foreigners in order not to lose face in front of them. The key concern, then, was whether the Vietnamese person nominated for the project could make it in the field, and for how long. With no general rush of candidates, the common understanding was that Vietnamese colleagues could take turns in case it was needed, while I was not allowed to be alone for the sake of cooperation.

Second, there was a financing question, too. The total budget for the Vietnamese-Hungarian academic cooperation *in all social sciences* amounted to eight weeks. In other words, funding could not cover more than two months for one person, provided that there were no other applicants for the budget! This fact explains why I spent only two months in 1985 and 1986 in the field. However, between 1987 and 1988, with an extra US$1,000 in funding, I was able to spend ten months in the field. With this breakthrough, I conducted the last four months of fieldwork in 1989. Unexpectedly, however, the political changes in 1989 put an abrupt end to our cooperation. I shall return to these details soon.

The Power of Friendship, Part 1

Starting our fieldwork in 1985, the first go was a test from both sides. From the Vietnamese side, questions arose, such as "What will the foreigner be like?" "How will he endure fieldwork hardships?" "Will he cause (political) 'problems'?" And from the other side: "What will the Vietnamese be like?" "How will our fieldwork go?" In the first year, there were three of us: my Vietnamese colleague and soon friend Vũ Đình Lợi, myself, and an interpreter. We worked with an interpreter because although Lợi had enrolled in a speedy English class, he did not trust his English; he could not talk with me, even less interpret for me. We solved the problem ingeniously, by conversing in writing on all sorts of scraps of papers, notebooks, etc. I still keep one sheet that I reproduce here (figure 11.1). During a village banquet where I had to give a toast, I noticed that Lợi moved aside and was busy writing. With suspicion, I openly asked him (in writing): "Do you have to give a report on/about me to your Institute and to the Department of Foreign Relations? Do you think, this report can influence their decision for the future?"[3] His reply: "After this journey I have to tell the all words for my Institute and about me and you." I marked "the all words" with a circle on the paper and asked again: "How can you do this? Did you write down what I said?" His immediate reply was "I write diary," whereof I remarked: "I write, too! But not for my Institute, but for myself." With Lợi's final phrase "I shall say thing advantage for you and for me," we ended our "conversation."

This sheet of paper movingly perpetuates the spirit of those years and our mutual concerns. Besides me, anybody might have taken this acknowledgment as a confirmation of suspicion, "Is this person a colleague? No, they are a sneak, an informer!" As for me, I have taken it as a *love confession*. Coming from a similar background, I had no doubts about being strictly controlled in a—however "brotherly"—communist

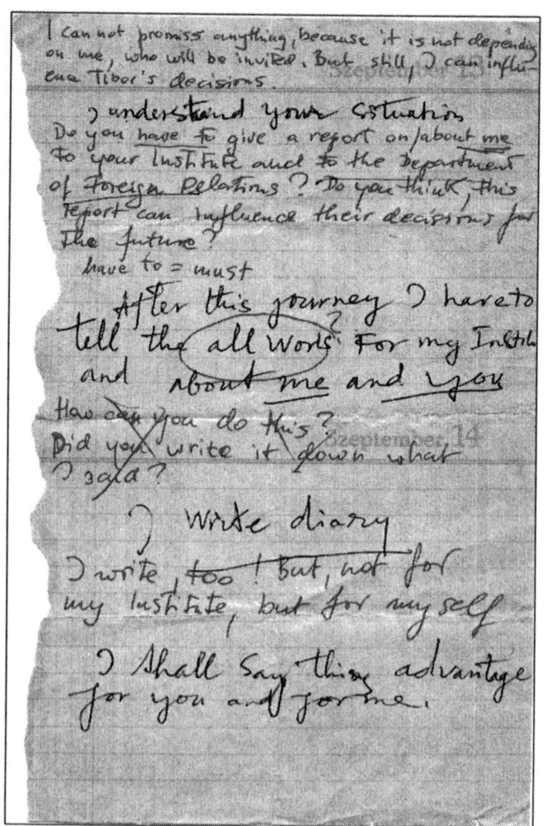

Figure 11.1. Written conversation between Lợi and the author (1985). In lighter color, one may read my questions and phrases; in darker color, the ones of Lợi. In reproducing our "conversation," I stuck to the original copy, notwithstanding grammatical mistakes. © G. Vargyas.

country. After all, vigilance and mistrust were two historical catchwords of communism in Europe; why should it be otherwise in Vietnam? The fact that my Vietnamese colleague openly admitted his duty of writing a report on me, on "the all words" I had said, proved his innocence and good will that was accentuated by his reassuring last sentence: "I shall say thing advantage for you and for me," meaning "Do not worry! I shall say advantage[ous]—i.e. beneficial things—for both of us."

I should admit, the first impetus of our friendship was given by mutual interest, a consideration we too often think is indecent, while trying to rule it out of our "proper" human interactions. Still, we know interest is practically present in all our personal relationships from love to friendship. Why should we be ashamed of it in this context? Lợi wished to come to Hungary, a dream in politically closed Vietnam, and I wished to return to Vietnam for a longer period of fieldwork. For me, it was vital to get a good echo at VASS through his report; for him, it was vital to get my sympathy and backing to come to Hungary. You help me, I help you! My first sentence on top of the paper points to this: "I can not promise anything, because it is not depending on me, who will be invited. But still, I can influence Tibor's [the director of my Institute] decisions." And I kept my word: through my direct intervention, Vũ Đình Lợi arrived the next year in Hungary for a six-month stay.

By virtue of these events, we became good friends, even accomplices. Whatever he could do, he did for me, and this was mutual. I still remember his terrified eyes when in 1986, he allowed me (*sic!*) for the first time to accompany a Bru friend to the forest. For him, a Vietnamese person, the forest was synonymous with danger, and he was literally *fully responsible* for my safety. We were late returning from the forest. He stood there, at the entrance of the trail into the forest, silent, waiting for me, shaking. A few minutes later, relieved, chatting, he showed me an unmistakable gesture of tying a rope around his neck smiling: "If you get into trouble, I shall be hung up."

A breakthrough came in February 1988, when we received a telegram calling him back to Hanoi. Curiously enough, this message did not say a word about me. Remember, we left Hanoi with two common understandings: (1) in case the fieldwork lasts too long, Vietnamese colleagues could take turns, and (2) I could not be alone. The great question was then, without a chaperone, what about me? Shall I return to Hanoi with him, or can I stay ("waiting" for an eventual chaperone relay)? The telegram, with its enigmatic wording, left the decision to us, or rather, to Lợi. And *this* turned out to be the loophole that influenced my fate once and for all.

After long discussions, torments, and sleepless nights, Lợi assumed the responsibility and decided to return alone. He knew that I would suffer should he force me to return, and I knew that my only chance for breaking the ice was to stay. And it came true! He departed and I stayed, and naturally the communist system had not shattered. Essentially, I think the core of the problem was that nobody wanted to bear responsibility, especially as the legal and other frames were not clear-cut. "Least said, soonest mended," but if there is only one person who takes the lead, things get set in motion. Obviously, this card was played by the Department of Foreign Relations, who were sympathetic and helpful but not otherwise willing to take any risks, leaving the decision to us. To cut a long story short, thirty-two years have passed since, but I am still moved by the daring step of my late Vietnamese friend, and I am beholden to him.

From this moment onward, everything went like clockwork. Lợi left February 8, 1988, and returned almost a month later. In the meantime, a telegram dated January 11, 1988 (*sic!*), reached me calling *both of us back* to Hanoi; it was sheer luck that we had not received it in time. On his return, Lợi brought a letter with him informing me that we had obtained extra funding from Hungary. As a sequel to all this, another telegram from the Foreign Relations Department of the VASS reached us and authorized me to stay for six more months. On April 5, we returned to Hanoi and remained away from Quảng Trị Province for six weeks. The second part of the fieldwork started in mid-May and lasted until the end of September, with a relay of Vietnamese colleagues comprising Trương Thụ and Vũ Đình Lợi. When Lợi left for a two-year scholarship in the Soviet Union, Thụ came again, although most importantly, I spent long periods alone in between. This was the happiest and most productive part of my fieldwork; I was already speaking Bru, alone in the village, living with a Bru family, moving freely around the whole region, and not hindered by any restriction (while going by the book).

The Bru Facing History

During my fieldwork, I soon became intrigued by the Bru's almost complete disinterest in history. As an anthropologist coming from Eastern Europe, where history and constant reinterpretation of past historical events was (and still is) at the center of sociopolitical life and political disputes, the Bru's almost total lack of historical remembrance was something that I could hardly accept and that called for an explanation.

The indifference was even more baffling considering that I was there hardly one decade after the end of the Vietnam War, an event of world historical importance that destroyed the life of the Bru in every possible aspect. Situated in the forested hilly border region between Laos and Vietnam, on both sides of the former Demilitarized Zone around the seventeenth parallel separating North and South Vietnam, they were heavily afflicted by the war, perhaps the most of all among highland minorities. During my stay, war was still lingering over us, and still, except for some by-the-way occasional remarks, I never heard a recollection of past historical events in public.

When musing about cultural traits relating to the (non)production of history, I noted the following lacks: (1) no endogenous writing system and no local chronicles or written historical documents; (2) no "native historians" or "keepers of tradition" (i.e., specialists with particular knowledge about and privileges over historical knowledge); (3) no named heroes or outstanding persons and/or heroic deeds, victories, and so on, in the past, and consequently no collective, public remembrance of history or historical events; (4) no formalized genealogies of ancestors, chiefs, rulers, or kings—a fact that is ruled out anyway by the acephalous character of Bru society and the common practice of teknonymy; and (5) no historical epic or widely circulating origin stories or any other folklore genres that could shed light on history. Though a few local historical legends do sometimes speak about migrations or origins and origin places, they are rare, not widely known, and poetically not well formulated. What is more important, they are never evoked publicly for substantiating a claim in disputes of juridical character or for arbitration. Overall, a would-be historian of the Bru's past would have to face a conspicuous lack of materials and documentation that a professional historian would be naturally used to dealing with. To give but one example of the difficulties in question, it has been impossible to geographically identify the Viên Kiều Mountain (the possible etymological forerunner of the Vân Kiều ethnonym used by the Vietnamese to denote the Bru) mentioned in historical sources between the sixteenth and nineteenth centuries.

Seemingly contrasting all of this, Bru religion, with its highly developed cult of the dead and ancestors, along with its concomitant periodical commemorative funeral feasts (symbolic secondary burials), seems to point in an opposite direction: to the religious importance of past generations (if not of the past itself). Indeed, in the course of the mortuary cycle, which lasts three generations (!) for each deceased, the memory of the deceased is periodically evoked: they are cared for, offered sacrifices and services, and, most importantly, purified. In theory, these practices could reflect a ritual attitude that is oriented toward the past. However, as I have argued elsewhere (Vargyas 2019, 10–12), there are a number of contradicting facts. First, the aim of the mortuary complex is to transform the *dead* (i.e., *historical* humans remembered with a name and a personality, imbued with personal memories) into *ancestors* (i.e., depersonalized, anonymous, far-off, *ahistorical* beings who merge, at the end of the cycle, into the figure of a primeval ancestral god or divinity called *yĩang Kaneaq*). Second, the cycle (i.e., the cult of the dead) lasts only for three generations. When the deceased no longer have descendants who knew them when they were alive, the cycle is closed. This termination occurs because the limit of *direct, personal recollection* of an individual in every human society, including the Bru, is three or (maximum) four generations.[4] When the personal memory of the deceased has vanished together with the people who knew them when they were alive, the dead are transformed into ancestors. The "conveyor-belt" leading toward Kaneaq is, however, always on the move: by the time the old dead leave it and enter ancestral divinity, there are new ones who step in and replace them. At the end of the cycle, the ancestors return among the humans in the shape of (the ancestral altar of) Kaneaq for good, in order to protect them. Third, the Bru deal with their dead only en masse, never personally, and even then only once a year during the yearly sacrifice for the "recent dead" (i.e., those who are not yet at the stage of being transformed into ancestors). The same holds true for the "ten-yearly" periodical, symbolic "reburials." While the names of the deceased are evoked, it is the recent dead as a category that are treated and commemorated at these occasions rather than the particular individuals. Funeral songs and some special rituals, as a rule, deal with human fate *in general,* but never with personal idiosyncrasies. No personal memories, deeds, or stories about the departed are evoked at funerals. And let us repeat, all of this occurs only once every ten years. Fourth, and finally, the Bru never visit graves and cemeteries. They have no prescribed dates in a month to do so, as there are among the Vietnamese, and there is no "all souls day" nor mention of the departed unless it is inevitable. In sum, everything seems to point toward deindividualization and ahistorization in favor of complete oblivion. The cult of the dead and the concomitant commemoration of the deceased aim, paradoxically, to erase the personal memory of the dead from collective remembrance and replace it with an anonymous ahistorical primeval divinity.

History of an Eighteen-Hour-Long Life History

Sharing the Bru's lives for good or ill, I had plenty of occasions to freely contact anybody. "Hanging about," I participated in events, conducted structured and semistructured interviews, and chatted in public and private, whether during rituals, communal work, or at home around the fireplace. I also had some key informants. Among them, my best friend, khŏi Sarăng,[5] was an uncommonly communicative, "extroverted" person for the notoriously shy Bru, a true connoisseur of Bru culture and custom. Owing to his position as a former village chief and his involvement in the war, he was widely knowledgeable about recent historical matters and was a prominent personality in every aspect among his fellow tribesmen. During our conversations, he made occasional remarks evoking his own life experiences as examples for a matter under discussion. For example, he spoke about his wife having a baby while he was imprisoned (Bru ways of dealing with misbegotten children), performing a shamanic ritual in a strategic hamlet behind a fence of barbed wire during the Vietnam War, gambling in spite of the state prohibition both in his home village and in the army, and so on. First, I did not pay particular attention to these stories apart from their illustrative value. But after a while, I realized that the mosaics I got to know added up to an unusually rich life history exemplifying not only his own fate but also possibly that of many Bru in general. I then started to make notes to remember them, entertaining myself with the plan for an eventual future recording. From the very first moment, I felt that his life story, if told by me and not worded by him with his matchless elegance and liveliness, would only amount to a colorless and tasteless skeleton that did not have any literary value.

However, for such an enterprise, a good command of the local language and complete confidence are needed—two things that I acquired progressively. Returning home in 1988, after ten months of fieldwork, I felt confident: at the next occasion I should be able to realize my hope of recording khŏi Sarăng. And in 1989, during my last fieldwork visit, I had taken along a small cassette player, which was easy to carry and hide, in addition to my cumbersome reel-to-reel tape recorder. This detail is worth mentioning because every time I motioned toward the big tape recorder, I was surrounded by an inquisitive crowd in a split second, mostly children looking for something happening. The small widget was thus a way of evading an undesirable audience.

After returning to the field, I was waiting for an opportunity to propose the plan to khỡi Sarăng. Then, on one occasion, when it was only the two of us in his guard hut on a swidden plot, I asked him about recording his story. To my great disappointment, his first reaction was immediate refusal unless "we leave out his friendship [i.e., involvement] with the Americans." He was strikingly open regarding his fears: "The Vietnamese will slaughter me!" (*yuan pơaiq kũq!*). Having no other choice, I accepted his conditions, hoping—which became true a few days later—that he would change his mind and consent to record his complete life history. On October 28, 1989, six weeks before the end of my fieldwork, we started recording his life history. We recorded in complete privacy, only the two of us in his hut on the swidden plot, over six to seven sessions until December 1, all of which occurred mostly at night. We started with less "touchy" topics and then chatted freely in any direction based on my notes and personal memories, exchanging ideas and opinions and asking for additional information, sometimes until sunrise. Even though khỡi Sarăng's fears dissolved progressively with time, I had to reassure him several times that I would not let anybody listen to any part of the recording, and that I would never publish a single word of it during his lifetime—a condition that I naturally accepted and complied with.

Khỡi Sarăng's fears were not irrational: his life was full of UXO or political discrepancies. The majority of what he talked about was then (and in some regards still is) considered a delicate subject. Born around 1940 in a village called Vung Khô near Khe Sanh, as a child, he encountered the French at the local French fort around 1947–1948. Being too young, he did not take part in the fights against them. In his youth, in the Second Indochina War (1955–1975), he got involved in the underground resistance, similar to many other Bru villagers. In 1959, he was imprisoned in Quảng Trị for "communist work." After two years in prison (1959–1961), he returned to his village and became village chief. Not concerned about his imprisonment, he continued working for the northern side, but when he had to flee because of it, he was let down despite earlier promises. Deeply disappointed, he switched to the South Vietnamese (American) side in 1965. In early spring 1965, he moved his entire village close to Khe Sanh, to the "fortified hamlet" by the airport next to the military base, in order to protect his fellow tribesmen. He enrolled in the American army, and from 1965 to 1968, he served as a mercenary, first undergoing a four-month military training in 1965, then a second one in 1967 in Pleiku. In 1968, when Khe Sanh

was besieged, he fled with his family to Cam Lộ, from where he continued on to a refugee camp in Kũa near Cam Lộ. He lived there from 1968
to 1972, until the communist takeover. In 1972, he moved back to his
home region, where he first met me in 1985. We saw each other for the
last time in 1989, as I did not return to Quảng Trị for almost thirty years.

The Problem with Transcription

Once a recording is finished, the next steps are transcription, translation,
and editing. Transcription on the spot proved impossible for me for several
reasons. First, we finished recording a few days before my departure. To transcribe an eighteen-hour recording of a free-flowing chat, particularly in the
case of a linguistically unfamiliar and unresearched tribal tongue, one needs
several months of intense work, especially without the help of bilingual assistants, dictionaries, or language manuals. In 1989, I merely had access to a
photocopy of the then only available Bru-Vietnamese dictionary (Hoàng Tuệ
1986). At the beginning of my field research, I did not speak Vietnamese or
Bru, leaving me with the choice to learn either Bru or Vietnamese. Although
I opted for the former, which proved to be a good decision for fieldwork, in
later years (e.g., working with the recording), I encountered many obstacles
related to not speaking the state language. And even if I was more or less
fluent in everyday Bru (with many mistakes, probably, and coupled with an
awful accent), transcription of a text with high literary quality, mixed with
many unknown Vietnamese (military, political, juridical, etc.) words, was a
hard task that further limited my abilities. Second, there were some technical problems, too: continuous rewinding and replay, which is inevitable for
transcription, ruins the machine (and rules out eventual future recordings);
it discharges the batteries (no electricity in the village in those days); and
generally, there is no place to withdraw to work in private, where no one can
hear the recording under transcription. In sum, I started the transcript only
at home, in Hungary, and it was soon interrupted for many reasons, leaving
it to incubate for nearly twenty years.

1989: "Year of the Turn"

The last year of the Vietnamese-Hungarian academic cooperation, 1989
came with tremendous changes of world political importance: the collapse of the Soviet communist system and later the Soviet Union itself, the
demolition of the Berlin Wall, the dissolution of the Warsaw Pact and of

the COMECON, and the transitional period from communism to capitalism in former Eastern Bloc countries. A great part of these changes happened while I was in the "bush." I learned about the dismantlement of the Berlin Wall in an Aeroflot plane taking off from Hanoi, and returned home by Christmas 1989, one night before the execution of dictator Nicolae Ceauşescu, general secretary of the Romanian Communist Party. The world was changing with lightning speed around us: old values and relationships were reevaluated, revalorized, or depreciated. Once a "friend" or "brother," Hungary had become a "traitor" to communism and, with it, to Vietnam—at least until the Renovation Period had made its impact. At the Hungarian Academy, the Eastern Bloc Countries subdivision of the Foreign Relations Department was soon dissolved and former "socialist" cooperation arrangements were depreciated. We "feasted our eyes on Paris and what was prepared for us."[6] However, with these changes, the only advantage of the old communist system, Hungary's privileged academic relations with Vietnam, slipped away too. Although I could return for conferences and short-term visits, I had lost my chance to complete long-term fieldwork in Vietnam for almost two decades. Moreover, once "poor communists," we soon turned into "poor capitalists." A Vietnamese friend commented: "Gábor, you are a dear old friend, but a poor one. Now the Japanese, the Swedish and the Americans are wooing us . . . and they bring money!"

In the Lure of History

Because of these unforeseeable world political events and the metamorphosis of my personal and professional life, the 1989 recording of khởi Sarăng's life history remained partly unfinished, and the work with it was interrupted. However, inspired and instigated by the themes of the recording and also by my formation as an Eastern European anthropologist, where ethnography and anthropology are considered historical sciences, I turned toward historical anthropology. In order to trace back the antecedents of all I had experienced in the field, I endeavored to collect every possible source relating to the Bru: travelogues from the end of the nineteenth century, colonial administrative and military reports, linguistic and other scientific (medical, geological, art historical, and, rarely, ethnographical) materials, ecclesiastic sources, and especially vast documentation on the Vietnam War. During two and a half years of scholarship in France (1991–1992, 1996–1997, and 1999), I also researched the archives of the École française d'Extrême Orient in Paris, uncovering unique documents from the beginning of the twentieth century relating to the Bru. My resulting book *In Search of the Lost Bru* (Vargyas 2000) is a summary of Bru ethnohistory, the process of getting to know them, and the history of research about them, covering a time lapse of approximately 120 years before my own fieldwork.

Meaningfully, some of the historical documents uncovered touch upon the questions I discussed with khỏi Sarăng on several occasions: the conspicuously pacific, "shy" political ideology of the Bru; their self-conscious evasion of any overt clashes with the surrounding state powers on the peripheries of which they live; their "weapons of the weak" (Scott 1985); and the lack of any political component in their ethnic identity. In an unpublished conference paper (Vargyas 1996), in my book (Vargyas 2000), and in a paper honoring Vietnamese-born French historian, Nguyễn Thế Anh (Vargyas 2008), I discussed the question of the Bru's state evasion years before it had become a debated topic following James Scott's (2009) *The Art of Not Being Governed*. I have repeatedly come back to this question (Vargyas 2016, 2017), arguing (albeit critically) in favor for Scott and refuting Oscar Salemink (2015). In earlier papers, I did not make mention of the life history even if my argumentation was partly based on it; in the past years, I reevaluated my strategy and began to exploit the material in thematic papers (Vargyas 2012, 2020).

Ethical Problems concerning Publication

The reason for my reticence hitherto was an ethical problem. Since the story was full of touchy political and ideological details, conforming to my promise, I not only refrained from publishing any of it during a quarter of a century but even stayed silent about the existence of this unparalleled document.[7] However, in 1996, following a UNESCO conference on intangible cultural heritage in Vientiane, Laos, I got back to the Bru on the other side of the border, and was struck by the sad news of khỏi Sarâng's untimely death.[8] Though this event in theory could have absolved me of my promise, I did not rush to publish for two reasons. First, the elapsed time was too short. I feared that the story could bring discredit—if not on khỏi Sarâng himself—to his relatives, the protagonists of the stories who are still alive, and to the Bru in general. Let us face it: notwithstanding the Renovation Period and ideological melting in Vietnam from 1985 to 1989, there were still inviolable political taboos in force (e.g., the cause of communism, the "anti-American war," or the everlasting fraternity and unity of the Vietnamese majority and the minorities). In this respect, khởi Sarâng's life is a true tickler insofar as he fought for a decade for the Việt Minh/Việt Cộng forces, before enduring two years of imprisonment for it (1959–1961). But, when he felt betrayed by them at a particular moment, he went over to the other side and spent some years as an American mercenary (1965–1968), before returning to his home region again in 1972. In Vietnam, as my second fieldwork visit in 2007 painfully illustrated, one may never be sure that political change will always turn out to be unidirectionally positive, foreshadowing democratization. Socioeconomic détente may also entail political hardening. Khởi Sarâng's life story could have been and may still be used against the Bru.

The second reason was a personal one, albeit not independent from the former: I did not want to risk my chances of being able to go back for a second, longer period of fieldwork. By then, I wanted to visit a resettled, doubly stigmatized Bru community in Đắk Lắk Province (Krông Pắc District, Ea Hiu commune). This community was resettled in 1972 during the war in a showy airlift rescue relocation project, as they were "allies" of the Americans (Nguyễn n.d.); the community was also stigmatized because most of them were Protestants, being the first converts of American proselytization among the Bru. If, as was highly probable, state censure would find Khởi Sarâng's story politically *not* correct, my hard-earned, protractedly built reputation as a "trustworthy" anthropologist would be lost forever. In this respect, let me note that I had received research permission in 2007—without any problems, in the course of a few days, alone among Euro-American anthropologists up to the present as far as I know—to spend half a year in what was then, and is still today, the most closed part of Vietnam, the area around the city of Buôn Ma Thuột in the Central Highlands. I feel thus substantiated to think that positive reports, echoes about our former activity (ending up in the files of internal security offices) that reflected our trustfulness, do (or did) play a role in Vietnam in granting us research permission.[9]

The Power of Friendship, Part 2: Second Fieldwork Visit among the Resettled Bru of Đắk Lắk, 2007

In 2007, after nearly two decades of unsuccessful attempts, I finally returned to Vietnam for a six-month period of fieldwork as an associated external research fellow for the project Kinship and Social Support in China and Vietnam (2006–2008), carried out by the Max Planck

Institute for Social Anthropology, Halle. This time I returned as a "rich capitalist," having the same financial circumstances as any "Western" anthropologist. I was also associated with the Institute of Cultural Studies, which was more dynamic then than other institutes at the VASS, and I was accompanied by a new associate, a dear friend and colleague ever since, Đinh Hồng Hải, from the same institute. I insisted on visiting the Bru of Đắk Lắk for two reasons. First, they were frequent protagonists of khởi Sarâng's stories, since they all fought on the same American side. Second, I wanted to assess cultural change, and they were the oldest resettled Bru community in Vietnam, living for thirty-five years among the Rhade/Ê Đê and Vietnamese as a relatively numerous yet still enclosed enclave of around 3,500 persons (Vargyas 2010, 2019).

The time has not come yet to tell all the details of this fieldwork visit. However, suffice it to say that a few years earlier, in 2001 and 2004, minority riots had taken place in the area of Buôn Ma Thuột that ended with a most unfortunate bloody retaliation (see Guérin et al. 2003, 1–7; Salemink 2003; Human Rights Watch 2002). As a consequence, the area was hermetically closed and militarily controlled, with an icy atmosphere far surpassing the "hard" period of the 1980s. Given the historical and political circumstances, I can consider myself very privileged to have received permission to enter the area and spend nearly half a year doing research there. But the fact remains that from the very first moment, I was subjected to an incredible degree of surveillance and restriction that made fieldwork practically impossible. Upon our arrival, a chief internal security policeman came to see us, introduced himself, and explained that I could not leave the house without being accompanied by him. We had to notify him a few minutes in advance by mobile phone, and only when he arrived (we never found out from where!) could we set out. We spent the first months of "research work" in a small team consisting of him, one or two of his subordinates, one or two local party or security leaders, Đinh Hồng Hải as research assistant, and myself. Moreover, detailed notes regarding our conversations were made (through bilingual locals) on the spot! It is natural that I had to abandon the idea of conducting any systematic fieldwork in such circumstances.

Appalled by this situation and not wanting to cause any inconvenience to my Bru friends, I decided to conduct research only at events that happened independently from us, in which we were allowed to participate (e.g., housewarming parties, funerals, agricultural work, etc.), focusing instead on "harmless" topics, my "plan B," which was compiling the transcript and translating "old folklore recordings"—khŏi Sarâng's life history! Of course, this work was not as harmless as we feigned it to be. But withdrawn to our house where we were only partially supervised, I could work more or less safely on the transcript, concentrating all my time and effort on this long-overdue project.

To be honest, I had prepared myself for this work anyway, knowing that the circumstances were favorable for such work. At the end of my stay, after a serious four-month race against time and ten to twelve hours of work per day withdrawn in my house, I returned to Hungary with the complete Bru transcript and its word-for-word Hungarian translation. A true vengeance for the icy circumstances.

This was, however, not without any thrill: I experienced "doorbell-dread,"[10] a Hungarian notion from the 1950s that I was familiar with only through belles lettres and documentary films. This idea relates to a fear of the secret police ringing the doorbell during someone's deepest sleep, at three or four in the morning, to take away "culprits" in black police cars. The doorbell was abrupt, but the dread was constant. One story will suffice to illustrate the atmosphere: Đinh Hồng Hải—who turned out to be not only a most helpful research assistant, a knowledgeable colleague, and a true friend but also a born bricoleur—installed an old-style dial-up internet line on our landlord's telephone.[11] A few days later the secret police chief warned our landlord that he could have "problems" because of us and that should "anything" happen, he was to bear responsibility. He came to see us nearly crying, showing his hands in handcuffs with an unmistakable gesture. At this point, Hải took a big breath and went to see the secret police chief. He assumed full responsibility for *me*, for *my* deeds, and *demanded* the use of internet for our purposes! Internal security forces were and are the most dreadful power, a state within the state in every former "communist" country, with no difference in Vietnam, especially then, and in Đắk Lắk. People shivered if they had to meet the security forces for any reason. I do not know of anybody in Vietnam who would have dared to do the same thing for me!

However much I was and still I am moved by his brave deed, from this moment onward I did not sleep well. I was not fearing so much for myself but for my landlord, for Hải, and for the Bru in general. What if the police found something objectionable in what I was doing? What if they realized the true nature of my work? At some points I was near to paranoia, near to what my colleague Nguyễn Tất Thắng had done in 1989 after our common field trip: he invited me to his home for dinner without written permission (at that time, we still needed one for meeting Vietnamese friends), and in full remorse after my departure, he went to the local police station and denounced himself.

But then, a thread broke. I could not contain myself anymore. One day our chief of (not so secret) police, a brilliant guy with whom we otherwise got on well, notwithstanding the power he represented, complained about "these histrionic and double-tongued Bru [cadres] who work for the present regime but praise the good old days [of the Republic of Vietnam]!" Then, in a sudden outbreak of ire, I gave him a lesson in history by recounting a tragic story in which two siblings on opposing sides of the civil war shoot at each other, and only come to recognize their mistake after a lethal wound is inflicted (a Bru story). There are no "goodies" and "baddies," just victims. This discussion was the moment when I irrevocably decided that khỏi Sarâng's life history should be published. According to my diary entry of June 21, 2007,

> [T]his story should introduce my planned book, roughly as follows: "One day, in 2007, when in a dark period of my life, in the field in Đắk Lắk, chatting in a coffee-shop with my dear (?) secret policeman-friend about Vietnamese history, I tried to explain to him the problem this book is all about . . . thirty-two years after re-unification and twelve to thirteen years after the death of khỏi Sarâng, the time has come to face all that happened. May this book help in realizing that the Bru and other minorities have been victims, who did not want anything but to survive in the longest and most cruel war of humankind since World War II."

Future Prospects

Here we are, after thirty years, with khỏi Sarâng's life history finally transcribed and translated. The ethical problems having dissipated, the question of what and how to publish could now be raised. There are technical questions and questions of principle. As for the latter, the cardinal one is whether the story should be published wholly and integrally in regard to its political sensitivity. When we discussed the matter in the field in view of an eventual Vietnamese edition, Đinh Hồng Hải proposed a kind of compromise, "to leave out a few problematic sentences but otherwise no problem." Even if I was and am still not sure whether this "minor" self-censorship would be enough from a political point of view, my immediate reaction was then and is now: "No way. If I waited until now, it was not for censoring khõi Sarâng or myself." The strength of the text—among others—resides in its integrity and straightforward style. It has to come out unexpurgated, without any alteration to its original phrasing.

This brings us, however, to a second, related question: In what way is this text "integral"? We have seen that the interview remained partially unfinished. In 1989, I planned to return the following year and make some additional recordings—a plan that unfortunately never was realized. But independently from the fact whether the missing details are minor or major as compared to the whole, when is a life history finished? When is it "complete"? Obviously, personal remembrance is influenced by a multitude of conditions. Among them, the context of storytelling is one that weighs the most, and we have seen the circumstances of it. Who knows what else khõi Sarâng could or would have told me, friendship or confidence notwithstanding, in other circumstances? His death and our unforeseeable fate have put an unfortunate end to our joint venture. There is no other choice than working with the material at our disposal. This is but one more reason in favor of an integral publication as much as possible.

A third principal question relates to the time lapse between data collection and scientific elaboration. Has the elapsed time changed the value of the material in any way? Will the fact that thirty years have passed since the recording necessarily mean that my interpretation of it will be different? For a historian, the first question does not even arise; there is always a time lapse between the document's creation and its scientific elaboration, independently from the amount of elapsed time. The life history of khõi Sarâng is, by its very nature, a historical document. My interpretation of it may prove to be (slightly or perhaps considerably) different today from what it would have been thirty years ago, owing to my personal and professional experiences and development since. But once the text is published in its entirety and its recording context is clarified, the reader will be able to critically evaluate my propositions and to reanalyze it as a source material. As far as I can see, the problems of interpretation are inherent due to our insufficient historical and cultural knowledge of the period in question.

Turning to the technical problems related to publication, the most difficult question is editing. The text is currently transcribed (in Bru) and translated (into Hungarian) in a form as near as possible to literal translation. It ramifies into many directions; it shifts in themes, times, and places; and sometimes there is a true dialogue, while at other occasions the recording runs for tens of minutes without interruption. There are also moments of repetition and overlap, with the same story sometimes told twice but with different accents and details. It has to be "smoothed" into a "coherent" and "continuous" "story script" (see Turner and Delisle, this volume). One organizing principle will surely be chronology. But as I focus on one interviewee's complete life history, and not on a particular aspect of many respondents' lives (see Pholsena, this volume), beyond the chronological perspective, editing into thematic chapters will probably prove to be necessary, too. And even then, the question will remain: What should be done with short fragments that do not fit anywhere? How should the integrity of the text be kept? Last but not least, there is a stylistic question, too: How should khởi Sarâng's typically Bru style be preserved? Shall I keep, for example, his word "ladder" (for entering Bru pile dwellings) when describing the decorated concrete *staircase* in an elegant multistory restaurant in Saigon where he was taken as a recompense by a South Vietnamese general who misappropriated his military pay?

Epilogue

I presented above a contextualized *longue-durée* history of my fieldwork in Vietnam, with special reference to an eighteen-hour-long life history recorded in 1989 and my ethnohistorical research. In recent years, the conceptual issue has been raised whether Southeast Asian socialist/communist countries were a peculiar terrain among anthropological fields, in which classical fieldwork methods were not applicable due to the sociopolitical conditions prevailing in them, necessitating the adaptation of new methods in order to "fit the challenges on the ground in socialist Asia" (Michaud 2010, 224; see also Turner and Daviau 2010; Turner 2013a; Luong 2006). Agreeing fully with this proposition, my case is an exception that confirms the rule. Alone among Euro-American anthropologists up to the present, I succeeded in carrying out classical long-term participatory anthropological field research among the Bru in the Central Highlands of Vietnam between 1985 and 1989 (but not really in 2007).

Additionally, we have seen how my positionality of being an "insider" Eastern Bloc European anthropologist in a "brotherly" communist country, Vietnam, impacted my opportunities. The advantages of it were and are clear: (easier) access to the field and an incontestably privileged position even if, being a "foreign" researcher notwithstanding, I had to make my painful way to the field just as any other "Western" researcher then and ever since. Another advantage may have been that coming from a similar political system, I was familiar with, and perhaps therefore endured more easily, the unusual (fieldwork) conditions: having to face and deal with an uncriticizable, antidemocratic political system and its representatives (party cadres, functionaries, police, etc.); waiting for authorizations; being accompanied in the field and controlled and supervised in many subtle or open ways; and enduring censorship and self-censorship, to mention but a few. As for disadvantages, there was the unavailability of any other part of the world for ethnographic research; the lack of funding; the obvious restraints in political, economic, cultural, and religious aspects alike; and last but not least, the historical knowledge of, and fear of, the abuses of the power.

Owing to the relatively early date (as compared to other papers in this volume) of my fieldwork, shortly before the Renovation Period and the general sociopolitical and economic opening heralding the advent of (inter)national development policies and an NGO project world, the more or less similar sociopolitical macro context and field procedures differently impacted those who came after me. I arrived through scientific cooperation based on political alliance and "fraternity," in the framework of academic cooperation, with openly proclaimed research aims encompassing classical anthropological fieldwork methods, and in a period of almost complete political closure. Those arriving a few years later in the next decade, in an incipient period of "double domination"[12] (Scott 1990), arrived perhaps in more favorable and open sociopolitical circumstances but lacked the same political and institutional "fraternal" background. Moreover, since they came mostly through NGOs and international development agencies aiming at delimited, short-term projects, they had to face not only the general macro context and limitations but also their own constraints owing to their agenda and methods (Turner 2013b; McAllister 2013; Daviau 2010).

Coming back to my own story, it may essentially be summed up in terms of three concepts proposed and discussed by Jean Michaud (2010, 223) regarding Southeast Asian "socialist" fields: creativity, reflexivity, and trust. As for the first two, we have seen the ways in which I succeeded in transcending my situation, getting through the system, making my way for long-term fieldwork. I do not pretend that any "insider"—Hungarian or other Eastern Bloc European anthropologist—would have responded in the same way I did, or that I have always given the most adequate responses. I am not even sure if I would react today in the same ways—though at large probably yes. There are no two identical situations.

Times change and even if we change with them, the supposed "bad" may later turn out to be the "better." In the 1980s, in Quảng Trị, notwithstanding the quasi-impossibility of doing social research in Vietnam, I was left completely free and unsupervised for long periods in the end, allowing me to follow a more classical approach to field research. The situation twenty years later in Đắk Lắk was dramatically worse, contrary to my expectations. In order to endure it psychologically and achieve results, besides perseverance and self-control, I also had "to adjust, circumvent and sometimes bend" (Michaud 2010, 223) the prevailing rules to a much greater extent than during my earlier fieldwork—a process in which my local research associates played an essential role.

This brings me to my most important point, the relationship with my Vietnamese counterparts and friends, ethnographers Vũ Đình Lợi and Đinh Hồng Hải. The point I wish to emphasize is that friendship and trust are vital ingredients. Whatever the relationship or difference between "social capital," "rapport," and "friendship" is, and whatever the doubts there are about genuine "friendship" in the European sense of the word[13] and "faking friendship" in the field (Driessen 1998; Duncombe and Jessop 2002; Glesne 1989), there is no denying the fact that strong interpersonal feelings of solidarity, respect, closeness, interdependence, and mutual trust mixed with tender emotions—a relationship that we commonly denote with the word "friendship"—may (and often do) arise between those working together in a locale for a long time.[14] One facet of this friendship and the trust it is based on, between the anthropologist and their local "informants" or "friends," is commonplace, being the methodological alpha and omega of our discipline, a compulsory part in every fieldwork manual (e.g., Watson 1999; Eriksen 1995; see also Rabinow 2007; De La Cruz and Gay y Blasco 2012). "However [. . .] trust may involve state officials and collaborators at all levels—academics, interpreters, librarians, guides, jeep drivers—who are far more likely to agree to help once they recognise one is a trustworthy person" (Michaud 2010, 224). Within the wide scale of possible relationships mentioned by Michaud, especially the one about our long-time "socialist" Asian local academic partners/collaborators/assistants, whose task or duty is to accompany us in the field, seems to me to be a neglected and very much underestimated question. Apart from some occasional remarks or half-page passing mentions or rare attempts "to give agency to others involved in the research project" (Turner 2010, 130; Turner 2013c; Daviau 2010, 202–203), there is hardly any literature available on the question. Yet what else if *this* is not a true "on the ground challenge in socialist Asia" (Michaud 2010, 224)? What else if *this* is not a question uniquely tied up with "socialist" Asian fieldwork conditions?[15]

Let me then close my chapter with some concluding remarks focusing on this question. I have conveyed above one episode of my lasting relationship with my Vietnamese anthropologist counterparts resulting from our common field research among the Bru. Obviously, relationships are never static, and friendships spanning over decades endure ups and downs, experiencing high points and vicissitudes and even true conflicts (Nagy 2018), just as any other human rapport (e.g., marriage). I do not wish to idealize our rapport, though death as the ultimate end of our life (in the case of Vũ Đình Lợi) inevitably arouses nostalgia. In this chapter, I presented and analyzed only one single facet of our relationship: my indebtedness to my Vietnamese colleagues/fellow anthropologists for their decisive role in "bending the rules" and enabling me to access the field. The story of our whole relationship remains to be told on another occasion.

From my personal experience, the lesson for me is the power of friendship. Similar to "good accounts," hardships endured together make good friends. Fieldwork, especially classical long-term participatory research, is a hard trial in every aspect, physically and psychologically alike, resembling military service or boarding school in its creation of strong bonds of comradeship. Those who endured it together and got on well in hard times will remain forever friends. Such was and is my case with my two Vietnamese colleagues who accompanied me during most of my fieldwork: Vũ Đình Lợi and Đinh Hồng Hải. It is high time to admit that I would have achieved much less without their constant help, understanding, and esteem, just as our mutual friendship relying on trust, whereby we overcame thousands of kilometers, cultural differences, and resulting life strategies. When thinking reflexively about my fieldwork, I shall never forget that when Sir Edmund Hillary became the first to summit Mount Everest, he had Tenzing Norgay, the Nepalese Sherpa, with him. His name should never be forgotten.

Notes

1. For the history and anthropology of the Bru in general, see Vargyas (2023).

2. I use "communist" in quotation marks here to remind readers that being a citizen of a communist country does not automatically indicate that a person is a communist.

3. I inserted here a grammatical explanation for Lợi ("have to = must") because I realized he had not understood everything.

4. To this question, see Assmann's (2011, 34–41) "communicative memory" as opposed to "cultural memory." The former "comprises memories related to the recent past [. . .] what the individual shares with his contemporaries" (36), and it is typically restricted to eighty to one hundred years. The latter is the long-term memory of societies that can span up to three thousand years.

5. Khởi Sarăng is a pseudonym I use in my publications for GDPR (the EU's General Data Protection Regulation) reasons.

6. This is a paraphrase of a well-known quotation from eighteenth-century Hungarian poet János Batsányi's "On the Changes in France," written in 1789.

7. For inherent dangers in publication, see Salemink (2013) and Vargyas (2018). In our countries, the usual deadline for declassifying documents is twenty-five years.

8. His exact birthday is not known, but he must have been in his fifties.

9. I could quote several cases when I learned that news of my public appearances and of what I said at conferences got back to Vietnam.

10. In Hungarian: *csengőfrász.*

11. In Ea Hiu, we lived in a rich Bru man's house in the center of the commune, some ten meters from the Communist Party's and the local government's offices. His landline was an extension of the office system, the only private telephone line in the commune. At the same time, however, we were experiencing the rapid spread of mobile phones.

12. Double domination: the state's political and economic marginalization of an ethnic minority by labeling it "backward" in an era of liberalized economic development.

13. See, for example, Driessen (1998, 132): "If we use the western definition of friendship [. . .]—stressing closeness, solidarity, absence of ulterior motives, reciprocity, impulsiveness in mutual choice, independence of social distinctions such as age, class, sex—only very few relationships in the field would qualify as such."

14. See, for example, Harrell and Li's (2013, 260–279) "textual desert—emotional oasis" metaphor on emotional engagement.

15. As far as I am aware, neither in former "socialist" Eastern European countries (including Hungary) nor in the Soviet Union was there a similar state imposition in effect for doing anthropological fieldwork.

References

Assmann, Jan. 2011. *Cultural Memory and Early Civilization: Writing, Remembrance, and Political Imagination.* Cambridge: Cambridge University Press.

Daviau, Steeve. 2010. "Conducting Fieldwork with Tarieng Communities in Southern Laos: Negotiating Discursive Places between Neoliberal Dogmas and Lao Socialist Ideology." *Asia Pacific Viewpoint* 51 (2): 193–205.

De La Cruz, Liria, and Paloma Gay y Blasco. 2012. "Friendship, anthropology." *Anthropology and Humanism* 37: 1–14.

Driessen, Henk. 1998. "Romancing Rapport: The Ideology of 'Friendship' in the Field." *Folk* 40: 123–136.

Duncombe, Jean, and Julie Jessop. 2002. "'Doing Rapport' and the Ethics of 'Faking Friendship'." In *Ethics in Qualitative Research,* edited by T. Miller, M. Birch, M. Mauthner, and J. Jessop, 108–122. London: Sage Publications.

Eriksen, Thomas Hylland. 1995. *Small Places, Large Issues: An Introduction to Social and Cultural Anthropology.* 2nd ed. London: Pluto Press.

Glesne, Corrine. 1989. "Rapport and Friendship in Ethnographic Research." *Qualitative Studies in Education* 2 (1): 45–54.

Guérin, Mathieu, Andrew Hardy, Nguyễn Văn Chính, and Stan Tan Boon Hwee. 2003. *Des montagnards aux minorités ethniques: Quelle intégration national pour les habitants des hautes terres du Viet Nam et du Cambodge?* Paris: L'Harmattan; Bangkok: IRASEC.

Harrell, Stevan, and Li Xingxing. 2013. "Textual Desert—Emotional Oasis: An Unconventional Confessional Dialogue on Field Experience." In *Red Stamps and Gold Stars: Fieldwork Dilemmas in Upland Socialist Asia,* edited by S. Turner, 260–279. Vancouver: UBC Press.

Hoàng Tuệ, ed. 1986. *Sách học tiếng Brũ Vân Kiều* [Bru Vân Kiêu language manual]. Hà Nôi: n.p.

Human Rights Watch. 2002. *Repression of Montagnards: Conflicts over Land and Religion in Vietnam's Central Highlands.* April 23. https://www.hrw.org/report/2002/04/23/repression-montagnards/conflicts-over-land-and-religion-vietnams-central-highlands.

Luong van Hy. 2006. "Structure, Practice, and History: Contemporary Anthropological Research on Vietnam." *Journal of Vietnamese Studies* 1 (1–2): 371–410.

McAllister, Karen. 2013. "Marginality in the Margins: Serendipity, Gatekeepers, and Gendered Positionalities in Fieldwork among the Khmu in Northern Laos." In *Red Stamps and Gold Stars: Fieldwork Dilemmas in Upland Socialist Asia,* edited by S. Turner, 165–184. Vancouver: UBC Press.

Michaud, Jean. 2010. "Research Note: Fieldwork, Supervision, and Trust." *Asia Pacific Viewpoint* 51 (2): 220–225.

Nagy, Zoltán. 2018. "Conflict and Fieldwork." *Acta Ethnographica* 63 (2): 345–359.

Nguyễn Trác Dĩ. n.d. *Cuộc Di Dân Sác-Tôc Bru Từ Quảng-Trị vào Darlac* [The resettlement of the Bru from Quang Tri to Darlac]. Saigon: Bộ Phát-Triển Sắc-tộc Ân-Hành.

Rabinow, Paul. 2007. *Reflections on Fieldwork in Morocco*, 2nd ed. Berkeley: University of California Press.

Salemink, Oscar. 2003. "Enclosing the Highlands: Socialist, Capitalist, and Protestant Conversions of Vietnam's Central Highlanders." Paper presented at the conference Politics of the Commons: Articulating Development and Strengthening Local Practices, Chiang Mai University, July 11–14, 2003, Thailand. http://dlc.dlib.indiana.edu/dlc/bitstream /handle/10535/1787/Oscar_Salemink_RCSD_paper.pdf.

———. 2013. "Between Engagement and Abuse: Reflections on the 'Field' of Anthropology and the Power of Ethnography." In *Red Stamps and Gold Stars: Fieldwork Dilemmas in Upland Socialist Asia*, edited by S. Turner, 241–259. Vancouver: UBC Press.

———. 2015. "Revolutionary and Christian Ecumenes and Desire for Modernity in the Vietnamese Highlands." *Asia Pacific Journal of Anthropology* 16 (4): 388–409.

Scott, James C. 1985. *Weapons of the Weak: Everyday Forms of Peasant Resistance.* New Haven, CT: Yale University Press.

———. 1990. *Domination and the Arts of Resistance: Hidden Transcripts.* New Haven, CT: Yale University Press.

———. 2009. *The Art of Not Being Governed: An Anarchist History of Upland South East Asia.* New Haven, CT: Yale University Press.

Turner, Sarah. 2010. "Challenges and Dilemmas: Fieldwork with Upland Minorities in Socialist Vietnam, Laos, and Southwest China." *Asia Pacific Viewpoint* 51 (2): 121–134.

———. 2013a. "Dilemmas and Detours: Fieldwork with Ethnic Minorities in Upland Soutwest China, Vietnam, and Laos." In *Red Stamps and Gold Stars: Fieldwork Dilemmas in Upland Socialist Asia*, edited by S. Turner, 1–21. Vancouver: UBC Press.

———, ed. 2013b. *Red Stamps and Gold Stars: Fieldwork Dilemmas in Upland Socialist Asia.* Vancouver: UBC Press.

———. 2013c. "The Silenced Research Assistant Speaks Her Mind." In *Red Stamps and Gold Stars: Fieldwork Dilemmas in Upland Socialist Asia*, edited by S. Turner, 220–238. Vancouver: UBC Press.

Turner, Sarah, and Steeve Daviau, eds. 2010. "Challenges and Dilemmas: Fieldwork with Upland Minorities in Socialist Vietnam, Laos, and Southwest China." Special issue, *Asia Pacific Viewpoint* 51 (2).

Vargyas, Gábor. 1996. "'We Have Accepted the Rule of Anybody That Has Come Here': On the Identity of a Vietnamese Minority in Transition; The Bru." Unpublished paper read at the international conference Asian Minorities in Transition: Diversity, Identities, and Encounters, December 12–15, Münster, Germany.

———. 2000. *A la recherche des Brou perdus, population montagnarde du Centre Indochinois.* Paris: Études Orientales/Olizane.

———. 2008. "Quiconque voulait s'imposer à nous, nous avons accepté son pouvoir." In *Monde du Viet-Nam/Vietnam World: Hommage à Nguyen The Anh,* edited by F. Mantienne and K. W. Taylor, 341–369. Paris: Les Indes Savantes.

———. 2010. "Resettled Ancestors: Religious Change among the Bru (in the Central Highlands of Vietnam)." In *Religion, Identity, Postsocialism: The Halle Focus Group 2003–2010,* edited by C. Hann, 130–133. Halle/Saale: Max Planck Institute for Social Anthropology (Department II).

———. 2012. "Caught in the Crossfire: The Bru and the Vietnam War as Reflected through Khŏi Sarâng's Life History." Unpublished paper read at the Second International Conference of Integrating and Developing European Asian Studies (IDEAS): National and Regional Identities: Appropriating the Past, February 1–7, 2012, Hong Kong.

———. 2016. "'Up' and 'Down': 'Zomia' and the Bru of the Central Vietnamese Highlands. Part I, Are the Bru 'Natives' in Zomia?" *Acta Ethnographica Hungarica* 61 (1): 241–258.

———. 2017. "'Up' and 'Down': 'Zomia' and the Bru of the Central Vietnamese Highlands. Part II, Fleeing the State or Desire for Modernity? Reflections on Scott and Salemink." *Acta Ethnographica Hungarica* 62 (2): 441–463.

———. 2018. "Fieldwork, Politics, Ethics." *Acta Ethnographica Hungarica* 63 (2): 323–344.

———. 2019. "Photoshopped Ancestors." *Max Planck Institute for Social Anthropology Working Papers* 194: 1–34.

———. 2020. "The Voice of the Lord from a Record Player (Vietnamese Highlands, 1960s)." *Acta Ethnographica Hungarica* 65 (1): 257–284.

———. 2023. "On Both Sides of the Annamese Cordilleras: The Bru of Vietnam and Laos." In *Routledge Handbook of Contemporary Highland Asia,* edited by M. Heneise and J. Wouters, 403–417. London: Routledge, 2022.

Watson, Conrad William, ed. 1999. *Being There: Fieldwork in Anthropology.* London: Pluto Press.

Contributors

Sylvie Beaud is currently working as an associate professor at the Faculty for Foreign Studies, Teikyo University (Tokyo). She obtained her PhD in anthropology at the Université de Paris Nanterre in 2012. Her research has focused on identity, politics, and ritual in China. She has also expanded her research field to personal development, New Age rituals, and esotericism. Throughout her research, whether in China, Japan, or elsewhere, she documents and analyzes the political aspects and forms of relational mediation at stake in rituals.

Vanina Bouté is a professor of social anthropology at the École des Hautes Études en Sciences Sociales (EHESS) and member of the Centre Asie du Sud-Est in Paris (Southeast Asia Centre, CASE-CNRS). She has been conducting anthropological fieldwork in northern Laos since 2000. She is the author or editor of numerous publications, including *Mirroring Power: Ethnogenesis and Dynamics of Integration among the Phunoy of Northern Laos* (Silkworm Books, 2018, translated from French), *Changing Lives in Laos*, co-edited with Vatthana Pholsena (NUS Press, 2017), and *From Tribalism to Nationalism: The Anthropological Turn in Laos—A Tribute to Grand Evans*, coedited with Yves Goudineau (NIAS Press, 2022). Her current research focuses on migration and the dynamics of change among highlanders living in the borders of northern Laos.

Sarah Delisle completed fieldwork in northern Vietnam for her master's degree program at McGill University, Canada. Her research focused on the impacts of extreme weather events in the northern uplands and the coping and adaptation strategies of Hmong and Yao ethnic minority groups. In collaboration with social enterprise Sapa O'Chau, she also worked as a research assistant on *Hmong Voices*, a National Geographic (US) Legacy Fund project. She currently works as the senior advisor for emergency management at McGill University.

Magnus Fiskesjö was educated in his native Sweden and at the University of Chicago, where in 2000 he received a joint PhD in anthropology and East

Asian languages and civilizations. Before that, from 1985 to 1991, he served in the Swedish embassies in Beijing (as cultural attaché) and in Tokyo; from 2000 to 2005, he was director of the Museum of Far Eastern Antiquities in Stockholm. Since 2005, he has taught in anthropology and Asian studies at Cornell University. His research interests include political anthropology, ethnic relations, ethnopolitics, archaeology, and heritage issues, above all in East and Southeast Asia. He recently published a book on the Wa people of the China/Burma frontier region, titled *Stories from an Ancient Land: Perspectives on Wa History and Culture* (Berghahn, 2021), and several articles on the ongoing genocide in Xinjiang, China.

Christian C. Lentz is an associate professor of geography at the University of North Carolina at Chapel Hill. He is the author of *Contested Territory: Điện Biên Phủ and the Making of Northwest Vietnam* (Yale University Press, 2019), winner of the 2021 Harry J. Benda Prize for outstanding first book in Southeast Asian studies. His articles have appeared in the *Journal of Peasant Studies*, the *Journal of Vietnamese Studies, Modern Asian Studies*, and other journals. His research and writing have been supported by the Association of Asian Studies, a Fulbright Fellowship in Vietnam, and a fellowship in the School of Historical Studies at the Institute for Advanced Study in Princeton, New Jersey. In addition to ongoing study of highland Southeast Asia, his current research traces political relations between Vietnam and Indonesia in the 1950s, exploring transnational alternatives to Cold War alignment and nation-state domination.

Jean Michaud is a professor of anthropology at Université Laval, Canada. Since the late 1980s he has conducted field research in several Asian countries, most importantly in Thailand and Vietnam. His research interests lie in understanding the rapport ethnic minorities have with modernity, the state, and market forces, in particular the long-term cultural and economic adaptation of indigenous populations to national and international pressures linked to globalization. He has published articles in *Current Anthropology, Anthropology Today, Human Organization*, the *Journal of Global History*, and *Ethnic and Racial Studies*, among others; some have been translated and published in China and Vietnam. He has authored, coauthored, edited, or coedited books with the University of Washington Press, the University of British Columbia Press, and Brill, among others, including the *Historical Dictionary of the Peoples of the Southeast Asian Massif*, 2nd ed. (Rowman & Littlefield, 2016). He has served as president of the Canadian Council for Southeast Asian Studies.

Pascale-Marie Milan (PhD 2019) is an associate researcher at the French Research Institute on East Asia (IFRAE/UMR 8043—France). She has been working with the Na people of southwest China since 2007. Her doctoral research focused on tourism and social change in the Na's institutionalized visiting system and kinship practices. She highlighted the transformation of their social organization and the rise of conjugal ties. While pursuing her research during a postdoctoral fellowship at the ÉFEO, she further explored kinship issues by comparing in detail kinship vocabulary and studying the different indigenous concepts of kinship, such as the house. She has written a monograph on the Na of Lijiazui (Barbier-Mueller/Somogy, 2016, in English and French).

Pierre Petit is a senior research associate at the Belgian National Fund for Scientific Research (FNRS) and a professor of anthropology at the Université Libre de Bruxelles (ULB). After his PhD dissertation on the rituals of the Luba of Katanga (1993), he investigated issues of material culture, ethnicity, urban anthropology, and research methodology in Congo. Since 2003, he has worked in Laos on the mobilities of highlanders involved in rural exodus and on the relations between the state and the ethnic minorities. His interest in historical anthropology appears in his last monograph, *History, Memory, and Territorial Cults in the Highlands of Laos: The Past Inside the Present* (Routledge, 2020) as well as in his current research on globalized iconographies of Catholic devotions and missionary medals. He is the editor of *Civilisations*, the main journal of anthropology based in Belgium.

Vatthana Pholsena is an associate professor and head of the Department of Southeast Asian Studies at the National University of Singapore. She worked as a research fellow in the Centre National de la Recherche Scientifique (CNRS; National Centre for Scientific Research) for over a decade, based at the Institut d'Asie Orientale (Institute of East Asian Studies) in Lyon and at the Centre Asie du Sud-Est (Southeast Asia Centre) in Paris. She is the author of *Post-war Laos: The Politics of Culture, History, and Identity* (ISEAS and Cornell University Press, 2006) and *Laos: Un pays en mutation* (Éditions Belin, 2011). Among other publications, she has also co-edited two books: *Interactions with a Violent Past: Reading Post-conflict Landscapes in Cambodia, Laos, and Vietnam*, with Oliver Tappe (NUS Press, 2013) and *Changing Lives in Laos*, with Vanina Bouté (NUS Press, 2017). Her current research investigates the contemporary experiences as well as the afterlife of the Cold War in the Lao-Thai borderlands.

Sarah Turner is a professor in the Department of Geography, McGill University, Canada. Her research focuses on the ways by which individuals who find themselves somehow marginalized, be it economically, politically, or ethnically, make a living in rural and urban Asia. Her current projects include a focus on ethnic minority livelihoods in the Sino-Vietnamese borderlands, including farmer everyday politics when faced with inappropriate agrarian programs and infrastructure projects. She also studies informal economy livelihoods and the resistance tactics of street vendors and motorbike taxi drivers in Hanoi, Vietnam. She has coauthored *Frontier Livelihoods: Hmong in the Sino-Vietnamese Borderlands* with C. Bonnin and J. Michaud (University of Washington Press, 2015) and is an editor of *Geoforum* and *Journal of Vietnamese Studies.*

Gábor Vargyas is a sociocultural anthropologist specializing in Southeast Asian and Pacific studies. He is a professor emeritus both at the Institute of Ethnology, Research Centre for the Humanities, Eötvös Loránd Research Network (formerly the Hungarian Academy of Sciences), Budapest, and at the Department of European Ethnology and Cultural Anthropology, University of Pécs, Hungary. He has conducted extensive field research in 1985–1989 and 2007 among the Bru (Vân Kiều) of Central Vietnam. He is the author of *A la recherche des Brou perdus, population montagnarde du Centre Indochinois* Les Cahiers de Peninsule No. 5 (Etudes Orientales, Olizane, 2000) and a number of articles on Bru ethnography and ethnohistory.

Wang Ming-ke is a professor in the Department of History, Peking University. He is also a corresponding research fellow at the Institute of History and Philology, Academia Sinica, Taiwan, from which he retired in 2022 after a thirty-seven-year research career. He has carried out extensive fieldwork among the Qiang and Tibetans living at the eastern fringe of the Tibetan Plateau. In 2014, he was selected as academician of the Academia Sinica. Currently he is writing a book on the relationship among human communities, historical memories, and civilizations.

Index